Nordic War Stories

Worlds of Memory

Editors:
Jeffrey Olick, University of Virginia
Aline Sierp, Maastricht University
Jenny Wüstenberg, Nottingham Trent University

Published in collaboration with the Memory Studies Association

This book series publishes innovative and rigorous scholarship in the interdisciplinary and global field of memory studies. Memory studies includes all inquiries into the ways we—both individually and collectively—are shaped by the past. How do we represent the past to ourselves and to others? How do those representations shape our actions and understandings, whether explicitly or unconsciously? The "memory" we study encompasses the near-infinitude of practices and processes humans use to engage with the past, the incredible variety of representations they produce, and the range of individuals and institutions involved in doing so.

Guided by the mandate of the Memory Studies Association to provide a forum for conversations among subfields, regions, and research traditions, Worlds of Memory focuses on cutting-edge research that pushes the boundaries of the field and can provide insights for memory scholars outside of a particular specialization. In the process, it seeks to make memory studies more accessible, diverse, and open to novel approaches.

Volume 7
Nordic War Stories: World War II as History, Fiction, Media, and Memory
Edited by Marianne Stecher-Hansen

Volume 6
The Struggle for the Past: How We Construct Social Memories
Elizabeth Jelin

Volume 5
The Mobility of Memory: Migrations and Diasporas across European Borders
Edited by Luisa Passerini, Milica Trakilović, and Gabriele Proglio

Volume 4
Agency in Transnational Memory Politics
Edited by Jenny Wüstenberg and Aline Sierp

Volume 3
Resettlers and Survivors: Bukovina and the Politics of Belonging in West Germany and Israel, 1945–1989
Gaëlle Fisher

Volume 2
Velvet Retro: Postsocialist Nostalgia and the Politics of Heroism in Czech Popular Culture
Veronika Pehe

Volume 1
When Will We Talk about Hitler? German Students and the Nazi Past
Alexandra Oeser

NORDIC WAR STORIES

World War II as History, Fiction, Media, and Memory

Edited by
Marianne Stecher-Hansen

berghahn
NEW YORK • OXFORD
www.berghahnbooks.com

First published in 2021 by
Berghahn Books
www.berghahnbooks.com

© 2021, 2024 Marianne Stecher-Hansen
First paperback edition published 2024

All rights reserved. Except for the quotation of short passages
for the purposes of criticism and review, no part of this book
may be reproduced in any form or by any means, electronic or
mechanical, including photocopying, recording, or any information
storage and retrieval system now known or to be invented,
without written permission of the publisher.

Library of Congress Cataloging-in-Publication Data

Names: Stecher-Hansen, Marianne, editor.
Title: Nordic War Stories: World War II as History, Fiction, Media, and Memory / edited by Marianne Stecher-Hansen.
Other titles: World War II as History, Fiction, Media, and Memory
Description: English-language edition. | New York: Berghahn Books, 2021. | Series: Worlds of Memory; 7 | Includes bibliographical references and index.
Identifiers: LCCN 2020054283 (print) | LCCN 2020054284 (ebook) | ISBN 9781789209617 (hardback) | ISBN 9781789209624 (ebook)
Subjects: LCSH: World War, 1939–1945—Scandinavia. | World War, 1939–1945—Scandinavia—Historiography. | World War, 1939–1945—Literature and the war. | World War, 1939–1945—Motion pictures and the war. | World War, 1939–1945—Influence. | War and society—Scandinavia—20th century.
Classification: LCC D763.S3 N6653 2021 (print) | LCC D763.S3 (ebook) | DDC 940.53/48—dc23
LC record available at https://lccn.loc.gov/2020054283
LC ebook record available at https://lccn.loc.gov/2020054284

British Library Cataloguing in Publication Data

A catalogue record for this book is available from the British Library

ISBN 978-1-78920-961-7 hardback
ISBN 978-1-80539-341-2 paperback
ISBN 978-1-80539-448-8 epub
ISBN 978-1-78920-962-4 web pdf

https://doi.org/10.3167/9781789209617

Dedicated to my past and present graduate and undergraduate students at the University of Washington, Seattle.

Ja - det haver så nyligen regnet,
og de træer de drypper endnu,
mangen eg er for uvejret segnet,
men endda er vi frejdige i hu.

(Yes, of late the rains have arrived
and drenched the trees where they stood,
many an oak has not survived
yet we're still valiant of mood.)

—Danish folk song, "Det haver så nyligen regnet," 1890, Johan Ottosen.
From *Højskolesangbogen*, 18th edition, nr. 497, stanza 5.1–5.4.
English translation courtesy of Tiina Nunnally.

Contents

List of Illustrations	x
Acknowledgments	xiv
Introduction Marianne Stecher-Hansen	1

Part I. War Historiography — 17

Chapter 1. Finland in World War II: Tragedy, Survival, and Good Wars — 21
Juhana Aunesluoma

Chapter 2. Danish Historical Narratives of the Occupation: The Promises and Lies of the 9th of April — 35
Sofie Lene Bak

Chapter 3. The Norwegian War Experience: Occupied and Allied — 49
Tom Kristiansen

Chapter 4. The Icelandic National Narrative and World War II: "Freedom and Culture" — 65
Guðmundur Hálfdanarson

Chapter 5. Sweden's Ambiguous War: Contradiction and Controversy — 81
John Gilmour

Part II. War Literature: Archive — 97

Chapter 6. Karin Boye as Ambivalent Spectator of Fascism — 101
Amanda Doxtater

Chapter 7. Isak Dinesen in Hitler's Berlin: Neutrality's Cloak in "Letters from a Land at War" — 116
Marianne Stecher-Hansen

Chapter 8. Sigrid Undset's Problematic Propaganda: The Call for Democracy in *Return to the Future*   136
Christine Hamm

Part III. War Literature: Canon   151

Chapter 9. Hans Christian Branner: Angst and the Existential Crisis of War in Denmark   155
Mark Mussari

Chapter 10. Crises of Memory in Norway's Occupation Novel: Sigurd Hoel's *Meeting at the Milestone*   169
Dean Krouk

Chapter 11. The Battle over Finnish Cultural Memory of War: Väinö Linna's *The Unknown Soldier*   185
Julia Pajunen

Chapter 12. Investigating Sweden's Postwar Neutrality: Ethics in Per Olov Enquist's *The Legionnaires*   202
Jan Krogh Nielsen

Chapter 13. The Allied Occupation of Iceland: Indriði G. Þorsteinsson's *North of War*   216
Daisy Neijmann

Part IV. War Cinema: Remembering and Forgetting   233

Chapter 14. *Somewhere in Sweden*: Quality Fiction and Popularized History in the World War II Television Series   237
Erik Hedling

Chapter 15. Icelandic Cinema and the American Military Presence: *The Girl Gogo, Atomic Station,* and *Devil's Island*   252
Pétur Valsson

Chapter 16. War Memory, Compassion, and the Finnish Child: Klaus Härö's *Mother of Mine*   269
Liina-Ly Roos

Chapter 17. The War Film as Cultural Memory in Denmark: *April 9th* and *Land of Mine*   282
Marianne Stecher-Hansen

Chapter 18. Acts of Remembering: Audiovisual Memory and the New Norwegian Occupation Drama   302
Gunnar Iversen

Chapter 19. Finland Returning to War on Screen:
The Unknown Soldier of 2017   314
John Sundholm

Epilogue   330

Index   333

Illustrations

Figures

Figure 1.1. Finland's relationship with Germany in 1941–44 was both close and tense. It became the topic of the most heated historiographical controversies in postwar decades. While the government insisted that the country was fighting a separate war against the Soviet Union, it could not hide the fact that Finland's war effort rested on its cooperation with Germany. On the occasion of Marshal Gustaf Mannerheim's seventy-fifth birthday, Adolf Hitler paid a surprise visit to Finland in June 1942, underlining the wartime bond between the two countries. Hitler is flanked by the marshal (*left*) and Finland's wartime president Risto Ryti (*right*). Courtesy of SA-kuva. 27

Figure 2.1. Barricades in Nørrebro, a working-class neighborhood in Copenhagen during the "General Strike" (*Folkestrejken*) in the summer of 1944. Although communists orchestrated the initial strikes, the riots and ravages were a spontaneous public outcry against the German occupiers and were neither under the control of trade unions, politicians, nor the resistance movement. Copenhagen was in a state of civil war. Danish police refused to stop the riots, but collaborators in German-controlled terror groups and militias fought against their Danish countrymen in the streets of the capital. In the memory of the Danes, the General Strike restored national pride and overshadowed the less heroic attitudes of the first years of the occupation. Unknown photographer. Courtesy of the Museum of Danish Resistance 1940–1945. 41

Figure 3.1. To arms! Norwegian conscripts—badly trained, desperately unprepared, and wholly inexperienced—were called up at the dawn of the German attack on 9 April 1940. Photograph of national servicemen after the aerial attack on Elverum, 11 April 1940, included in Olaf Tjønneland's renowned album from the campaign. Photographer: Olaf Tjønneland. Courtesy of Tom B. Jensen. 50

Fig. 4.1. "The Struggle": The eighth room of the exhibition titled "Freedom and Culture" surveyed the history of the Icelandic nationalist struggle in the period 1874–1944 through a demonstration of patriotic symbols, pictures of political leaders and events, and examples of patriotic poetry. Unknown photographer. Courtesy of the National Museum of Iceland. 66

Fig. 4.2. British soldiers in Reykjavík. A formation of British soldiers march through the center of Iceland's capital, Reykjavík, on the occupation day, 10 May 1940. Photographer: Helgi Sigurðsson (Courtesy of the Reykjavík Museum of Photography). 71

Figure 5.1. Aggressors and defenders? Swedish and German army guards appear relaxed on the border between neutral Sweden and German-occupied Norway in the winter of 1941, which was in stark contrast to the tense wartime relations between the two countries. The long border was better guarded on the Swedish side, as many Norwegian refugees discovered, due to Swedish concerns about German invasion, Quisling infiltration and British Special Operations Executive agents compromising Swedish neutrality. Photographer: Johan Karlsson, 1941. Courtesy of Bohusläns museum. 83

Figure 6.1. Leni Riefenstahl's film *Olympia I–II*, an elaborate documentation of the 1936 Berlin Olympic Games, evoked ambivalent commentary from the Swedish poet Karin Boye in her travel diary from Vienna in June 1938. In this sequence, female eurythmic dancers perform collectively in part II: *The Festival of Beauty*. Screenshot: Amanda Doxtater. 109

Figure 7.1. Karen Blixen (Isak Dinesen) listens with eyes averted and chin resting in her hand, photographed in Berlin on 19 March 1940. On the backside of the photograph, the baroness wrote, "From my visit in Berlin. Eager Nazis attempt to convert me." Unknown photographer. DAF Picture Service. Royal Danish Library digital archive. Courtesy of the Rungstedlund Foundation. 128

Figure 8.1. Sigrid Undset was determined to inform the American public about Norway's fierce fight for democracy. During five years in exile in the United States, 1940–45, Undset gave numerous lectures and press interviews. In her own words, she was a "propaganda soldier." Unknown photographer in the United States. Courtesy of Bjerkebæk, Lillehammer museum. 139

Figure 9.1. *Der brænder en Ild* (A fire is burning, 1944), original front cover of the underground anthology that includes Hans Christian Branner's first version of the short story "Angst," anonymously published by a clandestine press. The back cover reads, "This book may not be sold. But all who hold a copy in their hands ought to feel obliged in every way to support the freedom fight—also with money. Think of the prisoners! Help their loved ones! Find your place in the fight!" Illustrator anonymous. Published by Folk og Frihed forlag (People and Freedom Press). Courtesy of Marianne Stecher-Hansen. 157

Figure 10.1. Portrait of Sigurd Hoel in 1947, the year that *Meeting at the Milestone* was published. Although Hoel's novel quickly achieved canonical status as the classic work about occupied Norway, *Meeting at the Milestone* is a critical and problematizing literary representation of the period—a modern psychological novel that enacts a crisis of memory. Photographer: E. Rude, 1947. Courtesy of the National Library of Norway, Wikimedia Commons. 173

Figure 11.1. Graphic designer Martti Mykkänen (1926–2018), who became the leading name in postwar Finnish applied graphic arts, made the cover image of *The Unknown Soldier*. The image that is now an icon was an emergency order to WSOY with only a few days' notice in 1954. Cover image by Martti Mykkänen, from database of the publisher WSOY, courtesy of Raili and Riitta Mykkänen. 189

Figure 12.1. Baltic legionnaires behind barbed wire in the internment camp Ränneslätt, Sweden. A total of 146 Baltic refugee soldiers were extradited to the Soviet Union in January 1946, despite doubts that they would receive a fair trial there. The Swedish government officially apologized for the extradition in 1994. Per Olov Enquist's 1968 documentary novel *The Legionnaires* explores the political and ethical dilemmas posed by the extradition. Unknown photographer. Courtesy of Scanpix, SIPA USA. 203

Figure 13.1. The original Icelandic book cover for *North of War* (1971) portrays the essence of the Icelandic war experience: a scramble for money and a battle over male potency. Cover design by Auglýsingastofa Kristínar Þorkelsdóttur. 219

Figure 14.1. Popular singer Ulla Billquist—her song "Min Soldat" (My soldier) epitomizes Sweden's wartime atmosphere and military preparedness during World War II. Screenshot from the documentary film *When the Clouds Clear* (2016), directed by Lasse Zackrisson. Courtesy of Lasse Zackrisson. 239

Figure 15.1. *Devil's Island*: An American serviceman and his Icelandic bride pose for a wedding photo with her family in front of the abandoned army barrack that serves as the family home. The wedding attire of the couple contrasts the appearance of the bride's family, illustrating the difference between the life the bride is leaving behind in Iceland and the one waiting for her in the United States. Production still from *Devil's Island* (1996), directed by Friðrik Þór Friðriksson. Courtesy of Friðrik Þór Friðriksson. 264

Figure 16.1. Eero (Topi Majaniemi) peeking through a doorway at his Swedish foster parents in *Mother of Mine* (2005), directed by Klaus Härö. The use of doorways accentuate the "in-betweenness" of Eero, highlighting the homelessness of an evacuated Finnish war child in Sweden. Still from *Mother of Mine*. Screenshot: Liina-Ly Roos. 274

Figure 17.1. Poster for the Danish premiere of *Under Sandet* (titled *Land of Mine* in the English-language release) in early December 2015. The film enacts an inversion of the usual power hierarchy by depicting Danish soldiers harshly commandeering German prisoners—and it suggests that such brutal retribution may ultimately turn to compassion. In the featured image, the Danish sergeant Rasmussen (Roland Møller) cradles the young German prisoner Sebastian (Louis Hofmann). The promotional text states, "They survived the Second World War. Now they must survive the clean up." Courtesy of Nordisk Film. 295

Maps

Map 0.1. "Will Hitler Pick Sweden and Finland for Summer Fronts?" *Los Angeles Times*, 10 May 1943, Charles H. Owen. The American press speculates and solicits public support for the Allied war effort, as the tide of the war begins to turn against Nazi Germany. In the spring of 1943, neutral Sweden remains in a state of military preparedness while Finland is militarily allied with Germany in a grinding battle against the Soviet Union on its eastern border. Courtesy of David Rumsey Historical Map Collection, University of Washington Libraries. 5

Map 0.2. *World War II in the North Sea Area/US Naval Personnel Training Aid*, distributed 1944. North Sea region including Iceland, Norway, Denmark, Sweden, Finland, and northern Russia, Germany, northern France, and intervening land and sea areas. Shows aircraft invasion routes from the United States and United Kingdom, as well as German invasion route of Norway; also includes principal areas bombed by the Allies, principal areas of naval engagements, Allied air bases, Allied naval bases, and German targeted facilities. Courtesy of the Library of Congress, Geography and Map Division. 9

Acknowledgments

Many sincere thanks are due to numerous colleagues, friends, former students, and family members, whose inspiration and encouragement has been vital to the completion of this project. First and foremost, I owe an enormous debt of gratitude to each of the seventeen chapter contributors who in the spring of 2017 accepted my invitation to contribute original pieces to an edited volume, a project that had neither funding nor even a publisher at that point. I am particularly grateful to ten extraordinary scholars affiliated with leading Nordic universities—namely, Juhana Aunesluoma, Sofie Lene Bak, Guðmundur Hálfdanarson, Christine Hamm, Erik Hedling, Gunnar Iversen, Tom Kristiansen, Daisy Neijmann, Julia Pujanen and John Sundholm—because they gladly agreed to contribute to this collaborative study and complied readily with numerous editorial requests and deadlines, although we had never met in person—and most of us have yet to meet.

I also offer heartfelt gratitude to six North American colleagues, among them former graduate students, who enthusiastically contributed to the book, including Amanda Doxtater, Dean Krouk, Mark Mussari, Jan Krogh Nielsen, Liina-Ly Roos, and Pétur Valsson. Finally, I offer special thanks to John Gilmour at the University of Edinburgh, not only for his chapter contribution but also for his initial encouragement and suggestion to pursue Berghahn Books as the publisher.

Furthermore, I thank many colleagues and friends who offered suggestions and help along the way, especially Tiina Nunnally for invaluable professional advice and encouragement; Kristian Næsby, lecturer of Danish at the University of Washington, for film recommendations; Marianne Wirenfeldt Asmussen for critical feedback on my chapter on Isak Dinesen; Mark Mussari for his suggestion of the cover image; and Liesl Yamaguchi for her assistance in locating a scholar of adaptations of Linna's work. Not least I would also like to thank Meta, Kristian, and Gitte Brorsen, Jan and Karen Krogh Nielsen, Marianne Stølen, Marie Tetzlaff, Anett Wæber, and the Tranberg family for gracious hospitality in Denmark.

I must also express heartfelt gratitude to an entire generation of undergraduate and graduate students at the University of Washington who have contributed to this intellectual inquiry by means of inspired class presentations, countless outstanding term papers, and numerous exceptional senior essays as well as graduate seminar papers. Their engagement with various facets of the subject matter has added invaluable intellectual momentum to this book project.

Finally, but not least, I wish to thank my remarkable colleagues at the University of Washington, especially departmental chair Professor Andrew Nestingen and the divisional dean's office for the humanities for granting me research sabbatical in the winter and spring quarters of 2017; without professional leave from my regular teaching and administrative duties in the Department of Scandinavian Studies, this book would not have come to fruition. A special thanks also to Dan Mandeville of the University of Washington libraries whose prompt and helpful assistance never fails. My gratitude also extends to Georg and Nina Pedersen for their enormous generosity and foresight; the establishment of the *Georg and Nina Pedersen Endowed Faculty Fund for Danish Studies* will help support projects such as this one in the future.

I am also thankful to my close family members for cheering me on from the sidelines: especially Kirsten and Michael, and my sons, Andreas, Leif, and Viggo. Above all, I especially want to express my love and deepest gratitude to my mother Inger for her optimistic outlook, strong spirit, and cultivation of family, education, history, and communicative memories.

Finally, I wish to thank senior editor Chris Chappell, editorial assistant Mykelin Higham, and Lizzie Martinez at Berghahn Books for their patient guidance, professional assistance, and editorial advice. Again, I wholeheartedly thank the chapter contributors as well as Berghahn Books' editorial staff for their diligence and collegiality throughout the editorial and publication process.

—Marianne Stecher-Hansen
Seattle, 15 June 2020

Introduction

Marianne Stecher-Hansen

Where does an intellectual inquiry begin? In the late 1990s, I taught a graduate seminar at the University of Washington that dealt with Nordic literature and World War II. Is there such a thing as a Scandinavian war novel? We read literary works in the original Swedish, Norwegian, and Danish, such as Pär Lagerkvist's *The Dwarf* (1944), Vilhelm Moberg's *Ride This Night* (1941), Sigrid Hoel's *Meeting at the Milestone* (1947), Knut Hamsun's *On Overgrown Paths* (1948), and Isak Dinesen's *The Angelic Avengers* (1946). Connections to hardcore war literature seemed remote. My interest in the period was sparked by Thorkild Hansen's controversial documentary novel *Processen mod Hamsun* (1978; The case against Hamsun), about the postwar trial of Norwegian Nobel Laureate Knut Hamsun (1859–1952), which was the subject of my research at that time (Stecher-Hansen, 1997; 1999). The graduate seminar led to a course development grant from the Center for West European Studies in 2001; since then, I have regularly taught a course on "War and Occupation in the Nordic Region" at the University of Washington that has attracted many students from the Department of Scandinavian Studies and the Henry M. Jackson School of International Studies, particularly European Studies majors.

The project that began as an intellectual inquiry with graduate students coincided neatly in the 1990s with the emergence of a second (and eventually third) generation of World War II scholars in the Nordic countries, a tide that swelled with the *Historikerstreit* (historians' debate) on the European continent and a turn toward a "moral narrative" in revisionist approaches to World War II history. Since 2000, and simultaneous with increasing revisionism in World War II scholarship, the field of memory studies has flourished. These two paths of inquiry in history and memory studies are in many ways interconnected and related to a generational cycle in terms of the aging and passing of war witnesses, victims, and survivors.

From this generational perspective, my particular intellectual inquiry of the past two decades holds a connection to a parental past, because I belong to "the generation after" or *postgeneration* of World War II. As a first-generation American (born in Canada) of immigrants from Europe, I have some relationship to experiences of trauma and displacement as "inherited memory," "received history," or perhaps "postmemory," to use Marianne Hirch's term; I am the daughter of a generation of people who experienced the war and occupation with varying degrees of intensity and trauma. My parents were young adults while Denmark was occupied by its southern neighbor and historical foe, Germany. My late father spent the last year and a half of the war in military training in neutral Sweden, where he had fled by boat at night as a twenty-two-year-old engineering student and underground resistance member—and there he became a refugee soldier. This communicative memory became a clouded but indelible imprint in my childhood memory; the circumstances surrounding my father's escape to Sweden lacked a complete context.

These reflections are a point of departure for this collaborative scholarly project that seeks to investigate cultural memory of World War II as represented in various media, particularly in the historiography, literature, and cinema of the five Nordic countries. With the Nordic region serving as the geographic and political parameter, this study concerns the shifting preoccupations of collective and cultural memory of World War II, as evident in certain media: "nonfictional" media (historiography and travel writing) and fictional media (literature and cinema). I have made use of the opening reflections as an introduction to this study in order to illustrate the memory shifts and gaps about the war that occur over several decades. According to Jan Assmann, *communicative memory* "has a limited time depth which normally reaches no farther back than eighty years, the time span of three interacting generations" (2010: 111). While communicative memory is not the primary concern of this book, the passing of the war generation that stored, silenced, and selectively transmitted memories certainly represents an intense climatic change in the evolving field of cultural memory study.

This edited collection is primarily concerned with historiographical, literary, and cinematic narratives that represent forms of *cultural memory* that depend on public institutions of learning, transmission, and interpretation. In other words, it explores texts and mass-mediated expressions of cultural memory that sustain greater longevity and influence than the intergenerational *communicative memory* that lives in everyday conversations and interactions. At the present moment, communicative memories of World War II no longer inform the perceptions of the majority of individuals living today. Indeed, the oral communications that constitute a collective memory of the events of the war are largely extinguished. While a few war children, veterans, and survivors are still alive, the vast majority of individuals who were young adults or the age of military service have passed away. Nonetheless, it is obvious that the memoirists, politicians, filmmakers, journalists, intellectuals, literary writers, and veterans who published or produced work during the postwar decades, and thus disseminated and ritualized their war memories, have contributed to the formation of the institutionalized memory cultures of World War II over the past three generations.

Certainly, the experience of the Nordic countries in World War II (1939–45) belongs in a wider twentieth-century frame that includes World War I (1914–18). The constitutional monarchies of Denmark, Norway, and Sweden had maintained neutrality during the "Great War"—the centennial of the armistice was commemorated worldwide on 11 November 2018. The end of World War I and the international Treaty of Versailles of 1919 brought about territorial and political reconfigurations that healed some old wounds but also opened up new vulnerabilities—and eventually, and inadvertently, fueled the aggressive imperialist agenda of Hitler's Reich. In the Nordic region, the political outcomes related to World War I were also consequential. The outbreak of the Russian Revolution paved the way for the establishment of the Republic of Finland in early December 1917; however, the founding of the nation was immediately followed by a bloody civil war in 1918, in which approximately thirty-six thousand Finns perished—a traumatic experience of national disunity and class struggle that carried over into World War II. Also following World War I, Iceland became an independent state in 1918 after a long period of Danish rule (Iceland celebrated this "national centennial" in 2018); however, Iceland's new status meant a "monarchical union" with the Kingdom of Denmark and a shared foreign service (until the Republic of Iceland was founded in June 1944); however, when Iceland was occupied by the Allies in 1940, its ties with Denmark were, practically speaking, already severed by Germany's occupation. Also in the wake of World War I, the northern half of the Duchy of Schleswig (part of the Danish kingdom conquered by Prussia in 1864), populated by a Danish-speaking majority, was finally reunited with Denmark in 1920; however, often forgotten in national history are the thirty thousand Danes under German rule from this region who had been conscripted to fight in World War I for the German armed forces—Denmark's archenemy at the time. Such territorial and political reconfigurations—as well as others in the Nordic region—had significant bearing on political actions during the period as well as an impact on the subsequent formation of cultural memory of World War II.

The War in the North and Cultural Memory

How do some histories become and remain "active" in the working cultural memory of a nation or social group? Certainly, all memory is highly selective. "In order to remember some things, other things must be forgotten," states Aleida Assmann (2010: 97). There are blank spaces in the mental maps of the war—one needs to dismiss some things in order to make room for other things. What is actively disregarded or forgotten? The global conflict of 1939–45 led to distinct political consequences and postwar destinies for each of the five Nordic countries. The scope of this study is limited to five small countries: Denmark, Finland, Iceland, Norway, and Sweden. In fact, these were neutral nations in the northern periphery of Europe when the war broke out (and Iceland was still formally tied to the Danish kingdom).

The outbreak of the world war in September 1939 led to a "Race for Northern Europe" by the warring powers in order to control strategic positions and mineral resources (Häikiö 1983). Within just a few months, the entire Nordic and Baltic Sea region was clenched in the tight fist of a strategic power play between two totalitarian dictatorships: the Soviet Union and Nazi Germany. Since Stalin's Russia had engaged Finland militarily in late 1939, and Germany had occupied Denmark and Norway in early 1940, Sweden was sandwiched between these two warring powers with little wiggle room. Through a strategy of military preparedness and diplomacy, Sweden became the only Nordic state to maintain neutrality throughout the war. A fierce Nazi-Soviet grip around the entire Nordic region (excepting the territories of Greenland, Iceland, and the Faroe Islands) largely severed the Baltic Sea region from Allied aid or intervention during the war. The "War in the North" was a product of German and Soviet military aggressions, although due to the naval battles in the North Atlantic, there were also strong Allied interests in the region.

Of tantamount significance to the course of the war in the Nordic region was the German-Soviet Treaty of Nonaggression (often called the "Nazi-Soviet Pact") of 23 August 1939, which included a so-called "secret protocol" (signed by the Russian and German foreign ministers, hence called the "Molotov-Ribbentrop Pact") that delineated territorial spheres of influence; Hitler's Germany would take the western countries and Stalin would have free reign in Eastern Europe, including Finland and the Baltic states. The treaty was famously broken two years later by Hitler's massive, surprise advance into the USSR in late June 1941, called Operation Barbarossa (Häikiö 1983; Keegan 1989; Snyder 2010). It is less widely appreciated that the Nordic foreign ministers (with Denmark representing Icelandic foreign policy) issued a joint declaration of neutrality in May 1938 in the event of war. The Nordic countries had maintained neutrality in World War I, therefore most political

Introduction • 5

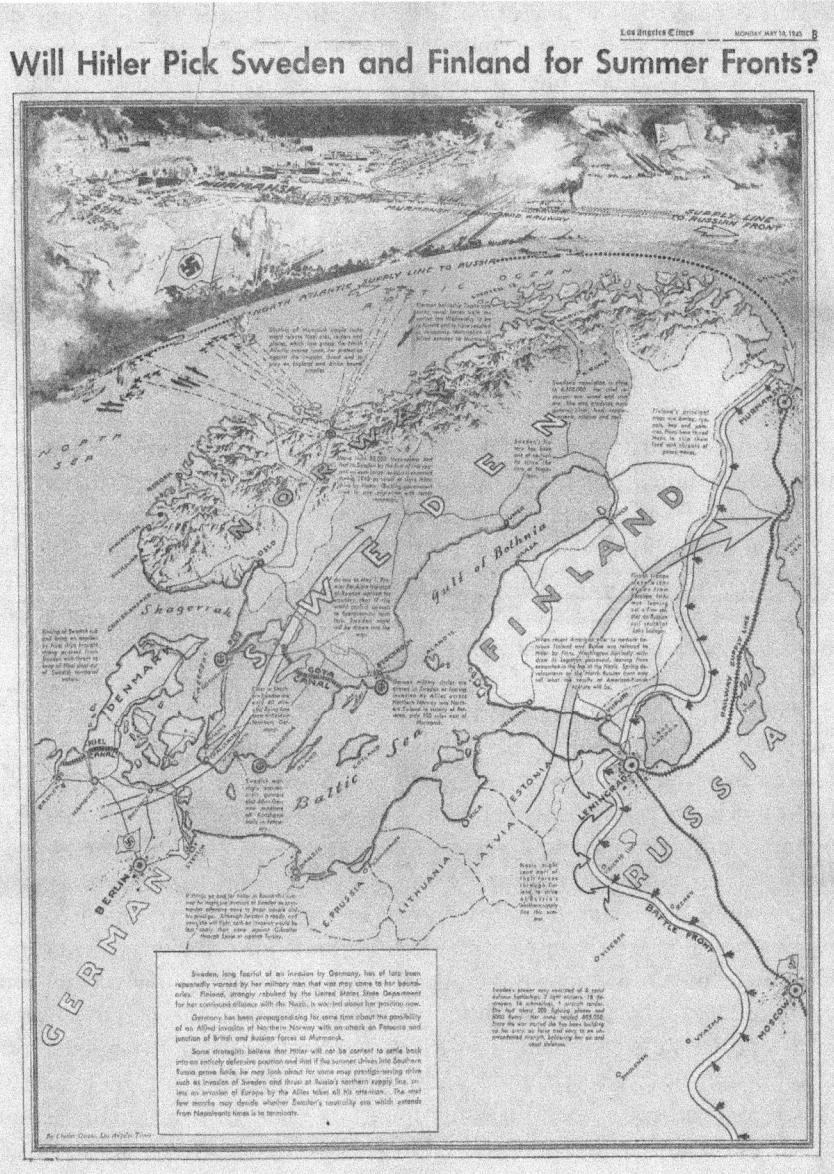

Map 0.1. "Will Hitler Pick Sweden and Finland for Summer Fronts?" *Los Angeles Times*, 10 May 1943, Charles H. Owen. The American press speculates and solicits public support for the Allied war effort, as the tide of the war begins to turn against Nazi Germany. In the spring of 1943, neutral Sweden remains in a state of military preparedness while Finland is militarily allied with Germany in a grinding battle against the Soviet Union on its eastern border. Courtesy of David Rumsey Historical Map Collection, University of Washington Libraries.

leaders assumed that neutrality would be respected in the impending conflict. The following April (over four months prior to the signing of the Nazi-Soviet Pact), Hitler's Germany offered nonaggression treaties to Denmark, Finland, Norway, and Sweden; only Denmark felt compelled to sign the nonaggression treaty with Germany in May 1939, whereas the other Nordic nations politely declined (Nordstrom 2000: 297).

Notably, the war in the Nordic region is marginalized in general accounts of World War II. John Keegan, for example, in *The Second World War* (1989) makes use of five succinct pages to cover the Russo-Finnish War and the German Campaign in Norway (Keegan 1989: 47–51). Nonetheless, the "War in the North" involved substantial military operations, large numbers of German military troops (particularly stationed in Norway and moving through Finland), and massive Soviet military offensives into Finland, which aimed to occupy the country (Overy 2013: 15). Why was the Nordic region pulled into the global conflict? The region held strategic naval ports (Norway's long coast and Finland's Arctic port in Petsamo) as well as the valuable mineral resources (particularly the iron ore mines in northern Sweden as well as nickel mines in northern Finland), significant for the warring powers and of strategic interest to both the Allied and Axis powers. In the west, the Norwegian coastal ports were significant for naval operations in the North Atlantic (the port at Narvik, which was vital for the flow of iron ore to Germany in the winter months, was destroyed by the British in April 1940 in the naval battle at Narvik). An Allied (Anglo-French) intervention plan in the winter months of 1940 failed to gain control over the iron ore mines in northern Sweden (the plan was actually never executed), leaving the region open to occupation. Finally, the German occupation of Denmark and Norway on 9 April 1940, including the territorial waters, ultimately left the entire Baltic Sea region cut off from the west.

Obviously these factors of war history are not the primary object of this project, but they serve as historical scaffolding and indispensable groundwork. Of greater interest is the working or active cultural memory that is conveyed by media and textual representations that have become the narrative "artifacts" of these varied national experiences. The study at hand investigates how histories are conveyed, contested, and mediated in national historiographies, literature (wartime and postwar), and cinema (particularly recent film). As will become evident in the chapters of this volume, the 1990s—given the fall of the Soviet Union and the end of the Cold War—marked the beginning of the widespread scholarly *Historikerstreit* in Europe and the emergence of a "moral narrative" regarding World War II among new generations of historians; these historical debates have not yet subsided (Keegan 1996; Snyder 2010). The tendency since the 1990s toward historical revisionism also holds true for the study of national historiographies in the Nordic region (Ekman and Edling 1997; Stenius, Österberg and Östling 2011; Gilmour and Stephenson 2013).

In this endeavor to pursue various approaches to historical narrative and cultural memory study of the Nordic region in World War II, there is also a place for the perspectives of New Historicism. Such an approach involves situating *texts* (historical/literary/cinematic) that are estranged from memory, or forgotten in the archives, in close proximity with historical contexts and reading them side by side with other discourses of the epoch. I propose that the narrative theory of Hayden White is relevant to a study of the master narratives of World War II in the Nordic region. White argues that historiography is *narrative* (he provocatively calls history "verbal fictions") and asserts that the historian makes use of "literary imagination," and, furthermore, that histories—and historiography itself—is subject to literary "emplotments": for example, romance, satire, comedy, or tragedy (White 2018). In other words, *emplotment* of narrative is not limited to literary fiction but also characterizes historiography. Here I refer to an influential 1978 essay by White, "The Historical Text as Literary Artifact." This is not to say that history is *fiction* (made-up facts), but it is to say that histories or historical narratives employ some of the features of literary fiction. For example, John Keegan implies that White's notion of "emplotment" applies to the established western narrative of World War II in his essay, "Do We Need a New History of the Second World War?" (Keegan 1997). Here Keegan suggests that World War II, as depicted by Anglo-American historians, has been "emplotted" as "a drama, its theme is that of heroic epic" that has been seen and studied in a certain "Churchillian one-way direction," and that "the war, under Churchill's playwright pen, became a drama in four acts" (Keegan 1997: 82–84). Indeed, such an one-directional *Churchillian* view (to borrow Keegan's term) of the victorious Western (i.e. British-American) powers in World War II is still very much present in cinematic productions; for example, in *Dunkirk* (directed by Christopher Nolan, 2017). Even though the motion picture depicts Allied forces trapped in a total military fiasco, the dramatic enactment becomes yet another narrative of heroic Allied victory. The Western democracies (mainly the United Kingdom, France, and the United States) often conveniently or passively forget that Stalin's Soviet Union, the archenemy in the Cold War period, was among the Allied forces and paramount to defeating Nazi Germany in the European theater of World War II.

While there are numerous historical facts and truths in the "Churchillian" history of World War II, it becomes an entrenched narrative and a cultural memory that both actively and passively ignores many episodes in the complex history of the period (Churchill 1948), including the Finnish military alliance with Nazi-Germany in the Continuation War of 1941–44; the Danish government's collaborationist policies, 1940–43; the role of Quisling's National Socialist Party in occupied Norway; and the profitable Swedish iron ore trade with Germany that lasted until January 1945 (Gilmour and Stephenson 2013; Nissen 1983; Rings 1982). Such World War II history indeed represents a master narrative that is lacking in "subplots to the main action" and is in need of "more secondary characters that widen the stage" (Keegan 1997: 84). According to John Keegan, this one-directional view ought to make room for the study and understanding of World War II as a series of regional conflicts within the greater global conflict. In other words, in the terms of war history and historiography, the present cultural memory project is elucidated by this concept of subplot and regional conflicts rather than by the neat bilateral lines of a global conflict that is illustrated by the following US naval training map of 1944.

In the context of the ongoing historical revisionism in the study of World War II, this project is broadly situated within the ever-growing field of memory study. The chapters in this volume employ a variety of approaches to critical theory and cultural memory study. In the following paragraphs, I sketch out a few of the key conceptions of cultural memory. By no means is this intended as a survey or overview of the field of memory study; I have attempted to draw out some of the critical perspectives that are relevant to this particular work.

In terms of organizational framing of the chapters of the volume, the Assmanns' critical apparatus has proved very useful; Jan Assmann offers a methodical illumination of Maurice Halbwachs's influential concept of *collective* memory by distinguishing between *communicative* memory (embodied, witnessed, intergenerationally transmitted) and *cultural* memory (archived, institutionalized, ritualized, mediated). More specifically, Aleida Assmann's definition of active and passive cultural "remembering" and "forgetting," as formulated in *Cultural Memory and Western Civilization: Functions, Media, Archives* (2011: 123), which distinguishes between "functional memory" and "storage memory," underlies the thinking behind the organization of this study. Further, Aleida Assmann's discussion of cultural memory in her essay "Canon and Archive" is employed in this volume by emphasizing the *active* and *passive* dimensions of both "remembering" and "forgetting" (Aleida Assmann: 2010: 99). Her observations are especially useful in sorting, examining, and reframing Nordic narratives about World War II that have been reiterated, repeated, commemorated, and institutionalized in the postwar decades. Further, in the context of the study of World War II, Assmann's understanding of "forgetting" is useful in situating those events and pasts that have been "passively forgotten" (that is, neglected, disregarded, or dispersed) as well as those events and materials that have been "actively forgotten" (that is, negated, destroyed, or censored). However, in the Assmanns' theory of memory, the family unit is the primary and privileged site for the transmission of embodied, communicative memories that are later institutionalized as cultural memory—this conceptual assumption is problematic as it does not

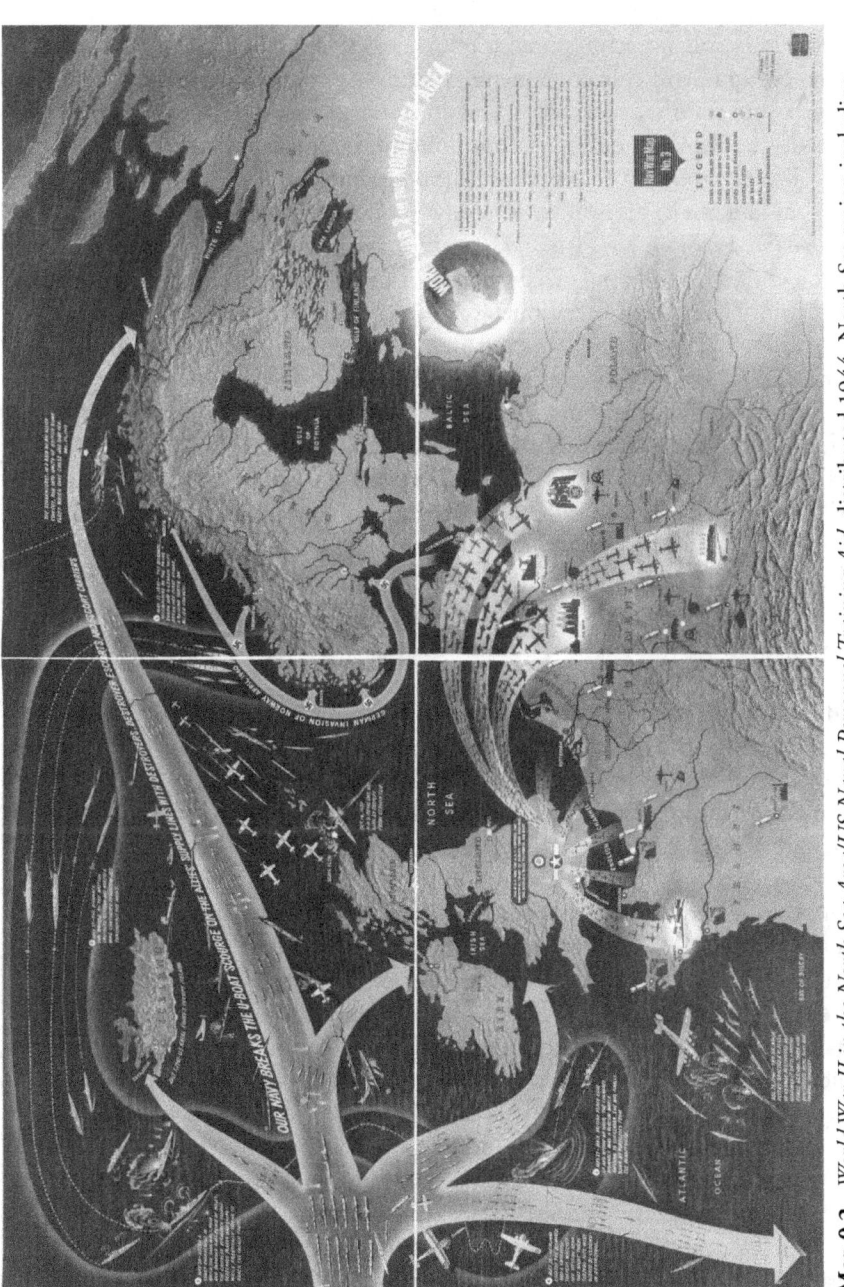

Map 0.2. *World War II in the North Sea Area/US Naval Personnel Training Aid*, distributed 1944. North Sea region including Iceland, Norway, Denmark, Sweden, Finland, and northern Russia, Germany, northern France, and intervening land and sea areas. Shows aircraft invasion routes from the United States and United Kingdom, as well as German invasion route of Norway; also includes principal areas bombed by the Allies, principal areas of naval engagements, Allied air bases, Allied naval bases, and German targeted facilities. Courtesy of the Library of Congress, Geography and Map Division.

account for the displacement, disruption, or erasure of family units that is inflicted by war on individuals and social groups.

Because this collaborative study employs varied approaches to historical narrative, cultural, and collective memory study—and, because this material deals with war trauma, military aggression and occupation and therefore histories of the displacement or victimization of different national (or social) groups—I draw attention to Michael Rothberg's notion of "multidirectional memory" as laid out in his influential study *Multidirectional Memory: Remembering the Holocaust in the Age of Decolonization* (2009). Rothberg's study serves as a corrective to popularized notions of the relationship between a collective memory and political, national, or ethnic identity, as one-directional or hereditary; Rothberg proposes instead that "we consider memory as multidirectional; as subject to ongoing negotiation, cross-referencing, and borrowing, as productive and not privative" (2009: 3). Rothberg argues for a rethinking of our conceptions of memory, particularly as they are relevant to postwar questions of "representation and recognition" in the modern world after the Holocaust, a world caught up in an ongoing process of decolonization (2009: 310). His insights on the interactive or "multidirectional" nature of cultural memory are applicable as well to this collaborative study of the particular memory formations of national identities in postwar Nordic narratives, especially when they rely on representations of nationally distinct World War II experiences.

Additionally, I would like to mention the significance of Alison Landsberg's pioneering study *Prosthetic Memory: The Transformation of American Remembrance in the Age of Mass Culture* (2004), as it is relevant on so many levels to the analysis of contemporary cinematic media dealing with World War II, and as it is also employed in chapter 19, which examines recent adaptions of the Finnish war film. Landsberg argues provocatively that modernity (and mass-mediated visual technologies) make possible an entirely new form of public cultural memory, which she terms *prosthetic memory*, that "emerges at the interface between a person and a historical narrative about the past, at an experiential site such as a movie theater or museum" (2004: 2). Landsberg depicts this modern mediated experience as a sensuous "moment of contact" in which a person "sutures himself or herself into a larger history" and thus acquires a "prosthetic memory" that has the "ability to shape that person's subjectivity and politics" (2004: 2), and that these artificially acquired memories, "like an artificial limb, are actually worn on the body; these are sensuous memories produced by an *experience* of mass-mediated representations" (2004: 20). Understandably—and considering Walter Benjamin's prescient observations in "The Work of Art in the Age of Its Mechanical Reproducibility," particularly his cautionary remark in the epilogue of 1939 regarding cinema's potential as a powerful medium of fascist propaganda—Landsberg demonstrates that such prosthetic or mass-mediated memories may function in social and historical contexts that are enormously problematic. (Such considerations are touched on in chapter 6, in the exploration of Karin Boye's ambivalent spectatorship of Leni Riefenstahl's 1938 film *Olympia*.) That said, the prosthetic memory also offers modern individuals and collectives opportunities for empathy and social change; Landsberg concludes her work by exploring the ethical dimensions of prosthetic memories, which "have the ability to alter a person's political outlook and affiliation as well as to motivate political action" (2004: 24).

Similar to other scholarly inquiries concerned with cultural memory and national identities, this project is invested in the multiple ways in which World War II experiences have been and are interpreted, mediated, and disseminated in the public sphere. An excellent example of cultural memory scholarship applied to World War II is that of Susan Rubin Suleiman, *Crises of Memory and the Second World War* (2006), particularly the notion of "crisis in memory," which is employed in chapter 10 that reads Sigurd Hoel's occupation novel through the lens of Suleiman's notion of a crisis in memory that both problematizes the knowledge of the past and questions the self-representation of a group of people in the present. Furthermore, Suleiman's analysis of Jean-Paul Sartre's work as a memoirist of Occupied France is generally thought-provoking in the context of this study of Nordic writers and war narratives. In her words, intellectuals and writers in their "acknowledged role as interpreters of public events, contribute significantly to the shaping of collective memories" (2006: 14). Suleiman demonstrates how Sartre exercised a significant role in interpreting France's World War II experience for the immediate postwar public; after the liberation, American magazines, such as *Vogue*, published Sartre's essays written in 1944–45, depicting the philosopher as a heroic figure of the underground French resistance movement (a role he never played). The situation of postwar France was problematic, given its collaborationist policies under the Vichy government (in some ways similar to Denmark's wartime policies); nonetheless, France claimed a seat among the victors at the postwar negotiating table. As an interpreter of culture, Sartre's essays played a significant role in reframing France's national wartime past in a favorable Allied context.

Lastly, an important contribution to contemporary nuanced understandings of cultural memory in relation to textual and visual representations is the work of Marianne Hirsch, *The Generation of Postmemory: Writing and Visual Culture After the Holocaust* (2012). Hirsch defines *postmemory* as an experience of the "generation after" (World War II), who bear the "personal, collective and cultural trauma" of their parental pasts. She postulates that some individuals who are born after the Holocaust to traumatized survivors or witnesses affectively experience postmemory:

> They "remember" by means of the stories, images, and behaviors among which they grew up. But these experiences were transmitted to them so deeply and affectively as to seem to constitute memories in their own right. Postmemory's connection to the past is thus actually mediated not by recall but by imaginative investment, projection, and creation. (Hirsch 2012: 5)

Thus, Hirsch's compelling notion of *postmemory* serves as both a corrective and a further elaboration of the Assmanns' typology of communicative and cultural memory, specifically because it accounts for the generation affected by displacement and war trauma—as Hirsch's theory addresses "the ruptures in memory transmission that are introduced by collective historical trauma, by war, Holocaust, exile, and refugeehood" (2012: 33). Under the Nazi regime in occupied Norway, the lives of thousands of ordinary civilians—not least Norway's Jewish citizens—were disrupted, threatened, and traumatized; families were displaced, and many individuals were forced into exile or deported to internment or concentration camps. Whereas in Finland (at war with the Soviet Union), the separation of young children from their biological families and evacuation to Sweden meant that an entire Finnish "generation after" (or *postgeneration*) has suffered acutely from the *postmemory* of the trauma of separation and displacement experienced by their parents as "war children"—a consideration taken up in chapter 16, which deals with the cinematic representation of the war child's trauma of displacement and homelessness in Klaus Härö's *Mother of Mine* (2005).

The Wartime Fates of the Nordic Countries

A close inspection of the Nordic region during World War II reveals five distinct fates and postwar destinies. These were vastly differing fates for the Nordic countries in the periphery of World War II, including occupation, resistance, neutrality, and military engagement (Gilmour 2013; Nissen 1983; Nordstrom 2000: 291–320). The Nordic countries were neither military aggressors nor leaders among "the great powers," obviously. However, neither were they passive. They (nation-states, political leaders, and individuals) were actors and agents; they made alliances, collaborated, engaged in combat as a belligerent (Finland), endured foreign occupations (Denmark, Norway, Iceland), resisted militarily (Norway), engaged in underground resistance and civil disobedience (Denmark, Norway), and acted as a neutral while also compromising that neutrality (Sweden).

The race for the north by warring powers largely ignored the pan-Nordic declaration of neutrality made in May 1938. When the war erupted in 1939, the cards fell as follows: Finland was engaged throughout the war as a belligerent (fighting three separate wars, two against the USSR—the second in alliance with Germany—and a third, the Lapland War, to drive the Germans out of northern Finland). Denmark (which had quickly capitulated) and Norway (which had fought a sixty-day war against the Wehrmacht forces) remained occupied by Nazi Germany for five long years. Iceland and the Faroe Islands, which were both still tied to the Danish kingdom, were peacefully occupied by the Allies (the British and the Americans). Only Sweden, caught by the Nazi-Soviet grip on its western border (by German-occupied Norway) and on its eastern borders (by the Soviet-Finnish conflict) maintained neutrality; however, Sweden's neutrality proved highly compromised by a "policy of concessions" that appeased German demands, including the profitable trade of iron ore (after the destruction of Narvik, the shipments continued via the Baltic Sea route) for the production of steel and the sale of ball bearings that fueled the Nazi German armaments industry. Only in 1943—after the tide of the war turned against Germany—did Sweden reform its refugee policy and engage in humanitarian operations that saved the lives of tens of thousands of persecuted peoples (including seven thousand Danish Jews), and also allowed the training of Danish and Norwegian troops on Swedish soil with the intent that they would be prepared, if necessary, to come to the aid of the Allied forces in a military "liberation" of the occupied countries.

In short, these are five entirely distinct political scenarios and wartime experiences that also led to differing postwar alliances and relations—for example, membership in the transatlantic military alliance NATO (North Atlantic Treaty Organization). Denmark, Iceland, and Norway were among the twelve founding member states in 1949, whereas Sweden and Finland remained neutral and nonaligned, and still today they stand outside the thirty NATO member states. In the European Union, Finland and Sweden are among only six EU member nations who have declared nonalignment with military alliances, including the NATO bloc. The transatlantic alliance on the one hand and the policies of nonalignment on the other are determined by the various geopolitical positions and national experiences of the Nordic countries in World War II, which contribute to the shaping of war narratives and national historiographies during the postwar decades and which still reverberate today.

In other words, given how each of the five Nordic countries experienced in World War II a distinct national political reality and postwar outcome, I determined to maintain national categories as organizational rubrics for the content of chapters in this volume rather than employ trans-Nordic themes and concerns to organize this collaborative study. Nevertheless, there is an effort throughout the chapters to offer intra-Nordic comparisons regarding political circumstances, national historiography, and cultural memory.

There are four parts to the volume, ordered as follows: (1) War Historiography; (2) War Literature: Archive; (3) War Literature: Canon; (4) War

Cinema. Each of these four parts consists of three to six original chapter contributions. Within the volume, I have provided "part introductions" that articulate the aim and content of each section and provide short chapter summaries. These short introductions also include the rationale for the internal ordering of chapters. Rather than order the chapters alphabetically by nation, as is often customary (for example, Denmark, Finland, Iceland, Norway, Sweden), I have determined to order the chapters according to the following principles. In War Historiography, the chapters are arranged chronologically according to the date of invasion or occupation (Finland, Denmark, Norway, Iceland, Sweden). In War Literature: Archive, they are also in chronological order, according to the date the text was originally *written*. Likewise in War Literature: Canon, the chapters are organized chronologically, according to the year the literary work was originally *published*. Finally, in War Cinema, the chapters are ordered according to the year that the films (or television series) were originally *produced*, beginning with the oldest and moving toward the most recent cinematic productions. I take full responsibility for any errors that were inadvertently introduced in the manuscript.

Marianne Stecher-Hansen (PhD, University of California, Berkeley, 1990) is Professor of Danish and Scandinavian Studies at the University of Washington. She has authored *The Creative Dialectic in Karen Blixen's Essays: On Gender, Nazi Germany, and Colonial Desire* (2014), and the critical commentary for *Karen Blixen: Værker; Skygger paa Græsset—Essays* (2020), and she has also edited *Danish Writers from the Reformation to Decadence 1550—1990* (2004) and *Twentieth-Century Danish Writers* (1999). She has also published *History Revisited: Fact and Fiction in Thorkild Hansen's Documentary Works* (1997).

References

Assmann, Aleida. 2010. "Canon and Archive." In *A Companion to Cultural Memory Studies*, edited by Astrid Erll and Ansgar Nünning, 97–107. Berlin: De Gruyter.
———. 2011. *Cultural Memory and Western Civilization: Functions, Media, Archives*. Cambridge: Cambridge University Press.
Assmann, Jan. 2010. "Communicative and Cultural Memory." In *A Companion to Cultural Memory Studies*, edited by Astrid Erll and Ansgar Nünning, 109–18. Berlin: De Gruyter.
Benjamin, Walter. 2018. "The Work of Art in the Age of Its Mechanical Reproducibility (1936–39)." In *The Norton Anthology of Theory and Criticism*, 3rd ed., edited by Vincent B. Leitch, 973–96. New York: Norton and Company.

Churchill, Winston. 1948. *The Second World War*. Vol. 1: *Gathering Storm*. Boston: Houghton Mifflin.
Ekman, Stig, and Nils Edling, eds. 1997. *War Experience, Self Image and National Identity: The Second World War as Myth and History*. Stockholm: Gidlunds Förlag.
Gilmour, John, and Jill Stephenson, eds. 2013. *Hitler's Scandinavian Legacy: The Consequences of the German Invasion for the Scandinavian Countries, Then and Now*. London: Bloomsbury Academic.
Häikiö, Martii. 1983. "The Race for Northern Europe, September 1939–June 1940." In *Scandinavia during the Second World War*, edited by Henrik S. Nissen, translated by Thomas Munch-Petersen, 53–97. Minneapolis: University of Minnesota Press.
Hirsch, Marianne. 2012. *The Generation of Postmemory: Writing and Visual Culture after the Holocaust*. New York: Columbia University Press.
Keegan, John. 1989. *The Second World War*. New York: Viking.
———. 1996. *The Battle for History: Re-fighting World War II*. New York: Vintage Books.
———. 1997. "Do We Need a New History of the Second World War?" In *War Experience, Self Image and National Identity: The Second World War as Myth and History*, edited by Stig Ekman and Nils Edling, 81–92. Stockholm: Gidlunds Förlag.
Landsberg, Alison. 2004. *Prosthetic Memory: The Transformation of American Remembrance in the Age of Mass Culture*. New York: Columbia University Press.
Nissen, Henrik, ed. 1983. *Scandinavia during the Second World War*. Translated by Thomas Munch-Petersen. Minneapolis: University of Minnesota Press.
Nordstrom, Byron J. 2000. *Scandinavia, since 1500*. Minneapolis: University of Minnesota Press.
Overy, Richard. 2013. "Scandinavia in the Second World War." In *Hitler's Scandinavian Legacy: The Consequences of the German Invasion for the Scandinavian Countries, Then and Now*, edited by John Gilmour and Jill Stephenson, 13–37. London: Bloomsbury Academic.
Rings, Werner. 1982. *Life with the Enemy: Collaboration and Resistance in Hitler's Europe, 1939–1945*. Translated by J. Maxwell Brownjohn. New York: Doubleday.
Rothberg, Michael. 2009. *Multidirectional Memory: Remembering the Holocaust in the Age of Decolonization*. Stanford, CA: Stanford University Press.
Snyder, Timothy. 2010. *Bloodlands: Europe between Hitler and Stalin*. New York: Basic Books.
Stenius, Henrik, Mirja Österberg, and Johan Östling, eds. 2011. *Nordic Narratives of the Second World War: National Historiographies Revisited*. Lund: Nordic Academic Press.
Stecher-Hansen, Marianne. 1997. "Art and Politics in *Processen mod Hamsun*." In *History Revisited—Fact and Fiction in Thorkild Hansen's Documentary Works*, 137–50. Columbia, SC: Camden House.
———. 1999. "Whose Hamsun? Author and Artifice: Knut Hamsun, Thorkild Hansen, and Per Olov Enquist." *Edda Nordisk tidsskrift for litteraturforskning* 3: 245–51.
Suleiman, Susan Rubin. 2006. *Crisis in Memory and the Second World War*. Cambridge, MA: Harvard University Press.
White, Hayden. 2018. "The Historical Text as Literary Artifact." In *The Norton Anthology of Theory and Criticism*, 3rd ed., edited by Vincent B. Leitch, 1463–80. New York: Norton and Company.

Part I

War Historiography

This first part of this volume addresses the World War II historiography of the Nordic region. Not only do these five chapters offer historical overviews of complex historical circumstances, they also delineate the dominant historical narratives as they pertain to the cultural memory of the war in each of the Nordic countries. The chapters here illuminate the master narratives of five distinct national historiographies that, as later demonstrated, inform and interact with the literary and media narratives about the war experience—often contesting the public cultural memories of the war years. Nordic scholars who specialize in the war history of Denmark, Finland, Iceland, Norway, and Sweden are the invited contributors of these chapters.

Finland was in fact the only Nordic nation that was engaged as a "belligerent" power throughout the entire period of the 1939–45 global conflict, fighting three "separate wars" (the Winter War and the Continuation War against the Soviet Union, and the Lapland War to drive the German troops out of its Arctic region). These wars cost the newly founded Republic of Finland dearly and inflicted collective trauma on the entire civilian population: over ninety thousand Finnish soldiers died in the hostilities, a half a million civilians were internally displaced, with approximately seventy thousand Finnish children evacuated to Sweden. Nonetheless, by successfully fending off Soviet occupation and defending its borders (which involved a 1941–44 military alliance with Germany), Finland preserved its sovereignty as a democratic republic. Finland did not fall to the Soviet Union and thus avoided the tragic fate of her Baltic neighbors Estonia, Latvia, and Lithuania. Hence, World War II is constructed in Finnish cultural memory as the "good war" or the unifying war. In chapter 1, Juhana Aunesluoma of the University of Helsinki argues that annual, institutionalized state commemorations of World War II (for example, the frequent televised showing of Edvin Laine's 1955 film classic *The Unknown Soldier* on 6 December) memorialize it as the "good war," the event that ultimately unified the Finnish nation, while at the same time actively silencing the public memory of the divisive civil war of 1918 (that had followed the founding of the republic in December 1917). Aunesluoma demonstrates how nationalist narratives of patriotism and heroism collide with a cultural memory of collective trauma, and he argues that since the 1990s there has been a neopatriotic turn in Finnish World War II memory culture.

The following two chapters illuminate the historical narratives of Nazi-occupied Denmark and Norway, respectively. On 9 April 1940, Denmark and Norway were invaded by numerous German military divisions, with Denmark serving as a mere stepping-stone to Norway. In chapter 2, Sofie Lene Bak of the University of Copenhagen unravels an intricate web of history and cultural memory in the experience of the occupied Danes. It is the story of a rapid surrender and a government policy of cooperation with Germany, which was gradually undermined by organized resistance and civil disobedience. German leaders had intended that Denmark would serve as the "model protectorate" for the Third Reich; the Danish parliament, police, and judiciary branch were allowed to remain in place (an illusion of democracy), operating according to an official Policy of Negotiation that lasted over three years, until late August 1943. This initial period of government collaboration was followed by increasingly organized resistance that ultimately allowed Denmark to join the table among the Allied victors in 1945.

In chapter 3, Norway's war experience is framed by Tom Kristiansen of the Arctic University of Norway as both "occupied" (albeit Norway fought a sixty-day war against German forces) and firmly "allied" (with a strong government-in-exile in the United Kingdom), a wartime status that gave rise to the long-established patriotic framework for Norway's war historiography. Kristiansen demonstrates how this postwar patriotic memory culture was gradually replaced, beginning in the 1970s, by more critically oriented, universalist approaches. New generations of historians have taken up previously omitted historical perspectives that had been neglected or actively negated.

Iceland's World War II experience is distinct from those of the European continent and the Scandinavian Peninsula. On 10 May 1940, Iceland—cut off from German-occupied Denmark (with which it shared a foreign policy)—was occupied by British troops, who were soon replaced by American military forces in 1941. The Allied occupation period came to be known in Icelandic parlance as the "Beloved War." The term is a reference to the economic prosperity and forces of modernity brought by the Allies that rapidly transformed the Icelandic nation and pushed it toward independence. In chapter 4, Guðmundur Hálfdanarson of the University of Iceland teases out the official institutionalization of the new nation's World War II narrative by means of a close reading of a historic exhibition catalogue, which had been produced for the museum exhibit "Freedom and Culture" celebrating the official founding of the Republic of Iceland on 21 June 1944. As the analysis of the 1944 catalogue demonstrates, the exhibition was intended to construct an official collective memory for the citizens of the new republic. Hálfdanarson argues that the World War II experience is notable for its relative absence in Iceland's official historiography, and that Iceland's official historical narrative treats the war as an isolated episode (even though the Allied occupation fundamentally transformed Icelandic society), because it does not fit neatly into the Icelandic grand narrative of freedom and cultural independence.

During World War II, Sweden successfully defended its neutrality and national sovereignty by means of a combination of robust military preparedness and skillful political diplomacy. In chapter 5, John Gilmour discusses the ambiguity of Sweden's experience in World War II and the contradictions and controversies that surround its wartime neutrality policies and are imbedded in postwar national historiography. Gilmour argues that ambiguity was in fact a defining tactic of neutral Sweden's social democratic prime minister Per Albin Hansson, whose unshakeable policy was to keep Sweden out of war by using a "negotiated neutrality," meaning an official Policy of Concessions that accommodated German demands. The wartime coalition government fulfilled its stated policy to keep Sweden out of war, and for decades historians have defended Sweden's wartime policies as "small-state realism." Due to neutrality, the Swedish welfare state had protected its citizens from the trauma and destruction of war; further, this meant that, when the tide of the war turned against Nazi Germany in 1943, the nation was in a position to offer humanitarian aid and shelter to tens of thousands of Jewish refugees as well as Danish and Norwegian resistance fighters. Nonetheless—particularly since the 1990s—Sweden as "bystander" and subsequently "rescuer" in World War II has fallen under continual scrutiny and engendered ongoing controversies.

Chapter 1

FINLAND IN WORLD WAR II

Tragedy, Survival, and Good Wars

Juhana Aunesluoma

To understand the centrality of the memory of World War II in Finland, one needs to do no more than open a television set on the country's Independence Day, 6 December. After the usual afternoon showing of Edwin Laine's classic 1950s film *The Unknown Soldier*, an adaptation of Väinö Linna's epic war novel, on the national broadcasting company YLE's main channel, the nation turns its gaze to the reception in the President's Palace in Helsinki. The reception is a peculiar mixture of formal state function and glittery ball, hosting close to two thousand invited guests dressed in evening gowns, white ties, and decorations. Broadcast live on Finnish television channels, the event has an audience of close to three million viewers in a country of five and a half million, making it the nation's most popular television program.

The evening follows a customary order. As the doors open, a line of older men and women first enter, some in uniform, most not. After they have greeted the presidential couple in front of a row of television cameras, a procession of other guests follows them into the spotlight. The nation then spends the next hours watching a succession of presidential handshakes—or, rather, a documentation of who has been invited this year and what the women are wearing. It is practically self-evident that veterans of World War II take the place of honor in the proceedings. That survivors of a nation's most significant military conflict are honored in this way on a national holiday is hardly an anomaly in international comparison. In Finland, however, World

War II commemoration serves a special purpose. Despite its tragic qualities, it is a good war to remember.

"In order to remember some things, other things must be forgotten," Aleida Assmann writes (2008: 97). Finnish Independence Day celebrations show how critical forgetting is, and also how selective any form of memory is. With each anniversary, one is struck by the absence of the historical context whereby Finland actually gained its independence. Spurred by the collapse of the Russian empire and the political chaos that ensued, the Finnish parliament declared independence in December 1917. The independent state was, however, socially and politically divided, and a civil war erupted in January 1918. Thirty-six thousand people (1 percent of the population) were killed in the conflict, making it one of the proportionately bloodiest civil wars in modern European history (Gerwarth 2017: 98–99).

In the interwar years, the War of Liberation of 1918—as the victorious side, the Whites, called it—was the war that was actively remembered. In the remembrance culture of the so-called first republic, the Whites' triumph over the revolutionary Reds in May 1918 sealed the nation's independence. That memory was manifestly a winner's memory, leaving aside the experiences of the vanquished, their suffering, and the perished on their side that greatly outnumbered those in the victor's ranks.

"In the memory of 1918 there were elements for both those, who wanted to remember and for those, who preferred to forget," writes Finnish scholar Heino Nyyssönen (2008: 214). The Whites celebrated 16 May 1918, the day of the victory parade in Helsinki, as the day when Finland truly became independent. With so many working-class men on the front, whose fathers or mothers had fought in the Red Guards in 1918, that tradition was abandoned during World War II. In 1945, with the reentry of the Communist left in Finnish political life, the center of attention shifted further. As the White memory culture became problematic, the country had a new, even greater conflict and a larger tragedy to cope with. Its struggle with the Soviet Union in 1939–44 eclipsed prior hardship and blurred earlier divisions of Finnish society, or so it seemed. In any case, World War II was a much better war to remember, as now Finland had not squandered its fortunes in internal strife but had successfully defended its independence. As a popular myth from the time of war has had it ever since, the Finnish nation regained its lost unity by fighting an external enemy.

In the mnemonic strategies of the postwar second Finnish republic, it was essential to overcome the divided memories of the first. World War II became the critical juncture where the newborn republic came of age, and despite its tragic nature, Finns devised their own, surprisingly unproblematic ways to commemorate it. Strong narratives and stable conventions were soon established to support institutionalized and consensual forms of remembrance.

The center of attention became not so much the state that represented historical continuity between the first and second republics but the people who had fought in the war. As fighting the war really had been a collective endeavor, with a standing army of more than half a million men and women at its peak in 1941–44, there were a large number of veterans of war to act as agents of memory. As late as 2004, one hundred thousand people were alive who had served at the front (Jokisipilä 2004: 23).

Remembering Finland's part in the world conflict required a nationwide exercise of forgetting in a way that was similar with other nations recovering from war (Judt 2002, 2008). But unlike in most other European countries, this did not happen in Finland because of what had come to pass during the war, but because of what had taken place before it. The day of 6 December became the moment when the whole nation could come together and join in new forms of collective remembrance and commemoration. However, instead of looking back to the birth pangs of the republic in the endgames of World War I and the civil war of 1918, the years 1939–44 provided a reference point and a transmission mechanism that connected the coming of the independent state to its present social and political shape.

The ways in which Finns simultaneously commemorate World War II and independence have been remarkably consistent for more than seventy years now. Without the need to forget a troubled past beyond World War II, and without the presence of a large number of veterans of war, these traditions might have taken on alternative forms. The veterans in Independence Day celebrations give past suffering and sacrifice a human face and remind us of the price paid for national survival. Relatively absent are glorifying tales from the front lines, battles heroically won or bravely lost. In their place are individual stories, usually of life after the war, survival, and recovery. The veterans give the day solemnity, but they do not spoil the party. After the ceremonial procession in the President's Palace early in the evening, it is time to dance.

Narratives of Three Wars

The annual independence celebrations take place with an increasing acuteness that a day is approaching when none of those who directly experienced the war will be left among us. While the memory of Finland's participation in World War II is gradually moving toward the realm of historical memory, with fewer and fewer Finns left with a personal connection to it, that memory shows no signs of fading. In Finnish historical culture, to use a broader concept involving both historiography and other representations of the past, the war years and their aftermath have long held a commanding position.[1]

Finland's experience of the world conflict has been discussed and represented in a large variety of accounts and narratives, all with their distinct features, actors, events, and turning points (Kinnunen and Kivimäki 2012). What is common to practically all of them is an understanding of Finland's part in World War II as a continuum of three different wars. Early on, the wars were given their own names: the Winter War, the Continuation War, and the Lapland War. This distinction was made to highlight the separateness of Finland's involvement in the global conflict. It underlines how the wars have been primarily understood in terms of Finland's own history, where a central theme has been the emergence of the Finnish state and nation, the history of its independence and survival. Still today, the wars serve as a collective myth supporting an idea of a unified nation forged in the crucible of war, a people earning the right for its existence in the international family of nation-states through its suffering and sacrifice (Meinander 2009: 392–98).

First came the Winter War (1939–40), when Finland defended itself against Soviet aggression.[2] After unsuccessful negotiations between Finland and the Soviet Union for territorial adjustments and Soviet military bases on Finnish soil, the Soviet Union attacked Finland on 30 November 1939 with the aim of establishing a Communist puppet government and subjugating the country under its rule. After 105 days of intense fighting and heavy losses on both sides, Finland managed to ward off the offensive and sue for peace in March 1940. Finland kept its independence, but peace came dearly.

The period of peace, with war raging elsewhere in Europe and with the Soviet Union tightening its grip over its western borderlands, was uneasy and short. As Finnish historian Timo Vihavainen has put it, "Since autumn 1940 Finland prepared for war, since peace was an option on offer only in the graveyard" (1998: 195). Fearful of Soviet intentions, Finland joined Germany's attack, Operation Barbarossa, on the Soviet Union in June 1941. During the Continuation War (1941–44), Finnish forces quickly regained the territories lost in the Winter War and advanced farther east. By the end of 1941, they formed a defensive line in the Karelian Isthmus, close to besieged Leningrad, and further north and east in Soviet Karelia. After a series of decisive battles in the summer of 1944, when Finland yet again stopped a Soviet offensive along the Eastern Front, it concluded an armistice and pulled out of the war. To fulfill the terms of the September 1944 armistice agreement, Finland turned its arms against its former ally Germany in the Lapland War (1944–45). The final terms of peace were settled in the Paris Peace Treaty of 1947.

While Finland avoided occupation and preserved its independence and democratic institutions, the wars saddled it with a heavy burden. More than ninety thousand soldiers and two thousand civilians died in hostilities. Territorial losses amounted to 10 percent of Finland's prewar territory. It had to pay reparations to the Soviet Union amounting up to 5 percent of Finland's gross national product, which took priority over its own postwar economic needs.[3] The government had to find new homes for more than four hundred thousand internally displaced persons, who for the most part were Karelian evacuees from the eastern territories ceded to the Soviet Union. A massive reconstruction task awaited. It gave the people both a physical purpose and a psychological escape, a sense of a *stunde null*, a year zero and a new beginning.

Postwar Revisionism

Despite a strong tendency to adopt a consensual grand narrative with a focus on the "people's war," the debate about the politics of Finland's involvement started as soon as the war ended. Finland's new political leaders, representing continuity in their domestic political color but marked discontinuity in their foreign policy views, sought to reassure the Soviet Union of their country's friendly intentions. In 1948, the two countries concluded a friendship, cooperation, and mutual assistance pact. Despite close ties to the Soviet Union, Finland pursued a policy of neutrality that aimed to secure its independence in the Cold War.

The new political orientation necessitated a clear break with the past, as well as a condemnation of the wartime leaders and their actions. In their revisionist view, colored by the needs of Finland's Cold War neutrality, postwar leaders accused their predecessors of "irresponsible adventurism" that had endangered the very existence of the nation. While the new foreign policy had the overwhelming support of the people and was favored across the political spectrum, views of the war varied in different segments of Finnish society. Many men and women who had served at the front continued to be suspicious of Soviet intentions in the postwar world, as they felt that none of the three wars had been Finland's fault. This put popular views of the war at odds with those that underpinned the country's new international position.

The most controversial issue was how Finland had ended up joining Germany in its attack on the Soviet Union in 1941, and why it kept on fighting on its side until late summer 1944. According to the official government line during the war, Finland sought to compensate for the losses it had suffered during the Winter War, and it fought in self-defense. Two postwar presidents, Juho Kusti Paasikivi (1946–56) and Urho Kekkonen (1956–81), were, however, both vocal in their criticism. According to them, the wartime leaders had been motivated by revanchism and had maintained a poor grasp of the geopolitical realities of the world at the time. They had never fully utilized the opportunities for negotiations and peace with the Soviet Union. Instead of joining Operation Barbarossa in 1941, Finland should have followed a policy of neutrality, just like Sweden had done. Furthermore, with the final outcome of the war in sight after Germany's debacle in Stalingrad, Finland should have aspired for a negotiated peace much earlier than it did. Touching an even more sensitive nerve, both presidents held the view that, with a failure of its diplomacy and with its unaccommodating stance toward Stalin's demands, Finland also bore its own responsibility for the outbreak of war in 1939. Paasikivi lambasted his predecessors that Finnish foreign policy had been conducted with gross negligence of the national interest, and he suggested a more realist alternative that would "recognize facts" and prioritize above anything else Finland's association with the Soviet Union in its foreign relations (Polvinen 1999: 28–29).

What the postwar revisionism meant in practice was put to test in the so-called war guilt trial in 1945–46. As a trust-building measure, and following the demands of the Allies that wartime leaders of Germany and its allies should be put to trial after the war, Paasikivi's government charged the wartime leaders for their decision to reenter and keep Finland in the war until 1944. Finland's wartime president Risto Ryti received a ten-year sentence in prison. A number of other leaders received shorter sentences. No death penalties were given, as the events stemmed from political decisions, not war crimes. War crimes were pursued in other trials, dealing with, among other things, the mistreatment of the civilian population in occupied Soviet Karelia and the deaths of Soviet prisoners of war in Finnish camps.[4] A notable omission among the list of persons convicted in the war guilt trial was the supreme commander of Finnish defense forces and the republic's first postwar president, Marshal Gustav Mannerheim (1944–46). By now a symbol of national unity, he had been instrumental in all the decisions the others were found guilty of in the war guilt trial, but he was spared as his presence was required as a moderating force to guide the nation from war to peace.

The trial was based on retroactive law, in itself a violation of what is commonly agreed to constitute a key principle of the rule of law: one cannot be convicted of a crime if it was not a crime at the time of the act. Not surprisingly, apart from the supporters of the left-wing parties, the trial was highly contentious among a significant part of the population. In their view, Ryti and others had hardly been guilty of anything else than doing their duty to defend the country in difficult circumstances. Although the sentences were lenient by European standards, anyone in Finland who felt that their nation as a whole had been treated unjustly in the war and in its aftermath could regard the imprisoned leaders as their martyrs.

What was significant, however, was that the trial gave the wartime leaders an opportunity to defend themselves and make their case, albeit within the parameters set by the court (Meinander 2011; Aunesluoma 2013). In the public proceedings and in written testimonials, a narrative of Finland having

Figure 1.1. Finland's relationship with Germany in 1941–44 was both close and tense. It became the topic of the most heated historiographical controversies in postwar decades. While the government insisted that the country was fighting a separate war against the Soviet Union, it could not hide the fact that Finland's war effort rested on its cooperation with Germany. On the occasion of Marshal Gustaf Mannerheim's seventy-fifth birthday, Adolf Hitler paid a surprise visit to Finland in June 1942, underlining the wartime bond between the two countries. Hitler is flanked by the marshal (*left*) and Finland's wartime president Risto Ryti (*right*). Courtesy of SA-kuva.

been dragged into the war against its own will was constructed. It is very likely that an apologetic version of wartime events would have emerged in any case soon after the war as a counterforce to the politically motivated revisionism, but a trial considered illegitimate in turn legitimated the defense's case beyond what it probably would have been in other circumstances. As they mounted their defense, the accused composed a rather extreme version of wartime events and decisions that stretched and omitted evidence as suited them, culminating in anything but a thorough and objective account of what had transpired. For anyone wishing to see Finland as a helpless victim of the war and the machinations of great powers, the defendants' case provided a selection of historical facts and arguments that could be used to support that interpretation for decades to come.

World War II Driftwood?

At the core of the interpretation was what later came to be known as the "driftwood theory" of Finland's reentry into the war in 1941.[5] According to this theory, events in the main theaters of the war and actions of powers beyond Finland's control had dragged Finland into war against the Soviet Union. The country was an object of aggression and not really a willing partner in Hitler's coalition, as the prosecutors suggested. Furthermore, it had fought its own "separate war" against the Soviet Union, and it had not joined in Nazi atrocities against Jews and other minorities.

After the trial, the defense's interpretation became the mainstay of historical accounts and memoir literature. It was repeated in the memoirs of the German wartime ambassador to Finland, Wipert von Blücher, who compared Finland's destiny to driftwood that was pulled into the torrent of great power politics, and thus it provided the key metaphor for Finns to describe their relationship with Hitler's Germany (von Blücher 1950). The English-reading public was also soon able to familiarize itself with the interpretation in Columbia history professor John H. Wuorinen's edited volume *Finland and World War II, 1939–1944*, published in 1948 in the United States (Herlin 1998). After resigning from the presidency in 1946, Marshal Mannerheim wrote his memoirs, in which the same line of argument was presented to a large audience in Finland (Mannerheim 1954). As the argument went, Finland had not been an active agent but a passive victim in the war. The new political leadership of Cold War Finland found it uncomfortable, but such was the strength of the argument that even President Kekkonen, who as minister of justice had been responsible for orchestrating the war guilt trial, ended up avoiding taking issue with it in his quarter century in office (Meinander 2011).

The tension arising from popular views of the war and Finland's new geopolitical position found outlets in public history and the war's cultural representations. While the Treaty of Friendship, Cooperation and Mutual Assistance and its application obliged Finns to forget the mutual animosity between the Soviet Union and Finland when looking at and thinking about the recent past, their gaze turned elsewhere—to the "people's war." The situation prompted artists and ordinary people to create their own histories of the war. From the mid-1950s onward and all the way to the present, this level of writing, experiencing, and displaying World War II history has made up the most voluminous and—when it comes to the wider public—probably the most accessible and influential part of all historical representations of it.

The critical point in the artistic expressions and representations of the war was Väinö Linna's novel *The Unknown Soldier*, published in 1954, as discussed in subsequent chapters in this volume. It was the first realistic fiction account of the war at the front and achieved immense popularity as soon as it was published. A film version became the biggest box office success in the history of the Finnish film industry. Characteristic of Linna's but also of other popular or artistic representations of the war, it took no explicit stand on the debate about Finland and Germany. By looking at the individual soldier's experience, it avoided the thorny issue of who fought with whom and for what purpose, and it removed politics almost completely from the picture.

Did Finland Choose War?

The calm around the driftwood explanation started to show its first cracks in the late 1950s. Utilizing German and Western archival materials, American and British historians C. Leonard Lundin, Anthony Upton, and Hans Peter Krosby challenged the driftwood thesis and brought it down in the late 1950s and 1960s (Lundin 1957; Upton 1964; Krosby 1967). According to them, it had been clear that the Finnish leadership had chosen war in 1941, planned their offensive operations in cooperation with the Germans, and taken a calculated risk to correct the wrongs of the Moscow Peace of 1940. Finnish historians, spearheaded by Professor Arvi Korhonen, who had assisted Risto Ryti in the trial in 1946, put up a defense but were eventually overwhelmed by documentary evidence and the compelling logic of the reinterpretation (Korhonen 1961).

If one accepted that the Finnish government had indeed chosen war in 1941, it opened up controversial questions over particular actions and personalities that had been avoided previously. A debate on and representations of, in particular, the forging of the alliance of a kind with Germany in 1941 and the events of summer 1944 thereafter began to revolve around concepts such as heroism, opportunism, ideology—all depending on the viewpoint of those conducting the argument. This debate, which has continued until this day, is not without ideological or moral undertones, and, however uneasy, it links the Finnish debate with international debates about the war's humanitarian dimensions, in particular the Holocaust (Holmila 2012).

The questioning of the validity of the driftwood thesis was connected to the cultural and intellectual milieu of the 1960s. The rising tide of left-wing movements and sentiments in national political life took one of its cues from criticism of the actions of the wartime generation. To accept the new interpretations of Finland's partnership with Hitler also indicated a political discontinuity. Finns should finally make a break with the war generation and the one that had preceded it. This process, however, remained in many ways incomplete. Continuities proved strong, and, on the level of historical culture, a sizeable tranche of opinion would still in the future show sympathy for the men on trial in 1946.

With Finnish agency accepted in principle among professional historians, the debate took different directions. In the 1970s and 1980s, historiography widened to cover the Finnish military occupation of Soviet Karelia, the mistreatment of its civilian population and Soviet prisoners of war, the war at the home front, its social and economic history, and the diplomatic history behind the wars, among other topics. In 2003, to use the words of Antero Holmila, "The Holocaust truly exploded into Finnish historical culture" with the publication of Elina Sana's popular book *Luovutetut* (The extradited) (Holmila 2012). Countering an earlier claim of eight Jews having being deported to Germany, Sana claimed that in fact forty-seven Jews were handed over to the Germans (Sana 2003). This sparked a heated controversy and a new wave of well-funded archival research establishing the extent to which Finnish authorities deported Soviet prisoners of war and civilians to Germany, deaths of civilians in internment camps, and the relatively high mortality rate of Soviet prisoners of war (Westerlund 2008; Kujala 2008). Another turning point was Oula Silvennoinen's doctoral dissertation in 2008 on the cooperation of the Finnish security police with their German counterparts. It established how they had been more involved and better informed about the murderous activities of the German *Einsatzkommando* (mobile killing squads) in northern Finland than had generally been assumed (Silvennoinen 2008).

Despite these trends in recent scholarship, and in particular with the end of the Cold War and the disappearance of the Soviet Union, scholars have identified a neopatriotic turn in Finnish World War II historical culture (Kinnunen and Jokisipilä 2012). In it, Finland's own, uniquely held war experience retakes center stage. In the culture of popular commemoration and representations of the war, this tendency has been discernible since the 1990s and does not show signs of weakening. In historiography, it has taken various guises. The battles on the Eastern Front in the summer of 1944 have been reassessed. As the country was saved from military occupation, it gained a "defensive victory," itself a part of the vocabulary of the military commanders at the front at the time. Revisiting Risto Ryti's original line of defense, neopatriotic historiography has been keen to emphasize Finland's involvement in World War II as a separate war. Unhampered by the foreign policy constraints of his predecessors, President Mauno Koivisto (1982–95), who himself had served at the front, became a high-profile defender of the decisions made by Ryti's government. According to Koivisto, their decision to reenter the war in 1941 was the only one that could be made with the information to hand, and in any case it saved the country and its people. If neutrality suited Finland well in the Cold War, it was not really an option on the table in 1941 (Koivisto 1998).

To this day, a tension exists between the views of the majority of historians and those of the general public. This has led to recurrent clashes with especially a younger generation of revisionist historians, who frame their work under the general heading of "new war history," and a public with more traditional views.

Conclusion: Politics and History

The ways in which Cold War–era Finns discussed and debated their involvement in World War II were to a large extent influenced by political developments in postwar Finland. To square the views of the war conditioned by postwar realpolitik, and the more popularly shared views of the wars as a necessary sacrifice, was not an easy task. The easiest strategy to cope with the trauma of war was to state that what had happened to Finland had more or less been inevitable, and in any case it had occurred beyond the influence of the decision-making powers of Finns themselves. The country's fate had not been decided in Helsinki, and not even on the battlefields, but in the chancelleries of power in Berlin, Moscow, and elsewhere.

This version of Finnish *Vergangenheitsbewältigun* (managing a problematic past) could not prevent the history and memory of the war from becoming politicized, with current developments in Finland's relationship with the Soviet Union setting the overall frame within which to evaluate its wartime behavior. Finland had fought, often heroically, and survived, but it had twice ended up on the losing side. It would not be given a third chance. What one thought about the politics of the war was connected to what one thought about the politics of the present, and about the appropriate strategies of how to cope with the Soviet Union in the postwar world.

This did not mean that there necessarily existed a forced silence in Finland about the war in general, or that its particular aspects were in public discourse suppressed by Finland's political elites. On the contrary, the war became right from the start a key element in Finnish historical culture and identity formation, a point of vigorous debate among historians and the general public, a salient feature in private and public memory and commemorative acts, and the topic of a variety of representations by artists, writers, filmmakers, and journalists.

However, some aspects of the war, especially its diplomatic and foreign policy dimensions, could not be discussed in a vacuum. As Finland's new international stance was founded on a policy of neutrality and accommodation with the Soviet Union, the war was considered to have taught the nation crucial lessons in the art of realpolitik, i.e., how to survive in a world dominated by great powers. For its postwar political leaders, a small, geopolitically vulnerable state had no other alternative than to seek the trust and friendship of its eastern neighbor. Open conflict with the Soviet Union, or, for that matter, any great power with a capacity of wielding its influence over Finland, was to be avoided by all means possible.

While Finns over time learned and were educated to appreciate this, a caveat was added: when trust fails, one can always fight to live another day. Finland had not been awarded its independence by outside powers in World War I; it had earned it on the battlefields of World War II. Its defenses withstood an overwhelming force twice, in 1940 and 1944, sparing the country from foreign occupation. With the passing away of the Soviet Union, and despite the coming to the fore of more troubling aspects of Finnish authorities' behavior in 1941–44, this aspect of the war continues to shape its memory. Postwar views of duty, survival, and heroism of ordinary Finns and their leaders still dominate it.

Juhana Aunesluoma (DPhil, University of Oxford, 1998) is Research Director at the multidisciplinary Centre for European Studies at the University of Helsinki. He has published extensively on Finnish twentieth-century history and Nordic and European post–World War II history, and he is the author of "Two Shadows over Finland: Hitler, Stalin and the Finns Facing the Second World War as History 1944–2010," in *Hitler's Scandinavian Legacy*, edited by John Gilmour and Jill Stephenson (2013).

Notes

1. On the concept historical culture, see Rüsen 1994; Torsti 2008.
2. For a general overview of Finnish military history in World War II, see Vehviläinen 2002.
3. The reparations burden was highest in 1945–48, with an average of 5 percent of GNP, and 2 percent in the remaining years 1949–52; Aunesluoma 2011: 95–98.
4. Deaths and violence in the internment camps of the civilian population in occupied Soviet Karelia and the mistreatment of Soviet prisoners of war in 1941–44 has been the object of several studies, beginning from the inquiries overseen by the Allied (Soviet) Control Commission in Finland in 1944–47. Despite an abundance of knowledge, it has been a topic of recent controversy, and in 2020 the Russian Federation set up a committee

of inquiry to study the matter accusing Finnish authorities of genocide. Rebuffing the claim, Finnish historians and the Finnish National Archives pointed out that a large body of detailed historical studies, archival evidence, and databases were readily available in Finland to anyone interested in the matter. The National Archives of Finland database of prisoners of war who died during the Winter War and Continuation War and of persons who died in civilian camps in East Karelia is available online at http://kronos.narc.fi/index.html. Nuorteva 2020.
5. A more detailed account of what is covered in the following sections in this chapter can be found in Aunesluoma 2013: 199–219.

References

Assmann, Aleida. 2008. "Canon and Archive." In *Cultural Memory Studies: An International and Interdisciplinary Handbook*, edited by Astrid Errl and Ansgar Nünning, 97–107. Berlin: De Gruyter.

Aunesluoma, Juhana. 2011. *Vapaakaupan tiellä, Suomen kauppa- ja integraatiopolitiikka maailmansodista EU-aikaan*. Helsinki: Suomalaisen Kirjallisuuden Seura.

———. 2013. "Two Shadows over Finland: Hitler, Stalin and the Finns Facing the Second World War as History 1944–2010." In *Hitler's Scandinavian Legacy: The Consequences of the German Invasion for the Scandinavian Countries, Then and Now*, edited by John Gilmour and Jill Stephenson, 199–219. London: Bloomsbury.

Blücher, Wipert von. 1950. *Suomen kohtalonaikoja: Muistelmia vuosilta 1934–44*. Helsinki: WSOY.

Gerwarth, Robert. 2017. *The Vanquished: Why the First World War Failed to End, 1917–1923*. London: Penguin Books.

Herlin, Ilkka. 1998. "Suomi-neidon menetetty kunnia—ajopuuteorian historia." In *Historiantutkijan muotokuva*, edited by Päiviö Tommila, 199–238. Helsinki: Suomen Historiallinen Seura.

Holmila, Antero. 2012. "Varieties of Silence: Collective Memory of the Holocaust in Finland." In *Finland in World War II: History, Memory, Interpretations*, edited by Tiina Kinnunen and Ville Kivimäki, 519–60. Leiden: Brill.

Jokisipilä, Markku. 2004. *Aseveljiä vai liittolaisia? Suomi, Saksan liittosopimusvaatimukset ja Rytin-Ribbentropin sopimus*. Helsinki: Suomalaisen Kirjallisuuden Seura.

Judt, Tony. 2002. "The Past Is Another Country: Myth and Memory in Post-war Europe." In *Memory & Power in Post-War Europe: Studies in the Presence of the Past*, edited by Jan-Werner Müller, 157–83. Cambridge: Cambridge University Press.

———. 2008. "The Problem of Evil in Postwar Europe." *New York Review of Books* 55(2): 33–35.

Kinnunen, Tiina, and Markku Jokisipilä. 2012. "Shifting Images of 'Our Wars': Finnish Memory Culture of World War II." In *Finland in World War II: History, Memory, Interpretations*, edited by Tiina Kinnunen and Ville Kivimäki, 435–82. Leiden: Brill.

Kinnunen, Tiina, and Ville Kivimäki, eds. 2012. *Finland in World War II: History, Memory, Interpretations*. Leiden: Brill.

Kivimäki, Ville. 2012. "Introduction: Three Wars and Their Epitaphs: The Finnish History and Scholarship of World War II." In *Finland in World War II: History, Memory, Interpretations*, edited by Tiina Kinnunen and Ville Kivimäki, 1–46. Leiden: Brill.

Koivisto, Mauno. 1998. *Koulussa ja sodassa*. Helsinki: Kirjayhtymä.

Korhonen, Arvi. 1961. *Barbarossa-suunnitelma ja Suomi: Jatkosodan synty*. Helsinki: WSOY.
Krosby, Hans Peter. 1967. *Suomen valinta 1941*. Helsinki: Kirjayhtymä.
Kujala, Antti. 2008. *Vankisurmat: Neuvostosotavankien laittomat ampumiset jatkosodassa*. Helsinki: WSOY.
Lundin, Charles Leonard. 1957. *Finland in the Second World War*. Bloomington: Indiana University Press.
Mannerheim, C. G. E. 1954. *Marskalkens minnen I–II*. Helsingfors: Schildt.
Meinander, Henrik. 2009. *Suomi 1944: Sota, yhteiskunta, tunnemaisema*. Helsinki: Kustannusosakeyhtiö Siltala.
———. 2011. "A Separate Story? Interpretations of Finland in the Second World War." In *Nordic Narratives of the Second World War: National Historiographies Revisited*, edited by Henrik Stenius, Mirja Österberg, and Johan Östling, 55–77. Lund: Nordic Academic Press.
Nuorteva, Jussi. 2020. "Genocide Investigation Launched in Russia Causes Confusion: Finland Investigated the Shortcomings of the Camps in East Karelia Immediately after the Continuation War." *Helsingin Sanomat*, 29 April 2020. https://www.hs.fi/mielipide/art-2000006491081.html.
Nyyssönen, Heino. 2008. "Commemorating Two Political Anniversaries in Cold War Finland: Independence and the Beginning of the Winter War." In *The Cold War and the Politics of History*, edited by Juhana Aunesluoma and Pauli Kettunen, 207–25. Helsinki: Edita Publishing and University of Helsinki Department of Social Science History.
Polvinen, Tuomo. 1999. *J.K. Paasikivi: Valtiomiehen elämäntyö 4, 1944–1948*. Porvoo, Helsinki, Juva: WSOY.
Rüsen, Jürn. 1994. "Was ist Geschichtskultur? Überlegungen zu einer neuen Art, über Geschichte nachzudenken." In *Historische Faszination: Geschichtskultur heute*, edited by Jörn Rüsen, Theo Grütter, and Klaus Füssman, 3–26. Köln: Böhlau.
Sana, Elina. 2003. *Luovutetut: Suomen ihmisluovutukset Gestapolle*. Helsinki: WSOY.
Silvennoinen, Oula. 2008. *Salaiset aseveljet: Suomen ja Saksan turvallisuuspoliisiyhteistyö 1933–1944*. Helsinki: Otava.
Torsti, Pilvi. 2008. "Why Do History Politics Matter? The Case of the Estonian Bronze Soldier." In *The Cold War and the Politics of History*, edited by Juhana Aunesluoma and Pauli Kettunen, 19–35. Helsinki: Edita Publishing and University of Helsinki Department of Social Science History.
Upton, Anthony. 1964. *Finland in Crisis 1940–1941: A Study of Small-Power Politics*. London: Faber & Faber.
Vehviläinen, Olli. 2002. *Finland in the Second World War: Between Germany and Russia*. Basingstoke: Palgrave Macmillan.
Vihavainen, Timo. 1998. *Stalin ja suomalaiset*. Helsinki: Otava.
Westerlund, Lars. 2008. *POW Deaths and People Handed Over to Germany and the Soviet Union in 1939–1955: A Research Report by the Finnish National Archives*. Helsinki: National Archives.

Chapter 2

Danish Historical Narratives of the Occupation

The Promises and Lies of the 9th of April

Sofie Lene Bak

At 4:15 A.M. on 9 April 1940, German troops crossed the overland border into Denmark. Simultaneously, a troop carrier passed the silent cannons atop the fortress of Copenhagen, and the General Headquarters in the capital were conquered in fifteen minutes. Large numbers of German bombers flew over the entire country. Denmark was not originally part of the German military campaign. The Danish policy of appeasement of the Nazi regime, the country's formal status of neutrality, and, ultimately, the signing of a nonaggression pact in May 1939 ensured that Germany did not need to use force in order to obtain what it could get through diplomatic pressure. However, increased Allied activity in the North Atlantic around Norway attracted German attention to the Nordic countries—and to Denmark, in particular, as a useful stepping-stone in its campaign against Norway, whose strategic position and pro-British orientation made it an important target. Military occupation of Denmark was a means to an end. In the early morning hours of 9 April, a memorandum was handed to the Danish government stating that Germany had taken over protection of the Kingdom of Denmark. It declared, nevertheless, that Germany had "no intention to violate the territorial integrity and political independence of Denmark."[1] Now the political and economic prospects depended on the reactions of the Danes. The Danish government issued a cease-fire order at 6:00 A.M. after sporadic fighting mainly near the southern

border of Jutland. The capitulation of Denmark was a reality before sunrise. What became known as the "peaceful occupation" of Denmark allowed the government to insist on the formal sovereignty of the kingdom and created a unique and illusory construction in a Europe controlled by Nazi forces. Denmark was not in a state of war with Germany in neither a formal nor practical sense. In principle, Denmark was still ruled by king, government, and parliament. The Danish courts, administration, and even the army and police maintained an independent status. The affairs of the two countries were conducted through normal diplomatic channels, namely the German embassy and the Ministry of Foreign Affairs, the Auswärtiges Amt, in Berlin. Denmark never came under the control of the Nazi Party or the SS.

The "promises of the 9th of April" was a standard reference to Denmark's right to govern its own internal affairs. The arrangement required a minimum of German soldiers and officials. In return, Denmark supplied Germany with provisions, weapons, machines for the metal industry, cement, and ships; in 1941, it outlawed the Communist Party and interned its members, eventually signing the Anti-Comintern Pact, which called for combating international communism. In 1940, the Danish foreign minister even suggested a monetary and customs union with Germany, with negotiations stranding on German disagreement. From a Danish perspective, wealth was attainable in the occupied territories of Eastern Europe, and plans for exploring the business opportunities in the German *Grossraum* were initiated immediately after the German attack on the Soviet Union in late June 1941. The willingness to negotiate had a decisive effect on the standard of living in Denmark, where the average calorie consumption remained even higher than in Germany throughout the occupation and the unemployment rate dropped from 24.9 percent in 1940 to null in 1942. To put it bluntly, "Denmark had a good war" (Østergård 2011: 51). To the Germans, Denmark served an ideological purpose as a model protectorate, a prototype for the new Europe ruled by the Third Reich.

Whereas most politicians struggled with defining the limits of negotiation, the foreign minister (1940–43) and prime minister (1942–43) Erik Scavenius was a champion of an activist policy, not only complying with German demands but also actively obliging and predicting German wishes in order to achieve goodwill in Berlin. Such goodwill was then exchanged for a mutual avoidance of three areas that the Danish government would never yield to: military contributions to Axis warfare; Nazi Party members in government; and persecution of the Jewish minority.

During the summer of 1943, a wave of sabotage and strikes directed at the German Wehrmacht swept the country. The uprising, which began among industrial workers, spread and was supported by a growing number of Danish resistance groups. When the Allies won the psychologically crucial victory at El Alamein and Stalingrad did not fall, the Danes believed the collapse of the German regime was imminent and looked forward to the prospect of an Allied invasion. Since the Danish authorities had lost control of the masses, Berlin issued an ultimatum to the government, demanding martial law, curfew regulations, and the death penalty for sabotage against the Wehrmacht. Presented on 28 August, it was promptly rejected by the government and by a united front of political parties. In the early morning of 29 August the *Oberbefehlshaber der deutschen Besatzungstruppen* in Denmark proclaimed that the Wehrmacht had assumed executive power and declared a state of martial law. The government and parliament resigned, the king was put under house arrest, and the officers and soldiers of the Danish army and navy were interned.

However, the diplomatic break was not absolute. The Danish police and the courts remained free of German influence. The permanent secretaries of the ministries stayed in their positions and now represented "official" Denmark—a modus vivendi that served both German and Danish interests in continuing the status quo. Yet, what has been termed the "August uprising" of 1943 marked the beginning of the end. The political restraints that had guided German conduct had been lifted, and terror campaigns against the enemies of the Reich began immediately. Only a few weeks later, plans for the mass arrest and deportation of the Danish Jews were initiated, and the death penalty and execution of Danish members of the Danish resistance was instantly enforced. By September 1944, the Germans had lost confidence in the ability and willingness of the Danish police to combat the resistance and dissolved the police force, deporting two thousand police officers to German concentration camps. In all, six thousand Danes were deported to German prisons and concentrations camps (compared to nine thousand Norwegians) (Barfod 1969). In the last months of the occupation, citizens in the larger cities, and most prominently in the capital of Copenhagen, were regularly caught in the fire between collaborators in German-controlled terror groups and the resistance, a fight on the threshold of civil war.

The Master Narrative

In the early morning hours of 5 May 1945, a resistance group seized the printing house of the Nazi newspaper *Fædrelandet* (The Fatherland). Accessing the printing facilities marked the beginning of a war of interpretation. The formerly clandestine newsagent *Information*, which assumed the facilities, was one—among many—in the immediate postwar years to publish a flood of books on the occupation. The countless books all shared one common feature: they honored the active resistance against the German occupation, whether or not these writers and journalists had actually supported the resistance during the occupation. As Denmark was liberated by foreign forces, the interpretation of who had contributed to the liberation and the de facto recognition as an Allied nation were matters of national urgency. For the politicians, who had accepted the capitulation in 1940 and supported cooperation with the Germans, several preconditions for reentering the political scene impended. On one hand, they had to embrace the resistance, arguing a symbiosis of active and passive resistance by evoking the allegory of "the shield and dagger," an analogy to French perceptions of the Vichy regime that suggested the government had shielded the population from brutalities of war, enabling the resistance to raise the dagger (Paxton 1972). On the other hand, the old politicians discreetly discredited the active resistance as political hooligans and radicals—at best politically immature, at worst dangerous and undemocratic. As to legislation, the parties in the war coalition enabled a juridical purge of collaborators, including the reintroduction of the death penalty for treason, which corresponded with the demands of the resistance. Moreover, they instituted a compensation law—uniquely inclusive in a European comparative perspective—that provided recompense for imprisonment, restitution of property, and support for reestablishment of health, homes, and careers. Among other things, the compensation legislation provided student grants to former members of the resistance (Bak 2012). In the first election after liberation, in October 1945, the Communist Party, admired for its contribution to and sacrifices in the resistance, won 12 percent of the votes, compared to 2 percent in prewar elections. By 1947, their share of the votes dropped to 7 percent, normalizing and stabilizing the political system in years to come (Bundgård Christensen et al. 2020: 718). The political pressure to investigate whether or not the politicians could be held responsible for the occupation was relegated to a parliamentary commission that concluded its work eight years later with a complete acquittal.

On the other hand, the resistance was abundant in legitimacy yet politically divided, and it sought to secure the legacy of the movement by cultivating a commemoration culture, which enacted monuments and memorials. It also fought battles against attempts to discredit the resistance, succeeding among other things in closing all investigations into the approximately four hundred political assassinations conducted by resistance groups during the occupation (Emkjær 2000).

The result of the complex political situation was a compromise, a master narrative that suited both parties. According to Danish collective memory, the population had been united by anti-German, pro-British sentiments; it also broadly supported active resistance, which shaped a bipartisan, democratically founded movement protected by the passive "hidden" resistance of the mainstream political establishment (Bryld and Warring 1998). The first generation of historians focused almost exclusively on the resistance movement. The dominant figure, Jørgen Hæstrup, himself a member of a resistance group, compiled an intensive collection of testimonies and sources resulting in the volumes *Secret Alliance*, published in English in 1976–77.[2] Similar endeavors were conducted by the Museum of Danish Resistance in Copenhagen, established in 1957. The master narrative guided the conclusions on the wide support for the resistance, a national unity, and the shield-and-dagger consensus. Similar to the rest of Western Europe, celebration of the resistance movement and the victims of political persecution washed away the shame of collaboration—but, it also long hindered the acknowledgment of the Holocaust, as victims of genocide were assimilated under a patriotic discourse that did not leave much room for mourning the dead or acknowledging the racist and anti-Semitic motives behind the persecution.[3]

A War of Words—Danish Historiography of the German Occupation

Not only has the master narrative informed the first generation of professional historians but it continues to define Denmark's historiography, in particular the discourses on the mechanisms and consequences of the Danish policy pursued during the German occupation. Danish historiography employs at least three concepts that refer to the policy. The differences are not purely semantic, but also reflect theoretical disagreement. The choice of concept provides an excellent clue to the ideological position of the various writers on the topic.

The historian Hans Kirchhoff introduced the term "Policy of Collaboration" (*Kollaboration*) into Danish historiography in 1979.[4] Briefly, it focuses on the compliance and opportunism of the Danish government, arguing that the policy was similar, in some respects, to that conducted in Vichy France, Norway, and Holland, regardless of whether active support and assistance to the German military machine was the intent or the result. Thus, Kirchhoff along with his generation of historians introduced a revisionist approach, focusing on the contrasts in an occupied country torn by social, political, and economic conflict. Another contemporary, Aage Trommer, researched the effects of the railway sabotage and indubitably demonstrated that the sabotage had infinitesimal effect on the course of the war (and how few the saboteurs really were), offending and angering veterans of the resistance. They were not appeased a few years later when Trommer further concluded that the members were not recruited broadly from the Danish population but were extremists from the political margins (Trommer 1971; Trommer 1973). Both Trommer and Kirchhoff stressed the profound and mutual hostility between the political establishment and the resistance groups.

The term "Policy of Negotiation" (*Forhandlingspolitikken*), on the other hand, stresses the exigencies and advantages of negotiation for Danish politicians. The term, coined by politicians who felt a need to defend their behavior after the war, was adopted by the first and second postwar generation of historians, who considered it important to correct the prevailing image of these figures as treacherous and pro-German.[5] By using the word "negotiation," the researcher implies that the Danish government and the German authorities were equal negotiating partners in a neutral, almost mechanical process of adjustment.

In recent years, the focus of most research has moved from the history of the resistance to less flattering aspects of Danish wartime history. Substantial new findings on the refugee policy of the 1930s, anti-Semitism, and Danish Waffen-SS volunteers at the Eastern Front have given historians fresh insights into the mechanisms and dilemmas of policymaking during the occupation,[6] and most historians now tend toward a third concept of "Policy of Cooperation" (*Samarbejdspolitik*). A term originating in the illegal press, it stresses the voluntary, active nature of the policy on the part of the Danes and signifies that the Danish political effort to balance German pressure with more active support and integration into the German *Grossraum* was in the interests of the German occupiers. The fiction of a neutral Denmark, the peaceful occupation, and the logic of a policy of cooperation served the political ends of both the Germans in Denmark and the Ministry of Foreign Affairs in Berlin. The Policy of Cooperation was a political goal in itself: it gave the Danish government some freedom of action and placed considerable restraint on the Germans. Compared to the debate on the Holocaust, the term combines the "intentionalism" implied by the concept of "negotiation," by stressing the national and democratic motives of the politicians, with the "functionalism" entailed in "collaboration," by underlining the activist nature of the policy and its actual consequences. As of the 1990s, the concept of collaboration all but disappeared from the historical debate, and with it, the suspicion cast on the Danish government for being pro-German or even crypto-Nazi. Most historians in the third generation, often born in the 1960s, favor a neo-consensus emphasizing that Danish politicians saw it as their primary task to keep Denmark and its democratic institutions free of the terrors of war and totalitarianism and to pilot the country through the occupation without destruction and civilian casualties. In sum, it was "a legitimate response of the weak to the attack by the superpower Germany" (Kirchhoff 2008: 11–12). However, unlike the "negotiation" school, most third-generation historians agree that the end was not without costs. As politicians agreed to downsize democracy in order to fit the German shoe, only too late did they realize that the population reacted to the damage to their souls that was caused by humiliation and surrender.⁷

Resilience and Solidarity: Collective Memory of the Occupation

During the war, Danes would hum the tune from the vaudeville melody "They Bind Our Mouths and Hands,"⁸ a song made famous by the jazz singer Liva Weel in 1940. The song is still intimately connected to the memory of solidarity and national unity during the German occupation and corresponds neatly with the master narrative. The narrative of resilience also affected individual memory, the structuring and selecting of which events to remember.

Figure 2.1. Barricades in Nørrebro, a working-class neighborhood in Copenhagen during the "General Strike" (*Folkestrejken*) in the summer of 1944. Although communists orchestrated the initial strikes, the riots and ravages were a spontaneous public outcry against the German occupiers and were neither under the control of trade unions, politicians, nor the resistance movement. Copenhagen was in a state of civil war. Danish police refused to stop the riots, but collaborators in German-controlled terror groups and militias fought against their Danish countrymen in the streets of the capital. In the memory of the Danes, the General Strike restored national pride and overshadowed the less heroic attitudes of the first years of the occupation. Unknown photographer. Courtesy of the Museum of Danish Resistance 1940–1945.

During the "General Strike" (*Folkestrejken*) in Copenhagen in the summer of 1944, following the Allied landing in Normandy, workers in Copenhagen went on a strike, and riots broke out throughout the city. The German put the capital city under siege and cut off water, electricity, and gas supplies. During the strike, ninety-seven civilians were killed and more than six hundred injured (Bundgård Christensen et al. 2020: 506). Only German restraints prevented a massacre. In the memory of those Copenhageners that lived through the occupation, the intense summer days in 1944 during a heat wave overshadowed other memories of an everyday life of adaptation and collaboration. An activist attitude engaged men, women, and children in building barricades, sharing and preparing food under the open sky, and celebrating in the streets. The event continues to play an important role in collective memory of the war. However, the activism displayed in the General Strike, and in similar riots the year before in the major cities of Odense, Esbjerg, and Aarhus, was far from the social and political attitudes held by a majority of Danes in the first years of the occupation.

Danes may have been clenching their fists in their pockets or giving the German soldiers "the cold shoulder" (*den kolde skulder*) but most, in all likelihood, supported the government policy. In March 1943, democratic elections were held with a historical turnout of 89.5 percent, which has never been surpassed since. Ninety-five percent cast their vote for the democratic parties in the cooperation coalition (Bundgård Christensen et al. 2020: 376). Active resistance was a choice for the political margins, and broader recruitment to the resistance groups only happened in the last months of the war, when an Allied victory was obvious and preparations began for the final battle for liberation. Intimate fraternization with soldiers from the German Wehrmacht was fiercely scorned during and immediately after liberation. Danish women, contemptuously called *Tyskertøse* ("German tarts") or *Feltmadrasser* ("field mattresses") were marginalized as ugly, unintelligent, socially disadvantaged, and promiscuous, and their inconvenient memories were excluded from the national consciousness. In 1994, the collective war memory was challenged by the revelation that at least 50,000 Danish girls and women had had romantic or sexual relations with German soldiers or personnel. This statistic is relative to the 635,000 women between the ages of 15 and 29 in Denmark during the war. Although the study by Anette Warring was extensively publicized, the estimated extent of fraternization never seems to have sunk into public memory. In a republished version in 2017, Warring further emphasized that 50,000 is indeed a most conservative estimate (Warring 2017; Warring 2006). Similarly, the economic benefits and extent of collaborating with the enemy was documented by a series of studies conducted by the younger generation of historians (Andersen 2005; Lund 2005), which were revealed in the press as shocking revelations and then quickly forgotten.

Still, the last years of the occupation did provide opportunities for heroic behavior, with the rescue of the Danish Jews in October 1943 being the most conspicuous example. Thousands of Danes engaged themselves spontaneously in warning, sheltering, and escorting Jews to the small fishing hamlets on the coasts of Zealand, as well as organizing and financing the transport to neighboring Sweden. Their actions served as a testament to the master narrative: a unification of resistance groups, the political establishment, and ordinary Danes in a joint effort to avert disaster. However, the logic of the cooperation policy did lead the government to accept informal discrimination of Danish-Jewish businesses and public employees, the first losing German import and export contracts, the second promotions to public offices (Halvas Bjerre 2017), and brought the permanent secretaries of the ministries alarmingly close to assisting the Nazi *Endlösung* with a proposal for a "voluntary" Danish internment of the Jews (Bak 2010). Still, in consistently dismissing any German talk of "a Jewish problem," the Danish politicians were in consonance with the vast majority of the Danish population, and the events in October 1943 and the later support for Danish-Jewish deportees still mark some of the finest hours of Danish history.

Nonetheless, revisionist research has substantiated that most fishermen received payment for transporting the Jews to Sweden, and recent scholarship has also stressed that paramount to Jewish survival was the conscious and strategic German restraint rather than Danish heroism.[9] As the policy of cooperation allowed for mutual concessions, the Danish government refused to accept anti-Semitic persecution, and the Germans in Denmark realized that mass deportation of Jews would make it impossible to work for a mutual understanding between the two nations. The Germans did not have freedom of action when it came to the Jews, and they complied because of the benefits of cooperation. In a neo-consensus interpretation, the protection of the Jewish community in Denmark was thus an undoubted achievement of the cooperation policy. The scholarly research of the 1990s and 2000s challenged the master narrative of a population united in resilience, solidarity, and support for the resistance. Although historical research on the occupation years enjoys vivid attention in the Danish press, the findings and critical conclusions had limited effect on collective memory. On the contrary, the master narrative was reinterpreted by the new millennium, turning occupation history into a potent political battlefield.

A New Moral Narrative

Throughout the Cold War, the mantra "Never again a 9th of April!" was a powerful reference in debates on NATO memberships, as the slogan became a *lieux de memoire*, deprived of any historical, analytic meaning and reduced to a simplified, symbolic expression of shared identity and national unity. The legacy of the resistance was also instrumental in debates on membership in the European Economic Community, and asylum and immigration policies (Bundgård Christensen 2013). However, with the fall of Soviet Communism in the 1990s, a redefined Danish foreign policy called for a showdown with the Danish neutrality policy in the twentieth century and, first and foremost, with the Policy of Cooperation during World War II.

In 2003, on the occasion of the sixtieth anniversary of 29 August 1943, which marked the end of the Policy of Cooperation, the liberal-conservative prime minister, Anders Fogh Rasmussen, denounced that strategy in an official statement as naïve, reprehensible, and cowardly. Looking back to that April morning in 1940 when the difficult decision to cooperate was made, Denmark's prime minister dissociated himself from what he termed a political and moral failure. Fogh Rasmussen's assault on the cooperation policy marked a previously unseen attempt of politicizing the past in order to legitimize the turn in Danish foreign policy toward active military engagement first in NATO operations in Serbia in 1999 and later in Afghanistan in 2002 and Iraq in 2003–7. It was not only a radical departure from the center-left coalition of Social Democrats and Social Liberals, which had dominated Danish politics since 1929, but a signal toward the formation of a new narrative replacing the postwar master narrative. Coined the "moral narrative," it dissolves the consensus between passive and active resistance and rejects the motivation, urgency, and rationale of the cooperation policy (Bundgård Christensen 2013). The debate following the statement highlighted a growing distance between professional historians and the general public as well as a decontextualizing of the past. The ironic fact that the prime minister was the leader of Denmark's liberal-conservative party (*Venstre*), which had historically represented the agricultural interests that profited intensively from the cooperation with Nazi Germany during the war, made no difference. Evidently, the past serves as a department store from which customers can buy anything and pick and choose as they please.

The selective use of the past was obviously not an exclusively right-wing phenomenon, as an incident in 2012 demonstrates. The socialist city councilor of Copenhagen headed a press conference to announce new road names for a fashionable apartment building complex on the city's waterfront. The road names commemorated prime ministers in the governments during the war, but due to "political and moral considerations," initial plans for naming a new street after the foreign minister and prime minister Erik Scavenius were rejected by the city council. The socialist city councilor motivated the rejection, stating that "by 1943 it must have been clear for the Danish politicians, that something was absurdly wrong south of the border. Scavenius closed his eyes and tried to negotiate Denmark through the crisis. Some may think that the end justifies the means. I don't think so."[10]

As the shield metaphor rusted, glorification of the dagger, the active resistance, has been unabated, as can be observed through a comparison of the reception of two recent on-screen representations of Danish resistance. Extremely popular in the box office, the Danish action film, *Flammen og Citronen/Flame and Citron* (2008), a biopic based on the infamous resistance fighters Bent Faurschou-Hviid and Jørgen Haagen Schmith, who assassinated political enemies of the resistance, portrays the protagonists as morally ambiguous characters, prone to blood thirst, mental breakdowns, and personal agendas. While some reviewers praised the film for its aesthetic value, other critics explicitly denounced it as a tainted distortion of the memory of resistance heroes. By contrast, reviewers perceived as sheer authenticity the uncritical admiration of a resistance group from Hvidsten in Jutland depicted in the film *Hvidsten Gruppen/This Life* (2012). The film portrays historical figures in a resistance group who were executed by the Germans in 1944. Their extraordinary status and political extremism was underplayed or ignored, with the dramatization instead being fueled by the tropes of the master narrative. The myth of the widespread resistance of the Danish people went almost unnoticed by reviewers, who paid homage to the film as an "opportunity to familiarize oneself with a realistic version of history" and called it "a war movie for the ordinary Dane."[11] It was the box office hit of the year.

Conclusion

The collective memory of resilience and solidarity during the German Occupation of 1940–45 still plays a prominent and instrumental role in forming Danish identity. No other historical topic attracts the attention and publishing zeal bestowed upon the occupation history. For two generations, historians have systematically challenged the master narrative of a population united in support for the resistance, deepening the chasm between professional historians and the general public. The moral narrative that evolved in the new millennium reflects a fragmented and selective knowledge of the past dictated by the needs and interest of the present. In a process of historicization—defined by the fact that the witnesses to the occupation are passing away—the use and abuse of the past enters a new phase, desperately needing historicization in terms of contextualization and hermeneutic appreciation of the scope provided to agents of the past. Collective memory of the occupation is increasingly instrumentalized politically as Danish society is presented with new real and perceived threats. In a memorial service at the scene of the terror attack at *Krudttønden* (The Powder Keg) Cultural Center, where an armed gunman killed one civilian and wounded three police officers in 2015, the old vaudeville tune from 1940 was once again evoked, as "they bind our mouths and hands" inspired a shared identity of resilience and solidarity in the audience. The moral narrative rejects the adaptation and negotiation of the war (and beyond) and neglects the motives and rationale of a policy limited in choices and resources. "The promises of the 9th of April" was an illusion utilized to protect democracy. The implicit lie is the fantasy of choices without consequence.

Sofie Lene Bak (PhD, University of Copenhagen, 2003) is Associate Professor of Modern History at the Saxo Institute of the University of Copenhagen. Her main field of research is the impact of the Holocaust in Denmark in terms of historiography, memory, and methodology. Formerly, Bak served as the curator for the Danish Jewish Museum, and she has authored several books and articles on World War II, the Holocaust, and anti-Semitism in Denmark, including *Nothing to Speak Of: Wartime Experiences of the Danish Jews 1943–1945* (2011).

Notes

1. "at Tyskland ikke har til hensigt nu eller i fremtiden at berøre kongeriget Danmarks territoriale integritet og politiske uafhængighed." Memorandum from the German government to the Danish and Norwegian governments, 9 April 1940. Printed in Alkil, 1946.
2. Hæstrup 1954; Hæstrup 1959, published in English as Hæstrup 1976–77.
3. See, for example, Judt 2005; Lagrou 1997; and, for Denmark, Bak 2001.
4. Kirchhoff 1979. In 2001, Kirchhoff modified his original denunciation in Kirchhoff 2001.
5. The most conspicuous example is Hæstrup 1966–71.
6. On the refugee policy, see Rünitz 2005; Kirchhoff and Rünitz 2007. On anti-Semitism, see Bak 2004. On Danish volunteers in the Waffen-SS, see Bundgård Christensen, Poulsen, and Scharff Smith 1998.
7. More recent examples: Andersen 2003; Lidegaard 2005; Bundgård Christensen, Lund, Wium Olesen, and Sørensen 2020.
8. "Man binder os på mund og hånd," lyrics by Poul Henningsen, music by Kai Normann Andersen.
9. See among others, Kreth and Mogensen 1995; Bak 2011; Kirchhoff 2013.
10. "Historiker: Det er småligt, at man ikke vil give Scavenius en vej," *Politiken*, 29 November 2012.
11. "'Hvidsten gruppen' går direkte i din DNA," *Berlingske Tidende*, 1 February 2012.

References

Alkil, Niels, ed. 1946. *Besættelsestidens Fakta*. Vol. 2. Copenhagen: J. H. Schultz.
Andersen, Steen. 2003. *Danmark i det tyske storrum: Dansk økonomisk tilpasning til Tyskland nyordning af Europa 1940–1941*. Copenhagen: Lindhardt og Ringhof.
Andersen, Steen. 2005. *De gjorde Danmark større: De multinationale danske entreprenørfirmaer i krise og krig 1919–1947*. Copenhagen: Lindhardt & Ringhof.
Bak, Sofie Lene. 2001. *Jødeaktionen oktober 1943: Forestillinger i offentlighed og forskning*. Copenhagen: Museum Tusculanum.
———. 2004. *Dansk Antisemitisme 1930–1945*. Copenhagen: Aschehoug.
———. 2010. "Between Tradition and New Departure: The Dilemmas of Collaboration in Denmark." In *Collaboration with the Nazis: Public Discourse after the Holocaust*, edited by Roni Stauber, 110–24. London: Stephen Roth Institute for the Study of Contemporary Antisemitism and Racism, Tel Aviv University, and Routledge.
———. 2011. *Nothing to Speak Of: Wartime Experiences of the Danish Jews 1943–1945*. Copenhagen: Danish Jewish Museum.
———. 2012. *Da krigen var forbi—De danske jøders hjemkomst efter besættelsen*. Copenhagen: Gyldendal.
Barfod, Jørgen H. 1969. *Helvede har mange navne, en beretning om koncentrationslejre og fængsler, hvor der sad danskere 1940–1945*. København: Zac.
Bryld, Claus, and Anette Warring. 1998. *Besættelsestiden som kollektiv erindring*. Frederiksberg: Roskilde Universitetsforlag.
Bundgård Christensen, Claus. 2013. "'The Five Evil Years': National Self-Image, Commemoration and Historiography in Denmark 1945–2010; Trends in Historiography and Commemoration." In *Hitler's Scandinavian Legacy, the Consequences of the German Invasion for the Scandinavian Countries, Then and Now*, edited by John Gilmour and Jill Stephenson. London: Bloomsbury Academic.
Bundgård Christensen, Claus, Niels Bo Poulsen, and Peter Scharff Smith. 1998. *Under Hagekors og Dannebrog: Danskere i Waffen SS*. Copenhagen: Aschehoug.
Bundgård Christensen, Claus, Joachim Lund, Niels Wium Olesen, and Jakob Sørensen. 2020. *Danmark besat. Krig og hverdag 1940–1945*. 5th ed. Copenhagen: Høst.
Emkjær, Stefan. 2000. *Stikkerdrab—Modstandsbevægelsernes likvidering af danskere under besættelsen*. Copenhagen: Aschehoug.
Halvas Bjerre, Jakob. 2017. "Samarbejdets diskrimination." *RAMBAM: Tidsskrift for Jødisk Kultur og Forskning* 26: 107–21.
Hæstrup, Jørgen. 1954. *Kontakt med England 1940–43*. Copenhagen: Thaning og Appels forlag.
———. 1959. *Hemmelig alliance*. Copenhagen: Thaning og Appels forlag.
———. 1966–71. . . . *Til landets bedste: Hovedtræk af departementschefstyrets virke 1943–1945*. Vols. 1–2. Copenhagen: Gyldendal.
———. 1976–77. *Secret Alliance I–III*. Odense: Odense University Press.
Judt, Tony. 2005. *Postwar: A History of Europe since 1945*. London: Penguin Books.
Kirchhoff, Hans. 1979. *Augustoprøret: Samarbejdspolitikkens fald*. Vols. 1–3. Copenhagen: Gyldendal.
———. 2001. *Samarbejde og modstand under besættelsen: En politisk historie*. Odense: Odense University Press.
———. 2008. *Sådan Valgte De, Syv Dobbeltportrætter Fra Besættelsens Tid*. Copenhagen: Gyldendal.
———. 2013. *Holocaust i Danmark*. Odense: University Press of Southern Denmark.

Kirchhoff, Hans, and Lone Rünitz. 2007. *Udsendt Til Tyskland: Dansk Flygtningepolitik under Besættelsen*. Odense: University Press of Southern Denmark.
Kreth, Rasmus, and Micheal Mogensen 1995. *Flugten til Sverige—aktionen mod de danske jøder oktober 1943*. Copenhagen: Gyldendal.
Lagrou, Pieter. 1997. "Victims of Genocide and National Memory: Belgium, France and the Netherlands 1945–1965." *Past and Present* 154: 181–222.
Lidegaard, Bo. 2005. *Kampen om Danmark 1933–1945*. Copenhagen: Gyldendal.
Lund, Joachim. 2005. *Hitlers spisekammer: Danmark og den europæiske nyordning*. Copenhagen: Gyldendal.
Nissen, Mogens R. 2005. *Til fælles bedste—det danske landbrug under besættelsen*. Copenhagen: Lindhardt & Ringhof.
Paxton, Robert O. 1972. *Vichy France: Old Guard and New Order 1940–1944*. New York: Columbia University Press.
Rünitz, Lone. 2005. *Af Hensyn Til Konsekvenserne: Danmark Og Flygtningespørgsmålet 1933–1940*. Odense: University Press of Southern Denmark.
Trommer, Aage. 1971. *Jernbanesabotagen i Danmark under den anden verdenskrig*. Odense: Odense University Press.
———. 1973. *Modstandsarbejde i nærbillede, det illegale arbejde i Syd- og Sønderjylland under den tyske besættelse af Danmark 1940–45*. Odense: Odense University Press.
Warring, Anette. 2006. "Intimate and Sexual Relations." In *Surviving Hitler and Mussolini: Daily Life in Occupied Europe*, edited by Robert Gildea, Olivier Wieviorka, and Anette Warring, 88–128. Oxford: Berg.
———. 2017. *Tyskerpiger*. 2nd ed. Copenhagen: Gyldendal.
Østergård, Uffe. 2011. "Swords, Shields or Collaborators? Danish Historians and the Debate over the German Occupation of Denmark." In *Nordic Narratives of the Second World War: National Historiographies revisited*, edited by Henrik Stenius et al., 31–53. Lund: Nordic Academic Press.

Chapter 3

THE NORWEGIAN WAR EXPERIENCE

Occupied and Allied

Tom Kristiansen

In a speech in September 1942, the American wartime leader President Franklin D. Roosevelt asked rhetorically if anyone was still wondering why the war was being fought. His answer—"Let him look to Norway"—instantly became one of the most celebrated passages in Norwegian history and has been proudly referred to ever since. Roosevelt did not present a soundbite, though. He followed the passage with something that amounts to a key to an explanation. Norway, he said enigmatically, was "at the same time conquered and unconquerable."[1]

At a time when there were more than three hundred thousand Wehrmacht personnel in Norway (Korsnes and Dybvig 2018: 5), it is easy to grasp what Roosevelt meant by "conquered," but what did he mean by "unconquerable" two years after Josef Terboven's *Reichskommissariat* (Reich Commissariat) and Vidkun Quisling's puppet government had been established by force, and a ruthless regime was well under way? Roosevelt's comment suggests that the answer is not to be found in the military domain but instead in the aspirations and attitudes of the population at large. Indeed, some four months earlier, in a radio speech in London on 17 May 1942, Norwegian Constitution Day, King Haakon VII had referred to his people's "unconquerable love for their Constitution" like the president implying the futility of military power.

That question—what was "unconquerable"—serves as a vantage point for this brief account of the main features of Norwegian war historiography and the country's diverse experiences from 1940 to 1945. They can be recapitulated in a few key points. Following the German surprise attack on 9 April 1940, Norway was forced out of neutrality—long considered an unwritten part of the 1814 Constitution. The sixty-two-day campaign that followed was fought by a coalition made up of British, French, Norwegian, and Polish forces. The evacuation of south Norway in early May and in the north in the beginning of June, carried through in an orderly manner without losses, was not caused by military defeat but the overall war development in the wake of the German attack on France and the Low Countries in May 1940.

The king and government, together with a small section of the armed forces, went into exile in Britain, and Norway thus became an active participant in the alliance against the Axis. The war contributions of *Hjemmefronten* (the Home Front), the merchant fleet, and the armed-forces-in-exile were fully integrated into the efforts of the Grand Alliance. When the war ground to a halt in 1945, Allied troops carried through a well-prepared and orderly assumption of power, installed a transitional regime without any turmoil, and

Figure 3.1. To arms! Norwegian conscripts—badly trained, desperately unprepared, and wholly inexperienced—were called up at the dawn of the German attack on 9 April 1940. Photograph of national servicemen after the aerial attack on Elverum, 11 April 1940, included in Olaf Tjønneland's renowned album from the campaign. Photographer: Olaf Tjønneland. Courtesy of Tom B. Jensen.

transferred all responsibilities to the Norwegian government in the autumn, well ahead of schedule. The repatriation of more than four hundred thousand German troops and some one hundred thousand prisoners of war and forced laborers started immediately, and an épuration legale was swiftly initiated. On the face of it, the nation was by far more unified in 1945 than on the eve of the German attack, which explains why the transition from war to peace went remarkably easily in Norway compared to many other European countries. True, Norway was profoundly divided because of the treasonous Quisling regime and the collaborators who took advantage economically and otherwise of the occupation. But they represented a clear minority (Andenæs, Riste, and Skodvin 1966).

Although World War II developed into a global struggle of which Norway was a part, the country's war experiences had several distinctive features. Among them were the huge German military buildup, the total destruction of the far north, and the heavy losses of seamen and ships. So was the quiet, stubborn, and sometimes violent resistance against the efforts to turn Norway into a Nazi state and include it in the Greater Germanic Reich. The country's war experiences may well be cast under two main headings: "occupied Norway" and "Norway-in-exile." But before presenting an overview of the period, let me give a brief account of the historiography.

War and Occupation: Memory and History

Unsurprisingly, the historiography on World War II is thoroughly influenced by the German bolt-from-the-blue attack and the ensuing campaign, the popular resistance to the occupation regime, and the government-in-exile's firm commitment to the Allied war effort (Corell 2010). However, during the seventy-odd years that have elapsed since the end of the war, the historical literature has undergone many shifts in perspective and topic (Dahl 2017). From the outset it took a trajectory quite similar to that of other occupied Western European countries. A patriotic memory culture—clearly in compliance with the zeitgeist—dominated the first three postwar decades. Emphasis was firmly put on how the unified nation stood up in heroic civil and military resistance and how the country contributed to Allied victory. The achievement of the vast Norwegian merchant fleet is invaluable and astonishing for a small country. The point of departure for most historians was the upper echelons of society, such as the government, the political elites, and the military leadership. That changed considerably over the years, and historiography widened its scope to include war stories from all levels and strands of society, eventually including representatives of the occupation regime and those who associated and collaborated with it in different ways.

An array of national-fanfare, multivolume, and leather-bound war histories adorned the bookshelves of Norwegian homes from the late 1940s. They were written by both academics, journalists, politicians, and officers, and many of the authors had played prominent roles in one way or the other before and during the war (Kjær 1946). This literature therefore aimed to serve as monuments, tributes, and official acts of remembrance in addition to historical accounts. Understandably, there was a great demand among people for literature that made sense of the war experiences and celebrated those who had made the biggest sacrifices. At that time it was still largely uncontroversial that the people who had led the nation through the most dramatic crisis since independence in 1814 were best suited for the task. However, the accounts were written with a scanty access to non-Norwegian written sources, which only became available in earnest from the 1970s. It is still impossible to determine whether this celebratory literature was deliberately constructed in order to beef up some actors while hushing, devaluing, or scotching other important actors or topics. It is probably most fair to regard the phenomenon as a product of a particular time.

The summer of 1940 witnessed the incipient beginning of Norwegian war historiography when the government-in-exile commissioned accounts in which it explained and justified its handling of the run-up to war, the campaign, and foreign policy dispositions to non-Norwegian readers (Lehmkuhl 1940). After the war, Parliament appointed a broad investigative commission to look into the government's and Parliament's conduct in 1940. The commission reports were essential in forming public opinion. Another commission was appointed by the armed forces to investigate the conduct of officers during the campaign, but its report was kept secret until 1979. The armed forces also established its own historical branch, in which officers who had participated from the 1930s set out to write their own history. In the period from 1952 to 1970 they issued eighteen volumes on the campaign, in addition to accounts of other aspects of Norwegian history before and during the war. A broad scholarly account and analysis of the government-in-exile's alliance, military and foreign policy, and internal history appeared in the 1970s (Riste 1973/1979). Moreover, a number of leading politicians, officers, and notables published their recollections well into the 1980s. True, these were volumes often written in self-appreciation and restricted to the political, legal, and military aspects of the war. These accounts gave war history a clear top-heavy inclination and were generally confined to politics, diplomacy, resistance, and warfare. In contrast to the military history of the war, both scholarly research and documentary and biographical accounts of the seamen and the merchant navy, and of the Home Front, were scarce up to the 1960s, with a few notable exceptions such as the pioneers of occupation history, Sverre Kjeldstadli (1959), Thomas Wyller (1958) and Magne Skodvin (1956).

The flood of war accounts reflecting the prevalent patriotic memory culture had been reduced to a trickle by the 1960s. Some voiced fear that war history was receding into the background of public attention as a result of the aging of prominent veterans. But the ebb was not to last. The first signs of a renewed interest could be noted in the late 1960s, as well as a significant widening of scope and topics. A new generation of scholars and documentarists, without a heavy load of vested interests, entered the center stage. The young scholars Hans Fredrik Dahl (1974) and Ole Kristian Grimnes (1977) were among the seminal forces in this process. The postwar patriotic memory culture was gradually replaced by a far more universalist, critical, and human rights-oriented approach.

Previously ignored or marginalized topics that began to be regarded as essential for the understanding of the era included the wide range of collaborations and Norway's integration into the Grossraumwirtschaft—the economic system that encompassed Germany, its allies, and the occupied countries. There was also important research into nonideological collaboration, the postwar treatment of women who had consorted with Germans and their offspring, or the children of Nazi Party members—many of whom innocently suffered humiliation after the war. Other uncomfortable topics that became subject of scholarly research were the Norwegian branch of the Lebensborn program, the assassinations carried out by the resistance movement and the widespread use of forced labor for tasks such as construction work, in which up to one hundred thousand people were engaged. Scholars likewise studied the involvement of Norwegian officials and police in the deportation of the Jews, arguably the most shameful episode of the war. Without much hesitancy, they were instrumental in both the registration, arrest, and deportation of the Jews (Bruland 2017). Even the German army's total destruction of the far north counties of Finnmark and north Troms, and the forced evacuation of the population, which had only attracted moderate interest for many years, became a central issue. All in all, there has been a marked increase in the interest in the war crimes of the Nazis, the plight of the victims, and the everyday life of ordinary people. The legal purge after 1945 was relatively uncontroversial for a long time, but there has been a renewed interest in investigating both the legal aspects of the process and the workings of the wartime judiciary.

The introduction of new topics and the renewed examination of old topics with new analytical tools have enriched the war literature immensely and broadened our understanding of the war substantially. Most importantly, there is at present a tendency to consider the responses to the occupational regime as a continuum stretching from armed to civil resistance, from enforced, pragmatic, and self-serving cooperation to ideologically inspired collaboration, rather than viewing them according to the former restricting dichotomy of resistance vs. collaboration.

War historiography has indeed become a geyser. On the one hand, it is characterized by a number of innovative documentary and scholarly contributions, which have vastly broadened our understanding of the era; on the other, it is characterized by popular accounts, both written and cinematic, occasionally in willful ignorance of seventy-five years of research. The latter are habitually presented with much fanfare in spite of their limited historical value. Popular culture time and again unravels the delicately knit mesh of insights and knowledge that scholarly, documentary, and fictional literature have meticulously constructed in the course of the postwar decades. This phenomenon is perhaps best illustrated by the 2017 feature film *The 12th Man*, as discussed by Gunnar Iversen in chapter 18 of this volume, obviously a generic war fantasy with an uncritical return to the patriotic memory culture. It attracted thousands of moviegoers but left historians nonplussed.

Occupied Norway

"Occupied Norway" may be accounted for under the subheadings "the occupation regime" and "the Home Front." The launch of the occupation regime in late September 1940—the German part and Quisling's government—was perceived as an outright provocation by the majority in a country that had experienced 126 years of peace and unchecked liberal development. The ambition to turn Norway into a Fascist state did not meet with any enthusiasm outside the small extreme right circles. Instead, the regime swiftly sparked scorn and civil disobedience. Despite the dual character of the regime, real power always resided firmly in the hands of the Germans. Vidkun Quisling (1887–1945) was essentially a figurehead with little real political clout, and he soon proved to be a liability to the Germans precisely because of the profound resentment he incited.

The German part of the regime was made up by a civilian and military component, the Reichskommissariat and the Wehrmacht. The initial German plan was to govern indirectly through a pacified Norwegian cabinet, in line with what took place in Denmark. The dramatic events on the first day of the attack made this unattainable because the sinking of the cruiser *Blücher* enabled the political authorities to escape Oslo. Quisling entered the national stage through a broadcast coup d'état—which tainted him irrevocably and changed the course of history. Unhesitatingly, the king refused to recognize Quisling, and the government refused to step down. They restated their decision to fight, and the ensuing campaign lasted for two months. On 10 June, three days after they had gone into exile, the commander in chief, General Otto Ruge, signed a capitulation agreement with the Germans (Kristiansen 2019). In the summer of 1940 there were negotiations between the occupier and a Norwegian administrative council in order to find an arrangement that was acceptable to both parties. The negotiations eventually collapsed, and as a result the Germans assumed full control on 25 September.

Josef Terboven (1898–1945) then became the dominant figure. He was a long-standing member of the Nazi Party, an active participator in the Sturmabteilungen (SA) from the mid-1920s, and an associate of Hitler. He was sent to Norway on 21 April on a fact-finding mission at a point when the fierce and relatively successful Norwegian resistance had infuriated Hitler. Three days later, Terboven was appointed Reich commissioner in Norway and thus became the supreme civil authority. He was empowered by Hitler himself and therefore independent of any German ministry or institution, including the armed forces. He guarded this privileged position cautiously throughout the war. In the wake of the collapse of negotiations in September, Terboven deposed the king and government and terminated the administrative council. Moreover, with the exception of the Fascists, all political parties were banned. That framework of the occupation regime was maintained throughout the war.

European countries under German occupation had vastly different experiences. There is a fundamental difference between the regimes imposed in Eastern and Western Europe. The regimes in countries like Belgium, Denmark, France, the Netherlands, and Norway could be exceedingly brutal but were nonetheless on another scale than the regimes in Poland, Ukraine, the Balkans, and the occupied parts of the Soviet Union. The Nazi ambition in Western Europe was to accommodate and integrate the populations and to exploit their assets. The majority populations were labeled as Aryan and consequently not subject to the enslavement, genocide, and deportations that peoples in the east suffered.

The Reich Commissariat was the civil administrative organization. Since the Norwegian bureaucracy continued to operate, it employed no more than around seven hundred people at the most. Its main office was in Oslo, but there were also branches distributed all over the country. Because the main task of the Commissariat was to guide and oversee the Quisling government and the Norwegian administration, there was a continuous rivalry between Quisling and Terboven. The Commissariat was the true representative of the Nazi regime in Norway. The regime also disposed of SS units and a considerable police force. They were placed under Wilhelm Rediess (1900–1945), making them a link in Heinrich Himmler's chain of command, but they were de facto a part of Terboven's regime.

The Wehrmacht was far more numerous than the Commissariat. It was mainly engaged in military and defense preparations and not in political, ideological, or party matters. In the military chain of command, it was far beyond Terboven's reach, but there was a strong rivalry between him and the commander in chief, Nikolaus von Falkenhorst (1885–1968), until the latter left Norway in 1944. The German military presence in the country was massive, reinforced from around 150,000 by the end of the 1940 campaign to a short-lived peak in November 1944 of more than 600,000 when German forces retreated from Finland via Norway. For a long period of time, the force counted, give or take, three hundred thousand personnel (Korsnes and Dybvig 2018: 5).

With the exception of eastern Finnmark, which was the rear and staging area of the Eastern Front, German land forces in Norway were primarily engaged in defensive activities. This could be seen in the building of more than three hundred artillery forts along the coast, which reflected the fear that an Allied invasion of the continent would start in Norway. Moreover the army units were rarely mobile, not on high alert, and never first rate operationally. The air force and navy, however, were active in the war in the Atlantic, in particular in attacking the Arctic convoys to Murmansk.

German military planners had never wanted, let alone included, Quisling's involvement in the *Weserübung* (Operation West). But his coup d'etat and Hitler's support made him a part of the occupation regime, as head of the puppet government and party Führer. Thus national aspirations had to be channeled through his party, which before the war had never been more than an obscure fringe group, albeit with many followers in high military circles. It had the ability to make boisterous provocations but not to attract enough votes to win a seat in Parliament. Quisling himself was a pompous, uncharismatic, and self-absorbed leader who aspired to be an original political thinker. Although he was an army officer by training, he had not seen active service since the end of World War I, after which he made a name for himself as a diplomat and secretary to the national hero Fridtjof Nansen. He founded his Fascist Party just a few months after he had stepped down as the exceedingly controversial defense minister in an Agrarian Party government in 1932.

The posture, jingoism, uniforms and banners, rhetoric, and rites of Quisling's party, Nasjonal Samling (National Union) 1933–45, were unmistakably inspired by mainstream European fascism. The party swiftly adopted Nazi viewpoints in racial and ideological matters, above all in its firm stance against liberalism, socialism, and democracy—and humanity, as it turned out. It only had some one hundred thousand supporters at the most, and at the start of the war it was in the doldrums. By high treason, Quisling established himself and his cohorts as an integrated part of the occupation regime (Kristiansen 2013). The German attack on the Soviet Union on 22 June 1941 gave the Quisling regime back its bearings. The war was perceived as a crusade against Bolshevism, which was just what it wanted—and needed. It aroused enthusiasm among regime supporters and gave them a sense of embarking on a historical mission. A good half year after the launch of Operation Barbarossa, Quisling's government was elevated to a so-called "national government" in February 1942 through a pretentious ceremony at the Akershus Castle in Oslo ("Statsakten") at which Quisling was appointed *Ministerpresident* (minister president). He believed this was the first step to the restoration of national independence under Fascist rule, but no redistribution of real power followed. Quisling remained a stuffed shirt.

The launch of the anti-Bolshevik crusade necessitated soldiers in the field. The Norwegian contribution was never significant, but it is nonetheless among the national embarrassments comparable to the regime's active involvement in the persecution and deportation of the Jews. The volunteers comprised both young women and men. A number of nurses were recruited, and they served both in Norway and Germany and on the front. After the war, they were quite indiscriminately regarded as collaborators and sentenced accordingly. Over the last couple of decades, there has been a tendency to regard their motives and deeds more forbearingly as a complex phenomenon. There is no doubt that many of the volunteers served in the German Red Cross, which was inseparable from the Nazi regime (Bay 2017). The vast majority of Norwegians fighting for the Germans, however, were the young men who voluntarily enlisted in the Waffen-SS, the military branch of Himmler's SS. The first three hundred joined the division "Wiking" in the winter of 1941, and they saw action in the early phase of Operation Barbarossa.

Recruitment only started in earnest in the wake of Barbarossa. The regime managed to muster a substantial force, although it had to scale back its ambitions. The significant growth in recruitment after the attack on the Soviet Union shows how important Nazi ideology and anticommunism were to the volunteers. Separate Norwegian units, such as the Norwegian Legion and the Light Ski Battalion, were eventually organized, and around 6,000 volunteers filled these units. Nearly all them ended up at the Eastern Front, where an estimated 850 were killed and an unknown number injured. In spite of their active service and sacrifices, their limited number and questionable military skills made them insignificant in a wider context. It is also noteworthy that Himmler only reluctantly incorporated non-German units into the SS, the spearhead of the Greater Germanic Reich. Any kind of national aspirations could obstruct the realization of this grand idea. Quisling on his part unrealistically regarded the Norwegian Waffen-SS as a step toward the restoration of national armed forces (Sørlie 2017: 322f.).

The establishment of the Norwegian Waffen-SS made the alarm bells sound in the resistance movement. Military service for the Germans was regarded as the ultimate form of collaboration. It became one of the resistance's vital tasks to obstruct the mobilization of Norwegians, both to the Eastern Front and as laborers. All in all, the dual occupation regime posed a lethal threat to all members and supporters of the resistance. The so-called Home Front faced the challenge of where to direct its efforts in order to achieve its goals without provoking senseless reprisals. "The Home Front" is a collective term for Norway's military and civil resistance: *Milorg* (military organization) and *Sivorg* (civilian organization). One should bear in mind that civil and nonviolent resistance were by far the most salient feature of the Home Front. There has been a tendency to underestimate its value and to overemphasize the armed resistance.

Norwegian historians identify three distinct phases of resistance. The years from 1940 to 1942 are characterized by fierce disapproval of the *Gleichsschaltung*, the occupation regime's efforts to Nazify Norway and integrate it into the Greater German Reich. This was essentially a nonviolent opposition to the regime's assault on the deeply rooted norms, values, and institutions of the liberal society. Even though Quisling's party experienced a significant growth in membership from the autumn of 1940, it provoked national institutions and organizations—such as the sports movement, the teachers, the Supreme Court, the Lutheran Church, the Labor movement and trade unions—to offer stubborn opposition to the regime's policy. The protests hardened the front between representatives of Norwegian society and the occupants. Since the opposition arose from a broad and heterogonous front, it was not particularly coordinated or coherent but nonetheless vocal and forceful.

The character of the second phase of resistance is quite different from the first. It covers the months from 1943 to mid-1944. While the regime had undoubtedly failed in its effort to win the hearts and minds of people and institutions, a new danger appeared on the horizon. It was feared that the occupational regime was planning to mobilize young people for labor service, and that this was a preparatory measure for mobilizing soldiers for the Wehrmacht. The resistance movement concentrated on disrupting the mobilization. Also emphasized in this phase was civilian resistance. Moreover, the Home Front and the government-in-exile had come to an understanding about aims and means in the struggle.

The last phase of World War II saw a shift to military resistance. This phase started in earnest in mid-1944 and lasted for the rest of the war. The Milorg leadership cooperated closely with the Allies and Norwegians in exile. The British decision from the autumn of 1942 to support Milorg instead of setting up a competing unit was also a seminal event in Norwegian resistance. The efforts of the Home Front, the government- and armed-forces-in-exile, and the British were coordinated. Milorg started to receive weapons and equipment from the United Kingdom, and the organization grew by leaps and bounds. In 1945 there were some forty-five thousand personnel under arms. But the Home Front was of little value without support from the outside.

Norway-in-Exile

The main constituents of "Norway-in-exile" were the merchant fleet, the king and government in London, the regular armed forces, and the refugee community in Sweden. By and by, the government learned to steer and coordinate these elements, and in combination they represented a formidable force, both because they embodied the aspirations of the majority of people and because their efforts were integrated into the cause of the Grand Alliance. It is notable that during the war, Norwegians living outside Norway proper not only represented the legitimate body politic but played the decisive national role for the first time in history (Riste 1987).

True, the government had had to escape, but it did not at all arrive empty-handed in Britain. At its disposal was a modern and efficient merchant fleet consisting of some one thousand vessels, operated by a professional, worldwide organization. It is estimated that about thirty-four thousand officers and seamen of the merchant navy served in the part of the fleet that was engaged in international trade in 1939. The fleet soon proved to be an invaluable asset that put the Norwegian government in a far more favorable position than the other exiled governments in London. Measured in population, gross national product, military power, and political clout, Norway was certainly a minor power. The merchant fleet, however, represents a remarkable exception.

With a population of barely three million people, Norway ranked fourth among the world's shipping nations. The abolition of the British Navigation Acts in the mid-nineteenth century had triggered a period of astonishing growth. A large part of the fleet served the British trade system, which significantly affected Norway's political and economic position in times of war. During the seven months leading up to the German attack, 58 Norwegian ships were torpedoed and 394 seamen lost their lives despite the country's neutrality. For officers and men of the merchant navy, the war started in September 1939.

The fleet was bound by contracts with the British. Both in World War I and the period from September 1939 to April 1940, Norwegian neutrality was in a fragile position and at the mercy of British policy and strategy. In 1940, 20 percent of the world's modern tankers were controlled by Norwegian shipowners, and a staggering 40 percent of the oil supply to Britain was carried on Norwegian keels. It goes without saying that these transports could not be discontinued in wartime. Although Norwegian ships sailed all over the world, most of the fleet was engaged in the Battle of the Atlantic.

In the early phase of the 1940 campaign, the government issued a Royal Decree in which the disposal—not the ownership—of all ships more than five hundred gross register tons was requisitioned. This governmental control lasted throughout the war. The administration of the fleet was handed over to a new agency, the Norwegian Shipping and Trade Mission, best known by its telegraph address Nortraship. The mission was placed directly under the Ministry of Supplies and was roughly organized like an ordinary shipping company.

Nortraship was an essential asset to the Allied war cause and put the Norwegian government in a favorable negotiating position. Above all, it provided the government with about 90 percent of its income, which came in addition to the gold reserves of the National Bank of Norway that were rescued during the campaign. These revenues paid for the renewal of the fleet, armaments, and the Norwegian state institutions in Britain. The fleet was worth a million men, wrote the journal *The Motorship*—more than a million, a US admiral added (Riste 1987: 114; Steen 1959: 120). Churchill duly praised it in a speech at the Royal Palace when he visited Norway in 1948. In the words of the British wartime leader, Norwegian sailors "maintained the life line between Britain and the United States," but "given at great cost." The Norwegian prime minister had confided to him about the loss of seafarers: "We felt as if they were our children."[2] The losses certainly represent a somber statistic. From April 1940 to May 1945, a total of 473 ships were sunk in international waters, in addition to 199 in domestic traffic. These numbers add up to a loss of 2.3 million gross register tonnage. Undoubtedly, most harrowing is the more than three thousand seamen who made the ultimate sacrifice.

The king and government arrived in London on 10 June 1940. In addition to the fleet, they had other assets. They were the only legal representatives of the country according to the Constitution and the emergency provisions passed by parliament shortly after the German invasion. Moreover, the government was recognized by the Western powers. One could argue that the solidarity between king and government and the unity of purpose was another asset. The British war cabinet had invited them to take refuge in Britain when the campaign in southern Norway drew to a close at the end of April. They only accepted a renewed invitation after the Allies had decided to evacuate northern Norway and left after having declared that the fight would continue in exile. As early as 26 July 1940 Norway formally entered into the wartime alliance with the signing of an agreement on military cooperation with the British. This was later replaced by a more inclusive agreement signed by foreign ministers Anthony Eden and Trygve Lie, which remained in effect for the duration of the war.

The Labor government, which had been in office since March 1935, was reinforced in exile by representatives of the Conservatives, the Liberals, the Agrarian Party, and the Home Front. This broad wartime coalition no doubt represented the best part of Norwegian society. At its offices in London, it maintained the peacetime departmental structure and was the uncontested representative of the Norwegian people. The main duties of the government could be summarized in a few points: to lead and coordinate Norway's war efforts at home and abroad, to promote national interests in the Alliance, to maintain close ties with the Home Front, and to prepare for the liberation of Norway and secure an orderly transition from war to peace.

The regular armed forces in exile had a dual assignment: to take part in the war under Allied command and to prepare for the resumption of control in Norway after a German defeat. The revenues from the merchant fleet put the government in a favorable position to develop its military power. The armed-forces-in-exile counted fifteen thousand personnel at the most, and eleven hundred lost their lives. From the start, the navy and air force were prioritized and put into active service under British operational command. The Norwegian Brigade in Scotland eventually counted around four thousand men, and was kept in reserve until liberation, although some units were occasionally made available for assignments under British command. The reasoning behind the prioritizing was simple. Navies and air forces were capital-intensive, not personnel-intensive, and the government had generous revenues but an insufficient recruiting base, which an army depended on.

During the war a community of Norwegian refugees gradually grew up in Sweden. The sixteen-hundred-kilometer-long border between Sweden and Norway cuts through an area of forests and wilderness, with a scattered population. Traditionally unguarded, the border is therefore porous and provided an emergency exit for Norwegians who wanted or needed to flee the country, including Jews, members of the resistance, people whose living conditions had deteriorated, and those who wanted to join the Norwegian forces in exile. A total of around fifty thousand people crossed the border to Sweden during the war.

Swedish neutrality made it extremely difficult for the government to support Norway openly. Until 1943, Sweden was forced to collaborate with a victorious Germany, without any other alternatives if the country were to keep out of the war and remain neutral. This position generated considerable bitterness among many Norwegians. But the Norwegians also had a lot to thank the Swedes for. Particularly during the final years of the war, after the change in Swedish policy in the wake of the German defeat at Stalingrad, Sweden assisted both the government-in-exile and the resistance in different ways. In addition to serving as a refuge or transit for people escaping occupied Norway, it permitted the establishment of the so-called Norwegian police troops, which in actual fact were regular infantry (Barstad 1991: 63). Around twelve thousand officers and men were organized and trained in Norwegian garrisons in Sweden. The troops were held in reserve to secure an orderly and peaceful transition after the anticipated German defeat. The Swedish government also provided Norway with generous material assistance. Prime Minister Johan Nygaardsvold, who had a humbling and embittering encounter with the Swedish government in 1940, was conciliatory shortly after the war. In June 1945, he said in an interview that since the "clouds of misunderstanding that had gathered over Scandinavia in the first year of the war had drifted away," he realized that "Swedish neutrality has been an asset for Norway."[3]

Conclusion: Why Unconquerable?

The German occupation of Norway started with a bang and ended with a whimper. In the end, the military masterminds had suffered a devastating and humiliating strategic defeat. There is little doubt that the vast majority of Norwegians experienced the occupation regime as characterized by unrelenting violence, cruelty, and repression, representing norms and values very few of them shared. It was therefore not only politically but also morally bankrupt in 1945.

The Norwegian commander in chief during the 1940 campaign, General Otto Ruge (1882–1961), spent five years as a prisoner of war in Germany. He was shattered by what he learned from home as the regime tightened its grip. An entry in his notebook on a bleak winter day in 1942 amounts to his explanation of why Norway, regardless of the military failure and political oppression, was "unconquerable." The occupation regime had so far ruthlessly clamped down on the clergy, the judges, the political left, the trade unions, the university professors, the students, and the teachers, but it had obviously provoked counterforces beyond its control. In Ruge's opinion, both Quisling and the Germans were "foolish to start a culture struggle," since in such a struggle "the oppressor is destined to lose, eventually."[4] That is exactly why the regime's nazification efforts failed. That is also why the Norwegians experienced that they were indeed "unconquerable" even after being militarily "conquered" (Kristiansen 2019: 398).

The relationship between the Home Front, Norway-in-exile, and Norway as a part of the Grand Alliance was uneasy. Mutual trust and cooperation only came about slowly and after endless trials and errors. The dynamics and relations between them eventually produced a mutually beneficial modus operandi. Another noticeable war experience is that this made the transition from war to peace surprisingly easy in Norway despite the overwhelming presence of the surrendered Germans, the Red Army liberators in the far north, and the British "Allied Mission to Norway." There were a few unfortunate incidents but no serious turmoil or actions of unchecked revenge, undoubtedly due to the preparations and unity of purpose of the parties involved. This created a political ferment with a long-term effect on Norwegian security policy: without the positive experience of participation in the wartime alliance, it is very unlikely that Norway would have left the tradition of nonalignment in peace and neutrality in war.

Tom Kristiansen is Professor of History at the Arctic University of Norway. Kristiansen's publications include numerous books and articles on Norwegian diplomatic, maritime, and military history. His latest book is the biography of the Norwegian commander in chief in 1940, *Otto Ruge: Hærføreren* (2019). He currently heads a five-year research project, "In a World of Total War: Norway 1939–1945," financed by the Research Council of Norway.

Notes

1. NARA, State Department 857.30, speech made by President Roosevelt at the Washington Navy Yard on the occasion of the transfer of the Royal Norwegian Navy Ship *Haakon VII*.
2. Churchill Archives, Cambridge, Churchill/WCHL 12/24/11: "WSC's Royal Dinner Address, Royal Palace, Oslo and speech by King Haakon VII, 11 May 1948."
3. Johan Nygaardsvold, *Norges Nytt*, no. 24, 22 June 1945, 17, "misforståelsens skyer som samlet seg over Norden i krigens første år . . . delvis [er] borte," innså han at "Sveriges nøytralitet var en lykke for Norge."
4. Otto Ruge's notebook III, written as a POW in Germany, October 1940–April 1945, "i en 'kulturkamp' taper alltid undertrykkeren til slutt," entry 7 March 1942; "Noget så dumt som å begynne en slik 'kulturkamp'!" entry 24 April 1942.

References

Andenæs, Johs., Olav Riste, and Magne Skodvin. 1966. *Norway and the Second World War*. Oslo: Johan Grundt Tanum Forlag.
Barstad, Tor Arne. 1991. "Norske flyktninger i Sverige." In *Broderfolk i ufredstid: Norsk-svenske forbindelser under annen verdenskrig*, edited by Stig Ekman and Ole Kristian Grimnes. Oslo: Norwegian University Press.
Bay, Eirik Gripp. 2017. *Himmlers Valkyrjer: Frontsøstrene på østfronten*. Oslo: Cappelen Damm.
Bruland, Bjarte. 2017. *Holocaust i Norge: Registrering, deportasjon, tilintetgjøring*. Oslo: Dreyer.
Corell, Synne. 2010. *Krigens Ettertid: Okkupasjonshistorien i norske historiebøker*. Oslo: Scandinavian Academic Press/Spartacus Forlag.
Dahl, Hans Fredrik. 1974. *Krigen i Norge*. Oslo: Pax.
———. 2017. *Krigen som aldri tar slutt: Én historie—mange fortellinger*. Oslo: Aschehoug.
Grimnes, Ole Kristian. 1977. *Hjemmefrontens ledelse: Norge og den annen verdenskrig*. Oslo: Universitetsforlaget.

Kjeldstadli, Sverre. 1959. *Hjemmestyrkene: Hovedtrekk av den militære motstanden under okkupasjonen*. Oslo: Aschehoug.

Kjær, Anders, ed. 1946. *Vi vil oss et land*. Oslo: Skandinavisk kulturforlag.

Korsnes, Kjetil, and Olve Dybvig. 2018. *Wehrmacht i Norge: Antall tysk personell fra april 1940 til mai 1945*. Tromsø: University library, Septentrio Report No. 4. Retrieved 3 April 2020 from https://septentrio.uit.no/index.php/SapReps/article/view/4575/4093.

Kristiansen, Tom. 2013. "Closing a Long Chapter: Norway's German Relations and the Third Reich, 1933–1945." In *Hitler's Scandinavian Legacy*, edited by John Gilmour and Jill Stephenson, 73–99. London: Bloomsbury.

———. 2019. *Otto Ruge: Hærføreren*. Oslo: Aschehoug.

Lehmkuhl, Herman K. 1940. *The Invasion of Norway*. London: Norwegian Government/Hutchinson.

Riste, Olav. 1973/1979. *London-regjeringa: Norge i krigsalliansen 1940–1945*. Vol. 1: *1940–1942: Prøvetid*. Vol 2: *1942–1945: Vegen heim*. Oslo: Samlaget.

———. 1987. *Utefront*. Vol. 7 of *Norge i krig: Fremmedåk og frigjøringskamp 1940–1945*. Oslo: Aschehoug.

Skodvin, Magne. 1956. *Striden om okkupasjonsstyret fram til 25. september 1940*. Oslo: Det norske samlaget.

Soleim, Marianne Neerland. 2018. *Sovjetiske krigsfanger i Norge 1941–1945: Antall, organisering og repatriering*. Oslo: Scandinavian Academic Press.

Steen, Erik Anker. 1959. *Norges sjøkrig 1940–1945*. Vol. 5. Oslo: Gyldendal.

Sørlie, Sigurd. 2017. "Norway." In *Joining Hitler's Crusade: European Nations and the Invasion of the Soviet Union, 1941*, edited by David Stahel and Lisa Lines, 317–340. Cambridge: Cambridge University Press.

Wyller, Thomas. 1958. *Nyordning og motstand: En framstilling og en analyse av organisasjonenes politiske funksjon under den tyske okkupasjoneen 25.9.1940–25.9.1942*. Oslo: Universitetsforlaget.

Chapter 4

THE ICELANDIC NATIONAL NARRATIVE AND WORLD WAR II

"Freedom and Culture"

Guðmundur Hálfdanarson

On 20 June 1944, an official exhibition surveying Iceland's history opened with fanfare at Reykjavík's secondary school in the center of the Icelandic capital, Reykjavík (Olgeirsson 1945: 427; *Morgunblaðið*, 21 June 1944, 2). The exposition had been hastily arranged to celebrate the founding of the Icelandic republic three days earlier, at the Iceland's primary *lieu de mémoire*, Þingvellir (Hálfdanarson 2000). The title of the exhibition, "Freedom and Culture," reflected its main theme, which was—according to the printed exhibition catalogue—to emphasize how "the flower, culture, can only grow in the terrain of freedom." Thus, by showing "glimpses from Iceland's cultural struggle and its struggle for freedom since the beginning of Icelandic history until the present day," the exhibition committee wanted to demonstrate that freedom meant "more than freedom from something, freedom from oppression, because it is also freedom to achieve something. Freedom to pursue cooperation and association, to law and justice, to independent cultural life. Freedom in this meaning is not anarchy, but a healthy and decent life" (*Frelsi og menning* 1944: 5–6; Olgeirsson 1945: 386). This point was driven home through tracing the story of the nation from its inception until the completion of the Icelandic fight for full independence, with each of the nine exhibition rooms dedicated to what was seen as an important stage or topic in the nation's history: "Beginning," "National Rule," "Explorations and Settling

New Lands," "Resistance," "Humiliation," "New Dawn," "Jón Sigurðsson," "Struggle," "Self-Determination" (*Frelsi og menning* 1944; Olgeirsson 1945).[1] The ultimate goal, the organizers declared, was to embed the official narrative of the Icelandic nation, as they presented it in the exhibition, into the minds of young Icelanders, or—in the words of one member of the exhibition committee, the socialist politician, Einar Olgeirsson—"to keep the legacy of the struggle [for Iceland's independence] alive, to turn the toil of past generations for freedom into a significant part in the life and consciousness of the emerging generation" (Olgeirsson 1945: 386). In this manner, the exhibition was meant to both construct an official collective memory for the citizens of the new republic and to convince those who were to inherit the land of the importance of "national freedom" and thus to arouse their desire to defend it against foreign encroachment.

The exhibition in Reykjavík was organized during an extraordinary period in Icelandic history, because World War II had caused a monumental transformation of the island's economy and social life. Through the centuries, the country had been placed "in the borderlands," to quote the American

Figure 4.1. "The Struggle": The eighth room of the exhibition titled "Freedom and Culture" surveyed the history of the Icelandic nationalist struggle in the period 1874–1944 through a demonstration of patriotic symbols, pictures of political leaders and events, and examples of patriotic poetry. Unknown photographer. Courtesy of the National Museum of Iceland.

historian Karen Oslund, and often described in accounts of foreign visitors as "a place that is just slightly off the edges of the map of the known world" (Oslund 2011: 169). These visions were shaped by the island's remote location in the mid–North Atlantic, far from both the old world in Europe and the new one in America, and also by Iceland's exotic landscapes and its inhabitants' perceived otherness, which had been described in countless travel books published in Europe and America (Ísleifsson 1996). The war, however, ended Iceland's isolation for good, as the British navy occupied the country on 10 May 1940, ostensibly to prevent German forces from snatching the strategically important island. Moreover, in July 1941, the United States took over the responsibility of defending the country, relieving Britain from stationing a substantial military force in Iceland (Whitehead 1999). The opportunity to use the island for their operations was of crucial importance to the Allied military forces, as it was later for the United States during the Cold War, because Iceland proved to be invaluable for securing and monitoring all communications between North America and Europe, both in air and on sea. During the war, considerable military presence in Iceland also brought great material advantage to the Icelanders and shifted their cultural gaze—at least for a while—from the European continent, which was mostly closed to them, toward North America. Thus, historians have come to the conclusion that if we are to select one particular date to mark "Iceland's entry into 'modernity,' then 1940, the year of the occupation, is the most obvious choice" (Kjartansson 2002: 220).

The historical significance of the war was further enhanced by the fact that Iceland became a fully independent republic during this fateful period, finally severing the ties with the Danish monarchy in 1944 (Hálfdanarson 2006). Since the late fourteenth century, Danish kings had ruled the island, first as a province governed through feudal relations with the continental metropole, but later as an integral part of a Danish empire. For most of that long period, the relations with Denmark had been widely accepted in Iceland as both inevitable and in Iceland's best interest. Thus, for the Icelandic elite, "Denmark" had been the primary point of reference for all of Iceland's relations with the world, as they sought their university education in Copenhagen and as Icelandic foreign trade was primarily conducted through Danish harbors. This had begun to change in the early nineteenth century with growing nationalist demands for political autonomy, but it proved difficult for a poor and small nation to escape its dependence on the former ruling nation. The war changed the situation completely, as the German occupation of Denmark in April 1940 and the British takeover in Iceland a month later made all economic and political communication between the two countries impossible.

In light of its historical significance for Iceland, World War II is notably more or less absent in the Reykjavík exhibition. In fact, the only mention of the conflict, raging both on the ocean around the country and over much of the globe, was to be found in a room recounting tales of Icelandic explorations and travels through the ages. Mixed with illustrations and texts explaining the "discoveries" of Greenland and America around the year 1000 were pictures commemorating the death of Icelandic fishermen killed by German U-boats off the Icelandic coast (Tómasson 1984: 150–60; Whitehead 2002: 200–201). The message was, the authors of the exhibition catalogue declared, that present-day Icelandic seafarers were in no way "inferior to their ancestors," because the same "manliness and honor" (*karlmennska og drengskapur*) lived in their hearts as had characterized the Icelandic seafarers of the past (*Frelsi og menning* 1944: 21; Olgeirsson 1945: 399). That is, the only reference to World War II in the exhibition highlighted the courage of Icelandic fishermen, who brought their valuable catch to the lucrative English market. It also pointed out how these hardy Icelanders displayed the same inner strength as their medieval compatriots, who allegedly had "found" America—and lost it again—around the beginning of the last millennium, thus implying that the nation's essence had not changed through the many centuries of its existence.

What needs to be explained here is the striking discrepancy between reality and the imaginary, or people's lived history after four years of military occupation and the Icelandic official collective memory, as it was expressed and produced in this commemorative exhibition. Outside of the exhibition halls, signs of war were ubiquitous: American soldiers marched in the streets of the capital, military camps were spread around the country, British and American airports had been constructed on the margins of Reykjavík's city center and close to the town Keflavik on the Reykjanes peninsula, and large convoys of ships, bringing armaments and other provisions from the United States to their European allies, stopped in Icelandic harbors so their crews could recuperate before the perilous journey across the Atlantic. Day after day, the war was also on the front pages of every Icelandic newspaper, describing the development of the conflict in minute detail. From descriptions of the historical exhibition in Reykjavík, however, it seems that its organizers deemed these momentous events to be unconnected to the narrative of the Icelandic nation, which had its own inner logic and particular purpose. The question is, therefore, why this silence, in light of the fact that World War II had clearly affected the country's history in such a fundamental way (Hálfdanarson 2011).

Make Iceland Great Again!

The second room of the historical exhibition in Reykjavík was dedicated to the so-called Commonwealth Period in Icelandic history, or the age of "National Rule" (*Þjóðveldi*), as it was termed by the organizers. It covered the time period from the point when Alþingi was established at Þingvellir in the early tenth century until Iceland came under the authority of King Haakon IV of Norway in the early 1260s. In the nationalist rendering of the Icelandic past, this was *the* glorious age of the Icelandic nation, or the time, to quote the romantic nineteenth-century poet, Jónas Hallgrímsson, when "heroes rode through the regions, while under the crags on the coastline / floated their fabulous ships, ferrying goods from abroad" (Ringler 2010: 101). For the first centuries of this period, the catalogue informs the reader, the leaders of the nation steadfastly opposed all foreign attempts to gain foothold on the island, both from Norwegian and Danish kings. In the end, however, the nation succumbed to outside pressure because of internal strife and disorder in the country itself. "Icelanders needed to be vigilant in order to preserve the free national rule," the authors of the catalogue reminded the visitors, because various "foreign rulers coveted Iceland and dispatched their messengers to lure the inhabitants to submit to their authority." According to the organizers of the exhibition, this was also a time of unsurpassed cultural vigor in Iceland, because the Icelandic sagas were composed in "the intense atmosphere of national rule." In these wonderful stories, the catalogue asserts, their unknown authors "managed to create a perfect image of their human environment, vast in substance, original in its form, classical in its art" (13–17). The implication here was that only a free nation could develop such cultural masterpieces, and therefore the true motto of this glorious era in the story of Icelanders, the authors of the catalogue suggested, was to be found in one line from an Old Norse mythical poem called "Grógaldr" (The spell of Gróa, or Gróa's chant), composed in Iceland during the late Middle Ages: "Sjálfr leið þú sjálfan þik" (You must be your own guide) (Larrington 2014: 257).

The moral of the story was, therefore, that the true aim of Icelandic politics was to gain and to preserve "national freedom," because it was only in a "free state" that the nation would be able to achieve its true potential, both as a political and cultural community. To prove this point, the exhibition contrasted the glory days of the Commonwealth Period to what happened following the country's entrance into a union, first with Norway and later with Denmark. In the distant past, the exhibition underlined, the Icelanders had been renowned for their cultural creativity and adventurous spirit, as Icelandic literati were sought after by foreign kings and Icelandic explorers traveled the world in search of fame and fortune. After freedom was lost, the nation's luck turned, and the sense of independence and enterprise was quelled in the nation. The main reason for Iceland's calamity was foreign exploitation, Icelandic nationalists maintained, as Danish kings levied heavy taxes on their subjects—not out of malevolence, the catalogue noted, but because "they were first and foremost kings of another nation, whose interest they wanted to take care of." Another reason for the national misfortune, according to the catalogue, was "growing despair and skepticism about the future, the legal and church language became mixed and corrupted, foreign laws flowed into the country, servility increased" (*Frelsi og menning* 1944: 28–30). Then, in the nineteenth and twentieth centuries, after centuries of decline and humiliation, Iceland's fortune turned again, and freedom was, finally, reclaimed through the strenuous and courageous efforts of a small cadre of national heroes. This process was on display in the last four rooms of the exhibition, exploring issues ranging from a "New Dawn" (*Dagrenning*) to "Self-Determination" (*Sjálfsforræði*). During the new era of national liberty, the authors of the catalogue stated, Icelandic society had developed at an astounding pace: "In 1874, we were still stuck in the Middle Ages; in 1944, we are a modern society"—that is, during the seven decades between the introduction of Iceland's first constitution in 1874 to the formation of the republic in 1944, the nation had been catapulted from a state of total stagnation into vibrant modernity. The last room of the exhibition showed how the nation had managed to improve its lot during the short period of national self-determination through copious illustrations of hydroelectric power plants, trawlers, state-of-the-art fish processing plants, wool factories, modern buildings, and statistical information mapping the dramatic decline in infant mortality in Iceland, and rapid population growth. "A nation capable of doing all this," the authors of the catalogue argued, "without encroaching upon other nations, deserves to be free and to live its life in peace" (*Frelsi og menning* 1944: 42; Olgeirsson 1945: 423–27).

According to this nationalist version of Icelandic history, self-determination, national culture, and the nation's material well-being are all interconnected elements, supporting and preconditioning each other in a virtuous cycle. In a speech celebrating the twenty-second anniversary of Iceland's sovereignty on 1 December 1940, Ólafur Thors, then minister of economic affairs and later prime minister in a number of Icelandic coalition governments, provided a perfect example of this line of reasoning. Speaking in the shadow of foreign occupation, the minister emphasized the importance of national self-determination for the Icelanders. "Everyone who studies Icelandic history," he declared, "will realize that Iceland cannot blossom without national freedom, no more than the plants of the earth can thrive without warmth and sunlight." Thus, he pointed out that the Icelandic literary jewels, which—he claimed—were considered to be among "the finest and most outstanding pieces of all literary works in the world," were written while the nation was free and in control of its own destiny. "After the Icelanders lost their national freedom," he continued, "their vigor and intellectual talent was paralyzed as they remained in the fetters of five centuries of captivity. As soon as the sun of liberty rose again, it was, however, as the nation's verve was set free and it headed toward new contests and achievements." Although British occupation had changed the course of Icelandic history for a while, Thors had the firm belief that this would only be a temporary phase that would pass. "We are certainly apprehensive and recognize how small we are and powerless," he admitted, "but we also recognize the strength of a small nation, which has, because of its origins, language, literature and historical development, sacred right, which will neither be obliterated nor ever taken away from it." His conviction was, therefore, that no matter which of the warring superpowers would be victorious in the war, "every indication was that the occupation would not have determining impact on Iceland's future" (Thors 1940).

In their nationalist strife, Icelandic politicians and commentators held the past up as an image of what the nation could accomplish if it were freed from foreign control. In the period of "national rule," Iceland had been recognized as an important hotspot of European culture, or so they argued, and comparable greatness was a goal to which the nation had to aspire. There were no illusions that the past could be resurrected, but the hope was that the nation would cleanse itself of the stigma of poverty and backwardness, which had tarnished its reputation for a long time—that is, to reclaim its rightful place in the pantheon of European civilization. But to become great again, the nation had to secure its political independence—on that issue all advocates of Icelandic nationality agreed. For this reason, World War II, with its military presence in Iceland and economic modernization, could only be envisioned as a temporary interlude in the nation's inevitable march toward the future.

Figure 4.2. British soldiers in Reykjavík. A formation of British soldiers march through the center of Iceland's capital, Reykjavík, on the occupation day, 10 May 1940. Photographer: Helgi Sigurðsson (Courtesy of the Reykjavík Museum of Photography).

Free at Last, Free at Last!

In May 1940, when the British military stepped on the Icelandic shore, the country they "invaded" had been a sovereign state for just over two decades. This had happened through the so-called Act of Union with Denmark, which came into effect on 1 December 1918. During the preceding decades, public authority had been slowly relocated from Copenhagen to Reykjavík in a few successive steps, as separatist nationalism became the hegemonic principle in Icelandic politics (Hálfdanarson 2006). The new arrangement between Denmark and Iceland was rather peculiar, however, as it established two sovereign states, tied together in a monarchical union, with the king of Denmark serving as the titular head of both of them. According to the Act of Union, Iceland had full sovereignty in both its domestic and foreign affairs, but the Danish foreign service implemented the Icelandic foreign policy on behalf of the Icelandic government. Furthermore, the Danish coast guard was required to patrol the Icelandic territorial waters as long as the former dependency needed Danish military assistance ("Dansk-íslensk sambandslög" 1918: 76; Thorsteinsson 1992: 76–88; Magnússon 2018).

The fear of surrendering the nation's precious and hard-fought freedom troubled Icelandic commentators from the moment it was finally achieved. "The nation may lose its independence and sovereignty again," wrote an unknown author in one of Reykjavík's newspapers on the day when Iceland celebrated the introduction of its sovereignty, "and it is the most sacred duty of all Icelanders to prevent that from happening, because if the nation gives up its independence again, then it will be lost forever" (*Vísir*, 1 December 1918, 1). This anxiety reflected both the profound belief in the crucial importance of national self-determination and acute awareness of its fragility. In the beginning, it was primarily fear of internal discord that sustained this anxiety, but as political tensions grew in Europe in the lead-up to World War II, the attention turned to external threats. As a small state, with no active military force, the only possible defense strategy Iceland had was to cling to the country's unconditional neutrality. This policy was written into the Act of Union, where the Danish government was obligated to announce to the world "that Iceland declares perpetual neutrality and that it has no war flag" ("Dansk-íslensk sambandslög" 1918: 79). The Icelandic government reiterated this policy in 1938 when it joined a pan-Nordic accord, where the five countries declared "their intention of applying similar rules of neutrality in the event of war between foreign Powers" ("Denmark-Finland-Iceland-Norway-Sweden" 1938: 141; Padelford 1938: 789). Declared neutrality had been the bedrock of Iceland's independence from the beginning, the editor of the Icelandic newspaper *Morgunblaðið* asserted just over a week after the British military forces had occupied the country with ease. "Our declaration of neutrality has been our 'Maginot-line,' which we have put our trust in," the unknown author continued, and when tested it had proved to be just as ineffective in keeping the foreign forces at bay as had the outdated fortifications on the European continent (*Morgunblaðið*, 19 May 1940, 5).

The British occupation put the Icelandic authorities in an awkward position. With the German seizure of Denmark on 9 April 1940, Iceland had finally broken all contacts with its former dominant power, opening a new era of full independence. The British conquest brought, however, Iceland's sovereignty to an abrupt end, as it placed the country under much more direct supervision than it had ever experienced during the centuries of Danish rule. This fact brought home the reality to the Icelandic authorities that in the new world of industrialized warfare, to quote *Morgunblaðið*'s editor again, "the existence of European small nations had become more uncertain, their life and independence more insecure." The Allied occupation or military protection of Iceland cannot, of course, be compared with the brutal German oppression in Norway and Denmark, and most Icelanders accepted it as unavoidable. The British commanders also promised from the beginning to honor Iceland's sovereignty and not to interfere in its internal affairs, and the US government reiterated that assurance. "The steps so taken by the Government of the United States are taken in full recognition of the sovereignty and independence of Iceland," President Roosevelt wrote in a message to the Icelandic prime minister just before the American forces arrived in Iceland, "and with the clear understanding that American military and naval forces will in no way interfere with the internal and domestic affairs of the Icelandic people; and with the further understanding that immediately upon the termination of the present international emergency, all such military and naval forces will be at once withdrawn, leaving the people of Iceland and their Government in full sovereign control of their own territory" (*New York Times*, 8 July 1941, 3). It was clear to everyone, however, that with tens of thousands of soldiers stationed on the island, the local authorities were totally at the mercy of the foreign military intruders. The future was, therefore, in doubt, and there was little that Iceland could do to shape its own fate. This prompted people to ask fundamental questions about the viability of the Icelandic nation-state. Was the time of sovereign, small states, shielded by accepted rules of noninterference in international law, over for good? Had Iceland escaped a subjugation to a Danish king simply to enter into a new and lasting control of the British Empire or the United States?

Polluted Blood and Corrupted Minds

In spite of these existential concerns, there was little doubt in most Icelanders' minds that they were placed in a privileged position during World War II.

Thus, generally it came as great relief to them to find out on the morning of 10 May 1940 that the occupation forces were British rather than German, and a constant stream of news in the Icelandic media, describing the brutal oppression of the Nazi forces in the countries they had occupied, reinforced that sense of good fortune (Árnason 1974; Whitehead 1980: 286–303). Iceland's geographic location was another factor in this story, as it shielded Icelandic society from most of the carnage and devastation of the war.[2] Therefore, it was not loss of life that worried the Icelandic public and policymakers the most, but rather what many regarded as the detrimental influences emanating from the soldiers stationed in the country. With so many foreign bodies present on the island, the morality of the Icelanders was at risk—and then, in particular, of those who were perceived to constitute the most vulnerable part of the nation, that is, women and the country's youth (Neijmann 2016; Hálfdanarson 2011).

The feeling was, therefore, that in spite of its distance from the European battlefields, the nation was engaged in an intense struggle for its survival. "Among other nations," wrote the editor of the organ of the social democrats in Reykjavík, published in the fall of 1941, "it is primarily the soldiers who are placed where people fight for the nation's life and death; here it is the women. Whereas other nations lose their sons in battles, either as fallen or crippled, the Icelandic nation loses its daughters. Some of them are worse than dead to the nation, while others are crippled beyond recovery" (*Nýtt land*, 5 September 1941, 2). The cause for this alarmist statement was a report, published a week earlier, on the moral conditions in Reykjavík (in daily parlance, this was called *ástandið*—or "the situation"—and hence the report, the "Situation Report"). The Situation Report was written by a committee of three eminent (male) public servants, chosen to investigate the relations between Reykjavík youth and the occupying forces. The state of affairs was deadly serious, the committee concluded, as there was a real danger that "a large class of prostitutes will be formed here, who will abandon our civilized life." The report did not propose any particular restrictions on the women's behavior but recommended that every Icelander would be encouraged to do her or his duty; it was imperative to guide public opinion in Iceland toward protecting "Icelandic nationality, Icelandic culture and Icelandic language," the committee declared, in order to preserve "Iceland as an independent civilized nation. The future of the Icelandic nation depends on one thing only: that the country's youth will not forget their civic duty "to their blood and soil" (*við blóð sitt og móðurmold*) (*Tíminn*, 29 August 1941, 346 and 348; *Morgunblaðið*, 28 August 1941, 5).

With a substantial number of foreign soldiers positioned in Iceland at a time when its total population was only around 120,000, the sense of moral decay consumed many of the Icelandic political and intellectual leaders (Björnsdóttir 1995; Baldursdóttir 2001). "Women in all countries are feeble when it comes to two social ills," wrote the politician and former minister of justice Jónas Jónsson in early September 1941, a few days after the publication of the Situation Report. "At the present time, women in all civilized countries have a hidden, but strong urge for living in cities . . . where most of them find neither joy nor fortune. Another frailty of women, related to the former, is that they are romantically attracted to foreigners, especially if they are dressed in uniforms" (Jónsson 1941). An important part of this critique centered on the fear of "racial mixing," which would inevitably pollute the "pure" Icelandic blood. During the interwar years, eugenics had been in vogue in Iceland, similar to America as well as the rest of Europe, both as a subject of "scientific" enquiry and the basis for social policy (Karlsdóttir 1998b, and 2005; Rydell 2010; Schneider 1990). To the Icelandic believers in "racial purity," women were a biological resource, which had to be protected—even from the protectors—in order to preserve the nation from eventual destruction (Karlsdóttir 1998a: 110–11; Magnúss 1947: 619–72; Whitehead 2013); in other words, "women's bodies belonged first to the nation and only then to themselves" (Stargardt 2015: 410). Agreeing with Jónas Jónsson on the attraction of foreign soldiers, Ágúst H. Bjarnason, professor of philosophy at the University of Iceland, warned his compatriots of the problems that sexual associations between Icelandic women and the soldiers could cause for the country. "Although there are many fine men in their ranks," he wrote in 1943 of the soldiers, "there are also many bad apples among them. Usually, it is also the most unscrupulous who seek out their counterparts of the female sex, and these relations can produce the most troublesome people" (Bjarnason 1943: 54).

It was not only women's bodies that these commentators thought to be in great peril but also the minds of Icelandic youth. "The university started a new activity by organizing *concerts* for the students and teachers," the rector of the University of Iceland announced in the fall of 1941, a few months after American forces took over the Icelandic military defenses. The aim of this initiative, he explained, was to open the world of classical music to university students, revealing to them "the difference between true music and the savage and rude tones called 'jazz,' which should be banned in any civilized society." The fact that Icelandic youth were exposed to "this degenerate music" in the dancehalls of Reykjavík, the rector observed, contributed "to the corruption and lack of restraint which afflicts our nation at the present and will eventually lead to its ruin" ("Háskólahátíð" 1943: 12). One can discern a deep anxiety about the nation's status in the perceived cultural hierarchy of the world in the rector's words. To him, Europe (white and Christian) was the only source of true civilization, and therefore the Icelandic intellectual elite had to be trained to appreciate European norms in order to secure Iceland's place in the camp of acknowledged civilized nations. For this reason, American influences were treated with great suspicion, and then especially those emanating from non-European cultural traditions. Jazz was the primary culprit, as it was described as "primitive" and "unrestrained" in the Icelandic media, and it appealed primarily to the young and immature. "Nations at a primitive cultural stage," wrote the musicologist and composer, Hallgrímur Helgason, "can only perceive basic rhythm through their outer ear. The highly developed emotional life of the Europeans produces inner rhythm, which we do not need to hear. The basic rhythm moves inside us, and we perceive its existence with our inner ear." To counteract the subverting influence of the primitive and decadent music, Helgason called for the resurrection of Icelandic traditional music, "which saturates the atmosphere with pleasure and happiness and ties us more firmly with the soil of our motherland [*móðurmold*]" (Helgason 1943).

Jazz had already reached Iceland in the 1920s, but the arrival of American soldiers in the summer of 1941 boosted its popularity among the country's youth. This posed a serious threat to Icelandic national culture, as Gylfi Þ. Gíslason, associate professor of business administration at the University of Iceland and later minister of education for the Social Democratic Party, argued in an article he wrote for the university students' journal in 1942. "American and Icelandic mentalities and attitudes differ greatly, and many of the American influences can, without doubt, be counted as undesirable and—stultifying [*heimskandi*]." Among the most disturbing cultural phenomena coming from America, Gíslason pointed out, was "the Negro music, called jazz . . . dreadful music which dulls people's senses, which unfortunately has had significant and corrupting influences on, among others, the youth in Reykjavík, their taste and even conduct." Iceland's strife for independence was not over, Gíslason reminded the students, and the protection of the nation's culture was a central part of that effort. "Now it is the students' role in the nation's struggle for independence," he continued, to prevent the stultification caused by American influences on the national culture, and "to combat all influences in this direction and to strengthen Icelandic culture" (Gíslason 1942).

The criticism of Icelandic women's interactions with British and American soldiers and of American cultural influences in Iceland were related because both focused on preserving the alleged "purity" and "essence" of the Icelanders, as it was expressed in their culture. The arrival of a great number of young foreign soldiers in Iceland amplified earlier disruptions of traditional Icelandic society, which were caused by rapid urbanization and industrialization during the first decades of the twentieth century. Towns and urban centers had for long been regarded as cradles of moral corruption, and with foreign bodies and cultural trends in the mix, the moral hazard was felt to be even more pressing. The Icelandic authorities had limited power to control the flow of soldiers to Iceland, although they were able to compel the American government to acknowledge the challenge by promising to send only "picked troops"—viz. "white"—to minimize the "danger to nation [of small population] from presence of a numerous army . . ." (*New York Times*, 8 July 1941, 3). They tried, however, to assert their power over young Icelandic women, opening a "reform home" in the countryside for young girls who had been compromised by "the situation." In the end, these efforts received limited popular support in Iceland, and the institution was closed in 1943. This does not mean that Icelanders generally approved of "the situation," historian Þór Whitehead concludes, but only that they were forced to accept their inability to do anything about it (2013).

Nation and Narration

"Nation is narration," writes the German historian Stefan Berger, paraphrasing the title of Homi K. Bhabha's influential collection of essays, *Nation and Narration* (Berger 2008: 1). What this entails is that nations are created through the stories that are recounted of their emergence and development, that they are, above all, "discursive formations" (Brennan 1990: 46). In other words, to quote Berger again, the "stories we tell each other about our national belonging and being constitute the nation" (2008: 1). The goal of the commemorative exhibition in Reykjavík in 1944 was, indeed, to tell the story of the Icelandic nation. It had developed—the organizers believed—from a glorious past, characterized by spectacular cultural achievements and national freedom in the Middle Ages, through centuries of economic and cultural decay under foreign rule, and it finally ascended into a period of renaissance after regaining its freedom in the early twentieth century. In the eyes of the organizers, freedom and culture were two sides of the same coin, and without the one, you cannot have the other (Sveinsson 1940). Furthermore, they perceived the nation as a metaphoric individual, who had been born as the first settlers of the island had formed an organized society in the tenth century and established vibrant cultural life in the twelfth and thirteenth. Placed on an isolated island, the imagined Icelandic community had preserved its cultural traits, expressed in a language that had survived relatively unaltered through the centuries, thus firmly linking the present with the past.

The narrative arc of this national(ist) history had already been determined at the beginning of the twentieth century through the works of authors like

Jón Jónsson, professor of history at the University of Iceland (see for example, Jónsson 1903; Hálfdanarson 2010). Icelandic schools inculcated his evolutionary model, tracing the history of Iceland from its medieval pinnacle through the travails of foreign subjugation, into generations of Icelandic students. The aim of the 1944 exhibition was to bolster the narrative's appeal to the Icelanders and thus fortify the newly born republic. At this moment, there were pervasive concerns among the cultural and political elites in Iceland that the young—seduced by the foreign military forces stationed in the country—were losing their connection with the past and thus compromising the nation's future. Furthermore, the war seemed to contradict the basic premise of the Icelandic national narrative, which claimed that "national freedom" was a necessary precondition for economic and cultural progress. The response was simply to erase the war from the Icelandic national narrative, because its creators thought it was irrelevant for the nation's long-term development. This may have influenced how World War II is remembered in Iceland. The war clearly affected Icelandic society in a fundamental way, but it is still regarded as an isolated episode in the evolution of Icelandic society and thus of limited consequence for the Icelandic grand narrative. This was not "our" war, although Iceland was lucky enough to be occupied by the victors, and therefore it is not an integral part of "our" history.

Guðmundur Hálfdanarson (PhD, Cornell University, 1991) is Professor of History and Dean of the School of Humanities at the University of Iceland. He has published extensively on modern Icelandic history, focusing on the construction of national identity and nationalist politics in Iceland. Among his publications are *Historical Dictionary of Iceland* (1997), *Íslenska þjóðríkið—upphaf og endimörk* (The Icelandic nation-state—origins and limits, 2001), *Europa 1800–2000* (coauthor, 2003).

Notes

1. In Icelandic: *Upphaf, þjóðveldi, landafundir og langferðir, viðnám, niðurlæging, dagrenning, Jón Sigurðsson, barátta, sjálfsforræði*. Jón Sigurðsson was the unquestioned national hero of Iceland, best known for formulating the Icelandic demands for self-determination during the mid-nineteenth century.
2. It is estimated that 225 Icelanders lost their lives because of the war, most of whom perished at sea after German attacks on Icelandic ships (Magnúss 1950; Tómasson 1984).

References

Árnason, Hans Kristján. 1974. "Ísland í höndum nasista hefði þýtt ósigur Bretlands." *Lesbók Morgunblaðsins*, 15 September, 4–5.
Baldursdóttir, Bára. 2001. "'Þær myndu fegnar skipta um þjóðerni': Ríkisafskipti af samböndum unglingsstúlkna og setuliðsmanna." In *Kvennaslóðir: Rit til heiðurs Sigríði Th. Erlendsdóttur sagnfræðingi*, edited by A. Agnarsdóttir, E. H. Halldórsdóttir, H. Gísladóttir, I. H. Hákonardóttir, S. Matthíasdóttir, and S. K. Þorgrímsdóttir, 302–17. Reykjavík: Sögufélag.
Berger, Steven 2008. "Narrating the Nation: Historiography and Other Genres." In *Narrating the Nation: Representations in History, Media and the Arts*, edited by Stefan Berger, Linas Eriksonas, and Andrew Mycock, 1–16. New York: Berghahn Books.
Bjarnason, Ágúst H. 1943. *Vandamál mannlegs lífs*, vol. 1. Reykjavík: Háskóli Íslands.
Björnsdóttir, Inga Dóra. 1995. "Island: Uheldige kvinner i et heldig land." In *Kvinner, krig og kjærlighet*, edited by D. Ellingsen, A. Warring, and Björnsdóttir, 149–96. Oslo: Cappelen.
Brennan, Timothy. 1990. "The National Longing for Form." In *Narrating the Nation*, edited by Homi Bhabha, 44–70. London: Routledge.
"Dansk-íslensk sambandslög." 1918. *Stjórnartíðindi fyrir Ísland: Árið 1918*. Reykjavík: Ísafoldarprentsmiðja.
"Denmark-Finland-Iceland-Norway-Sweden: Declaration Regarding Similar Rules of Neutrality." 1938. *American Journal of International Law*, Supplement: Official Documents, 32(4): 141–63.
Frelsi og menning: Sýning úr frelsis- og menningarbaráttu Íslendinga í Menntaskólanum í Reykjavík í júní 1944. 1944. Reykjavík: Ríkisprentsmiðjan Gutenberg.
Gíslason, Gylfi Þ. 1942. "Forheimskun og hervernd." *Stúdentablaðið*, 1 December, 3–6.
Hálfdanarson, Guðmundur. 2000. "Þingvellir: An Icelandic 'lieu de memoire.'" *History and Memory* 12(1): 5–29.
———. 2006. "Severing the Ties—Iceland's Journey from a Union with Denmark to a Nation-State." *Scandinavian Journal of History* 31(3–4): 237–54.
———. 2010. "Sagan og sjálfsmynd(ir) þjóðar." *Glíman* 7(1): 113–35.
———. 2011. "'The Beloved War': The Second World War and the Icelandic National Narrative." In *Nordic Narratives of the Second World War: National Historiographies Revisited*, edited by Henrik Stenius, Mirja Österberg, and Johan Östling, 79–100. Lund: Nordic Academic Press.
"Háskólahátíð." 1943. *Árbók Háskóla Íslands: Háskólaárið 1941–1942*, 9–15. Reykjavík: Háskóli Íslands.
Helgadóttir, Herdís 2001. *Úr fjötrum: Íslenskar konur og erlendur her*. Reykjavík: Mál og menning.
Helgason, Hallgrímur. 1943. "Jazz-músík og siðræn uppeldisáhrif." *Straumhvörf* 1(3): 80–83.
Ísleifsson, Sumarliði. 1996. *Ísland, framandi land*. Reykjavík: Mál og menning.
Jónsson, Jón. 1903. *Íslenzkt þjóðerni*. Reykjavík: Sigurður Kristjánsson.
Jónsson, Jónas. 1941. "'Ástandið' í Reykjavík: Tvær leiðir til úrbóta." *Tíminn*, 2 September, 350–51.
Karlsdóttir, Unnur B. 1998a. *Mannkynbætur: Hugmyndir um bætta kynstofna hérlendis og erlendis á 19. og 20. öld*. Reykjavík: Sagnfræðistofnun Háskóla Íslands, 1998.
———. 1998b. "'Kynbætt af þúsund þrautum.'" *Skírnir* 172(2): 420–50.
———. 2005. "'Vönun andlegra fáráðnlinga . . .' Ófrjósemisaðgerðir á Íslandi, 1938–1975." *Saga* 43(2): 7–46.
Kjartansson, Helgi S. 2002. *Ísland á 20. öld*. Reykjavík: Sögufélag.
Larrington, Carolyne. 2014. *The Poetic Edda*. Rev. ed. Oxford: Oxford University Press.

Magnúss, Gunnar M. 1947. *Virkið í norðri*. Vol. 2: *Þríbýlisárin*. Reykjavík: Ísafoldarprentsmiðja.
———. 1950. *Virkið í norðri*. Vol. 3: *Sæfarendur*. Reykjavík: Ísafoldarprentsmiðja.
Magnússon, Skúli. 2018. "Fullveldishugtakið í íslenskum rétti frá 1918 til samtímans." In *Frjálst og fullvalda ríki. Ísland 1918–2018*, edited by Guðmundur Jónsson, 129–72. Reykjavík: Sögufélag.
Neijmann, Daisy. 2016. "Soldiers and Other Monsters: The Allied Occupation in Icelandic Fiction." *Scandinavian-Canadian Studies* 23: 96–120.
Olgeirsson, Einar. 1945. "Sögusýningin." In *Lýðveldishátíðin 1944*, edited by Alexander Jóhannesson, 381–430. Reykjavík: Leiftur.
Oslund, Karen. 2011. *Iceland Imagined: Nature, Culture, and Storytelling in the North Atlantic*. Seattle: University of Washington.
Padelford, Norman J. 1938. "The New Scandinavian Neutrality Rules." *American Journal of International Law* 32(4): 789–93.
Rydell, Robert W. 2010. "The Proximity of the Past: Eugenics in American Culture." *Modern Intellectual History* 7(3): 667–78.
Ringler, Dick. 2010. *Bard of Iceland: Jónas Hallgrímsson, Poet and Scientist*. Reykjavík: Mál og menning, 2010.
Schneider, William H. 1990. *Quality and Quantity: The Quest for Biological Regeneration in Twentieth-Century France*. Cambridge: Cambridge University Press.
Stargardt, Nicholas. 2015. "Wartime Occupation by Germany: Food and Sex." In *The Cambridge History of the Second World War*. Vol. 2: *Politics and Ideology*, edited by Richard J. B. Bosworth and Joseph A. Maiolo, 385–411. Cambridge: Cambridge University Press.
Sveinsson, Einar Ólafur. 1940. "Frelsi og menning." *Stúdentablaðið*, 1 December, 3–5.
Thors, Ólafur. 1940. "Fullveldisræða." *Morgunblaðið*, 3 December 1940, 5–6.
Thorsteinsson, Pétur. 1992. *Utanríkisþjónusta Íslands: Sögulegt yfirlit*. Vol. 1. Reykjavík: Hið íslenska bókmenntafélag.
Tómasson, Tómas. 1984. *Heimsstyrjaldarárin á Íslandi*. Vol. 2. Reykjavík: Örn og Örlygur.
Whitehead, Þór. 1980. *Ófriður í aðsigi*. Reykjavík: Almenna bókafélagið.
———. 1999. *Bretarnir koma*. Reykjavík: Vaka-Helgafell.
———. 2002. *Ísland í hers höndum*. Reykjavík: Vaka-Helgafell.
———. 2013. "Ástandið og yfirvöldin: Stríðið um konurnar 1940–1941." *Saga* 51(2): 92–142.

Chapter 5

SWEDEN'S AMBIGUOUS WAR

Contradiction and Controversy

John Gilmour

The Nordic countries were neutral in 1939. They had hoped to replicate the same conditions that kept them conflict-free as onlookers during the bloody carnage of World War I (Wylie 2013: 605). Unfortunately for them, the ambitions of Hitler and Stalin coupled with a scornful disregard for neutrality swept three of the four countries into the war—two into German occupation and the remaining one, Sweden, into an uneasy island of peace surrounded by a turbulent sea of resistance, collaboration, and conflict in the bordering countries of Norway, Denmark, and Finland. Sweden was effectively isolated from the west. To enable a wider understanding when assessing Swedish conduct during World War II, there are two facts and two uncertainties that should be considered. The facts are firstly that World War II was an imperial war fought for territory and security; it was not a war fought for freedom and civil rights. Secondly, the great imperial powers had little consideration for smaller nations if their actions did not meet with the wartime needs of those powers; they were expendable (Rothwell 2005: 117). The Swedish leadership fully appreciated both these facts. The uncertainties are firstly that Sweden did not know who would win World War II until after 1943; until then, Sweden had to reckon with the possibility of a Nazi-dominated Europe. Secondly, Sweden could not be confident that Finland, its former province and defensive buffer against the Soviet Union, would preserve its independence. This concern ranked high in Swedish consideration of its relationship with all the belligerents until September 1944.

Ambiguity is one of the most useful tools in the politician's box of tricks. Being able to say one thing and imply another is of great advantage when trying to maintain leadership of a group with a spectrum of views. The deft use of ambiguity was one of the defining characteristics of neutral Sweden's leader during World War II, the veteran Social Democratic politician Per Albin Hansson, known to Sweden's citizens simply as "Per Albin." His unshakeable policy was to keep Sweden out of war using "negotiated neutrality" unless its sovereignty was threatened (Johansson 1984: 413). The Swedish nation contained a range of views on how the government should conduct a neutral policy toward the belligerent powers during World War II, and Per Albin walked a proverbial tightrope to enable his coalition government to fulfil its stated policy to keep Sweden out of war.

It was only some years after the war ended that the reputation of Per Albin and his government foundered on the unambiguity of the genocidal crimes of Nazi Germany. Black and white replaced shades of gray. In this short overview, I shall focus less on the ebb and flow of the tides of war and instead attempt to explain the reasons for Sweden's conduct between 1939 and 1945, and also why that became the subject of such bitter continuous debate that colors the country's attitudes to that war in the current millennium.

Swedish Conditions

Most non-Swedes fail to appreciate the importance of Finland to Sweden between 1939 and 1944. Finland formed the buffer against the dreaded Soviet Union, and as a former Swedish province, its people remained closely related to Sweden. Thus, when Russia, by then an ally of Nazi Germany, invaded Finland in November 1939, there was public alarm and outrage in Sweden; alarm at the prospect of a new border with the Soviet Union and outrage at a totalitarian power grab against a Nordic neighbor. However, Per Albin kept a cool head, and the only concrete assistance provided was armaments and volunteers. About seventy thousand Finnish children, called *krigsbarn* (war children), were transported to Sweden. Sweden's status in the conflict moved from neutral to noncombatant, but, importantly, Sweden was not drawn into the great power conflict. An uneasy peace was brokered in March 1940 (the Treaty of Moscow), which lasted until Hitler invaded Russia in June 1941 (Operation Barbarossa), at which time Sweden was forced to allow the German *Engelbrecht* Division to transit Sweden from Norway to Finland. Support for Finland in Sweden then diminished due to Finnish military cooperation with Germany to recover lost territory. When in 1944 Finland was again threatened with Russian occupation, Sweden acted to broker a peace that preserved Finnish independence and thus the buffer protecting

Sweden. In the subsequent expulsion of German forces from Finland, Sweden again provided a haven from the military conflict for Finnish civilians. There were those in the Swedish government who wanted a more active role for Sweden in Finland, but that policy was opposed by others who wanted to avoid conflict with the Soviet Union. Nevertheless, Finland was a major distraction for a country that had the Wehrmacht camped on its western borders with Norway and Denmark.

War with Germany was a constant factor for the Swedish leadership to consider. Hitler's ravages throughout Europe had convinced the Swedes that they could never be entirely safe from attack. They knew that the dictator had no sympathy with democratic Sweden despite King Gustav V's assurances that the country was resolutely neutral. Hitler commented in March 1943 that Sweden now supported the enemy, and even if they were too clever and careful to show it openly, they "try to trip me up whenever possible," obviously realizing "that I can do nothing to them" (Carlgren 1973: 393n177).[1] The Swedes were also unaware that the German military believed as early as 1940 that it would be too expensive to attack Sweden as it would require

Figure 5.1. Aggressors and defenders? Swedish and German army guards appear relaxed on the border between neutral Sweden and German-occupied Norway in the winter of 1941, which was in stark contrast to the tense wartime relations between the two countries. The long border was better guarded on the Swedish side, as many Norwegian refugees discovered, due to Swedish concerns about German invasion, Quisling infiltration, and British Special Operations Executive agents compromising Swedish neutrality. Photographer: Johan Karlsson, 1941. Courtesy of Bohusläns museum.

between twenty and forty German army divisions to do so (Zetterberg 2013: 103–4). Yet, Sweden's defensive capability on the ground was poor, and in the air it could only deploy a small number of obsolete machines, leaving the country open to bombing attack, a threat that was deployed to secure transit concessions. The country needed to demonstrate military as well as political resolve, and it did this in two ways: mass conscription and rearmament.

The Swedish army was mobilized and its conscript reserves called upon at several tense points during the war. This meant that the whole country, not just the professional soldiers, was affected by the war. This mass mobilization had important military, economic, and social implications for Sweden. Firstly, the conscripts had to be equipped, trained, and quartered throughout the country. Equipment had been run down during the disarmament in the 1920s and 1930s, and so many conscripts (and their anxious relatives) were openly derisive of Per Albin's famous speech in October 1939 claiming that "our preparation is good."[2] The equipment shortages forced the pace of rearmament by Swedish industry, which of course needed some foreign materials such as rubber and fuel which could only be imported with the negotiated cooperation of the Allies and Germany. However, war work soon led not only to the reduction in unemployment, which had blighted the 1920s and 1930s but also to a shortage of labor. Women and refugees from Norway and Denmark were deployed to fill in for conscripted men, which altered the social position of women in Swedish society. There were also frantic attempts to buy military equipment from the belligerents that was largely inadequate. If Sweden wanted guns, aircraft, and warships, it would have to manufacture them itself. This is not the place to go into the statistics and development of military hardware that so enthralls some military historians and present-day reenactors.[3] It is, however, true to say that Sweden was better equipped in 1945 than in 1939. By then, the air force had 580 operational aircraft compared to only 122 in 1940 (Bengtsson 2014: 213).

Just as important as the equipment was the leadership, attitudes, and capabilities of the men in charge of Sweden's defense, and here there were many "question marks." When Finland was attacked in 1939, many of the senior officers pressed the politicians to join the struggle to defend Finland against their traditional enemy, Russia. When this failed to shift the resolve of Per Albin to keep Sweden out of the war, they again tried unsuccessfully, with some "activist" political support, to persuade the government to join the German attack on the Soviet Union in 1941. The army in particular exhibited an admiration for German militarism, but they could not match German tactical ability. The cautious, elderly commander in chief, Olof Thörnell, even accepted a German decoration in October 1940. Per Albin in particular wanted to minimize the risk of attack by reassuring the Germans that Sweden had no hostile intentions, and the appointment of Thörnell did just that.

However, Thörnell's acceptance of the Order of the German Eagle created consternation among the Swedish public and tainted the reputation of an otherwise loyal soldier. The Social Democrats had the reactionary military in their sights when the Coalition Government inaugurated a series of reforms designed to democratize the forces, and for the duration of the war the politicians kept firm control over the actions of the military. Sweden was never going to be a victim of military adventurism. There were small numbers of casualties due to operational problems such as accidents rather than by engagement with the belligerents, but the shared conscript experience had a leveling effect on Swedish society.

Food and fuel followed defense as a main concern for the Swedish authorities. Sweden had starved in the latter years of World War I due to the Allied blockade of Europe, and the strain on society was severe. Much interwar activity was devoted to planning for this eventuality again, and this was one area that Per Albin was correct to say that the country was well prepared. Rationing of food and fuel was introduced early in the war and again did much to reduce the inequalities between classes. Unlike World War I, the government also put a priority on negotiating with the belligerents to secure trade deals that would keep the country going, and it is that trade with Germany that contributed to Sweden's reputation as a country that supported the Nazi war effort. The Allies understood the necessity for this trade, but contemporary and postwar critics have not. Sweden remained on short rations throughout but did not suffer the famine that struck German-occupied Europe later in the war.

There were critical Danish and Norwegian voices that, far from accepting that Sweden had enjoyed a lucky escape from their fate, envied the Swedes their privileged neutrality (the same as they had hoped for themselves) and looked for suspected Nazi collaboration among the Swedish elite. Norwegian prime minister Nygaardsvold instructed his representative in Stockholm to deliver a letter to Per Albin, which included, "As long as I live and breathe, Sweden will never be seen as part of Scandinavia but as a knave that stood in the service of Germany . . ." (Nygaardsvold 1998: 156–57).[4] The diplomat wisely did not deliver it. These voices found sympathetic audiences in London and Washington that further stoked the feeling that Sweden was failing to stand fast with its Nordic neighbors and the Western democracies in their struggle against the Nazi behemoth.

None of the belligerent powers welcomed a neutral Sweden, but after the occupation of Denmark and Norway, only Germany realistically could convert Swedish neutrality into war by invading the country. If Germany could achieve its strategic objectives without expending scarce military resources on occupying Sweden, it would not attack. The Swedish leadership of course did not know that. The Western Allies lacked the military means and the strategic ambition to defend Sweden against Germany, yet Britain and later the United States resented the relationship that Sweden was forced to have with Germany. However, they, like the Soviet Union, could only criticize impotently while tolerating and attempting to limit Swedish trade and transit concessions. Some of the troop transit concessions conceded to Germany under pressure during the first phase of the war when Germany was winning were privately accepted as un-neutral by Per Albin. These were gradually withdrawn when the Wehrmacht began to retreat. Trade with the Third Reich was also scaled down under Allied pressure when the tide of war had turned against Germany.

Within Sweden too, critical voices were raised in opposition to the wartime policies of Per Albin's coalition. On one side, there was criticism of what was seen as an overly supine approach to the abhorrent Nazis, for example in the restriction of press articles and artistic expression critical of German actions in occupied Europe. On the other side, there were those who believed that it was timely to support the German invasion of Russia in order to eliminate the age-old threat to Sweden from the east. Stalin's crimes of mass executions of innocent Russians and use of slave labor camps in the Gulag were already known to Swedes in the 1930s, whereas the extent of the genocidal crimes of Hitler and his henchmen were only gradually revealed as the war proceeded. Therefore, some Swedes believed that Hitler offered a shield from communist atrocity without fully realizing that the Nazis represented an equally existential threat to a democratic Sweden and that they were likewise criminal in their selective racial, minority, and political persecutions.

The main trading relationship that Sweden had with Germany was the continuation of the peacetime export of iron ore and ball bearings, both of which clearly and undoubtedly contributed to the German war effort. What is less well known is that Swedish trade with Germany was subject to Allied agreement through bilateral negotiation and that the Allies recognized Swedish dependence on Germany for the coal that fueled the factories to rearm Sweden. Similarly, Germany accepted that the Allies were the main source of petroleum for the Swedish military and permitted tankers through an otherwise tight blockade.

The transit of German troops through Sweden between 1940 and 1943 is often portrayed as a willing concession by the Swedish leadership to assist the German war machine. It is further implied that Sweden knowingly permitted the transport of German troops to fight the Norwegian forces in Narvik in June 1940 and even permitted the transport of Jews to concentration camps in Germany. Neither allegation is correct, but it is true that Per Albin's government permitted the transit of one German division from Norway to Finland in 1941 to invade Russia. This was the nadir of Sweden's concessions to Germany under extreme pressure at the height of the Nazi success, but neither was that Swedish concession nor German success ever repeated despite the German call for Sweden to participate in their "crusade against Bolshevism." In this regard, it is often forgotten that while thousands of Norwegians and Danes did respond to that call, only a few hundred Swedes did so (Nestler et al. 1996: 166; Gyllenhaal and Westberg 2010: 257). About nine hundred Swedish merchant seamen also died in Allied service (Gyllenhaal and Westberg 2010: 208).

The Holocaust

The Holocaust is today the defining episode of World War II for many people, and its characteristics allow for simplistic "good and evil" narratives, both factual and fictional. Yet during the war and for many decades after, it was generally regarded as only one of the many human tragedies that the war brought to the world. As Tony Judt, the eminent European historian (who lost Jewish family members in the Holocaust) wrote,

> For many years, Western Europeans preferred not to think about the wartime sufferings of the Jews. Now, we are encouraged to think about these sufferings all the time. . . . But for historians, this is misleading. . . . It is hard to accept that the Holocaust occupies a more important role in our own lives than it did in the wartime experience of occupied lands. (Judt 2015: 134–35)

This was true of neutral Sweden also. Prior to World War II, Sweden had exercised broadly similar immigration policies to the rest of the west when Jewish refugees from Nazi persecution in Germany, Austria, and Czechoslovakia began to seek asylum abroad: admit a very few and hope that other countries accept them instead (Svanberg and Tydén 1997: 201–2). The dire economic conditions of the 1930s made governments very sensitive to their citizens complaining about "foreigners taking their jobs." Add ever-present populist anti-Semitism and powerful professional self-interest from doctors and dentists, and the Western democracies failed to accept Jewish refugees in the numbers needed to avert the catastrophe that followed. Sweden and the other Scandinavian countries followed suit.

Both the Swedish public (despite German pressure to restrict reporting) and the Swedish foreign ministry were fairly well informed about the repression in Germany and Austria. This, however, did not create widespread pressure on the government to alter its restrictive immigration policy. As the war progressed after 1939, the atrocities in the occupied territories were also reported, again with little effect (Svanberg and Tydén 1997: 178–80). It was not until 1942 when the Norwegians failed to prevent the transportation of 763 Norwegian Jews—739 to their deaths in extermination camps (despite the valiant attempts of the Norwegian resistance to take as many as possible over the Swedish border)—that public opinion and government policy changed in Sweden (Svanberg and Tydén 1997: 248). As this became gradually known outside official circles, widespread Swedish indignation was based on a rather convoluted view that the oppression of "Scandinavian Jews" was somehow more worthy of outrage than that of Eastern European and German-Austrian Jews. The official Swedish response focused more on behind-the-scenes attempts to rescue as many as possible rather than high-profile protests. Indeed, sympathetic non-Nazi contacts in the German Foreign Office had revealed that Nazi foreign minister Ribbentrop had ordered the Stockholm Embassy not to discuss the issue of the Norwegian Jews with Sweden. Accordingly, the senior German Foreign Office diplomat in Berlin warned the Swedes that the result of any official Swedish protest "could be merely negative and a Swedish intervention would mainly be to the detriment of the Norwegian Jews . . ." (Koblik 1987: 197–98).[5] The Swedes then redirected their rescue efforts into Red Cross rather than official diplomatic channels, but, strikingly, Sweden had now become a sanctuary for any Jewish refugees from Nazi oppression: Swedish government immigration policy had been changed by the actions of Norwegian collaborators in concert with German authorities. Yet Sweden has been criticized for "not speaking out" against oppression of the Jews when there is clear evidence to indicate that this could be counterproductive. Also, the Western Allies could afford to be vocal in their condemnation of Germany, whereas encircled, vulnerable Sweden had to consider the consequences on coal and oil supplies, military retaliation, and territorial integrity.

Swedish sanctuary offered hope to the Danish Jews when in September 1943, the Germans seized direct control of the country, planning to round up and exterminate Denmark's almost eight thousand Jews (Svanberg and Tydén 1997: 312). In striking contrast to Norway's collaborators, there was a major rescue effort by a large section of the Danish population that resulted in almost all the Jews being transported by fishing vessels over to Sweden where official reception centers welcomed and resettled them there. The Germans were able to declare Denmark *judenfrei* (free of Jews).

Later in the war, the low-key approach of rescue rather than protest by Swedish authorities paid off in two initiatives, one in Hungary and one in Germany, that saved thousands of Jews. First, in Hungary in July 1944, the impending transportation of the country's Jews led to King Gustav V sending a message directly to the country's dictator Horthy (bypassing the occupying Germans), pleading with him to use his influence to save the Jews from "victimization." This (together with other messages) held up the action temporarily, and Swedish businessman Raoul Wallenberg arrived in Budapest two days later to make one of the most remarkable interventions of the Holocaust (Carlsson 2006: 268–73). Wallenberg is widely renowned as the Swede who rescued the most Jews. He was in business with a Jewish Hungarian and was familiar with the country. He used passports, influence, and property to protect Jews from deportation to concentration camps. Firstly, he issued thousands of Swedish protection passports (*Schutz-Pass*) to Jews, which identified the bearer as a Swedish citizen awaiting repatriation. Surprisingly, these documents were accepted by the German and Hungarian authorities. They afforded actual protection against the transports. Secondly, Wallenberg negotiated with and bribed German and Hungarian officials to allow those holding *Schutz-Pass* be treated as Swedish citizens. Thirdly, he used the funds he had brought with him to rent buildings as Swedish diplomatic territory to accommodate about seventeen thousand of these new "Swedish citizens" (*Räddningen Budapest 1944* 1997: 215). Wallenberg was assisted by the Swedish Red Cross and the Swedish minister. When the Russians occupied Budapest in January 1945, they found over twenty thousand Jews under Swedish protection. Wallenberg was then seized by the Russians as a suspected spy for the United States, and he is believed to have died in prison in the Soviet Union in 1947.

In the second instance in 1945, the Swedish government decided on 10 February to send Count Folke Bernadotte of the Swedish Red Cross to Germany to negotiate the release of Norwegian and Danish concentration camp prisoners with the Holocaust's architect, Heinrich Himmler. Due to Hitler's violent reaction to an earlier deal with Switzerland, the whole operation was kept low-key. Bernadotte met Himmler on 19 February and secured agreement that the Red Cross would repatriate the weakest Scandinavian prisoners. Three hundred Red Cross medical staff and drivers were gathered and one hundred repainted vehicles, the "White Buses" requisitioned from the Swedish army. The buses entered Germany via Denmark, and by 30 March they had assembled Scandinavian prisoners in the relative safety of Neuengamme camp in north Germany. The evacuations to Sweden began on 3 April, and the Swedes were joined by a parallel expedition from Denmark. With Swedish support, a Jewish negotiator now succeeded in securing Himmler's agreement to the evacuation of Jewish women from Ravensbrück camp in addition to the Scandinavians already evacuated. In the end, between thirty-five hundred and sixty-five hundred Jews, mainly women, were evacuated to Sweden and Denmark (Svanberg and Tydén 1997: 370–71).

The complexities of moral ambiguity in wartime conduct even extend to this humanitarian operation. Historians' attention has turned away from those who were rescued to those who were not and why. What was the moral basis for initially rescuing only Swedish and Danish citizens, and, relatedly, what was the likelihood of Himmler offering to free other nations' prisoners? What was the rescuers' culpability for inadvertently transporting other prisoners out of Neuengamme, some to die in other camps, in order to accommodate the Scandinavian prisoners in transit? Would more of them have survived the SS death march of nine thousand to the coast after the rescuers had departed? Would some or all of them have been among the three thousand murdered in Neuengamme camp before the march? Would some or all of them have been among the seven thousand march survivors who died when the RAF sank the vessels that they had been loaded onto? Were the RAF morally responsible for their deaths also? Were the RAF morally responsible for the dead and wounded rescuers in attacks on the buses? Were they legitimate targets in a war zone? These tragic and desperate events defy simplistic moral judgments, which frequently ignore the context and circumstances in which decisions were made by men and women negotiating with genocidal criminals and risking their lives on behalf of others. Little did they know that decades later, they had also risked their moral reputations (Boritz et al. 2015: 102–9 and Persson 2002: 338–39).

How then should the much-criticized Swedish response to the Holocaust be viewed? In terms of the enormity of the Holocaust, the statistics of Jews rescued are meager yet meaningful. By these actions, Sweden fell clearly into the "rescuer" category of Holocaust actors, having been a "bystander" up to 1942. No Swedish authorities delivered Jews into Nazi hands, unlike the police collaborators in Norway. By adopting a low-profile response and adeptly using the Red Cross, neutral Sweden provided a distinctive haven for about thirty thousand Jewish refugees. Critics must ask themselves whether all of this could have been achieved had the Swedish government adopted the high-profile but almost certainly ineffective open condemnation of Nazi atrocities that critics demanded. Sweden might well have gained a better moral image, but at the expense of Jewish lives. Nonetheless, it is certainly true that the Holocaust was not central to the concerns of the Swedish leadership and the country's authorities. As Tony Judt remarked about the Holocaust, "For practically everyone else the war had quite different meanings: they had troubles of their own" (Judt 1997: 134).

External Threats

Swedish cultural and political sympathies had changed somewhat since 1914–18 when there was evident empathy with Germany's position among the ruling political and aristocratic classes. This was hardly surprising given the extent and depth of the relationship with Germany from the time of the Hanseatic League and, later, the Protestant Reformation and the Thirty Years' War. However, the relationship was complicated by cultural, religious, and family ties. One further unappreciated ambiguity was that Swedes could be simultaneously anti-Nazi and pro-German. People like Sven Grafström (a diplomat who had a German wife) detested what the Nazis had inflicted on Germany but still regarded many Germans as friends. Others (such as many Finns) saw Germany as the only power to limit the Russian existential threat. Yet after 1933, the Swedish public and their leaders were sickened by Nazi excesses against political opponents and Jewish citizens.

The years between the wars had seen a Westernizing of Swedish popular culture through cinematic and musical influences, and German culture was no longer the dominant influence (Östling 2016: 234–35). This, however, did not deter the Nazis from bombarding Sweden with propaganda and attempting to lure Swedes into "cultural exchanges" with Nazi organizations. The Swedish government attempted to counter this infiltration by operating a version of cultural neutrality that at best restricted the extent of Nazi propaganda and at worst left Sweden open to the charge of placing Allied material about war aims, the struggle for military supremacy, and the horrors of occupied Europe on the same moral level as Nazi conquest, admiration of the Wehrmacht, and perverted ideological views on Jews, Slavs, and minorities. The Swedish government also restricted reporting of Nazi atrocities, particularly in the earlier part of the war when Germany was ascendant, on the basis that such publication riled the notoriously thin-skinned Nazis (analogous to the present North Korean regime) and created avoidable disputes with Germany when Sweden was attempting to avoid invasion and limit German pressure on its trade and neutrality. It was simply easier to institute a form of self-censorship than to indulge in wrangling with the Germans over publishing reports that some felt would have little or no effect on Nazi abuses. Media often overvalues its restraint on abusive politicians by the exposure of criminal behavior when, in most cases, the abuse continues. In the case of the Nazis, they simply dismissed such exposure as part of the wider "Jewish-Communist conspiracy" against the German people.

Despite any sign that their criticism and reporting had any restraining effect on Nazi actions, two editors continued to challenge the authorities with their publications: communist Ture Nerman with *Trots Allt!* (Despite everything!) and liberal Torgny Segerstedt with *Göteborgs Handels- och Sjöfarts-Tidning* (Gothenburg's trade and maritime news). An exasperated Per Albin noted in his diary, "We can't risk conflict with another country (Germany) so that one man (Segerstedt) can publish what he pleases,"[6] which indicated the pressure that Per Albin felt to secure Sweden from war with Germany (Wahlbäck 1972: 129). The ideologically driven publishers had no such misgivings and today are regarded by many as heroes for speaking out against Nazi tyranny.

The Swedish cultural community was also subject to restraint from the government, and in one notorious case, a Stockholm cabaret producer, Karl Gerhardt, was targeted by the authorities for staging a provocative revue that used the Trojan Horse as a metaphor for German influence on Swedish policy. Further, Vilhelm Moberg's historical novel, *Ridd i Natt!* (1941; translated as *Ride this Night*, 1943) was the basis for a theater production; Moberg's work offers an analogy of German oppression. Other theater productions included light revues with popular artistes like comedian Nils Poppe. The Swedish wartime public preferred escapism rather than drama in their choice of film, theater, and literature, but one production of *The Merchant of Venice* was notable for its unusually sympathetic portrayal of Shylock the Jewish merchant, who is normally a standard Shakespeare villain. This interpretation was a Swedish recognition of the suffering of Jews in occupied Europe.

The Swedish government also fretted about the espionage and sabotage potential of the belligerents in Sweden. Aware that there was a high risk of them seeking to influence Swedish policy, impair Swedish defense and inflict damage on each other's interests in Sweden, a huge internal security organization Allmänna Säkerhetstjänsten (STJ) was set up to prevent this. Phone tapping, mail tampering, agent shadowing, and surveillance were used to gather evidence and prosecute aliens and Swedes involved in illegal activity. The British in particular hated the STJ, referring to them as the "Svestapo," because it was mainly British activities to support resistance in occupied Denmark and Norway that were affected. This led to the accusation that the STJ were pro-Nazi, but there is little evidence to support this. Damagingly, they did exchange some information with the Gestapo about communists. These were on an equal footing with Nazis as a threat to Swedish security due to their sponsorship from the Soviet Union, but the Swedes avoided any closer entanglement with the notorious secret police.

After 1945: "Small-State Realism" and the "Moral Narrative"

By the end of the war, Sweden had faced down attempts by the British and French to infiltrate their troops into Sweden under the pretext of helping Finland (while avoiding being drawn into a war with the Soviet Union); refused German demands for troop transit to Norway until the Norwegians surrendered; negotiated with both sides to maintain Swedish industry and fuel supplies; provided a safe haven for thousands of Scandinavian and European Jews; permitted and supported the recruitment, training, and arming of Norwegian and Danish forces in Sweden; and ended transit and trade with Germany under pressure from the Allies with all decisions taken by a democratically elected Coalition Government representing all major parties. Why then did Sweden find itself faced with growing postwar condemnation of its wartime record?

After 1945, Swedish politicians were rather smug about their wartime accomplishments in remaining out of a damaging war while holding out for an Allied victory. This was seen as a triumph of skillful Swedish diplomacy and a refusal to buckle under Nazi pressure, but rather undervalued the fact that the Allied armies took the pain while trade with Germany, albeit necessary, contributed in some way to German war effort. Even worse, following the revelations about the industrial extermination of Jews and others, Sweden could be accused of "not doing enough." Yet throughout the postwar period up to the 1990s, the pragmatic "small-state realism" narrative of minimal yielding to German threats and then withdrawing all concessions was dominant and accepted. In 1991 Maria-Pia Boëthius, a polemical journalist, challenged this interpretation and introduced an overdue moral questioning of the accepted narrative of "small-state realism." For example, was it right that Sweden should have traded with Germany? Such questions proliferated over the following decade and in 2000 the government launched a twenty-million-kronor research program to uncover any further unpublished evidence of inappropriate activity. It can be said that the academic results of this program have been impressive in providing further focused analysis and assessment studies.[7] Yet this search for evidence of a conspiracy of silence about Sweden's relationship has produced meager results. Nothing has emerged that seriously challenges the defensible self-interest that prevailed in Swedish wartime policy over ideological or moral imperatives.

The impact of World War II on Sweden has nevertheless been substantial. The somewhat flexible policy of neutrality was vindicated and mutated into nonaligned moral superiority during the Cold War. Additionally, wartime rearmament propelled Sweden into becoming a significant arms supplier. As Johan Östling has shown, postwar Sweden expunged any remaining taint of Nazism from its cultural and academic arenas and introduced educational reforms designed to promote questioning democratic citizenship rather than authoritarianism (Östling 2016: 187–88). A hangover similar to "survivor's guilt" has permeated Sweden to the extent that many Swedes are either reluctant to discuss World War II or state outright a standard view that "we had supported Germany and our neutrality policy made us morally guilty for the war and the Holocaust" (Björkman 2005).[8] Perhaps that is a measure of the success of the educational reforms, but I agree with the veteran Sweden historian Alf W. Johansson when he commented, "Something has gone wrong with the Swedish view of World War II" (Johansson 2014: 16–21).[9] Tony Judt perhaps offers the answer when he writes, "And so, if we teach the history of the Second World War above all—and sometimes uniquely—through the prism of the Holocaust, we may not always be teaching good history" (Judt 2016: 134).

Sweden's flexible neutrality was an effective defense during World War II, but it created contradictions and controversies that persist today in historical and popular culture. By pursuing policies that involved interaction with Nazi Germany, Sweden was demonized by its neighbors and the Allies during and after the war. Swedish historians failed to deal with the ethical issues involved, and a moral narrative gained traction following the end of the Cold War. Sweden's wartime policy has largely been rejected by Swedes today, and recent immigration policies can be seen as an attempt to atone for Sweden's wartime conduct. In 2017, one Swede supporting foreign vagrants said, "When I was little, I recall that we had Jews who came from Germany and asked Sweden for asylum. Among others, the inhabitants of Skåne refused—and we know how that went" ("Tiggeriförbud" 2017). [10]

John Gilmour is Honorary Fellow in Scandinavian Studies at the University of Edinburgh and the author of *Sweden, the Swastika and Stalin* (2010), with an updated Swedish edition *Hitler, Stalin och Sverige* (2016). Gilmour also published (with coeditor Jill Stephenson) *Hitler's Scandinavian Legacy* (2013).

Notes

1. "alla möjliga krokben för mig". . . "att jag ej kan göra dem något."
2. "Vår beredskap är god."
3. See, for example, the Beredskapshistoriska Föreningen, "an independent association who portrays the Swedish conscript soldier during 1939–1945" [*sic*].
4. "at så lenge jeg lever og ånder så skal aldrig Sverige bli betraktet som en del av Norden, men som en ruterknekt som står i Tysklands tjeneste."
5. ". . . kunde blott bliva negativt och en svensk intervention skulle över huvud taget snarast vara till skada för de norska judarna …"
6. ". . . man kan inte riskera en konflikt med annat land för att en herre skall få producera sig honom lyster."
7. See for example B. Karlsson, "Om handeln mellan Sverige och Tyskland 1938–45—Den svenska skogsindustrins problem," paper presented at a research conference in Lübeck, 11–12 November 2005.
8. "vi hade stött Tyskland och vår neutralitetspolitik gjorde oss moraliskt skyldiga till kriget och Förintelsen."
9. "Något har gått snett i den svenska synen på andra världskriget."
10. "När jag var liten minns jag att vi hade judar som kom från Tyskland och bad Sverige om skydd. Bland annat de besuttna i Skåne nekade—och ni vet hur det gick."

References

Bengtsson, Sven-Åke. 2014. *En svensk tiger*. Stockholm: Svenskt Militärhistoriskt Biblioteks Förlag.
Björkman, Jenny. 2005. "Nollpunkten för vår tideräkning." In *Populär Historia* 5. Malmö: Bonnier Publications International AS.
Boritz, Mette, Mads Blom, Per Mouritsen, Galit Peleg, and Cecilie Wallengren. 2015. *De Hvide Busser*. København: National Museet.
Carlgren, Wilhelm M. 1973. *Svensk utrikespolitik 1939–1945*. Stockholm: Allmänna förlaget.
Carlsson, Erik. 2006. *Gustaf V och andra världskriget*. Lund: Historiska media.
Flyghed, Janne. 1992. *Rättsstat i kris: Spioneri och sabotage i Sverige under andra världskriget*. Stockholm: Federativ.
Gyllenhaal, Lars, and Lennart Westberg. 2010. *Swedes at War*. Bedford, PA: Aberjona Press.
Johansson, Alf W. 2014. "Var vi så fega egentligen? Något har gått snett i den svenska synen på andra världskriget." In *Respons* 1 (March). Stockholm: Tidskriften Respons.
Judt, Tony. 2015. "The 'Problem of Evil' in Postwar Europe." In *When the Facts Change: Essays 1995–2010*. London: Penguin Press.
Koblik, Steven. 1987. *"Om vi teg, skulle stenarna ropa": Sverige och judeproblemet 1933–1945*. Stockholm: Norstedt.
Nestler, Ludwig, Wolfgang Schumann, and Werner Röhr. 1996. *Europa unterm Hakenkreuz: Die Okkupationspolitik des deutschen Faschismus 1938–1945. Band 8: Analysen, Quellen, Register*. Berlin: Hüthig Verlagsgemeinschaft.
Nygaardsvold, Johan. 1998. *Dagbøker 1918–48 og utvalge brev ogpapirer 1916–52*. 31 December 1940. Edited by Harald Berntsen. Oslo: Ascheoug.
Persson, Sune. 2002. *Vi åker till Sverige: De vita bussarna*. Stockholm: Fischer & Co.
Räddningen Budapest 1944. 1997. Rapporter ur UDs arkiv. Stockholm: Fischer & Co.
Rothwell, Victor. 2005. *War Aims in the Second World War*. Edinburgh: Edinburgh University Press.
Svanberg, Ingvar, and Mattias Tydén. 1997. *Sverige och Förintelsen: Debatt och dokument om Europas judar 1933–1945*. Stockholm: Arena.
"Tiggeriförbud i Vellinge—bra eller dåligt?" 2017. *Sydsvenskan*, 18 September. Retrieved 21 September 2017 from https://www.sydsvenskan.se/2017-09-18/live-debatt-tiggeri forbud-i-vellinge-bra-eller-daligt.
Wahlbäck, Krister. 1972. *Regeringen och kriget: Ur statsrådens dagbocker 1939–41*. Stockholm: Prisma.
Wylie, Neville. 2013. "Life in Plato's Cave: Neutral Europe In WWII." In *A Companion to World War II*, edited by Thomas W. Zeiler and Daniel M. DuBois. Malden, MA: Wiley-Blackwell.
Zetterberg, Kent. 2013. "The Case of Sweden." In *Hitler's Scandinavian Legacy: The Consequences of the German Invasion for the Scandinavian Countries, Then and Now*, edited by John Gilmour and Jill Stephenson, 101–127. London: Bloomsbury Academic.
Östling, Johan. 2016. *Sweden after Nazism*. New York: Berghahn Books.

Part II

WAR LITERATURE: ARCHIVE

The texts examined in this part of the volume are examples of Scandinavian wartime travel writing, essayistic journalism, and personal narrative. The three writers are widely recognized women of the period: the Swedish modernist poet Karin Boye (1900–41), the internationally recognized Danish storyteller Isak Dinesen/Karen Blixen (1885–1962), and the Norwegian novelist and Nobel Laureate Sigrid Undset (1882–1949). These writers are not ordinarily associated with World War II literature or scholarship. Further, the texts examined in this part of the book are not celebrated or canonized literary works, but neither are they entirely forgotten. I would argue that these wartime texts belong to cultural "storage memory" or the "archive." One could say that they exist in the literary storehouse (i.e., the library) and belong in the passive dimension of preservation and scholarship. In other words, the selected texts have not functioned in the active dimension of continuous publication, circulation, and interpretation that constitutes canonization. Thus, the chapters in part II seek to reframe these texts in a World War II context and to engage them in conversation with other wartime discourses rather than allow them to remain isolated in the narrow rubrics of authorship and biography.

The three chapters of part II offer close readings and analysis of the following texts: Karin Boye's 1938 travel journal *Resedagbok i Grekland: Från Hitlers Berlin till Apollons Olympia* (Travel diary in Greece: From Hitler's Berlin to Apollo's Olympia) alongside her letters from the Third Reich on the eve of the outbreak of World War II; Isak Dinesen's essay "Letters from a Land at War" ("Breve fra et Land i Krig," 1948), originally written in the spring of 1940 as newspaper chronicles from Hitler's Berlin; and Sigrid Undset's *Return to the Future*, a work of propaganda, originally published in an English translation in the United States in 1942 (the original text was first published in Norway after the war in 1945, as *Tilbake til Fremtiden*), about the author's escape from occupied Norway and journey to the United States.

In the spring of 1938 Karin Boye traveled to Greece through Hitler's Germany and Austria on the brink of World War II. Boye's encounter with National Socialism was mediated through a screening in Vienna of Leni Riefenstahl's film *Olympia* about the 1936 Berlin Olympic games. In chapter 6, Amanda Doxtater explores Boye's travel journal from the period and the poet's position as an ambivalent spectator who was both attracted and repelled by the Fascist spectacles of the Third Reich. The chapter positions Boye's observations, and the modernist aesthetic of her literary work, in relation to Sweden's neutrality.

In March 1940 Isak Dinesen/Karen Blixen traveled to wartime Berlin. Internationally recognized for her *Seven Gothic Tales* (1934) and *Out of Africa* (1937), Dinesen was to write a series of chronicles about conditions in the New Germany—but the author's observations were not published because Germany occupied Denmark in April 1940. Chapter 7 investigates the historical context for the writing of Dinesen's "Letters from a Land at War" and argues that the text makes use of irony in oblique criticism of the totalitarian regime, psychology of conformism, implicit racism, and imperialistic agenda of Hitler's Germany.

In April 1940 Sigrid Undset fled Norway soon after Germany's occupation. Living in exile in the United States during the war years, Undset became a fierce advocate for Norway's fight for democracy and freedom from Nazi tyranny. *Return to the Future*, published in the United States, is both a work of wartime travel writing—about Undset's months-long journey east to America—and a clever piece of Allied propaganda. In chapter 8, Christine Hamm argues that Undset constructs a national romantic picture of Norwegians that will appeal to Americans, alongside an enemy representation of treacherous and slavish Germans that was intended to galvanize Allied sympathies for Norway's cause.

Although the literary oeuvre of these three women is recognized and celebrated, these particular texts have often vexed literary scholars and biographers. They have not circulated widely because they have appeared controversial, uncomfortable, or inscrutable. In the case of Boye's travel journal, it was finally published decades after the war; in the case of Dinesen's essay from Hitler's Berlin, it was first published in Denmark after the war in 1948; in the case of Undset's book, although it was published in Norwegian after the war, it remains largely unknown in Norway.

Nevertheless, these texts are important and deserve to be lifted from the archive of scholarship because they offer wartime observations on the totalitarian regime, propaganda, and performing arts and cinema of the Third Reich from early perspectives in the war (respectively in 1938, 1940, and 1942), that is, from various ideological vantage points (ambivalent, neutral, and firmly Allied) that were voiced well before the tide of war had turned against Germany. The three texts represent women writers who are positioned as "neutral" Scandinavian outsiders observing German National Socialism and the mass psychology of Fascism (in the case of Boye and Dinesen), or as a Norwegian citizen observing the German Wehrmacht as the enemy invader as well as the wartime societies of the communist Soviet Union and Imperial Japan (in the case of Undset). Whereas the texts of Isak Dinesen and Karin Boye are ambivalent or strained by efforts at neutrality, Sigrid Undset's emotional work of propaganda speaks directly in the interest of occupied Norway's fierce fight for democracy. These chapters are arranged chronologically in the order that the texts were originally written (rather than by the date of publication): chapter 6 addresses Karin Boye's prewar travel journal and letters; chapter 7 examines Isak Dinesen's essay written in 1940; and chapter 8 investigates Sigrid Undset's *Return to the Future*, published in 1942 at the peak of hostilities.

Chapter 6

KARIN BOYE AS AMBIVALENT SPECTATOR OF FASCISM

Amanda Doxtater

On the evening of 17 June 1938, Swedish poet and author Karin Boye (1900–1941) went to the movies in Vienna.¹ The film she saw was *Olympia*, part I: *Festival of the Nations* and part II: *Festival of Beauty*, Leni Riefenstahl's elaborate documentation of the 1936 Olympic Games held two years earlier in Berlin. The extraordinary cinematic spectacle of athletes from all over the world competing before roaring crowds lasted four hours. Boye consumed the spectacle of Nazism as well, imbricated with the classical iconography of the games themselves: the classical Greek statues and ruins with which Riefenstahl's cinematic homage to youth and beauty opens eventually transform into the neoclassical fascist architecture of the stadium, the image of Adolf Hitler opening the games, and the swastikas waving. She watched opening ceremonies in which the Swedish team marched prominently onto the track, second in line behind Germany. When Boye eventually left the theater and stepped into her present moment, the spectacle would continue in a Vienna thick with Nazi banners; the *Anschluss* had taken place only a few months earlier. Boye's stop in Vienna was but a brief layover on a journey that took her through a continent on the verge of World War II and along a route reminiscent of the path by which the Olympic torch had been brought north. Along with Berlin, Boye made short stops in Prague and Vienna, then traveled via Bucharest to Istanbul, finally to arrive in Greece and Crete, where she spent nearly two months on a scholarship from the Swedish Academy. Only days after seeing *Olympia* in Vienna, she would cast her eyes upon its ancient ruins in Greece. Describing her trip through the continent in a letter to the academy shortly thereafter (21 July 1938), she noted that the timelessness of Greece offers a reprieve after Berlin, Prague, and Vienna where "something was changing, and it weighed on my nerves: the oppositions were so great and threateningly ominous, leaving one feeling mercilessly enclosed in the context of one's contemporary moment that it was altogether too much" (Boye 2000: 293).[2]

In his introduction to *Travels in the Reich*, Olivier Lubrich observes that "foreigners in a totalitarian dictatorship are in an *ambivalent position*. They are simultaneously in the midst and at a distance. Ethnology might call this situation an extreme case of 'participant-observation'" (Lubrich 2010: 7). Boye is a case in point. Her reactions to seeing *Olympia* in Vienna on 17 June, recorded in a travel diary she kept along her journey (later published as *Resedagbok i Grekland: Från Hitlers Berlin till Apollons Olympia* [1994, Travel diary in Greece: From Hitler's Berlin to Apollo's Olympia]) reveal her to be an ambivalent spectator not only of her contemporary moment, but of Nazi spectacle writ large.[3] It reads as follows:

> In the evening I watched Leni Riefenstahl's Olympia I and II, in other words an undertaking of almost four hours. But it was magnificent! She has learned from the greatest Russians. The way she can make everything exciting, the way she can capture the essential in a glance is remarkable. And beautiful! Peculiar with the foreign races, how pure, how beautiful, how uniquely dignified they were as they played their parts here before the crowds of Aryan-fanatics: the Negros superior in running, the Japanese winning all of the endurance competitions—and a bronze medalist rider from the U.S.A., surely a Jew. All of their faces were so genuine and sympathetic and they approached their tasks so dispassionately. The film didn't persuade me to believe in the Third Reich, but in sports. So, it probably was propaganda. (Boye 1994: 16–18)[4]

Boye is clearly drawn to the film. Her reference to the greatest Russian filmmakers (presumably the masters of montage such as Sergei Eisenstein and Dziga Vertov) suggests an appreciation of *Olympia*'s formal innovations: its cinematography, editing, and composition. She admires the beauty of the performing athletes, their elegant bodies and dramatic exertions, and the way their faces exude a concentrated dignity. And she is drawn to something of the spectacle that is the film itself, as an aesthetic object or experience capable of capturing something "timeless" or "essential," something apart from the historical present (an impulse not entirely at odds with the neoclassical historical narrative of the Third Reich that Riefenstahl's film propounds). At the same time, Boye clearly distances herself from the film as propaganda for the Third Reich.[5] Her references to non-Aryan victors implicitly condemn the Reich's racial ideology, and she remains wary of the way that Nazi spectacle forces athletes to play roles they might not otherwise have chosen. Boye's own position as a spectator is similarly conflicted. While she differentiates herself from the crowds of "Aryan fanatics" avidly watching the games from the stands, she also avidly consumes the film herself.

One of Sweden's most cherished poets, Boye is not generally read as a consequential observer of World War II. She took her life in 1941, before the monstrosities of World War II came fully to light, which likely contributes to this. But Boye did have significant firsthand experience with the rise of the Third Reich. In addition to her brief journey over the continent in 1938, she also lived in Berlin for eight months in 1932–33 (first January to October 1932, and then September to November 1933) where she witnessed the Weimar Republic draw its last breaths as the Nazi Party gained power.[6] Boye's travel diary, along with these earlier encounters with the Third Reich, further reveal her as spectator at once intrigued and repulsed by fascist spectacle.

Scholarship on Boye has also underplayed her interest in film and the scenes of (film) spectatorship that recur throughout Boye's oeuvre. At times references to the cinema appear as a logical part of a novel's fictional world, for instance in the cosmopolitan cityscape of Stockholm in Boye's novel *Astarte* (1931), in which young women listen in rapt attention like moviegoers captivated by a suspenseful film, almost against their will. But it also recurs expressionistically, as in *Kris* (1934; translated as *Crisis,* 2020), when Boye describes the devil as speaking with the grating, tinny voice of an announcer in a public service film. More recent scholarship has expanded our image of Boye from a poet to a public intellectual who yearned "for an art that united modernism and leftist radicalism, psychoanalysis and politics, activism and personal development" (Svedjedal 2011: 338).[7] Interesting to me is the extent to which cinema might function as such a conciliatory art. In what follows, I take a closer look at Boye looking at the Third Reich—primarily as a cinema spectator, but also as a modernist, left-leaning intellectual, a queer woman, and an ambivalent (and "neutral") Swedish bystander. I draw upon Boye's real-world encounters with national socialism (documented in her Berlin work: criticism, essays, and letters she wrote during her travels, and the 1938 travel diary) and scenes of spectatorship in two of her most well-known novels—her formally experimental autobiography *Crisis* and her dystopian novel *Kallocain* (1940), set in a totalitarian future—to illuminate some of the tensions in Boye's work between the personal and the public, the aesthetic and the political that occur throughout her oeuvre.

Projecting Boye's intellectual and emotional life into Riefenstahl's idealization of fascism in *Olympia I–II*, illuminates moments when Boye's personal development coincides—uncomfortably—with contemporary discourses about cultural development and type. Like many other intellectuals who visited the Third Reich, Boye saw fascism as political, but perhaps more fascinating as an emotional, aesthetic, and psychological phenomenon—a perspective that becomes impossible after the Holocaust. For example, the passage in the travel diary immediately preceding her response to Riefenstahl's film reads,

> 17 June Vienna: Midmorning: wandered around. Horrible gray skies and the constant threat of rain, as the entire trip thus far. Theater week: Banners with swastikas everywhere, swastikas on all of the Aryan stores, on the parish bulletin boards etc. Ate dinner in a little café with swastikas in the windows outside and filled with happy Jews inside. In the bank there was a portrait of Hitler that conveyed more than all of the caricatures, serious, ascetic, almost beautiful in a way: one human-type against another, one life-attitude against another, the tightly-wound against the fluid. (Boye 1994: 16–18)[8]

In this scene, Boye paints herself as a privileged observer of this teeming café in which allegiances are spatialized: inside (Jewish) and outside (Third Reich). The passage signals the absurdity of these two disparate worldviews coexisting in such proximity at the same moment. Boye's neutrality allows her the mobility to choose sides, and there is no question where she chooses to sit. Yet her reaction to the portrait of Hitler is unnerving. We can read it in the vein of many outside observers of the Third Reich who sought to comprehend the source of his charisma. Alternatively, the passage also suggests that Boye identified with some aspect of its contradiction, with managing irreconcilable, opposite impulses within a single person, the condition that drives the modernist crisis of subjectivity in Boye's novel *Crisis*. Given that this novel is propelled by the main character's largely inexpressible queer desire, seeing its mechanism mapped onto the face of Hitler is evocative to say the least. A letter Boye wrote later that same day raises further questions about how such a laden representation as the portrait could be imbricated into the intense self-exploration of her own ambivalence. Boye writes, "I was gripped with the same feeling I presume a radiant national socialist would have if he suddenly discovered that he was one hundred percent Jewish. Can you imagine? Of course, my heart lies entirely with the other side. 'O wretched man that I am! Who will deliver me from this body of death?'" (Abenius 1951: 318).[9] On one hand, Boye's logic is false. There is no subject position that aligns with the "other side" in the dehumanizing fascism of the Third Reich. Being denied one's humanity does not constitute a position to choose. On the other hand, it would be a mistake to dismiss Boye's reaction as clear evidence of underlying sympathy to fascism. Given that Boye's crisis was also infused with religious overtones, she might be citing the Apostle Paul as a warning about Hitler's own seductive zealotry. Or her confusion might point toward fascism's demand for a kind of literal self-contradiction. In short, Boye's ambivalence deserves a closer look.

A Spectator behind the Scenes

Sometimes Boye's writing functions as something like historical flypaper onto which impressions stick. Boye was one of many foreign journalists and literary figures to travel through the Third Reich, some publishing travelogues or journalism from an insider perspective, others leaving traces in unpublished diaries or letters. Boye didn't move to Berlin with the intention of reporting on the political situation, but rather to escape public life in Stockholm, where she was well known, and write. Still, the political situation in Berlin seeps into her letters from this period, sometimes as a simmering, oppressive tension, other times as sardonic background. In a letter to her friend Erik Mesterton, she asks him to forgive her lack of correspondence by writing, "You must have thought that I was either dead and buried, shot by Nazis, or that I'd embraced life in Berlin so much that I forgot all of my old friends" (Boye 2000: 208).[10] That her family had cultural ties to Germany (her grandfather was German) and that she spoke and translated from German might have made Boye something of an insider in Berlin, but she still refers to herself in one letter as a tourist whose full comprehension of the situation was limited as an outsider. Taken together, Boye's letters present her as a poor but privileged, neutral-ish observer taking the temperature of emotional reality of the city, sometimes almost inadvertently.

Like her letters home from Berlin in 1932–33, Boye's travel diary from 1938 reads at times as a conventional, if elegant, travel log composed of sketches of casual encounters with fellow travelers, philosophical meditations, and ideas for future work. Alongside masterful landscape descriptions are quotidian references to travel accommodations, missed train connections, heat, and pesky insects. Fascism and antifascism are embodied here in Boye's often banal encounters with people espousing an ideology, people for whom she displays something like ethnographic curiosity. She meets a pleasant (if ultimately tedious) Austrian woman whose redeeming qualities are her pacifism and opposition to Hitler. A sailor working on an Italian ship who took war for a kind of sport and believed Jews to be the root of all evil provides a case study for the dull-wittedness of "average" fascism. Other times, Boye expressed her dismay at unfolding events in ways that were both explicit and dramatic. The sight of the yellow benches in Berlin in 1938, the only ones where Jews were allowed to sit, caused her to break down in a flood of tears on the street.

Propaganda also interested Boye, both in terms of its mass consumption and psychology. Some of the (few) articles Boye published from her first stay in Berlin look specifically at fascist propaganda in popular culture. In 1934, Boye wrote a two-part newspaper article looking at Nazi popular literature—a piece inspired by watching the filmic adaptation of one novel,

Hitler Youth Quex (1933).[11] Boye critiques the film's characterization and narrative elements, noting that despite being well-made and well-acted, it suffered for its blatant anti-Semitism and utterly schematic female and communist characters. She finds similar characterization in other Nazi novels she analyzes (Boye 1992: 117–23). Other literary observers from Scandinavia, such as Isak Dinesen (Karen Blixen) were also interested in film propaganda. Dinesen's "Letters from a Land at War," intended to be published after a visit in the spring of 1940, as discussed in the following chapter by Marianne Stecher-Hansen, documents how film propaganda, among other cultural institutions, was affected by the Third Reich. Entering the country as a designated foreign journalist, Dinesen was guided by an escort from the Ministry of Propaganda, which included a backstage look at the filming of a scene with Swedish actress Zarah Leander playing Mary Stuart—the fateful moment of her capture by Bothwell. Mary Stuart was forced to experience this capture again and again, take after take, which constituted a veritable hell in Dinesen's eyes. While Dinesen and Boye differed on their appreciation of cinema (Dinesen expressing a vaguely aristocratic disdain of the popular form typified by the garish torture of this would-be queen and Boye being more amenable to popular culture), each sought to understand its function as propaganda. For each writer, the temporality of cinema afforded a way of conceptualizing the contemporary moment as a peculiar repetition of the past in the bodies of actors or performers.

Dinesen's behind-the-scenes glimpse into Nazi film production would uncannily echo Boye's treatment of film propaganda several months later in her 1941 dystopic novel *Kallocain*. The narrator of the novel, Leo Kall, a scientist living in Chemistry City #4 in the totalitarian, militaristic "worldstate" develops a truth serum to test the loyalty of its citizens. When he runs out of voluntary human subjects upon which to test it, he travels to the propaganda ministry to request that a recruitment film be produced, only to discover that the project is already in the works. Curious, Kall stumbles into a kind of focus group at the Film Palace in which a psychologist specializing in film propaganda stands lecturing to various insider officials about the relative effectiveness of happy vs. unhappy endings on recruitment. Despite being a loyal subject, the experience unexpectedly rattles him. Kall's invention has annihilated any possibility of individual interiority in the worldstate; secrets are no longer possible. But at the same time, through his testing of the truth serum, a seductive, gentle "fellowship" (*gemenskap*) is revealed as spreading organically through the worldstate. Its members gather wordlessly to enact rituals of trust and human connection that threaten the very integrity of the state. Kall, as a kind of accidental-yet-complicit observer of film propaganda being created, illuminates something of Boye's ambivalence toward cinema as a medium with the potential to be complicit in the radical violation of individual autonomy while at the same time potentially engendering new publics and new forms of human connection that transcend the state.

A Face in the Crowd

The notion of a new, regenerative collectivity or fellowship—a key figuration in Boye's later prose—relates to her as an interwar cultural radical and modernist in the 1930s whose work contributed to the intellectual environment in which the Swedish welfare state would emerge. Part of the ambivalence of her gaze at fascism stems from being drawn to moments when it interfaced with the possibility and promise of that collective, regenerative project in Sweden.[12] At stake for Boye was the question of how to honor both the individual and the collective. Boye's appreciation of *Olympia*'s spectacle might have derived from the film's ability to combine the granular with a vision of masses. The film accomplishes this formally, through variation in shot scale, for instance, editing together shots of individual faces in close-up and extreme long shots of crowds. *Olympia* also brings together a remarkable diversity of camera placements, from aerial shots to ground-level footage, and unites disparate temporalities, from slow-motion, to sculptural bodies played in reverse, to lightning-quick montage. *Olympia*, in other words, encapsulated something of Boye's own desire to integrate individual and collective, albeit in the name of a national socialist ideology she detested.

In her response to *Olympia*, Boye emphatically distinguishes herself from "the crowds of Aryan fanatics" in the film. Interestingly, she had firsthand experience of such crowds. In Berlin in 1931–32, Boye moved in circles of left-leaning Scandinavian intellectuals interested in the mass psychology of fascism. These included Norwegian Nic Hoel (née Waal), a Reichian psychoanalyst, and Vilhelm Scharp, whom Boye knew from Uppsala where they had been active in Clarté, an international organization advocating pacifism and socialism in the 1920s. Scharp, a lecturer of Swedish in Berlin who eventually became an anti-Nazi activist, was especially eager to tap into Berlin's zeitgeist and experience fascist spectacle firsthand. To this end, Boye, Scharp, and Hoel attended a Nazi campaign rally on the eve of the 12 March 1932 elections. Scharp had supposedly exploited his family connections to Hermann Göring's Swedish relatives to gain admittance. During the event held in Berlin Sportpalats, a vast indoor arena in Schöneberg, Göring's persuasive oratory recounted the names of fallen Nazi soldiers. Boye purportedly watched in a kind of intoxicated fascination, and raised her arm in a Sieg heil (Abenius 1951: 203–4).[13] This scene of spectatorship has been interpreted as evidence of Boye's poetic susceptibility to the same hypnotic lure of Nazism affecting the masses around her. Her fascination derived in part from Boye's interest in understanding how collective ritual worked upon unconscious drives: Eros and Thanatos. Swiss author Denis de Rougemont, another of the many author-spectators who attended Nazi rallies during this period, makes the relationship between political spectacle and sex explicit, writing, "The reoccupation of the Rheinland is a kind of sexual act, just as much as a political one. How else is the bizarre euphoria that is in the air, in the movements of the crowds, in the glances exchanged, and the comments tossed around to be explained?" (de Rougement, as quoted in Lubrich 2010: 85). The three Scandinavians, that is Boye, Hoel, and Scharp, were situated as spectators in the gallery. As "neutral" spectators observing from a vantage point from which they could look down over the demonic fury of thousands of excited, fanatical faces, they played their part in the spectacle.

As this scene illustrates, Boye's initial time in Berlin allowed her the opportunity to experience something of the erotic excitement of *Olympia*'s crowd shots. It also enabled interaction at the more intimate level of a close-up. Boye was a hyperattuned *self-spectator* of her own mind and body who alternated between intellectual analysis and portrayals of the chaotic realities of inner emotional life in a way that few Swedish poets did (Enander 1995: 271). Boye underwent psychotherapy in Berlin for depression related partly to what she referred to as her overactive death drive and partly to negotiating her sexuality.[14] She had been in a short, relatively amicable marriage to economist Leif Björk and had had previous relationships with both men and women, but eventually she found a psychoanalyst in Berlin who encouraged her to embrace her desire for women rather than trying to cure her inversion.[15] Thus, amid the rise of fascism, Berlin (and its nightlife) paradoxically also afforded Boye new freedoms to live as a lesbian, which she did for the remainder of her life. It was in Berlin that she met Margot Hanel, a young German-Jewish woman whom she later helped to immigrate to Sweden as her wife (a very bourgeois thing to do, she quips in one letter).[16] Berlin was a complex, contradictory space for Boye with innocent Jews being accosted in the streets, violent clashes between Nazis and communists, and also new personal freedoms and desires.

In her autobiographical novel *Crisis*, written not long after her initial time living in Berlin, Boye effectively reworks the erotic fanaticism of the seated crowd (as in the Nazi rally, or later in *Olympia*) into a scene of collective fellowship grounded in queer desire. Boye's twenty-year-old protagonist, Malin Forst, a hyperintelligent, religious woman attending a teacher's training college, undergoes a crisis of faith. The epiphany that brings Malin's crisis to consciousness occurs one morning when she sits among her fellow students and her eyes fall upon her beautiful classmate, Siv, sitting several rows in front of her. Or rather, Malin's gaze falls upon the back of Siv's neck, which Boye describes in neoclassical terms, as a column. Amorphous lesbian desire is channeled into an exquisite contentment and sense of reprieve. Eventually, this subtle elation subsides, leaving Malin with the courage to face the clashing oppositions within her: good and evil, submission and resistance. (At one point her character literally splits into dialogue between Malin I and Malin II.) The novel integrates Malin's crisis of desire into other recognizable iterations of interwar, modernist crisis: terror at the incomprehensible devastation of World War I; various failures of bourgeois values; and the inadequacy of words, representation, and form. This crisis also engenders the possibility for renewal and rebirth out of destruction. Not unlike what will later be figured in *Kallocain,* in *Crisis,* Malin's gaze prompts the insight that she belongs to a kind of mystical collectivity of people who recognize one another in the crowd, at a glance. Malin refers to this queer fellowship in terms also employed by the Third Reich, calling it "My people!" (*Mitt folk!*) (Boye 1934: 233).

Boye's ambivalence watching *Olympia* in Austria, four years after *Crisis* was published, likely derived in part from the eroticism of the film's fascist fantasy. We can imagine Boye being drawn to the idealization of the female body in the film (and perhaps the memories of Weimar Berlin that it conjured up) while at the same being repelled by its use in a national socialist

Figure 6.1. Leni Riefenstahl's film *Olympia I–II*, an elaborate documentation of the 1936 Berlin Olympic Games, evoked ambivalent commentary from the Swedish poet Karin Boye in her travel diary from Vienna in June 1938. In this sequence, female eurythmic dancers perform collectively in part II: *The Festival of Beauty*. Screenshot: Amanda Doxtater.

context. Discussion of *Olympia*'s homoeroticism typically revolves around scenes featuring men, such as the opening of part II, in which Riefenstahl's camera lingers on a group of young, nude, Aryan men sweating and swatting each other with birch branches in the close proximity of a sauna before they dive into a pristine lake. But as Terri Gordon discusses in "Fascism and the Female Form: Performance Art in the Third Reich," the film's female figures also bear an interesting history of Nazi ideology. One sequence of eurythmic dancing, for instance, begins with a closely framed low-angle shot of a single dancer moving her arms rhythmically in the sun and then cuts out, further and further, to an extreme long shot revealing thousands of women in geometric formation filling a stadium—a quintessential scene of mass ornament, drawing on Sigfried Kracauer's theorization. Gordon further contextualizes this sequence within German *Körperkultur*, the cult of the body that began in the late nineteenth century, one that brought together artistic and cultural movements on the left and mystical nationalism on the right. This helps explain the Third Reich's paradoxical use of expressionist dance—something more easily associated with Weimar decadence (Gordon 2002: 186). German pioneers of modern dance (*Ausdruckstanz*) Mary Wigman and Rudolph Laban were originally commissioned to choreograph the opening ceremonies for the 1936 Olympics, but Wigman's call for mystical dance (even though she conceived it herself as very much in the service of the German state) ultimately proved too threatening for the party. If the iteration of Wigman dance that made its way into Riefenstahl's film could inspire a collectivity perceived as transcending the state, perhaps *Olympia*'s eurythmic dancers offered Boye a visual corollary to the wordless, mystical connections she explores in *Crisis* and *Kallocain*, as appealing and organic resistance to the oppressive logic of totalitarianism.

A Spectator in Time: Greece

Boye also sought to locate these organic, mystical connections in time. As a modernist, being able to represent her own historical moment in relation to the past became a key aesthetic concern for her. In some of the most evocative passages of her 1938 travel diary, Boye contemplates the present moment in architecture and sculpture by witnessing traces of the past persisting within it. In Prague, a city that enchanted and inspired her, she describes peering through the centuries as if they were transparent stones. Past and present can also grow seamlessly into one another, "the old roots from the 900s put forth new shoots, and the new Prague grows out of the old. Without disturbing one another. And yet I've also never felt the literally breathtaking depth of centuries that I have here" (Boye 1994: 8).[17] Greece constituted a particularly laden geography for Boye, having studied Greek and Latin in her youth. The villages on Crete that she admires for their "originary-ness" (*ursprunglighet*) (Boye 2000: 293) take her out of time, but also confirm her notions of cultural teleology and development.[18] She describes rural life on Crete, for instance, as replete with charmingly "simple" people whose lives harken back to the way Swedes lived in the previous decades. Artifacts from antiquity could also literally take her breath away. Boye's diary includes several desirous moments gazing at classical statuary and ruins in Greece. She stares so long at a statue of Apollo that she feels exhausted in her diaphragm, as if having taken too many deep breaths (Boye 1994: 67).

Watching Riefenstahl's depiction of historical time and statuary in the opening of *Olympia I*, after visiting Prague but before arriving in Greece, must have been an uncanny experience for Boye. *Olympia I* opens with an evocative imbrication of past and present via the overinvested topos of ancient Greece. The soundtrack is magisterial. Initially, the camera tracks boldly through the ruins of Greek temples around dramatically lit, soft-focus classical statues portraying mythological figures Medusa, Aphrodite, Achilles, Paris, and Apollo. Eventually it comes to rest on the Myron's discus thrower, which, through live action mixing and superimposition, begins to move, transforming into a live athlete. The subsequent shots of moving bodies are as idealized as the classical statues. The film enacts the sensual pleasure of gazing at bodies, an erotic gaze that will persist throughout the film. Low-angle shots depict nearly nude men, larger than life, throwing the javelin or gracefully tossing and catching the shotput against a vast sky. Following this, nude female athletes moving rhythmically in graceful, abstract shapes that will eventually transmogrify into the Olympic flame that will then be carried north, over land, by runners through silhouetted models of European capitals until it reaches the space of the neoclassical Nazi stadium in Berlin.[19] A timeless classical past is animated, embodied, and carried symbolically into the present moment to ignite it. In other words, Riefensthal accomplishes cinematically what Boye yearns to in words. Seeing time visualized in this way must have taken Boye's breath away even as its ideology landed like a blow to the stomach.

Fellow Swedish modernist Pär Lagerkvist would also enlist classical Greece to stand in for Western civilization in his antifascist manifesto "Den knutna näven" (The clenched fist, 1934). Employing an implicitly Eurocentric notion of progress and enlightenment, he argues that Nazism emerges paradoxically as European at the same time that it stands as a grotesque violation of its core values: progress, freedom, and enlightenment. Boye is interested in this paradox as well, and at times she also calls the teleology into question. After a visit to the national museum in Greece, she ponders whether artistic representation actually does correspond to any linear notion of cultural or racial development. "Does art's orientation have anything to do with its *stage* of culture or with its *species* of culture or with racial temperament at all?" (Boye 1994: 44).[20] Greece, for both Swedish authors, ultimately remains sacred. Lagerkvist calls for Europe not to abandon what the monstrous current regime has besmirched but rather to return to the heritage that persists deep beneath it, resulting in a temporal paradox: "Our future now, as always, lies in our past" (Lagerkvist 1989: 197).[21]

Boye's Ambivalent Reception

The ambivalence of Boye's own response to fascism is reflected, to some degree, in her critical reception. Considered largely as a poet rather than a novelist, essayist, or cultural critic, Boye's work has often been read biographically. Until fairly recent scholarship redeemed her as a central figure of interwar modernism in Sweden (Domellöf 1986), she had largely been cast as a poet of the existential, the emotional, the universal. In imagining Boye as an observer of her contemporary moment, many scholars often project onto her person the weight of a retrospective desire, capacity, or failure to have *seen* or *seen through* Nazism. Oftentimes she is willfully cast as a sympathetic, naïve spectator. In his immense literary biography on Boye, *Den nya dagen gryr: Karin Boyes författarliv* (2017, The new day dawns: A literary biography of Karin Boye), Johan Svedjedal writes, "Even though she obviously opposed Nazism, she sometimes tended (as many other of her contemporaries did) to regard it with an indulgent look that in retrospect can seem naïve" (Svedjedal 2017: 340).[22] Though Boye scholarship overwhelmingly represents her as critical of Nazism, these representations are often qualified in some way. Boye's political radicalism is tempered by her draw toward neurosis, for instance. Boye's sensitive nature as a poet can make her unconsciously susceptible to Nazism (Abenius 1951) or cause her to be so terrified by fascism that the feelings of helplessness it produces overwhelm her fragile psyche (Hammarström 1997: 202–6). One finds adamant readings of Boye as an antifascist: Boye as clearly opposed to Nazism, with her treatment of communism being more ambivalent (Gustafsson Rosenqvist 1999: 86), and Boye as a resoundingly eloquent—and resolutely outspoken—critic of totalitarianism (Enander 1995). Or at the other end of the spectrum, Boye as complicit: a public figure who didn't speak out explicitly enough because she harbored secret affinities for National Socialism, a combination that resulted in her being a "wannabe modernist" (Luthersson 2002: 269). The protean way in which Boye has been represented in relation to World War II—a beloved, queer cultural figure whose antifascism is not entirely beyond qualification—raises questions about what such figurations of spectatorship, in a cultural archive that continues to come to light, might contribute to larger conversations about Sweden's continually evolving understanding of its position as a "neutral" bystander-spectator of World War II.

Amanda Doxtater (PhD, University of California, Berkeley, 2012) is Assistant Professor and the Barbro Osher Endowed Chair of Swedish Studies at the University of Washington. Her translation of Karin Boye's *Kris* (1934) is published as *Crisis* by Norvik Press (2020). Doxtater's monograph in progress is titled *Tears in Ice: Tracing the Body in Carl Th. Dreyer's Art Melodrama*; her research interests include melodrama theory, performance and translation studies, gender and representation, design-thinking, and public humanities.

Notes

1. I am deeply grateful to SOCE for their invaluable support, and to Marianne Stecher-Hansen for her brilliant editorial insight and patience.
2. "Det var en växling, som tog på nerverna: motsatserna var stora och hotfullt ödesdigra, och man kände sig så obönhörligt inmurad i sin samtids sammanhang, att det var åtskilligt för mycket." Thank you to Madeleine Engström Broberg at Svenska Akademin for scanning a copy of this letter for me. All translations are my own unless otherwise noted.
3. See Boye (1994). Archeologist and classicist Paul Åström edited and published this facsimile edition of the diary in 1994, interested largely in its references to classical culture. To date it remains untranslated into English and has received relatively little scholarly attention.
4. "På kvällen såg jag Leni Riefenstahls Olympia, I och II, alltså bortåt fyra timmars sysselsättning. Men det var storartat! Hon har lärt av de största ryssarna. Hur hon kan göra allt spännande, hur hon kan fånga det väsentliga i en glimt, är märkvärdigt. Och vackert! Egendomligt var det med de främmande raserna, hur rena, hur vackra, hur särpräglat förnäma de spelade sin roll här inför den arisk-fanatiska publiken: negrerna överlägsna i löpning, japanerna sega i alla uthålighetstävlingar—och en tredjeprisryttare från U.S.A., säkert jude. Alla ansikten var så äkta och sympatiska inför de sakliga uppgifterna. Filmen har inte kommit mig att tro på Tredje riket, men på idrotten. Så nog var det propaganda."
5. Riefenstahl had a certain amount of independence in making the film, yet maintained close ties with the Nazi Party; see Downing (2012: 40–44).
6. Boye had also traveled abroad on two other occasions. In 1928 she participated in a trip to the Soviet Union, which seems to have tempered her belief in bringing about social renewal by revolutionary means (though she continued to study Marxism and maintained her interest in Soviet literature), and to Yugoslavia in 1930 with her husband at the time, Leif Björk.
7. "strävan efter en konst som förenade modernism och vänsterradikalism, psykoanalys och politik, activism och personlighetsutveckling."
8. "17 juni Wien: Förmiddagen: kringströvande. Gräsligt gråväder med regnhot, som hela resan hittills. Teatervecka: hakkorsfanor överallt, hakkors på alla ariska butiker, i sockenuppslagen etc. Åt middag i ett litet kafé med hakkors i fönstren och fyllt med glada judar innanför. I banken fanns ett Hitler porträtt, som sade mer än alla karikatyrer, allvarligt, asketiskt, nästan vackert som det var: människotyp mot människotyp, livshållning mot livshållning, den hårt anspända mot den flyttande."
9. "... jag greps av en känsla, som jag förmodar en glödande nationalsocialist skulle ha, om han plötsligt upptäckte att han var hundraprocentig jude. Förstår du det? Hela mitt hjärta

är ju hos de andra. 'Jag arma människa, vem frälser mig ur denna dödens kropp?'" This passage is Romans 7:24.
10. "Du tror väl antingen att jag är död och begraven, skjuten av Nazis, eller att jag så med liv och lust går upp i Berlinlivet att jag glömt alla gamla vänner."
11. See also, "Emotional Engineering: Hitler Youth Quex (1933)" (Rentschler 1996: 53–69).
12. For a brilliant reading of the interface between fascism and literary modernism in Norway, see Krouk (2017). For discussions about how racial ideologies are inextricable from the Swedish welfare state project in the 1930s, see Rudberg (1998) and Habel (2002).
13. Not doing so, Abenius explains, would have put her in mortal danger. Svedjedal (2017) offers an invaluable reexamination of the sources upon which the standard reception of Boye's life and work have been rehearsed. He refers to a note by Scharp remarking after his interview with Abenius that she had misrepresented his depiction of the scene in her biography of Boye.
14. For an analysis of Boye's work that focuses on her overactive death drive and her suicide, see Jansson (2017).
15. This was her third stint in analysis. First was Alfhild Tamm, a Freudian in Stockholm, then Walter Schindler (for two months in Berlin), and then Dr. Lampl in Berlin. Nic Hoel connected Boye and Lampl.
16. Hanel committed suicide only months after Boye did.
17. "de gamla rötterna från 900-talet bär bara nya skott, det nya Prag växer ur det gamla utan att de skämmer varandra, och ändå har jag aldrig haft en så bokstavligt hisnande känsla av århundradenas djup som här." After this, Boye remarks that had she been born in Prague, she likely would have been a burning (*glödande*) nationalist, but in a good way, not a gorilla in boots (i.e. a Nazi) but rather a modern follower of Huss pursuing freedom of thought. Boye admires Jewish culture in Prague, including its ancient synagogue and city hall where the gold chains of the Jewish ghetto used to be locked every night, and now hung as a reminder to politicians of a past not to be repeated.
18. While Boye does mention Ataturk in Turkey and the dictatorship in Greece (noting that the group of young students she travels with on Crete are all republicans), she only mentions it in passing in her travel diary. The contemporary political situation in southern Europe is of secondary concern to her.
19. The 1936 Olympic Games were the first to incorporate the torch ceremony—now a standard element (Downing 2012: 70).
20. "Har konstens inriktning något att göra med kultur*stadiet* eller med kultur*arten* eller med rastemperament överhuvud? [Visit to National Museum, Athens 7 July]."
21. "Vår framtid ligger nu som alltid i vårt förflutna" (Lagerkvist 1949: 91).
22. "Även om hon var självklar motståndare till nazismen, tenderade hon ibland (som många andra samtida) att betrakta den med ett överseende som i efterhand kan verka naivt."

References

Abenius, Margit. 1951. *Drabbad av renhet, En bok om Karin Boyes liv och diktning*. Stockholm: Bonnier.
Agius, Christine. 2012. *The Social Construction of Swedish Neutrality: Challenges to Swedish Identity and Sovereignty*. Manchester: Manchester University Press.
Boye, Karin. 1934. *Kris*. Stockholm: Bonnier.

———. 1940. *Kallocain*. Stockholm: Bonnier.
———. 1992. "Nazistisk skönlitteratur I, II." In *Det hungriga ögat: Journalistik 1930–1936; Recensioner och essäer*, edited by Gunnar Ståhl, 117–23. Stockholm: Legus.
Boye, Karin, and Paul Åström. 1994. *Resedagbok I Grekland: Från Hitlers Berlin till Apollons Olympia*. Studies in Mediterranean Archaeology and Literature. Pocket-book; 128. Jonsered: P. Åström.
Boye, Karin, and Helgeson, Paulina, 2000. *Ett verkligt jordiskt liv: brev*. Stockholm: A. Bonnier.
de Rougement, Denis. 2010. "The Dream of Sixty Million People." In *Travels in the Reich, 1933–1945: Foreign Authors Report from Germany*, edited by Oliver Lubrich, 79–90. Chicago: University of Chicago Press.
Dinesen, Isak. 1979. "Letters from a Land at War." In *Daguerreotypes, and Other Essays*, edited by P. M. Mitchell and W. D. Paden, 88–137. Chicago: University of Chicago Press.
Domellöf, Gunilla. 1986. *I oss är en mångfald levande: Karin Boye som kritiker och prosamodernist*. Umeå/Stockholm: Umeå universitet.
Downing, T., and the British Film Institute. 2012. *Olympia*. 2nd ed. New York: Palgrave MacMillan; on behalf of the British Film Institute.
Enander, Crister. 1995. *Relief: Författarporträtt*. Stockholm: Legus.
Gordon, T. J. 2002. "Fascism and the Female Form: Performance Art in the Third Reich." *Journal of the History of Sexuality* 11(1): 164–200.
Gustafsson Rosenqvist, Barbro. 1999. *"Att skapa en ny värld": Samhällssyn, kvinnosyn och djuppsykologi hos Karin Boye*. Stockholm: Carlsson.
Habel, Ylva. 2002. "Modern Media, Modern Audiences: Mass Media and Social Engineering in the 1930s Swedish Welfare State." Unpublished dissertation, Stockholm University, Stockholm, Sweden.
Hammarström, Camilla. 1997. *Karin Boye*. Stockholm: Natur och kultur.
Jansson, Peter. 2017. *Själens krypta: En essä om Karin Boyes självbiografiska roman Kris*. Göteborg: Lindelöws bokförlag.
Koepnick, Lutz. 2008. "0-1: Riefenstahl and the Beauty of Soccer." In *Riefenstahl Screened: An Anthology of New Criticism*, edited by Neil Christian Pages, Mary Rhiel, and Ingeborg Majer O'Sickey, 52–70. New York: Continuum.
Krouk, Dean. 2017. *Fascism and Modernist Literature in Norway*. Seattle: University of Washington Press.
Lagerkvist, Pär. 1949. *Prosa: Bödeln—Den knutna näven—I den tiden—Den befriade människan*. Stockholm: Bonnier.
———. 1989. *Five Early Works*. Lewiston, NY: Edwin Mellen Press.
Lubrich, O. 2010. *Travels in the Reich, 1933–1945: Foreign Authors Report from Germany*. Chicago: University of Chicago Press.
Luthersson, Peter. 2002. *Svensk litterär modernism: En stridsstudie*. Stockholm: Atlantis.
Rentschler, Eric. 1996. *The Ministry of Illusion: Nazi Cinema and Its Afterlife*. Cambridge, MA: Harvard University Press.
Rudberg, E. 1998. *The Stockholm Exhibition of 1930: Modernism's Breakthrough in Swedish Architecture*. Stockholm: Stockholmia Förlag.
Svedjedal, Johan. 2011. *Spektrum 1931–1935: Den svenska drömmen; Tidskrift och förlag i 1930-talets kultur*. Stockholm: Wahlström & Widstrand.
———. 2017. *Den nya dagen gryr.: Karin Boyes författarliv*. Stockholm: Wahlström & Widstram.

Chapter 7

ISAK DINESEN IN HITLER'S BERLIN
Neutrality's Cloak in "Letters from a Land at War"

Marianne Stecher-Hansen

It is not widely known that "Isak Dinesen"—the nom de plume of Danish writer Karen Blixen (1885–1962)—visited Hitler's Germany in early 1940, shortly before Denmark was occupied, or that she, after the war in 1948, published her observations in an essay titled "Letters from a Land at War." It is furthermore remarkable that the political philosopher Hannah Arendt (1906–75), who had fled Nazi Germany in 1933 and escaped occupied France to settle in the United States in 1941, came to know and admire Isak Dinesen's literary work while living in New York. In *The Human Condition* (1958: 175) Arendt attributes a quotation to Isak Dinesen—"All Sorrows can be borne if you put them into a story or tell a story about them"—and makes other references to Dinesen in her works of political theory (Wilkinson 2004: 78). In a review essay published in the *New Yorker*—and republished in *Men in Dark Times*[1]—Arendt suggested that storytelling had forged the Danish writer's wisdom:

> Storytelling, at any rate, is what in the end made her wise—and, incidentally, not a "witch," "siren," or "sibyl," as her entourage admiringly thought. Wisdom is a virtue of old age, and it seems to come only to those who, when young, were neither wise nor prudent. (Arendt 1968: 109)

It is evident that Arendt appreciated Dinesen's sagacious literary tales and had cause to question the author's public image as a "witch" or "sibyl." Indeed, the perception of "Baroness Blixen" as a conservative icon is difficult to destabilize, as the former director of Denmark's Karen Blixen Museum, Catherine Lefebvre, laments: "The revolutionary side of Blixen is often neglected as the image of the noble and highly educated Baroness does not coincide with this characteristic" (Lefebvre 2016: 103). However, it is precisely in Dinesen's often overlooked essays that her heretical and occasionally "revolutionary" perspectives are given voice (Stecher-Hansen 2020, 2014).

Hannah Arendt and Isak Dinesen are two intellectual, wise and "disobedient" women of the twentieth century whose paths crossed once, although they did not meet face to face. Dinesen, a celebrated figure in intellectual and literary circles in the United States at midcentury, made her first and only visit in 1959 to North America. Over several months, she made numerous public appearances (as well as televised interviews and radio broadcast readings), including at the Ninety-Third Street YMHA (Young Men's Hebrew Association): *The Poetry Center*, where Hannah Arendt attended at least one storytelling performance that left a lasting impression (Lefebvre 2016: 103; Wilkinson 2004: 82).

Regardless of her familiarity with Isak Dinesen's literary tales, Hannah Arendt would not have been familiar with the "Letters from a Land at War" (originally published in Danish as "Breve fra et Land i Krig"). Although Dinesen's wartime visit to Germany is briefly mentioned in *Titania* (1967)— the biography by Parmenia Migel, which Arendt reviewed for the *New Yorker* in 1968—"Letters from a Land at War" first appeared in English in 1979 (after Arendt's death) in *Daguerreotypes and Other Essays*, a translation that features Arendt's review essay as the foreword. Furthermore, a German translation of Dinesen's essays was first available in 1991, as *Mottos meines Lebens* [Mottos of my life] by "Tania Blixen." One might wonder whether or not Arendt—had she read "Letters from a Land at War"—would have appreciated some of Dinesen's wartime observations from the Third Reich.

In this chapter, I argue that Dinesen's text operates under a "cloak of neutrality" in order to make use of irony in an oblique and sagacious critique of the totalitarian system, psychology of conformism, racism, and imperialistic culture of the Nazi regime that she witnessed in wartime Berlin. It would not be accurate to argue that Dinesen is "ambivalent" in her reactions to Hitler's Germany, because "ambivalence" (in the psychological sense of the word) would imply an emotional engagement—that is, both attraction and repulsion. In "Letters from a Land at War," the middle-aged Danish writer formulates a perspective on Nazism with lucid rationality that might best be characterized as neutral, aesthetic, and distanced. Although Dinesen's observations are not politically engaged (the text makes deliberate use of neutrality both as a narrative strategy and as a political position), the text contains an implicit political assessment that denounces the "forced will" of the German National Socialists and the political agenda of Hitler's regime. In the following analysis, I seek to demonstrate that Dinesen's essay represents Nazism as a fanatic "religion" practiced by a mass cult of blindly zealous followers and depicts the state-sponsored arts and cultural activities as propaganda in the service of a totalitarian state.

Unlike Sigrid Undset's *Return to the Future* (the subject of chapter 8), which was written as propaganda in the service of the Allied cause at the peak of the war in 1942, Dinesen's "Letters" from Berlin never served as wartime propaganda—neither for the Allied powers, nor for the German occupiers in Denmark (although the author's assigned German escorts in Berlin certainly had such a purpose in mind). In fact, Dinesen's chronicles from Hitler's Germany were never published during the war. Instead, Dinesen's "Letters from a Land at War," which first appeared in print after the war in the Danish literary journal *Heretica* in 1948, constitute a wartime critique of the Nazi totalitarian regime that remains largely unknown—in the terms of cultural memory study, one could say that it is "archived" or belongs to "storage memory" (Assmann 2010: 99; Assmann 2011: 123–24). "Letters from a Land at War" has often proven difficult for biographers and scholars, because Dinesen's wartime account of the Nazi regime—when ripped out of the historical moment—appears controversial or inscrutable to postwar readers.

Such texts are important and deserve to be lifted out of the figurative archive of scholarship and put into conversation with contemporaneous texts. In *Travels in the Reich, 1933–1945: Foreign Authors report from Germany*, Oliver Lubrich points out that that "travel reports have a value not only as authentic representations but also as contemporary constructions" (2010: 1–2). In the case of Dinesen's "Letters," they offer critically astute observations on the Nazi regime from an early perspective in the war (the spring of 1940), before alliances were shored up and before the tide of war had turned against Germany in 1943. As Lubrich notes, "Reports by foreign visitors open up new perspectives on European history. . . . Because they register the reality of life in Nazi Germany through the eyes of an outsider, they report it in a different way than contemporary German witnesses have portrayed it" (2010: 2). Indeed, "Letters from a Land at War" is valuable because Dinesen positions herself as a neutral Scandinavian outsider and as an educated woman (similar in ways to Swedish poet Karin Boye in her 1938 travel book, as discussed in the previous chapter) who observes the totalitarian system, the mass psychology of fascism, and the propagandistic arts of the Nazi Reich from the critical vantage point of a neutral, northern neighbor.

Travel to the Third Reich: Neutrality's Cloak

Throughout her literary career, both publicly and in private letters, Dinesen consistently maintained that she took no interest in politics; therefore, the ideological dimension of Dinesen's authorship has vexed some of her biographers and literary critics. In *Isak Dinesen's Art: The Gayety of Vision*, Robert Langbaum—whom Arendt credits as "by far her best critic" (1968: 100)—offers the following appraisal of Dinesen's letters from Hitler's Germany:

> Her criticism of Nazi totalitarianism shows that her own political ideas are in the tradition that has produced modern liberalism—that she is really in her political thinking recalling liberals to their true tradition and their true ideals. The thing that appals her about Nazi society is that it glorifies will power, that its achievement is not a growth but a mechanical *tour de force* that suppresses the human and natural desire out of which, for her, all good things come. (1964: 199)

On the other hand, two decades later, Judith Thurman in *Isak Dinesen: The Life of a Storyteller*, appraises Dinesen's "Letters from a Land at War" less favorably, criticizing the essay as "simply too lofty, too personally exempt, too privileged and cautious to give the sinister facts any of their real gravity or importance," and remarks that "a certain style is inadequate to a certain subject, at a critical point in history" (1982: 291–92). In Denmark, critical studies of Karen Blixen published over the decades have most often overlooked her chronicles from Berlin.

Why did the Danish writer choose to travel to Nazi Germany at the beginning of the war? Already in 1938, following the horrifying reports of *Kristallnacht*, Dinesen's British publisher, Constant Huntington—encouraged by the excellent reception of *Out of Africa* (1937)—wrote to the Danish writer to urge her to go to Germany to write a book "on conditions there," remarking that "such a book would prove a most important contribution to the cause of international understanding" (Blixen 1996: 287). This initial plan to travel to Germany did not come to fruition; however, about a year later, in late 1939, following the outbreak of the war, Dinesen eagerly pursued plans for a series of articles from Berlin, Paris, and London. In late May 1939, Denmark had signed a nonaggression treaty with Nazi Germany, and, at that point, in an effort to maintain neutrality, Danish authorities implemented some censorship in order to reduce criticism of Nazi Germany in the press. In November 1939, Dinesen, with the help of her attorney Erik Petri, negotiated arrangements with Scandinavian publications: the Danish daily *Politiken* in Copenhagen, Bonnier in Stockholm (which managed two Swedish weekly journals) and *Tidens Tegn* in Oslo. The Danish writer was to spend one month in each city and provide four chronicles from each of the warring capitals: Berlin, London, and Paris. By early February 1940, Dinesen had secured visas to all three countries (Günter 1985: 61).

Due to the course of the war, the assignments to Paris and London never materialized. Dinesen flew to Berlin on 7 March 1940 (although in the published essay her departure is dated 1 March) and returned home to Denmark on 2 April 1940, merely a week before German forces occupied Denmark on 9 April. Upon her return to Denmark in April and early May of 1940, Dinesen completed the writing of the four chronicles contracted by the Danish daily *Politiken*. However, due to the occupation, conditions had changed in Denmark upon her return from Germany, and Dinesen resisted the publication of the chronicles in *Politiken*. The Danish public would now certainly take offense at any remarks in the chronicles about Denmark's "neutrality" (which had been violated) or about the helpfulness or "courteousness" of the German people. With concerted effort, Dinesen and her attorney convinced editor Niels Hasager (1888–1969) at *Politiken* not to publish the chronicles (Günter 1985: 66). Nevertheless, Dinesen received the contracted payment of 2,400 Danish crowns for her work. She then put her manuscripts aside until after the liberation. In the published foreword, she claims that "I let my *Letters from a Land at War* lie for eight years without looking at them" (Dinesen 1979: 91). That claim is only partly true, but the point is that the chronicles were never published in Denmark during the war.[2]

Private letters reveal that Hitler's Germany was a topic of discussion in the Dinesen family during the late 1930s. A particular interest in Germany seems to have been prompted by Karen Blixen's sister Ellen Dahl, who made visits to Hitler's Germany in the 1930s and wrote enthusiastically about her experiences to family members. The author herself makes a notable reference to the charismatic lure of Hitler in a letter of 1 June 1938 to her aunt:

> I believe that Hitler is to a great degree brilliant—perhaps really what one in a sense would call a genius—not so much by personality as by a quite mysterious connection with the people and the times. (Blixen 1996: 278 [my translation])[3]

Notable in this sentence is the interest in the mass appeal of Hitler, "his mysterious connection with the people and the times." About his "magnetism" Dinesen also later remarks in her published essay, "It is strange to think, that the spirit of a single man, just like a magnet which is dragged over a collection of metal fragments, can rearrange and transform a society" (Dinesen 1979: 105).[4] However, the admiration for Germany's new leader expressed in this letter of June 1938 is mitigated by an explicit rejection of "this new German spirit," which Dinesen finds intolerable, stating that it is "exclusively emotional" (Blixen 1996: 278 [my translation]).[5]

In the summer of 1938, the Danish writer, like the majority of Europeans, had no premonition of the terrible course that anti-Semitism would take in Germany. The letter that refers to Hitler's charisma is written before *Die Kristallnacht* took place on 9 November 1938. Dinesen's interest in the figure of Hitler is characteristic of Europeans in the 1930s. Germany's new leader aroused curiosity and fascination, and—unfortunately—he was admired initially by many who considered him a political reformer. For example, the Swedish travel writer Sven Hedin, an avid German sympathizer who was fearful of Soviet aggression, visited Nazi Germany repeatedly between 1935 and 1943, meeting with Goebbels, Himmler, Ribbentrop, and Hitler himself (Lubrich 2010: 203). The Danish silent cinema actress Asta Nielsen, a celebrated diva in Berlin where she cultivated her career from 1911 to 1937, had tea and conversation in 1933 with Goebbels and Hitler.[6] Nielsen at one point expressed admiration for Germany's new leader before returning permanently in 1937 to Denmark where accusations of Nazi sympathies plagued her for years after the war (Allen 2012).

The responses of Nordic visitors to Hitler's Germany in the 1930s are as varied as the many personalities involved. Such distinguished Swedish writers as Gunnar Ekelöf and Pär Lagerkvist, who both traveled through the Third Reich in the 1930s, were quick to assess the imminent dangers of the new Germany and to warn against them. The Danish playwright and pastor Kaj Munk (1898–1944), also a notable figure of the period who visited the Third Reich, initially admired Hitler (and Mussolini) and traveled to Berlin already in 1933 to applaud the new regime. However, like many Danish writers of the 1930s, Kaj Munk soon became alarmed by Nazi anti-Semitism; he became an outspoken voice against Hitler's Germany in occupied Denmark and suffered the consequence. On 4 January 1944, the bold pastor-playwright was arrested at his parsonage at Vedersø, shot in the head by Nazi henchmen, and thrown into a ditch (Daugbjerg 2011).

Dinesen writes in the foreword to "Letters from a Land at War," published in *Heretica* in 1948, that she had let her chronicles lie for eight years without looking at them. She adds, "In reality I had forgotten that I had written them" (Dinesen 1979: 91).[7] Indeed, critics and postwar readers might question whether a text written about Nazi Germany before the occupation—not to mention before the Holocaust—would remain untouched by an author who published it three years after the war. It is possible that Dinesen made some minor editorial revisions to the original manuscripts written in 1940.

The "foreword" to the essay, which Dinesen added in 1948, offers some insights into the strategies of a cautious and artful narrator. Dinesen claims that she contacted the editor of the Danish daily *Politiken*, Mr. Hasager, on 3 September 1939, on the very day of the war's outbreak, regarding an assignment as a correspondent. Dinesen does not mention any previous plans or interest in traveling to Germany; she states that she told the editor that "I had no insight into politics and no political flair," and argues that "I was an honest person, and perhaps an impartial layman's observations from a politically turbulent time would in the future have a certain interest as a *document humain*" (Dinesen 1979: 89).[8] Written in 1948, it is interesting to note the choice of the words "in the future." When Dinesen writes the "foreword" after the liberation, she is deliberately writing for posterity. In touching on the most sensitive and politically explosive topic of her day, Dinesen strives for a studied historical distance to the subject matter. Reassessing her chronicles after the war, she predicted the objections of her future readers and emphasized again that her observations on Nazi Germany were recorded and that the chronicles were written (a partially truthful claim, as she completed them in early May 1940) while Denmark was still "neutral," that is, *before* the occupation[9]:

> Perhaps the readers will feel that I have expressed myself with unreasonable indirection, where I could have spoken out in a straightforward manner. They must take into consideration that the letters were written before the Occupation. Denmark was at that time still neutral, and there were considerations to be made which later disappeared. (Dinesen 1979: 91–92)[10]

In March 1940, Dinesen had indeed believed—as did many at the time—that Denmark, and the other Scandinavian countries, would be allowed to maintain neutrality as they had been in World War I. The occupation came as a shock.

About offers to meet high-ranking Nazi bureaucrats (perhaps Hitler himself), Dinesen suggests in the foreword of the essay that she was reluctant and ultimately did not take advantage of the opportunity:

> If I had been a true Journalist, I would have accepted the Third Reich's repeated offers to meet its great personalities face to face. I now wish that I had taken advantage of them. . . . At one point, I responded yes, but later sent apologetic regrets. Something in the idea must have rubbed me the wrong way to a great degree. (Dinesen 1979: 91)[11]

This explanation has been disputed by Martin Günter, who suggests that it was likely not Dinesen who sent regrets, but the other way around. Apparently, Hitler's full calendar of meetings in March 1940, filled with "cultural personalities" such as Sven Hedin, indicates that it is more likely that the leader himself canceled an interview (if there was one) with the visiting Danish baroness and writer, whose name was unfamiliar to him (Günter 1985: 71). At any rate, Isak Dinesen was not aggressive in her duties as a "foreign correspondent" for *Politiken* in Nazi Germany; the fact that she never did meet any of the so-called "great personalities" of the Third Reich attests to caution or skepticism. It is noteworthy, however, that Dinesen did allow herself to be interviewed by the Nazi Party's daily *Völkischer Beobachter* (People's Observer) in late March 1940. The interview was published in Germany on 5 April 1940 (after the author had returned to Denmark) but was apparently never read by Dinesen; in this highly censored and translated interview, the Danish writer expresses a remarkable combination of admiration and "lack of understanding" for the Third Reich (Brundbjerg 2000: 71–73;).[12]

Dinesen deliberately positions herself as a neutral outsider in Germany, and this consistent perspective becomes an effective narrative strategy in her chronicles from the Third Reich. Her view of Berlin is not as a citizen from a weak or threatened neighbor to the north; instead, her perspective brings the reader a kind of "aerial" or otherworldly view of wartime Berlin. Her vantage point is distant, originating in remote times and places in history, and in that manner, the chronicles achieve a protective "cloak of neutrality."

The Old Hero in Bremen: German Fare

Dinesen opens her wartime letters with a curious homage to "en gammel ven" (an old friend) in Germany, the general Paul von Lettow-Vorbeck (1870–1964). In fact, the author interrupted her stay in Berlin in order to pay a visit to the old general in Bremen. Dinesen's acquaintance with the general originated in 1913, when Paul von Lettow-Vorbeck traveled to Africa to serve as commanding general in German East Africa in 1914–18. Dinesen made his acquaintance on board the ship to East Africa in 1913 and bid him farewell in Mombasa on 14 January 1914, the day of her wedding to Bror von Blixen-Finecke. The general and Dinesen did not meet again in Africa. Twenty-five years later, General von Lettow-Vorbeck wrote to Dinesen in the summer of 1939, stating that he had recently read *Out of Africa* and kindly pointed out that Dinesen had misquoted a poem by Goethe (Blixen 1996: 296–98). Eventually, in late January 1940, Dinesen replied to the general's letter, and this correspondence led to her visit to Bremen in late March 1940, an experience she describes in the first part of the essay.

In this first chronicle, Dinesen immortalizes General von Lettow-Vorbeck as an "Old Hero in Bremen" describing him in mythic proportions, as a symbolic representation of old imperial Germany: "He belonged to the old days. I have not since met any German, by whom I received such a strong impression of what imperial Germany was and stood for" (Dinesen 1979: 120).[13] Dinesen shapes von Lettow-Vorbeck into a literary character that illustrates her notion of the chivalrous enemy, writing that the German general was admired and respected by the English forces in Africa "not only a skillful commander and a brave soldier, but because he was such a *chivalrous enemy*" (Dinesen 1979: 93; emphasis added).[14] During World War II, Paul von Lettow-Vorbeck served Hitler's Germany.[15] However, for the Danish writer, in March 1940—on the occasion of the old general's seventieth birthday—the chronicle served as a representation of a "chivalrous enemy," a characteristic belonging to another era of warfare.

The opening letter, "An Old Hero in Bremen" may strike the reader as an unnecessary digression from observations from Nazi Germany.[16] It is the most sympathetic of Dinesen's letters from Germany—and, given the context of the private visit to Bremen, there are reasons for this deliberate or feigned friendliness. At first glance, Dinesen's piece about von Lettow-Vorbeck seems pure nostalgia for the old colonial Africa. However, the portrait of von Lettow-Vorbeck as a representation of "chivalrous" old Germany juxtaposed with the willful National Socialists in the subsequent chronicles comes to serve another purpose. The essay at this point introduces a pattern for the treatment of the topic of Hitler's new Germany by constructing a series of implicit contrasts: the contrast between imperial Germany (the colonial architecture and atmosphere of Bremen) and Nazi Germany (the inhuman neoclassical structures of Berlin); between the old chivalrous "enemy" (General von Lettow-Vorbeck) and the faceless masses of the totalitarian state (the Nazi clergy of Berlin); between warfare driven by individual passions and one determined by the force of a collective will. The pattern is consistent throughout the entire text, which gradually and cleverly builds an oblique yet consistent denunciation of Hitler's new Germany.

In her homage to the German general, and in references to the "courteousness" of the people of Bremen, Dinesen expresses sympathy for the former Germany. She describes her arrival in Bremen late at night where the ordinary people are boundlessly helpful. About a dinner at the general's home, Dinesen writes, "Among the guests was the painter, Professor Horn, who is the father-in-law of Rudolph Hess. Out of courtesy toward me, the German party spoke English, something similar would not have happened to me in England" (Dinesen 1979: 97).[17] Although superficially the remark is sympathetic to German hospitality, it also underlines the fact that Dinesen herself did not speak German, that she was truly an outsider in this gathering.

These deliberate efforts at neutrality remind the reader that Isak Dinesen had associates and acquaintances on both sides of the fence when World War II broke out; that, despite the war, the author was always concerned about the international market for her books; and that, when the chronicles were originally drafted in 1940, she was painfully aware that the ultimate outcome of the war was uncertain. This sober fact is demonstrated by Dinesen's consistent efforts during the war to publish *Winter's Tales* (1942) in Germany. Two of Dinesen's *Winter's Tales* were in fact published in 1943 in German translations, namely "The Pearls" in *Berliner Illustrierte Zeitung* (Berlin Illustrated Newspaper or BIZ) and "The Sailor-Boy's Tale" in *Europäische Revue* (European Review), as demonstrated by Poul Behrendt (2013: 140; 145). However, despite a signed contract of July 1943, the German translation of the complete collection of literary tales by "Tania Blixen," (as she would be known in Germany) never appeared in print; on 12–13 September 1944, the Allied fire-bombing of Stuttgart decimated the author's German publishing house—a fortuitous strike for Dinesen's postwar legacy (Behrendt 2013).

Nazism's Faceless Zealots

Dinesen's most astute observations on Nazism are articulated in the second chronicle, "Great Undertakings in Berlin" ("Store Foretagender i Berlin"). After praising the impressive courtesy of her assigned German escorts,[18] Dinesen offers an analysis of the fanatic zealousness of the "clergy" of the totalitarian state: "Its men and women all look like one another—faith radiates from their faces, they are untiring and zealous unto death, without doubt or hesitation in their souls" (Dinesen 1979: 103).[19] Making an analogy to the clergy of the early Catholic Church, Dinesen describes the faceless conformity and blind dedication of Nazi bureaucrats and their followers. The text depicts how the masses of citizens are organized into large "voluntary" social organizations, such as the Reichsfrauenbund, Volkswohlfahrt, and Arbeitsfront. In particular, she describes the fourteen-million-member Reichsfrauenbund (State Women's Organization), headed by Frau Scholtz-Klink, a typically German lady in appearance with blonde braids wound around her head. Dinesen questions the methods of the "block-guard" of the women's organization with the following ironic commentary:

> I never really found out what kind of methods the *Reichsfrauenbund* has up its sleeve to force its will, in case someone refuses obedience. . . . When I asked, they answered me, "It never happens"—and that answer was perhaps in itself just as instructive as any explanation. (Dinesen 1979: 104)[20]

Most insightful is Dinesen's observation that the Third Reich represents a form of social revolution, which gave power to the masses of Germans who had not previously held power, including women: "It struck me that the women who are now governing the entire German femininity are a type which, until the arrival of the Third Reich, had little opportunity to wield power" (Dinesen 1979: 105).[21] Further, the comment suggests that this proletarian class of woman, who now tenaciously holds onto power for the first time—a new variety of social revolutionary—is particularly fierce in wielding its power. For Dinesen, the militarism of the totalitarian regime forces an unnaturally "masculine" culture upon its entire citizenry, as she reflects later in *Shadows on the Grass*: "When in 1940 I was in Berlin . . . woman—and the whole world of woman—was so emphatically subdued that I might indeed have been walking about in such a one-sexed community" (Dinesen 1961: 3).

In her essay, Dinesen moves from a discussion of the rigid, internal organizations of the totalitarian state to a discussion of its external structures, namely the architecture and worldview of Nazi Berlin. In an ironic and essentialist description of the new German mentality, she emphasizes the predilection for structure, systems, and statistics. She suggests that the magnitude and size of the neoclassical structures of Berlin is evidence of an unnatural urgency: "It is a superhuman, an inhuman tempo. This is not a growth, it is a *tour de force* and there is fear somewhere. One doesn't know whether it is in the viewer or in the architects" (Dinesen 1979: 106).[22] The author argues that this display of powerful structures in Hitler's Berlin is not an organic "growth," spontaneously produced by instinct and desire. Nazi Berlin is a *tour de force* driven by fear and anxiety; the tempo of construction reflects a dangerous single-mindedness. Religious devotion for Nazi bureaucrats and officials, writes Dinesen, consists of a "passionate worship" of systems, structures, and statistics.

Working from a position of neutrality and distance, Dinesen maps her depiction of the Nazi movement onto other cultural topographies. Seeing Nazism as a kind of fanatic religious movement, she transposes images of the Catholic clergy as well as the "young Mohammedan movement" that "went forth to conquer the world" (Dinesen 1965: 108) onto the German National Socialists. As a form of travel writing, it is notable that Dinesen specifically maps Nazism onto a symbolic topography of Arabia and Africa, by means of a comparison between early Islam and Nazism as fanatic religious movements, writing that "the Word Islam means submission, which is the same thing that the Third Reich expresses with its upraised arm. Yours in Life and Death" (Dinesen 1979: 108).[23] However, Dinesen does not stop at a simple comparison; she observes further that "the half-moon is a nobler symbol than the swastika" (Dinesen 1979: 108).[24] Dinesen points out that the racist credo of Nazism is infertile, that it lacks reciprocity and the capacity for cultural exchange (which she admires in Islam). This understanding is reiterated in her comment: "But Islam was a belief in God. It could both give and take, of all its power. It wanted to save the whole world, if the world would accept it" (Dinesen 1979: 110).[25]

Dinesen's commentary reaches beyond random observations and begins to develop a model for an interpretation of Nazism. Having employed the analogy of the early Catholic Church and the medieval crusaders as well as the nascence of Islam in the eighth century, Dinesen offers a historical perspective on the phenomenon of Nazi fanaticism in the twentieth century. Moreover, Dinesen ultimately concludes that the "religious madness" of Nazism is a perversion of genuine religious passion, symbols, and rituals into a cult of hero worship by which a totalitarian leader is able to seduce and manipulate the masses. In other words, Nazism employs the outward trappings of religious devotion without its sacred core; it is a perversion of religious devotion, one without God. It would appear, Dinesen suggests, that the National Socialists have usurped the human capacity for genuine religious faith with an escapist credo of racism. In "Letters from a Land at War," Dinesen thus describes this ideology of racism as dangerously menacing, and ultimately infertile and self-destructive:

> But the cultivation of race retreats into itself, and even its triumphal march becomes a vicious circle. It cannot give and it cannot receive . . . despite the great hopes for the future which are upheld here, there is only limited perspective in the vista of Nazism. . . . The people, or the masses of a people, have risen in a new, surprising, and frightening way. They stand against the heavens with a monumental force, and cast a mighty shadow in front of themselves, and none of us knows, how far that shadow will reach or over whom. And yet, the viewer thinks that ultimately the people are standing in their own light. (Dinesen 1979: 111)[26]

Here, as in several other passages in this text, Dinesen voices an unequivocal denunciation of Nazism despite her stated intentions to maintain "neutrality." The text sharply underlines the fact that both the Crusaders and the early Muslims were driven by a fanatic belief in a divine order rather than by a credo of racism. It is precisely the absence of a divine presence (whether it be God or Allah) that Dinesen as an artist finds most distressing in Hitler's Germany; this is one of the main points underlying her observations in the final two chronicles.

Propaganda and the Artist

In the third letter, called "Strength and Joy" ("Kraft og Glæde"), Dinesen makes use of deliberate irony in the choice of this title, a reference to the Nazi recreational or leisure organization Kraft durch Freude (literally "Strength through Joy"), an organ of the German Arbeiterfront (Labor Front) in the 1930s. The focus of this chronicle is Dinesen's observation that art and leisure, forced on the masses in the service of the Nazi political agenda, can only produce propaganda ("*l'art pour la Nation*") and never genuine art ("*l'art pour l'art*"), nor any real joy for that matter. In a broader scope, the chronicle offers a searing commentary on the Nazist distortion of a Nietzschean "Will to Power" and its sterile, racist mentality and aggressive worldview. That Blixen titles the chronicle, "Strength *and* Joy" might indicate another topic of the third chronicle, namely the dangers of a false or distorted relationship between words and facts in the service of propaganda.

In its poignantly satirical representation of a National Socialist mentality, "Strength and Joy" is the most ironic of the four chronicles as it reproduces Dinesen's conversations with young Nazi German bureaucrats. This chronicle accomplishes more than an illustration of differing worldviews; it openly satirizes the aggressive political ambitions and humorless mentality that Dinesen identifies in the young German National Socialists:

> The young Germans nearly always got the last word when we talked together. For no matter how clearly they presented their arguments, there was always

Figure 7.1. Karen Blixen (Isak Dinesen) listens with eyes averted and chin resting in her hand, photographed in Berlin on 19 March 1940. On the backside of the photograph, the baroness wrote, "From my visit in Berlin. Eager Nazis attempt to convert me." Unknown photographer. DAF Picture Service. Royal Danish Library digital archive. Courtesy of the Rungstedlund Foundation.

> something to which I had to respond: "We foreigners cannot understand that." Then they said: "But you will come to understand it. We are going to demonstrate it to the world." The difference between us lay very deep, but when we were far enough along in a debate, we struck it. (Dinesen 1979: 115–16)[27]

In this illustration of differing worldviews, Dinesen juxtaposes the rigid Nazi German belief in the strength of the will (*viljens kraft*) with her own philosophical belief in destiny (*skæbne*), which she euphemistically refers to in the text as "*la grace de Dieu*" (the grace of God).

From the carefully constructed narrative position of the politically neutral observer, the third letter also attempts sympathetic insights into conflicting worldviews of the British and German warring powers. Dinesen ventures that the roots of German aggression lie in the moral defeat of World War I as much as in any specific political ideology. She proposes that in the English attitude lies a special kind of "confidence in God's grace, which one calls humor," whereas the German belief in the omnipotence of the will is a reaction to the punitive Treaty of Versailles and the loss of "the belief in God's Grace for Germany" (Dinesen 1979: 119).[28]

One can draw a straight line from Dinesen's observations on German exertions of a "will to power" to her discussion of propaganda and the dismal state of the arts in the Third Reich. Without any connection to the divine (or metaphysical realm) there can be no art, according to the Danish writer. Art in the service of a nation and a political agenda is only propaganda. The chronicle concludes with a description of a visit to the Nazi film studio UFA-Stadt by Babelsberg, where a production of *Maria Stuart* is being filmed. Other than the opportunity to meet the famous Swedish actress Zarah Leander (1907–81), a leading film star for UFA until 1943, Dinesen experiences the spectacle of the German film industry under the Third Reich as "Dante's Hell, above earth" (Dinesen 1979: 122).[29]

The fourth and final chronicle from Berlin, "The Stage" ("Skuepladser") was written after Dinesen returned from Germany to Denmark. In a May 1940 letter to her attorney, Dinesen states that she had lost all enthusiasm for the project and that she no longer wished to write about the Third Reich.[30] This last chronicle, written in occupied Denmark, is no less critical of Hitler's Germany. In "The Stage," Blixen makes an effort to continue the discussion from the third chronicle concerning propaganda and the arts in the Third Reich. It is a disparagingly critical review of the state of the arts; according to Dinesen, the visitor to Berlin finds neither a dramatic production nor a musical performance that meets sophisticated standards. Nazi Germany can neither produce a proper *King Lear* nor an elevated Beethoven's Fifth Symphony. Dinesen offers opinions on the cultural life of Nazi Germany, such as the following:

> The Germans indeed appropriate foreign classical art in their own way, like a great power; and a stranger from a little country who sits and listens to them while they talk about the matter can feel a bit ill at ease. Shakespeare, they say, is in reality Germanic by virtue of his mighty humanity; Shaw is Germanic in his clear understanding of the problems; Ibsen is Germanic in his search for truth and bitter idealism. . . . Hans Christian Andersen is invited in, for he is of course German in his spirit; Søren Kierkegaard is the same because of the depth of his mind. (Dinesen 1979: 130)[31]

Dinesen's observations about the cultural life in the Third Reich are sharply ironic in such passages. The text makes clear that the Third Reich is no place for true artistry and that the imperialistic ideology of the aggressive New Germany will ultimately crush indigenous artistic and literary legacies of smaller nations, such as Denmark and Norway. Also noteworthy in the fourth chronicle about the theatrical arts is Dinesen's provocative discussion of the performance of Georg Büchner's tragedy, *Dantons Tod* (The death of Danton), in which she evokes other "revolutionary times." As earlier in the essay, Dinesen maps her depiction of the Nazi Reich onto an earlier historical epoch and location—in this instance she evokes the bloody French revolution with its Reign of Terror. Dinesen's observation about the drama's three main characters, the "triumvirate of the classical revolution—Robespierre, Danton, Marat" (Dinesen 1979: 132)[32] seems to allude to the impending downfall of the current "revolutionary" leaders of the Third Reich and their very own reign of terror: Hitler, Goebbels, and Himmler come to mind.[33]

"Letters from a Land at War" reveals Dinesen's sharp eye for the essential characteristics of National Socialism: its life-negating discipline, inherent sterility, racism, and self-destructive momentum—the essay concludes by suggesting that conflicting worldviews and warfare are perhaps an inevitable aspect of human civilizations. On this level, Dinesen's essay (think of her conversations with the Nazi bureaucrats about the will, about joy and strength) can be understood as the juxtaposition of the values of one culture (a small, neutral nation), against those of another (the aggressive imperialist). Rather than offer despicable representations of the Nazi Germans as "mentally ill" subhumans (such as they are represented by Sigrid Undset in *Return to the Future*), Dinesen paints her German conversation partners as human adversaries, albeit often unthinking bureaucrats and zealots, with whom she engages in a civilized duel of words. In "Letters from a Land at War," Dinesen does not depict Hitler's Germany as populated by heinous monsters but rather by banal bureaucrats and uncritical zealots who are following "the leader." What would Hannah Arendt have thought of Dinesen's characterization of the Nazi German mentality that ultimately led to such crimes against humanity? It seems that Dinesen's representation of Berlin's unthinking and zealous bureaucrats corroborates Arendt's famous notion of the "banality of evil," coined in her reporting for the *New Yorker* on the Adolf Eichmann trial in Jerusalem (Arendt 1963).

Postwar Memory: Authorship and Legacy

On 4 June 1945, in the month after the liberation and the lifting of censorship, Karen Blixen wrote joyfully to her esteemed British publisher Constant Huntington (the father-in-law of the celebrated English major Brian Urquhart), with the following words: "What happiness it is to see English uniforms in the streets and on the roads, instead of German—no, I believe one must have been through these five years really to understand it, and it will be too long to begin to tell you about it" (Blixen 1996: 422–23 [my translation]). It ought to be noted that Dinesen's perspective on the blind fanaticism of Nazism in Germany, which she formulated in her essay, is expressed succinctly in a private letter of May 1946 to her sister Ellen Dahl. Her personal reflections on Nazism are quite consistent with the views expressed in "Letters from a Land at War"; at the same time, they are explicitly critical of the Nazi regime. In 1946, Dinesen describes Nazism as "a fanatic and consciously subjective view of life" and states that humanity has never before witnessed such a fanatic view "practiced with greater cruelty" or "tolerated with less resistance, than has occurred during the Nazi-period in Germany" (Blixen 1996: 445 [my translation]).[34] Postwar, Dinesen attempts to describe the *væsensforskel* (essential difference) between Nazi criminals and ordinary "gangsters." The difference lies, she proposes, in the adherence to a quasi-religious or fanatic ideology that organizes and justifies the crimes of a totalitarian state. Further, Dinesen argues that the conditions that made possible the hegemony of Nazism in Germany are the same as those that have preceded other "states of emergency" historically and in our own day, namely: "An idea or a principle, which is proselytized or held as absolute and holy in and of itself, with the determination that this idea or this principle ought to, and must be, carried through" (Blixen 1996: 445 [my translation]).[35] Thus, the implicit or "cloaked" critique of Nazi Germany, which is evident in the chronicles of 1940, shifts to a direct condemnation of such a "fanatic and consciously subjective view of life" in her postwar letter.

Nevertheless, the brutal realities and complexities of World War II perhaps do not fit neatly within aesthetic vision of Dinesen's literary fiction. Her representations of the soldier or the "chivalrous enemy" are a far cry from plainclothes resistance members and citizens engaged in acts of civil disobedience who were motivated by political conscience and moral imperatives. The reality of foreign troops on Danish soil may have brought Isak Dinesen into a bind with regard to her aesthetic ideals and personal freedoms. Unlike Norway's Sigrid Undset, Dinesen was not ideologically committed at the outset of the war. Striving to keep her literary pursuits free from politics, Dinesen responded cautiously to the occupation by maintaining an apolitical or "neutral" aesthetic detachment, a position that she refined in her chronicles from Germany in early 1940. During the occupation, Dinesen continued to cultivate her artistic freedom under a cover of masks, pseudonyms, and constructed artistic persona. One thinks here of her parodic Gothic novel *The Angelic Avengers* (1946), published in 1944 at the height of German censorship in Denmark as *Gengældelsens veje*, under the pseudonym Pierre Andrézel. As an intellectual, Dinesen valued most highly the individual rights and freedoms that she knew could never exist under a totalitarian regime. Reflecting on the war in 1946, she wrote to her sister Ellen Dahl: "I feel as if I am the servant of words and ideas . . . for me, the repression of free thoughts and words is the final and fateful blackout" (Blixen 1996: 445 [my translation]).[36] Whereas some critics may have found lacking in published contributions an unequivocal condemnation of Nazi Germany, this chapter situates Dinesen's "Letters from a Land at War" as an astutely indirect denunciation of

Nazism and the conditions in Hitler's Germany, as experienced firsthand by the author in early 1940. Isak Dinesen was certainly no Nazi-German sympathizer, but neither was she any outspoken critic of Denmark's wartime collaborationist policies nor of the later German occupational regime. Nonetheless, it is beyond doubt that Dinesen recognized Hitler's Germany as a conformist, racist and doomed dictatorship and that she articulated her conviction in her postwar essay that the individual, the artist, and genuine art can never thrive under such repressive regimes.

Marianne Stecher-Hansen (PhD, University of California, Berkeley, 1990) is Professor of Danish and Scandinavian Studies at the University of Washington. She has authored *The Creative Dialectic in Karen Blixen's Essays: On Gender, Nazi Germany, and Colonial Desire* (2014), and the critical commentary for *Karen Blixen: Værker: Skygger paa Græsset—Essays* (2020), as well as edited *Danish Writers from the Reformation to Decadence 1550–1990* (2004) and *Twentieth-Century Danish Writers* (1999). She has also published *History Revisited: Fact and Fiction in Thorkild Hansen's Documentary Works* (1997).

Notes

This chapter is partially adapted from an article originally published in *Scandinavian Studies* 82(1) (spring 2010). Copyright 2010 by *Scandinavian Studies*. Used with permission of the University of Illinois Press.

1. Published originally in the *New Yorker*, 1968, as a review essay of Parmenia Miguel's *Titania: The Biography of Isak Dinesen*, and republished in Arendt, *Men in Dark Times* (New York: Harcourt, Brace and World, 1968).
2. My review of materials in the Karen Blixen archives at the Royal Danish Library reveals that in 1947 the author completed a typescript, titled "Breve fra et Land i Krig: Marts 1940," for publication in the Danish journal *Frie Ord* (Stecher-Hansen 2014: 110), but that this issue of the journal was never published.
3. "Jeg tror jo om Hitler, at han er i høj Grad genial—maaske virkelig, hvad man, i én Betydning kan kalde et Geni—ikke saa meget ved noget personligt Indhold som ved en aldeles mystisk Føling med Folket og Tiden."
4. "Det er underligt at tænke paa, at en enkelt Mands Væsen, ligesom en Magnet, der bliver ført henover en Samling Metalstykker, kan omgruppere og forvandle et Samfund" (Blixen 1965: 134).
5. "dette nye tyske væsen, er udelukkende emotionelt" (my translation).
6. I thank my colleague Kristian Næsby for drawing my attention to this interesting detail.
7. "I Virkeligheden havde jeg glemt at jeg havde skrevet dem" (Blixen 1965: 120).
8. "Jeg havde ingen Indsigt i Politik og ingen politisk flair. Men jeg var et ærligt Menneske, og maaske kunde ogsaa en fordomsfri Lægmands Optegnelser fra en politisk mægtig bevæget Tid engang i Fremtiden faa en Slags Interesse som document humain" (Blixen 1965: 119).

9. This claim is accurate, excepting the fourth letter titled "Skuepladser" (The stage), which Dinesen completed in May 1940 upon her return to Denmark, as I have demonstrated in previous scholarship (Stecher-Hansen 2010: 84–86).
10. "Maaske vil Læserne ogsaa finde at jeg har udtrykt mig urimelig snørklet hvor jeg kunde have talt lige ud. De maa da tage i Betragtning at Brevene er skrevet *inden* Besættelsen. Danmark var dengang endnu neutralt, og der var Hensyn at tage som siden fald bort" (Blixen 1965: 121).
11. "Hvis jeg havde været virkelig Journalist vilde jeg have modtaget Det Tredje Riges gentagne Tilbud om at se dets store Personligheder Ansigt til Ansigt. . . . En enkelt Gang svarede jeg ja, og sendte senere med en Undskyldning Afbud. Noget i Tanken maa have været mig i for høj Grad imod" (Blixen 1965: 121).
12. In the interview, "In Berlin traf ein: Karen v. Blixen-Finecke aus Kopenhagen," Dinesen is reported to have stated that "Ich habe das Bestmögliche getan, zu lesen, zu sehen, zu hören, zu begreifen! Das Verständnis muß kommen" (Brundbjerg 2000: 73) [my translation: I have done the best possible to read, to see, to hear, and to understand! The understanding must come].
13. "Han hørte til i den gamle Tid, og jeg har ikke truffet nogen anden Tysker, gennem hvem jeg saa stærkt har faaet Indtryk af, hvad Kejsertidens Tyskland var og stod for" (Blixen 1965: 122).
14. "ikke alene som en genial Feltherre og en tapper soldat, men fordi han var en saa *ridderlig Fjende*" (Blixen 1965: 122; emphasis added).
15. Paul von Lettow-Vorbeck returned from Africa to Germany in 1919 and participated in a failed coup d'état against the Social Democrats in 1920; as a result of participation in the coup, he was dismissed from military service. In 1928, he was elected to parliament; in August 1939, Paul von Lettow-Vorbeck was rehabilitated by Hitler and reappointed as general.
16. Dinesen's homage to Lettow-Vorbeck is informed by a laudatory article, "General von Lettow-Vorbeck," written by Ludvig Boell, in celebration of the general's seventieth birthday, published 20 March 1940, in *Völkischer Beobachter* (the daily newspaper of the Nazi Party 1923–45), during her visit to Bremen (Günter 1985: 71–72).
17. "mellem Gæsterne var Maleren, Professor Horn, som er Rudolph Hess' Svigerfader. Af Artighed mod mig talte det tyske Selskab engelsk, noget tilsvarende kunde ikke være hændt mig i England" (Blixen 1965: 127).
18. A Danish-speaking guide, Mrs. Hein from southern Schleswig, was assigned to accompany Karen Blixen daily during her entire stay in Berlin (Günter 1985: 69).
19. "Dens Mænd og Kvinder ligner alle hinanden—Troen lyser dem ud af Ansigtet, de er utrættelige, nidkære indtil Døden, uden Tvivl eller Tøven i Sjælen" (Blixen 1965: 132–33).
20. "Jeg fik aldrig rigtigt at vide, hvilke reelle Magtmidler, *Reichsfrauenbund* har i Baghaanden til at drive sin Vilje igennem i Tilfælde af, at der nægtes Lydighed. . . . Naar jeg spurgte, svarede de mig: 'Det sker aldrig'—og dette Svar var maaske i sig selv lige saa oplysende som nogen Forklaring" (Blixen 1965: 133–34).
21. "Det slog mig, at de Kvinder, der nu regerer hele den tyske Kvindelighed, er af en type, som inden Det Tredie Riges Komme kun har haft ringe Mulighed for at faa Magt" (Blixen 1965: 134).
22. "Det er et overmenneskeligt, et umenneskeligt Tempo. Dette er ikke en Vækst, det er en tour de force, og der er Angst et Sted, man ved ikke ret, om det er hos Tilskueren eller hos Bygmestrene" (Blixen 1965: 135).
23. "Ordet Islam betyder *Hengivelse*, det er vel det samme, som det Tredje Rige udtrykker i sin Haandsopsrækning: Din i Liv og Død" (Blixen 1965: 137).
24. "Halvmaanen er et ædlere Tegn end Hagekorset" (Blixen 1965: 137).

25. "Men Islam var en Tro paa gud. Den kunde baade give og tage, af al sin Magt, den vilde frelse hele Verden, hvis Verden vilde tage imod den" (Blixen 1965: 139).
26. "En Racedyrkelse løber tilbage i sig selv, og selve dens Sejrsgang bliver en circulus vitiosus. D e kan ikke give og ikke tage imod . . . tiltrods for de store Fremtidshaab der holdes op her, er der da kun et kort Perspektiv i Nazismens Vista. . . . Et Folk, eller en Masse i et Folk, har rejst sig paa ny, overraskende og forfærdende Maade, det staar imod Himlen med monumental Kraft, det kaster en vældig Skygge foran sig, og ingen af os ved, hvor langt denne Skygge vil naa at falde, eller over hvem af os. Og dog, tænker Beskueren, er det tilsidst sig selv, som dette Folk staar i Lyset" (Blixen 1965: 140).
27. "De unge Tyskere fik saa godt som altid det sidste Ord, naar vi talte sammen. For hvor klart de end fremsatte deres Argumenter, saa var der bestandig noget deri, hvortil jeg matte svare: 'Det kan vi andre ikke forstaa.' De sagde da: 'Men det vil De komme til at forstaa. Vi skal bevise det for Verden.' Forskellen imellem os laa meget dybt, naar vi kom langt nok ind i en Debat, stødte vi paa den" (Blixen 1965: 144–45).
28. "'Tillid til Guds Naade, som man kalder Humor" and "Troen paa Guds Naade for Tyskland" (Blixen 1965: 148).
29. "Dantes Helvede, ovenpaa Jorden" (Blixen 1965: 151).
30. Karen Blixen's letter to her lawyer Erik Petri, dated 30 May 1940, published with her collected letters (Blixen 1996: 322–23), in which she states that the last chronicle was written after her return to Denmark and after "decisive events" of 9 April had taken place.
31. "Tyskerne tilegner sig dog Udlandets klassiske Kunst paa deres egen Maner, paa Stormagtsmaner, og den Fremmede af en lille Nation, som sidder og hører til, mens de taler om den, kan nok blive lidt beklemt tilmode.—Shakespeare, siger de, er i Virkeligheden Germaner i Kraft af sin vældige Menneskelighed, Shaw er Germaner i sin klare Sans for Problemerne, Ibsen er Germaner i sin Sandhedssøgen og beske Idealisme . . . H. C. Andersen bliver budt indenfor, han er jo tysk gennem sit Gemyt, Søren Kierkegaard er det gennem sit Sinds Dybe" (Blixen 1965: 158–59).
32. "Af det klassiske Revolutions-Triumvirat: Robespierre, Danton, Marat" (Blixen 1965: 161).
33. I acknowledge and thank Julius Rodriguez, master's student in Germanics at the University of Washington, for this insightful interpretation.
34. "Menneskeheden aldrig har set et fanatisk og bevidst subjektivt Livssyn praktiseret med større Grumhed, eller taalt med ringere Modstand, end det er sket under Nazi-tiden i Tyskland" (Blixen 1996: 445).
35. "En Idé eller et Princip, der forkyndes and hævdes som absolut og i sig selv hellig, med Beslutningen om, at denne Idé eller dette Princip bør og skal føres igennem" (Blixen 1996: 446).
36. "Jeg føler mig som Tankens og Ordets Tjener . . . for mig er den Fri Tankes og det fri Ords Undertrykkelse den endelige og skæbnesvangre Mørklægning" (Blixen 1996: 446).

References

Allen, Julie. 2012. "Tea with Goebbels and Hitler: Asta Nielsen in Nazi Germany." *Journal of Scandinavian Cinema* 2(3): 333–41.

Arendt, Hannah. 1958. *The Human Condition*. Chicago: University of Chicago Press.

———. 1963. *Eichmann in Jerusalem: A Report on the Banality of Evil*. New York: Viking Press.

———. 1968. "Isak Dinesen, 1885–1963 [sic]." In *Men in Dark Times*. New York: Harcourt, Brace and World.
———. 1979. "Isak Dinesen, 1885–1962." In *Daguerreotypes and Other Essays*, vii–xxv. Chicago: University of Chicago Press.
Assmann, Aleida. 2010. "The Dynamics of Cultural Memory between Remembering and Forgetting." In *A Companion to Cultural Memory Studies*, edited by Astrid Erll and Ansgar Nünning, 97–107. Berlin: De Gruyter.
———. 2011. *Cultural Memory and Western Civilization: Functions, Media, Archives*. Cambridge: Cambridge University Press.
Behrendt, Poul. 2013. "En skæbneanekdote fra *Berliner Illustrierte*: Omkring *Vinter-Eventyrs* udgivelse og udslettelse i Hitler-Tyskland." *Danske Studier*: 138–82.
Blixen, Karen. 1944. *Gengældelsens Veje*, as Pierre Andrézel. Copenhagen: Gyldendal.
———. 1965. "Breve fra et Land i Krig." In *Essays*, 118–66. Copenhagen: Gyldendal.
———. 1996. *Karen Blixen i Danmark: Breve 1931–1962*. Edited by Frans Lasson and Tom Engelbrecht. Vol. 1. Copenhagen: Gyldendal.
Brundbjerg, Else. 2000. *Samtaler med Karen Blixen*. Copenhagen: Gyldendal.
Daugbjerg, Søren. 2011. *Kaj Munk and Germany—Theater and Politics*. Translated by Brian Young. Port Townsend, WA: New Nordic Press.
Dinesen, Isak. 1961. *Shadows on the Grass*. New York: Random House.
———. 1979. "Letters from a Land at War." In *Daguerreotypes and Other Essays*, translated by P. M. Mitchell and W. D. Paden, 88–137. Chicago: University of Chicago Press.
———. 1986 (1946). *The Angelic Avengers*, as Pierre Andrézel. New York: Penguin Books.
Günter, Martin. 1985. "Karen Blixen i Hitlers Berlin." *Cras: Tidsskrift for kunst og kultur* 42: 57–72.
Langbaum, Robert Woodrow. 1964. *Isak Dinesen's Art: The Gayety of Vision*. New York: Random House.
Lefebvre, Catherine. 2016. "Accidental Tourists: Some Thoughts on Blixen, Arendt, and Disobedience." *Scandinavica* 55(1): 100–105.
Lubrich, Oliver, ed. 2010. *Travels in the Reich 1933–1945: Foreign Authors Report from Germany*. Translated by Kenneth Northcott, Sonia Wichmann, and Dean Krouk. Chicago: University of Chicago Press.
Migel, Parmenia. 1987. *Tania: A Biography and Memoir of Isak Dinesen*. First published as *Titania*, 1967. New York: McGraw-Hill Books.
Stecher-Hansen, Marianne. 2010. "Soldier's Daughter: Karen Blixen on Nazism—*Breve fra et Land i Krig*." *Scandinavian Studies* 82 (1): 53–94.
———. 2014. *The Creative Dialectic in Karen Blixen's Essays: On Gender, Nazi Germany and Colonial Desire*. Copenhagen: Museum Tusculanum Press.
———. 2020. "Efterskrift: Erindringsfortællinger og Essayistik." *Karen Blixen Værker—Skygger paa Græsset & Essays*, 515–92. Copenhagen: DSL/Gyldendal.
Thurman, Judith. 1982. *Isak Dinesen: The Life of a Storyteller*. New York: St. Martin's Press.
Wilkinson, Lynn R. 2004. "Hannah Arendt on Isak Dinesen: Between Storytelling and Theory." *Comparative Literature* 56 (1): 77–98.

Chapter 8

SIGRID UNDSET'S PROBLEMATIC PROPAGANDA
The Call for Democracy in *Return to the Future*

Christine Hamm

At the time of World War II and Norway's occupation on 9 April 1940, Sigrid Undset was the most internationally celebrated Norwegian author besides Henrik Ibsen. Undset had been honored for her historical novels set in medieval Norway—*Kristin Lavransdatter* (1920–22) and *Olav Audunssøn* (1925–27)—with a Nobel Prize for Literature, and her fiction was widely read in North America, Scandinavia, and German-speaking countries. In addition, Undset was a sharp critic of Norwegian social life, and she published extensively in Norwegian newspapers. During the 1930s, she had written many articles against Nazi Germany, criticizing, for instance, the treatment of disabled children and warning against the dangers of Nazi ideology.[1] As an outspoken intellectual and Nobel Laureate, Sigrid Undset was a "person of interest" to the occupying German forces. In the spring of 1940, Undset feared that the Wehrmacht would press her to give talks or readings on the radio and that she might be forced to collaborate with Hitler's Germany in this manner. Therefore, it became necessary for her to flee occupied Norway.

One of the few books Sigrid Undset wrote after her exile carries the striking title *Return to the Future*. What does it mean? What is "the future" and from where is one supposed to return to it? The book, which was first published in 1942 in the United States by Alfred A. Knopf (in an English translation), and later in Norwegian as *Tilbake til fremtiden* (1945), contains Undset's personal memoir of her escape in April 1940 and her long journey eastward to reach the United States in August of the same year. The structure of this "memoir" follows the escape route the author took from Lillehammer through northern Norway, and then through Sweden, Russia, and Japan. The first four of the five chapters are titled accordingly, "Norway, Spring 1940," "Sweden, Summer 1940," "Fourteen Days in Russia" and "Japan en passant," as they each describe the situation in these countries at the time and render Undset's impressions. In the last chapter, titled "Return to the Future," Undset has finally arrived in San Francisco, crossed the States, and settled down in Brooklyn, New York. As it becomes clear, the future is however not America; for Undset, the future is a reborn, democratically governed Europe. The "return" will come when the occupied countries that have been put to ashes by the totalitarian German and Russian regimes rise up again in the future.

This chapter argues that Undset's personal memoir about her journey from Norway to America is a clever piece of Allied propaganda. Undset wants her American audience to fight Germany and the Axis Powers and free her country.[2] She produces a picture of Norwegians that will appeal to Americans, alongside an enemy representation of Germans that will galvanize Allied sympathies. Fueled by the sorrow of her personal loss and her hatred toward the Nazi Germans and Soviet Russians, she appeals to the Allies to defeat the totalitarian regimes, partly using her enemies' own rhetoric against them. She ironically contests the Nationalist Socialist ideology of "Blood and Soil" and argues that the Norwegians, contrary to the Germans, have a right to own their country because they have tilled the soil and fished the seas for centuries. She also shuns Hitler's ideas of the Germanic "master race," depicting the Nordic people as fundamentally different from the Germans and, ironically, as morally and physically superior to any so-called "Aryan race." Arguing from an essentialist position, Undset mimics the propaganda of the totalitarian regimes, which she attacks and draws appalling pictures of the Nazi Germans, Soviet Russians, and Imperial Japanese. Undset concludes *Return to the Future* by casting doubt on the idea that these countries will ever become democratic and peace-loving nations. Thus, Undset's explicit agitation for freedom and democracy is heavily undermined by her own hatred toward the Axis powers, which the Atlantic charter wants to destroy. As a propaganda narrative in the service of the Allied cause, *Return to the Future* is both energized and undermined by the author's passionate emotional engagement. The uncomfortable complexity of this piece of writing explains why the book has received very little academic interest since the war.

Considering the historical situation in 1941, Undset's appeal to American citizens to support the fight for a free Europe and underlying hatred toward Nazi Germany are understandable. As stated in the preface to the Norwegian edition *Tilbake til fremtiden*, which was published in Norway after the liberation in 1945, Undset wrote most of the text in the summer and fall of 1941, at the point in time when Nazi troops had massively invaded Soviet Russia (Operation Barbarossa in late June 1941); England was suffering under German attacks from the Luftwaffe, and the United States had begun to consider its entry into World War II (which occurred on 8 December 1941, following the Japanese attack on Pearl Harbor). Months earlier in the spring and summer of 1941, Undset impatiently wanted the Americans to join the British forces, and she longed to see Norway again as a free country. In fact, Undset's text closely interacts with the negotiations between U.S. president Roosevelt and British prime minister Winston Churchill and their mutual plans for the Atlantic region after the war. A major goal of Undset is to ensure a place for Norway in the future North Atlantic association.

A statement dealing with the goals of the Allied forces for the postwar world was pronounced on 14 August 1941 in Placentia Bay, Newfoundland, and called "The Atlantic Charter." *Return to the Future* questions whether it will be possible to realize the goals of the charter. Will the Allied nations (Great Britain, France and, later, United States, and Soviet Union) fighting the Axis powers (Germany, Japan, and Italy) ever be able to establish freedom and democracy again? Will they be able to prevent the wish for territorial gains and to work for a world free of fear? The first page of Undset's final chapter, titled "Return to the Future," contains a clear call for the work for democracy. After the Americans have helped to defeat Nazi Germany, Undset argues that it will be necessary to assist the defeated populations:

> [R]ebuild health in nations where millions of people have been destroyed by undernourishment and naked starvation, by hatred and by abnormal living conditions, by inhuman and nerve-shattering experiences—where a generation of children has had the worst imaginable conditions in which to grow up during their formative years. (Undset 1942: 208)[3]

It is Undset's explicit goal to support the strategies of the Allied forces in the West in order to build up again what she calls a "healthy" Europe. At the same time, Undset clearly understands that the suffering in the occupied European countries will produce hatred against Germany and that it will be a real challenge to get the European nations to live peacefully together again.

Undset's focus on the next generation is hardly surprising considering that she had been dealing all her life with questions concerning children's education and upbringing (Hamm 2013). The cultural role she gives to family life is visible throughout her entire authorship. In the famous speech on the Fourth Commandment, held for students in Trondheim in 1914, Undset argues for the rights of children, among these the right to inherit a culture from their parents. Only if parents live in such a way that children can grow up respecting them will they become good citizens as well as good human beings (Undset

Figure 8.1. Sigrid Undset was determined to inform the American public about Norway's fierce fight for democracy. During five years in exile in the United States, 1940–45, Undset gave numerous lectures and press interviews. In her own words, she was a "propaganda soldier." Unknown photographer in the United States. Courtesy of Bjerkebæk, Lillehammer museum.

2004a: 122–45). During the war, however, Undset was forced to witness a generation of children growing up without the benefit of cultural traditions.

Undset pursues two explicit goals when writing *Return to the Future*: to urge the United States to join the Allied cause in Europe, and to ensure Norway a place in the North Atlantic alliance. Her approach is strategic, since her goals were not as easy to achieve as it might seem today. As Undset discovered upon her arrival in San Francisco on 26 August 1940, the image of Norway at that time was not favorable (Skouen 1982: 38). In fact, most Americans believed that the Norwegians had surrendered quickly to the German occupying forces, without any resistance. This image had been produced by an American foreign correspondent named Leland Stowe, who happened to be in Oslo on the infamous date of 9 April 1940. However, it soon became clear to Undset that Stowe did not speak Norwegian and had little idea about what had really gone on around him, since he had spent most of 9 April in the basement of the American Embassy.

Naturally, Stowe's misinformed reports were especially hurtful to Undset, since her eldest son Anders had been killed in battle during the first weeks of the German invasion while desperately trying to defend Lillehammer with little weaponry. As biographer Sigrun Slapgard has documented, Undset was so provoked by Stowe's inaccurate reporting that she approached her publisher Alfred A. Knopf to inquire how she might rectify the reporting on Norway's resistance. Knopf urged her to write a book in order to "render the facts and tell about her own escape and experience" (Slapgard 2007: 448).[4] In fact, during her stay in the United States, Sigrid Undset considered herself a "propaganda soldier" (Slapgard 2010: 29), fighting for Norway's cause by giving talks (mostly at universities and Scandinavian association meetings, but also speaking for radio broadcasts on WNYC in Manhattan), giving press interviews, and writing articles as well as her memoir about the escape from Norway.[5] In *Return to the Future*, however, Undset not only tried to render a true picture of the German invasion and Norwegian resistance to her American readers but also produced a narrative that argues for the necessity of fighting all forms of totalitarianism without mercy. The author accomplishes this by turning the ideological propaganda of totalitarian regimes against them, using both irony, parody, and inversion as rhetorical devices. The following analysis will demonstrate Undset's subversive narrative strategy.

A Norwegian National Romantic Narrative in the Melodramatic Mode

The first chapter of Undset's memoir ("Norway, Spring 1940") opens with a national romantic perspective on the symbiotic relationship between the

Norwegian landscape and the Norwegian people. The author maintains that the Norwegians are peace-loving because they had to concentrate for centuries on clearing their land of stones. Invoking Ivar Aasen's famous poem "Nordmannen" (The Norwegian),[6] she informs her American readers that the Norwegians were so busy working their soil, which was covered with rocks and stone, that they had no time for war and did not dream of gaining more territory. Drawing on the idea of a nation's essential soul as produced by history and culture, Undset consciously counters the biologically based racism of Nazi ideology. According to Undset's argumentation, Norwegians were not born "strong and morally superior" but had become so over the centuries due to the farmers' and fishermen's struggle for life in harsh natural surroundings.[7] Contesting the blood-and-soil ideology of the German Nationalist Socialists in this way, Undset claims that the Norwegians "earned" their country, and therefore the Germans had no right to it whatsoever. Furthermore, the Norwegians were ready to defend their Norway—even at impossible odds:

> We Norwegians had become a peaceful people. . . . And we are only about three million people—about as many as live in Brooklyn—to work and administer this country from which it is so difficult and heavy a task to win a living. (Undset 1942: 5–6)[8]

Undset continues by recounting that three million Norwegian citizens were taken by surprise when Germany occupied the country on 9 April 1940. She describes in detail how she spent the morning of 7 April in Oslo, giving a speech to Norwegian students, and later attending the theater and a dinner. She recalls how her Finnish foster children (child war refugees from the Winter War in Finland) awaited her upon her return to Lillehammer. Finally, she mentions how quickly her own son Anders decided that he has to defend his country, although it seemed quite hopeless, and that her younger son Hans joined the medical corps by bicycle. In this way Undset initially employs the genre of the memoir in order to establish herself as a reliable narrator as well as a kind and engaging person.

Undset's narrative strategy in the first chapter of *Return to the Future* is a mixture of the memoir with an essentialist depiction of a hardworking and peace-loving people formed by the harsh and beautiful nature and climate of Norway. However, at closer inspection, Undset's admirable picture of the Norwegian people as healthy and morally superior may strike the modern reader as exaggerated and even ridiculous. For instance, *all* Germans in Undset's book only think of enriching themselves during their stay in Norway, and *all* Norwegians are helpful and understanding. Using a melodramatic mode of excess, Undset appeals to her readers' emotions and turns her descriptions of various people into a simple, dramatic contrast between good and evil.

In *Return to the Future*, Norwegians are generally depicted as self-controlled, well-behaved, and kind, and Undset portrays the entire country as if it were one living and breathing body. At one point, Undset is transported by a little sailing ship from Åndalsnes heading for Narvik. She stresses the community between Norwegians by telling about their almost wordless attunement: although the little group of refugees has no leader, they seemingly always decide what to do together ("[W]e kept far out to sea, and in the early morning we lay in at the harbor of the farthermost lighthouse" [Undset 1942: 42]).[9] In a subtle way, Undset creates the impression that she is participating in steering the boat, since she talks about the way of sailing in such a familiar and competent way. When it turns out that the group of refugees cannot pursue their journey by boat because it is too dangerous to sail through the fjords farther north, they are helped to escape by ski. Due to her poor physical condition and her heavy body, Undset cannot perform the trip herself, so she is pulled on a sleigh to Sweden by a couple of young men. But she nevertheless manages to include herself in the picture of the typical Norwegian by repeatedly talking of "we Norwegians." And the Norwegians are portrayed not only as helpful, but also as smart, strong, and healthy.

In contrast to the healthy Norwegians, the Nazi German soldiers are described as ugly and physically unfit for battle, and wearing spectacles: "There were an unbelievable number of bowlegged, narrow-shouldered, flat-footed individuals, with broad, dropping bottoms . . . it naturally seemed very remarkable that so many wore glasses." In Norway, Undset claims, one hardly sees younger people with spectacles (Undset 1942: 78).[10] Obviously parodying the Nationalist Socialist propaganda of the Germanic race's "magnificent physique" (Undset 1942: 78), Undset depicts the Norwegian people as physically fit and morally superior, thus distinguishing them from the "ugly" German soldiers whose self-proclaimed superiority as a "master race" (*Herrensfolk*) is ridiculed.

In the second chapter ("Sweden, Summer 1940"), Undset relates how she is forced to wait in Stockholm for her son Hans after having successfully escaped Norway. Finally united, mother and son must accept that Norway is an occupied country, and that they must find a way to reach the United States, which had earlier extended an invitation to the author. Staying with her Swedish colleague, the writer Alice Lyttkens, Undset observes that all her Swedish friends are resolutely against the Nazis. Neutral Sweden was reluctant to accept a transit agreement with Germany, which allows German soldiers to travel by rail through Sweden to occupied Norway or to the Finnish front. Further, most of the Swedish population lives in a state of uneasiness, Undset claims, because they cannot feel safe from attack by the great warring powers, either by the USSR or by Nazi Germany. Although she considers Sweden among the democratic nations, Undset nevertheless cannot refrain from criticizing Sweden's wish to remain neutral, and expresses scorn for the childish effort to seek revenge on the Germans by allowing their houses to remain unpainted as a passive act of protest.

Totalitarian Russia and Japan: Travelogue and Trauma

Whereas the opening chapters on Norway and Sweden draw on Undset's cultural authority and her own personal experience of the invasion, the text changes tact in her effort to give a picture of Russia and Japan in chapters 3 and 4. Employing the genre of travelogue, these chapters are characterized by Undset's effort to render her impressions of foreign countries from the position of an outsider. Undset claims that she first was curious when entering the Soviet Union, since so many of her young fellow countrymen and colleagues had hailed communist Russia in the 1920s. In *Return to the Future*, Undset stages the meeting with communism by giving the role of the naïve and admiring Norwegian to her twenty-year-old son Hans, who soon discovers that Russia is not any utopia and that it is far from the dreams of Western writers and intellectuals. According to Undset, Hans soon realizes that the Russian revolutionary experiment has misfired. In the end, he is totally disillusioned.

Undset's narrative about her journey through Russia is strongly influenced by the historical fact that the Soviet Union, during the weeks she traversed it in the summer of 1940, was still in alliance with the Axis powers (the Nazi-Soviet Pact had been signed 23 August 1939); Undset was traveling through enemy territory. Furthermore, Stalin's Russia was already seen as an archenemy to Scandinavians because of the Soviet offensive into Finland in late November 1939, which initiated the Winter War and, consequently, the Continuation War. The violation of Finnish territory by the USSR was a traumatic experience for most Scandinavians.[11] Undset was among those Scandinavian citizens who offered to host Finnish child war refugees (the so-called *krigsbarn*) in order to protect the younger generation from the Russian military offensives in Finland. Of course, Undset could not forget this reality when traveling though Stalin's Russia.

Undset's resentment toward Stalinism is evident in her descriptions of Moscow. For instance, she describes how people are housed in very tight spaces, often sharing beds with others while working shifts in the many factories. Moscow is dusty and stinks, the buildings are crumbling, and no one takes away the garbage. The toilets in the yards are without proper plumbing and sanitation. Undset sees no shops offering goods, and the people are mostly occupied by walking. Page after page, Undset focuses on the poor living standard in the Soviet Union, creating a questionable picture of a communist country with which the Americans—by the time of the publication of *Return to the Future* in 1942—had joined into alliance (in December 1941, i.e. after the bombing of Pearl Harbor, when the United States joined the Allies, which included the USSR). Undset consciously renders her impressions of a nation that does not know, and even does not care, about the dangers of not cleaning themselves and their surroundings. Reading Undset's memoir in 1942, Americans must have felt the need to distance themselves immediately from Soviet Russia and the Russian peoples.

Further, Undset's description again bears open characteristics of an essentialist argumentation about a people founded on culture and political system. Supporting a totalitarian regime, Undset's argument goes, the Russians are giving up their individuality and their freedom, and, as a consequence, they are no longer able to think by themselves and take care of themselves. Communism stresses the collective to such a degree that it kills every individual impulse. Undset recounts that she imagines when walking with others in the streets in Moscow that people may be "infected" by the bacillus of this communist suppression. In other words, she depicts communism as a disease:

> Still Hans and I had ample time to wander about in Moscow. And I imagined, I could feel, there is something hypnotic in collective life, one loses oneself in a way when one moves with a stream of totally strange people with whom one cannot talk, whose faces tell one absolutely nothing. (Undset 1942: 96)[12]

Undset points to the danger of being hypnotized by collectivism and stresses the possibility of becoming immune to it. In this, she obviously plays on American fears of Communism as spreading and infecting the European democracies.

Thus, in *Return to the Future*, Soviet Russia is generally presented as a backward state lacking in economic and social development and falling hopelessly behind the Western democratic nations. While some outsiders might expect progress after the Bolshevik Revolution and greater civil rights, Undset sees people in Russia as behind the times, holding onto ideas that the Western democracies had left behind in the nineteenth century. In other words, for Undset, Soviet Russia is no better prepared for the future than Germany. Obviously, Undset intends to warn her American readers against seeing Russia as a political ally, even though the USSR has joined the Allied forces and opposes Nazi Germany as the enemy.

Considering her American audience, Undset concentrates on emphasizing the differences between Norwegians and Russians. However, her effort to draw out the differences between citizens of democratic countries and citizens living under totalitarian regimes occasionally seems comical. For instance, Undset's scorn for communist propaganda and its effects becomes obvious when she describes the cows in the Russian countryside, which she observes from her train window: "[t]he Russian cows seemed to be collectively inclined—they always walked or stood packed together in a tight cluster. . . . I never saw a Russian cow behave like our individualistic ones . . . (Undset 1942: 118).[13] Undset's observations become absurd, revealing her deep-seated hatred for Stalin's Soviet Union.

The wartime impressions of Imperial Japan are less emotionally targeted. When Undset and her son Hans arrive in Japan, she soon becomes aware of the fact that the Japanese still support patriarchy. Undset is totally ignored by Japanese tour guides who only talk to her young son Hans, even when she is the one who asks the competent questions. Undset therefore gives up on the effort to talk to the guides and keeps quiet, always holding herself behind her son, as she comments in ironic despair: "So I did as the Japanese women do: followed the male head of my family at a respectful distance and in silence" (Undset 1942: 179).[14] At the same time, she is surprised that the living standard is much higher in Japan than in Russia, in spite of the ongoing war in China.

Most importantly, though, the chapter on Japan gives Undset the opportunity to reflect on the influence of Christianity on the development of Western democracies. Part of what she finds is the absence of a belief in Jesus Christ and Christian solidarity of all humans. On the other hand, Christianity only supports democracy in those countries where the will to freedom has been traditionally strong, such as in the region of the North Atlantic; Undset claims, "It was the peoples along the coast of the Atlantic Ocean who, first and foremost, had this longing for freedom, this determination to make the community more spacious and build it on an increasingly reciprocal basis" (Undset 1942: 193–94).[15] But the democracies have also been unbelievably naïve in thinking that all other countries would be glad if their inhabitants also would be free. The wish for freedom is not found everywhere, claims Undset in *Return to the Future*. Countries formerly colonized by the British and French, for instance, have reacted against being invaded and occupied, even in cases when the inhabitants ultimately experienced more freedom than they had before the Western colonization.

Without the harsh prejudice that characterizes the observations on Soviet Russia, Undset criticizes Japan for its imperial regime. She has heard about the Japanese fear of the police, and of the many victims of the war in China. The citizens of wartime Japan are suffering and very poor, even if their houses look better than the houses in Soviet Russia. Nevertheless, it seems as if Japan has a potential for Undset; she claims that under the influence of Western ideology, this cultivated nation would be able to produce democratic thinking by itself. Undset is not able to understand Russia due to her emotional relationship to the Soviet invasion of Finland, but she manages to appreciate imperialistic Japan, observing that the Japanese people share with the Norwegians a love for wood and flowers.

Hope and Despair: Undset's Essayistic Reflections on the Future for Democratic Europe

In the final chapter, "Return to the Future," Undset leaves behind both the genre of the memoir and the travelogue and adapts the style of a polemical essay, which pleads for a future for the Western democracies. She begins with a warning, quoting a Norwegian proverb: "Do not sell the hide before the bear has been shot" (Undset 1942: 207).[16] She warns of the danger in planning a new democratic future for Germany. According to Undset's polemic, German history has shown that the Germans are unable to live peacefully together with other nations. Of course, she knows that the "work of rebuilding a society of free nations and free human beings" (Undset 1942: 210)[17] will be difficult because Hitler's Germany has produced so much hatred in other countries. Hatred is a sterile emotion, and it will threaten the project of rebuilding Europe from the ashes of war, observes Undset. What is needed is a better understanding of the German "soul," she claims, suggesting that a soul might be understood and may be treated, psychoanalytically: "We conceive of the souls of nations as individuals, personalities" (Undset 1942: 218).[18] However, her description of the German soul then becomes itself heavily influenced by her own hatred toward the Germans. Using the vile Nazi rhetoric about the Jewish people against the Germans themselves, Undset describes the German people as essentially psychically crippled, as psychopaths.[19] In the same way as the Nazis "diagnosed" Jews as sharing certain psychic traits, Undset diagnoses Germans as generally loving servitude. Undset ventures that the German soul suffers from a sadomasochist longing for a dictator to deify and serve:

> No single note in the ingenious play upon the deepest strings of the German people's souls which Adolf Hitler has carried on is more ingenious than precisely this: that he has demanded to be worshipped as a godlike being. Thereby he met a German need since time immemorial, a need which was already the chief motif in the German medieval poems about the Niebelungs' tragic fate, the yearning for an unconditional subjection under a master. (Undset 1942: 222)[20]

Because the German psyche is dominated by the wish to be suppressed, Hitler could win the masses for his cause. At his point in the polemic, Undset's argumentation transitions from an essentialist perspective, based on culture and landscape, to biological and psychical essentialism. When it comes to Germany, she no longer attempts to explain the people's soul as based on the political system and their culture in combination with the natural surroundings, but "diagnoses" the fundamental character traits that make the Germans embrace certain political regimes. Undset interprets German militarism as a kind of natural response to the German demand for keeping psychic chaos under control. Quoting her article on women and war written already in 1918 ("Kvinnene og krigen"), Undset claims that militarism becomes the uniform worn by a sick people: "I wonder if the German people do not need militarism as the lobster needs its shell—the hard exterior is an armor enclosing a soft, boneless body" (Undset 1942: 219).[21]

Motivated by her personal hatred toward the Nazis, Undset presents a despicable enemy representation to her American readers. Germany is a "sick" nation of the mentally ill, which Undset doubts will ever be cured. Adapting the propaganda devices of her enemies, Undset seeks to persuade her American readers to feel disgust and hatred by creating the appalling image of the German "lobster" crawling over everything in its way. Thus, although Undset explicitly recognizes hatred as the unfortunate outcome of the war, she herself evokes affects in her readers in order to engage them in the emotional battlefield.

In this final chapter, Undset also argues for universal ideas. Democracy is considered an absolute, which must be supported under all conditions, and a principle not to be compromised. Democracy needs to be fought for in any circumstance. This includes equal rights for all citizens, respect for the people and its government, and discussion as the only way to find solutions for all manner of problems (Undset 1942: 241). Undset surprisingly compares democratic thinking to a scientific method, in which one must patiently discover the best results. On the other hand, she observes that totalitarian regimes rely on fantasies and dreams, which are supported by quasi-scientific methods, such as Nazi Germany's false promise of a utopian society, which was supported by a racist ideology. For Undset, democracy is the future, and a return to the future goes through America: "Now it is only across America that the road leads back to the future—that which we from the European democracies call future" (Undset 1942, 203).[22] However, for Undset, America is not the future, but the route to it, back to Norway. And it is the Norwegians who are well prepared to rebuild Europe, if the reader trusts Undset: they are used to hard work, they never give up, as they have over centuries built and rebuilt homes in places ruined by forces of nature such as storms, heavy rains, and other challenges of the climate.

In summary, *Return to the Future* opens as a memoir about Undset's escape from Norway. However, underlying the surface of this wartime memoir and travelogue is a work of clever and subversive propaganda, published at a key moment of the war and aimed deliberately at American readers. Parodying and inverting the vicious propaganda of the German National Socialists, as well as that of the Soviet communists of her time, Undset counters the racist ideologies of her enemies with her own polemic based on a conception of culture. However, her effort to depict the Norwegians as morally superior to the "mentally ill" Nazi Germans as well as to the "hypnotized" Russian communists produces national caricatures, which in the eyes of modern readers might prove to be contraproductive to the Allied aims at rebuilding Europe. Absorbed by personal grief and desperation, Undset evokes feelings of hatred in order to reach her aim—American help for the British forces fighting against Germany. Ultimately, *Return to the Future* serves as problematic propaganda for the Allied project of working for democracy in Europe, because the author's own emotional investment in her cause tends to obfuscate the narrative.

Christine Hamm is Professor of Scandinavian Literature at the University of Bergen, Norway. Hamm's publications include monographs on compassion and melodrama in Amalie Skram's work (*Medlidenhet og melodrama*, 2006), and on Sigrid Undset's literary representation of parents (*Foreldre i det moderne*, 2013).

Notes

1. See, for instance, her comment on Ragnar Vold's critique of German ideology, published in *Morgenbladet* 15 December 1939 (Undset 2004b).
2. We know little about the contemporary reception of the book in America. On the basis of the letters Undset wrote to her sister Ragnhild in Stockholm, however, Björn Fontander claims that both *Return to the Future* and Undset's other memoir of the same year, *Happy Times in Norway*, which focuses on her children's life before the occupation, were loved by American readers (Fontander 1992: 166).
3. "Det blir å bygge op sundhet igjen i nasjoner, hvor millioner mennesker er blitt ødelagt av underernæring og naken sult, av hat og av abnorme levevilkår, av umenneskelige og nerveslitende oplevelser,—hvor en generasjon av barn har hatt de verst tenkelige forhold å leve op under i grunnleggende alder" (Undset 1945: 173).
4. ". . . fortelle med saklighet om de faktiske forhold, fortelle om sin egen flukt og erfaring."
5. Marie Maman gives an overview of Undset's activities in the United States (Maman 2000).
6. Ivar Aasen's poem "Nordmannen" is very famous since it is one of the most popular National songs of Norway "Mellom bakker og berg." The poem was printed in a final version in the third edition of Aasen's collection of poems, *Symra* (1875).
7. Note that such forms of cultural or social constructivism that characterize Undset's thinking must be criticized for being deterministic and leading to a problematic form of

national essentialism. The idea that a nation's climate, history, and culture necessarily lead to the development of specific "essential" character traits in the people parallels the idea that biological or racial characteristics determine a people's behavior. Applied to a discussion of national difference, critics ought to question Undset's underlying assumption that cultural specificity necessarily grounds national essence.

8. "Vi norske var blitt et fredelig folk. . . . Og vi er bare tre millioner mennesker—omtrent så mange som det bor i Brooklyn" (Undset 1945: 9).
9. "[V]i holdt langt ut til havs, og tidlig på dagen la vi inn i havnen ved et av de ytterste fyrtårn i leden" (Undset 1945: 40).
10. "Men mellem karene selv var det utrolig mange hjulbente, sidrumpede og bredrumpede, smalskuldrede, plattfotede individer. For nordmennene var det selvfølgelig særlig påfallende at så mange bar briller,—i Norge er det relativt ualmindelig å se folk under 45 med glassøine" (Undset 1945: 68).
11. Many former Norwegians communists stopped agitating for their cause when Soviet Russia showed its real face and invaded Finland. See, for instance, Vidar Sandbeck's description of his communist father in *Far* (1984), who is devastated by learning of the Finnish war.
12. "Likevel fikk da Hans og jeg rikelig med tid til å vandre rundt i Moskva. Og jeg innbilte mig, jeg kunde føle, det er noe hypnotiserende i kollektivt liv—en taper sig selv på en måte, når en driver slik med strømmen av vilt fremmede mennesker som en ikke kan snakke med, hvis ansikter absolutt ingenting sier en" (Undset 1945: 81–82).
13. ". . . kuene i Russland [lot] til å være kollektivt innstillet,—alltid gikk eller stod de, pakket sammen i tett klynge. . . . Aldri så jeg en russisk ku opføre sig som våre individualistiske" (Undset 1945: 101).
14. "Så gjorde jeg som de japanske kvinnene og fulgte efter mannfolket mitt i ærbødig avstand og taushet" (Undset 1945: 150).
15. "Det var folkene langs Atlanterhavskysten først og fremst som hadde denne frihedslengselen, denne viljen til å gjøre samfundet rummeligere og bygge mere og mere gjensidighet" (Undset 1945: 163–64).
16. "Selg ikke huden, før bjørnen er skudd" (Undset 1945: 172).
17. "Arbeidet for å bygge op igjen et samfund av frie nasjoner og frie mennesker" (Undset 1945: 175).
18. "Vi oppfattter nasjonenes sjeler som personligheter" (Undset 1945: 182).
19. Undset is able to point to very few German intellectuals, whom she suspects by that time to be spread all around the world, living isolated from each other (if they have not been killed in a concentration camp). These Germans are excluded from the general characteristics.
20. "Intet enkelt grep i det geniale spill på den tyske folkepsykes dypeste strenger, som Adolf Hitler har drevet, er mere genialt enn nettopp dette,—at han har krevet å bli dyrket som et guddommelig vesen. Dermed imøtekom han et urgammelt tysk krav,—et krav som er ledemotivet allerede i de tyske middelalderdiktninger om Niebelungenes nød, driften til betingelsesløs underkastelse under én herre" (Undset 1944: 184–85).
21. "Mon ikke det tyske folk trenger militarismen som hummeren trenger sitt skall,—det utvendige hårde panser om sitt myke, benløse legeme" (Undset 1945: 182).
22. "Efter å ha flyktet fra naziinvasjonen i Norge, gjennom Sovjet-Russland og Japan, visste jeg, å komme til Amerika blir allikevel å komme inn på hjemveien igjen. Nu er det bare over Amerika at veien fører tilbake til fremtiden. Det som vi fra de européiske demokratiene kaller fremtid" (Undset 1945: 171).

References

Fontander, Björn. 1992. *Undset, Hamsun och kriget*. Stockholm: Carlssos.
Hamm, Christine. 2013. *Foreldre i det moderne: Sigrid Undsets forfatterskap og moderskapets grammatikk*. Oslo: Akademika.
Maman, Marie. 2000. *Sigrid Undset in America: An Annotated Bibliography and Research Guide*. Lanham, MD: The Carecrow Press.
Moi, Toril. 1999. *What Is a Woman? And Other Essays*. Oxford: Oxford University Press.
Skouen, Arne. 1982. *Sigrid Undset skriver hjem: En vandring gjennom emigrantårene i Amerika*. Oslo: Aschehoug.
Slapgard, Sigrun. 2007. *Sigrid Undset: Dikterdronning*. Oslo: Aschehoug.
———. 2010. "Based in Brooklyn." *Scandinavian Review* 97(1): 22–30.
Undset, Sigrid. 1942. *Return to the Future*. Translated by Henriette C. K. Naeseth. New York: Alfred A. Knopf.
———. 1945. *Tilbake til fremtiden*. Oslo: Aschehoug.
———. 2004a. "Hedre din far og din mor." In *Essays og artikler 1910–1919*, edited by Liv Bliksrud, 122–45. Oslo: Aschehoug.
———. 2004b. "De falske ideologier." In *Essays og artikler 1930–1939*, edited by Liv Bliksrud, 946–49. Oslo: Aschehoug.

Part III

WAR LITERATURE: CANON

The third part of this study deals with canonized literary representations of the war experience, published in Nordic literatures during the immediate postwar decades, specifically between 1947 and 1971. These chapters investigate canonized literary works or "classics" that have remained active in the working cultural memory of World War II by means of publication, translation, anthologized editions, and adaptations. Having passed rigorous processes of selection over the postwar decades, these works have become literary artifacts and have secured a lasting place in the cultural memory of Nordic societies. The chapters in this part of the volume investigate literary works that grapple with national reckoning and collective memory of the war experience. In other words, these texts engage representations, on an individual or collective level, of complicity, collaboration, or passivity; furthermore, they serve as indictments of government wartime policies or as representations of resistance or military sacrifice. There are few depictions here of heroism or battlefield grandeur; these are works that engage ethical dilemmas and existentialist perspectives and that often come to function as postwar apologia. The various readings demonstrate how these literary narratives shape, complicate, or trouble the nation's cultural memory of war. Part III of this study consists of five chapters; again, the readings are arranged chronologically according to the original publication date of the central literary work.

The first two chapters deal with the earliest postwar literature of liberated Denmark and Norway. Hans Christian Branner's novella *Angst*, first published in an anonymous collection (by an underground press) in 1944, and later in 1947, is an expressionistic, nightmarish exploration of Denmark's collective postwar psyche. In chapter 9, Mark Mussari relates Branner's *Angst* to the collective Danish memory of the occupation—as framed by the research of Claus Bryld and Anette Warring; further, Mussari demonstrates how Branner's existentialist fiction resists the whitewashing of political and personal collusion, as his angst-ridden characters hold up an insistent mirror to the reader.

In Norway, Sigurd Hoel's postwar novel *Meeting at the Milestone* (1947) is a canonized literary representation of the occupation period; at the same time, it constitutes a modern psychological novel that offers a problematizing representation of Norwegians during the occupation—questioning why some became collaborators or joined the far-right National Socialist party. Rather than reinforcing the framework of patriotic historiography and national unity, the novel disrupts such cultural memory. In chapter 10, Dean Krouk of the University of Wisconsin-Madison reinterprets this classic that deals with a traumatic period of the national past through Susan Rubin Suleiman's concept of a "crisis in memory," demonstrating that such crisis functions on both the collective (national) level and the individual (protagonist-narrator) level of this complex literary work.

Absolutely central to Finland's cultural memory of World War II is Väinö Linna's novel *The Unknown Soldier* (1954), recently published in a new English translation as *Unknown Soldiers* (2015). In chapter 11, Julia Pajunen investigates the extraordinary status of this hard-boiled war novel, depicting the experience of ordinary Finnish soldiers in Finland's Continuation War against the Soviet Union. A repeated narrative discourse enacted by new editions, translations, and adaptations (both cinematic and theatrical), *The Unknown Soldier* is inextricably entrenched in the working cultural memory of Finland in World War II. Making use of Astrid Erll's understanding of cultural memory as well as Linda Hutcheon's theory of adaptation, Pajunen demonstrates how the narrative of *The Unknown Soldier* became embedded in an institutionalized commemoration of national unity and an integral part of a patriotic cultural discourse, which are now strangely dislodged from the original 1954 novel by Linna. Thus, this reading demonstrates how Finland's cultural memory appropriates this canonical war novel by actively "remembering" some of its characters and dialogue while "forgetting" Linna's sardonic depiction of the meaningless deaths of the soldiers and the futility of war itself.

In the case of Sweden, it is difficult to speak of either occupation literature (as in Denmark, Norway, or Iceland) or of a war novel (as in Finland). In Sweden, postwar literature dealing with World War II often involves coming to terms with the wartime government policy of concessions. Thus, chapter 12 addresses Per Olov Enquist's documentary novel *The Legionnaires* (1968), an early foray into the ongoing postwar scholarly debates on Sweden's wartime neutrality policies and public controversy that gained full-scale momentum in the 1990s. The novel investigates the 1946 extradition of Baltic military refugees from Sweden to the USSR (the "Legionnaires" were primarily Latvian and Estonian Waffen-SS conscripts who had been drafted or recruited by Germany to fight against the Soviet Union during World War II); Enquist's documentary narrative is told in the voice of an "investigator" who examines archival material and interviews in order to uncover a traumatic episode in the nation's immediate postwar experience. Reading through the lens of ethics theory, Jan Krogh Nielsen demonstrates how Enquist's literary representation of political and ethical questions surrounding the Baltic extradition runs parallel to the deeper national debate about Sweden's bystander position in World War II.

In Iceland, the Allied occupation is not such a frequent topic in postwar literature and film; however, in 1971, the novelist Indriði G. Þorsteinsson published *North of War* (1971), a novella that crystalized a narrative of Icelandic cultural memory of the war. In chapter 13, Daisy Neijmann of the University of Iceland illuminates how the cultural memory of the war is perceived in terms of impotence and loss rather than gain, and that it is often portrayed in highly gendered and sexualized terms. Neijmann's analysis complicates the Icelandic cultural memory of the Allied occupation—a period that had caused a complex moral, cultural, and identity crisis for the new nation—and demonstrates how Þorsteinsson's novella *North of War* gives narrative shape to Iceland's war experience and articulates the standardized Icelandic narrative of the Allied occupation, which has been incorporated into cultural memory.

Chapter 9

HANS CHRISTIAN BRANNER
Angst and the Existential Crisis of War in Denmark

Mark Mussari

In *Besættelsestiden som kollektiv erindring* (The occupation as collective memory), Claus Bryld and Anette Warring associate angst with a specifically Danish sense of nationalism. For the Danes, the national, they write, has always been bound with angst (Bryld and Waring 1998: 17). The authors see the origins of this association in Denmark's defeat in the Second Schleswig War to Germany (Prussia) at Dybbøl in 1864, and in the fear that this loss would be a prelude to more defeats and possibly the end of Denmark as a nation-state. From this perspective, the German occupation of 9 April 1940 looks like the beginning of the end. Bryld and Warring employ postwar texts to illustrate the thematizing and mythifying of the five-year occupation and, especially, Denmark's revisionist position as a member of the Allied Forces (it was not, as it initially signed a nonaggression pact with Germany) and all Danes as members of the resistance (which, obviously, they were not).[1] Bryld and Waring observe, "The occupation had become a link in some imagined solidarity or a part of the collective memory" (1998: 181).[2] Through this ongoing revisionism, manifesting itself in newspaper articles and documentaries, many Danes could repress more equivocal responses to the occupation and create what Sofie Lene Bak refers to in chapter 2 as a "master narrative."

Addressing the complexity of the Danish response to the war in much of his fiction, H. C. Branner (1903–66) would not allow for the conflict resolution attained by mythifying history during or after the occupation.

Branner's fiction moves in the opposite direction: instead of erasing contradictions or whitewashing political and personal collusion, his angst-ridden characters hold an insistent mirror up to readers, a mirror reminding them that the struggle producing angst is an internal one, not simply a national or political one. Lurking behind this approach is the persistent message that the end of the war will not alleviate all angst. In *Being and Nothingness*, Sartre observes that "anguish is distinguished from fear in that fear is fear of beings in the world whereas anguish is anguish before myself . . . my being provokes anguish to the extent that I distrust myself and my own reactions in that situation" (Sartre 1984: 65). Therefore, for Branner, the war alone does not dictate angst; the acute environment reinforces and compels angst already present within each character.

In 1944, Branner contributed a short story titled "Angst" to the illegal publication *Der brænder en Ild* (A fire is burning), a collection of short stories, poems, and essays written anonymously by some of Denmark's most prominent authors at the time (including Tove Ditlevsen, Knud Sønderby, Kjeld Abell, and Martin A. Hansen) and published during the German occupation.[3] The back cover tells readers not to sell the book, to think about prisoners of war, and to support "Frihedskampen—ogsaa med Penge" (the fight for freedom—with money, too). Branner based the illegal "Angst" on his earlier short story "Trommerne" (The drums), from 1942. The illegally produced "Angst" also points to the later, longer postwar novella also entitled *Angst*,[4] a meld of both "Trommerne" and the illegal "Angst," and first published in 1947. Branner's lifelong engagement with the concept of angst comes as no surprise to anyone familiar with his oeuvre; his characters frequently find themselves alone and disoriented in an oneiric world of expressionist imagery. They are dissociated, fragmented, fictional ciphers for Branner's sense that modern people—in the mid-twentieth-century meaning of modern—are split, divided souls trapped between the long arm of childhood and the emptiness of an object-obsessed contemporary life. They are born into angst just as Branner felt he was born into war. In a talk given on New Year's Day in 1959, he recalled that as a child, in 1914, "the war had come into my life and it has been there ever since. My childhood was lost to it. My entire youth consisted of the time after the war, the time between wars, and the time before the war. That too was lost in the Great War, and now—in my late manhood—it is the time of the Cold War" (Branner 1959: 31).[5] This consciousness of war pervades a number of his characters, many of whom find themselves in distraught personal situations caused, at least in part, by the war and occupation.

In the 1944 version of "Angst," the narrator informs us at the start that he is suffering from insomnia; his attempts at dreaming of landscapes dissolve into wartime images of long, dark corridors and locked doors, behind which

Figure 9.1. *Der brænder en Ild* (A fire is burning, 1944), original front cover of the underground anthology that includes Hans Christian Branner's first version of the short story "Angst," anonymously published by a clandestine press. The back cover reads, "This book may not be sold. But all who hold a copy in their hands ought to feel obliged in every way to support the freedom fight—also with money. Think of the prisoners! Help their loved ones! Find your place in the fight!" Illustrator anonymous. Published by Folk og Frihed forlag (People and Freedom Press). Courtesy of Marianne Stecher-Hansen.

lie people on cots. They too lie awake in the darkness, listening to the sounds of heavy boots, rattling keys, barked commands, and a scream. The narrator suddenly finds himself in a car on a train, a car packed with people on their way to a camp surrounded by barbwire and men in black uniforms. Now, he explains, the angst "is burning dry behind my eyes" (Branner 1944: 50).[6] The narrator gets up, rolls down the blinds (as many Danes did during the occupation), and lights a lamp. The narrator alludes to warnings about arrests and hostages; the sound of a car pulling up and a door opening convince him he's about to be taken in the night, but it turns out to be merely his neighbors coming home. Surrendering to fear, he insists, only empowers one's enemy:

> You're dealing with an enemy who is deeply familiar with all the negative forces in humanity. Superstition, cowardice, ignorance, mendacity, *schadenfreude*,

love of destruction, lust for sensation, blind egoism.... You have helped him with your silence and passivity, your tendency to spread doubt and uncertainty all around you, your callousness to others' sufferings. Even at this very moment you are working for his cause by poisoning the air with your fear. (Branner 1944: 51)[7]

Branner has broken the fourth wall to speak directly to the reader. Utilizing second person, addressing not a departed lover as in the other two versions but instead the contemporary Dane during the occupation, he pulls the reader into the story and thus the story into the reader. He accomplishes this feat by creating a voice inside the character, one that metaphorically advises him to let angst's black sediment sink to calm (Branner 1944: 51). Yet, the interior voice only receives attribution once, and the "you" it is directed at quickly merges with the "you" who is the reader.

In the expanded *Angst* from three years later, in 1947, the narrator, in an agitated state because of the war and occupation, discusses a letter he is composing solely in his head. He won't write it down, a sign of the character's paranoia, because he fears it will fall into the "wrong hands" (Branner 1947: 7) and be used against him. He then envisions his lover obsessing about the letter, turning it over again and again in her hand, the object becoming "a thing that can be held in the hand and looked at and touched" (Branner 1953: 7–8).[8] even more than something she reads. The narrator also insists that her ideas of him will dictate how she reads the letter, which over time will become only a "confirmation of everything you already know about me" (Branner 1953: 8).[9] Eventually, she will take the letter out when she no longer feels any of her own angst, when peace (*Freden*) finally arrives, he says, thus connecting the letter to the war: "So you will be carrying that letter like a dead thing you cannot get rid of although it no longer belongs to you" (Branner 1953: 9).[10] The use of this image indicates Branner's merging of wartime angst and authorial impotence; it recalls Kierkegaard's illegible letter in his parable from *Enten/eller I* (Either/or I) in the section "Silhouettes." In that parable told by Kierkegaard's narrator "A," a man possesses a letter, which he believes contains information regarding his life's very happiness—but the writing is pale and fading, bordering on illegible. "A" observes: "Then, presumably with anxiety and agitation, he would read it most passionately again and again and at one moment deduce one meaning, at the next moment another..." (Kierkegaard 1987: 190). Yet the letter will ultimately become so illegible as to be meaningless, until all that is left to the man reading the letter are the tears in his eyes. The letter, an object, has become secondary to the man's state of mind, his emotions, that is, his anxiety in the loss of certainty.

The man-and-letter parable illustrates that an emotional state is not about the object (the steadily dissipating object of grief) but rather about grief. For

Kierkegaard, angst ultimately arises in a religious context: a person is aware that she must eventually stand before God in all eternity, thus lending her decisions eternal consequences (Kierkegaard 2014: 75).[11] On the other hand, for Heidegger, the progenitor of many twentieth-century existential concepts of angst, angst develops from a person's consciousness of finitude, of one's mortality, of the ultimate nothingness (Heidegger 1996: 245).[12]

Branner, the War, and Angst

As an author writing in the 1940s, Branner uses the war as a catalyst to an angst that brings forth realizations about more than simply the mutability of life or the reality of death. Like the letter in Kierkegaard's parable, the war is in some ways not really the issue: a person's loss of meaning and sense of despair have merely been heightened by the acute situation of living under the German occupation. For Branner's narrator in *Angst* (1947), a more Sartrian version of angst occurs when he finally leaves his apartment and takes a train through darkened Copenhagen. After handing a man his ticket, only to be met by a dissociated mouth opening to say something it never does, the narrator boards a train where a strange man in a black hat holds a newspaper "in hateful desire." The headline "screams" of a hundred thousand men dying on the Eastern Front. The man then sends the narrator a threatening look; the narrator soon realizes everyone in the train is holding up a newspaper, divorced from each other. The narrator tries to escape, from car to car, but each one is filled with the same people staring threateningly at him over the edge of their newspapers. If hell is other people for Sartre, a coupé full of beings-in-themselves, for Branner it is a passageway through which the narrator must push, eventually disembarking into the "safety . . . in the city's dark throngs."[13]

The narrators in "Trommerne" and the two versions of "Angst" give voice to the modern person too attached to things. Branner depicts people attached to physical objects as what he on more than one occasion refers to as "dead grown-ups" (an approach that reaches its apotheosis in the figure of the sedentary Thomas in the author's postwar novel *Ingen kender natten*, from 1955). Early in the postwar version of *Angst*, the narrator repeatedly hopes that his "familiar things . . . will make the sound of the drums disappear completely" (Branner 1947: 14).[14] Later, after his belligerent train ride, he overhears people on the street talking in the darkness: one comments that "we can get good cakes again," and another boasts that he knows where "you can buy all the woolen socks you need" (Branner 1947: 43).[15] The voices concur that they should not be complaining—one even admitting he has been hoarding sugar and another describing the pleasure he feels burying his hands in his private stash of coffee beans. "We have everything!" one finally exclaims. The narrator hurries past them, because he finds something unpleasant about hearing "crazy" people talking together. The difficulties of the occupation, in terms of resources, have been trivialized by some Danes' selfish notions of comfort.[16] More importantly, the scene undermines the popular sense of mass resistance constructed by many postwar historians.

In Branner's fictive universe, the war has shaken the narrator and created a colorless world of dry white fear and black sticky death. Throughout his writing, Branner avoids direct scenes of war, and readers rarely encounter a German soldier in any of his works. Maria Krysztofiak sees this approach as characteristic for the aestheticizing of World War II in Danish literature: "Danish authors portray the war only in very loose connection to the concrete political situation; if anything, it is regarded as a phenomenon of civilization, one that is evident to both the single individual and all of society" (Krysztofiak 1983: 139).[17] Instead, Branner employs imagery normally associated with German Expressionism to unsettling effect: a heavy dependence on black and white, nightscapes, blinking lights, craters, towers, faceless masses, tunnels, etc.[18] This emphasis on threatening environments in shadowy images of distortion owes much to the art and film created during the height of German Expressionism in the 1920s. Wherever they appear, these images are driven by anxiety; subjective and often antimimetic, they foreground the individual's mental state and his or her increasing discomfort with World War I and the devastation of its consequences. In "Expressionism: A Health Warning," David Elliott cites "the dichotomy and pathetic distance between the untrammeled freedom of nature and the seductive alienation of the city" as the crux of Expressionism (Elliott 1993: 43).[19] He points specifically to *Die Brücke*, the first group of German expressionists (founded in 1905), and their move in 1911 from the nature surrounding Dresden to Berlin, where they "experienced as well as depicted the alienation of the great Metropolis" (Elliott 1993: 43). Urban scenes become nightmarish landscapes filled with lurid colors and the jagged outlines of woodcuts.

In the postwar *Angst* (1947), the narrator wanders in his own nightmarish urban setting, reflecting both the state of his mind and the long, dark night of the occupation. At one point he follows a man in a red woolen scarf into "a mumbling darkness" (Branner 1947: 45), where something black and formless crawls out of a doorway.[20] Before long, uniformed figures come by, one by one and two by two: "It was as if they flared up in an instant and turned into ashes, disappearing like gray apparitions into a tall white building . . . a train of lifeless shadows" (Branner 1953: 46).[21] Yet, throughout these scenes, the narrator continues to pursue the throng; longing for communality, he follows them wherever they lead. "I said to myself that I would stay in the stream and feel a part of it, but at the same time I was afraid for I had the feeling that it was breaking up, it increased its speed toward something big and unknown waiting in the darkness—a jubilant boundless freedom or a horror without name, perhaps a vertical fall down into the abyss" (Branner 1953: 51–52).[22] Although the narrator wants to become one with the stream of people, he fears the "freedom" the throng moves toward in the dark. Freedom—the freedom of choice—presents something frightening; the vertigo of possibility, a favorite image of existentialists (cf. Kierkegaard's dizziness), leaves the individual hovering over an abyss.

In his apostrophe to his absent lover, the narrator in the postwar *Angst* traces the evolution of his beliefs for her (and the reader): "At first I was talking about belief in God, and then about belief in the human being and his unknown destination, and at last only about belief in the multiple meaning of life itself. Now all these things are behind me, now I am trying again to believe in God. But if you ask the name of my new God there is no name, and if you want to know something about my new belief then there is nothing to know" (Branner 1953: 10–11).[23] Branner's narrator vacillates between an existential angst believing in nothing and one longing to fill the void left by bankrupt belief systems that have led to the war. In this sense, the narrator has defined himself, in mid-twentieth-century terms, as a humanist in the pejorative sense professed by Nordahl Grieg in *Ung må verden ennu være* (May the world stay young): a weak, bloodless, emotionally cold person living in the "dead dust" of books.

In his talk "Humanismens krise" (The crisis of humanism), given at the Student Union in Copenhagen in 1950, Branner observed that humanism had come to mean uncertainty and indecision in a time of thoughtless action (Branner, 1950: 8). Using responses to World War II as a touchstone, Branner wants to move the humanist out of the academic or idealist sphere and into a two-sided reality. In his talk he explains: "A humanist is one who presupposes faith in people, as he respects the individual person as an end in and of itself but who simultaneously recognizes his spiritual and material connection with all of humanity and stands by his part of the responsibility for this community" (Branner 1950: 13).[24] In "Angst," the narrator's wife berates him for fearing the Gestapo when, in reality, the Gestapo has no idea who he is: during the occupation he hasn't contributed to helping anyone in any meaningful way. Therefore, his angst arises not from fear of eternal consequences for action taken, not from any simple consciousness of his own death, but from his inert, removed, and solely intellectual state of being.[25] Whereas Kierkegaard insists on the primacy of the single individual, Branner makes clear in "Humanismens krise" that "faith in a transcendent principle can no longer free the individual from the angst of responsibility. The individual person's salvation has become humanity's salvation" (Branner 1950: 27).[26] Any religious efforts must now be united with social consciousness; a person's moral imperative has become a universal responsibility. In 1950, reflecting on the disastrous consequences of World War II, Branner cannot free individuals from their place in society, in community, or in the world. Angst arises not from simply looking inward: it arises from weakness and self-obsession at odds with one's connection to others, an individual moral responsibility to society—to humanity.

No Man Knows the Night

In 1955, Branner reworked many of the dominant issues in "Trommerne" and the other versions of "Angst" into his novel *Ingen kender natten* (translated as *No Man Knows the Night*, 1958), one of Denmark's most effective postwar novels dealing with the German occupation.[27] Told mostly in a stream-of-consciousness style, *Ingen kender natten* vacillates between two characters: the communist resistance fighter Simon, who is fleeing the Gestapo, and Tomas, the alcoholic son-in-law of a wealthy manufacturer and collaborator during the war. In Simon and Tomas, Branner has split the inner dialogue of his "Angst" protagonist into two characters, yet again emphasizing the contradictory and conflicting Danish positions during the war. Both characters are driven by their own versions of angst: Tomas paralyzed and anesthetized in a limbonic state of inertia, and Simon full of political platitudes yet fleeing and fearful of taking too much action. In many ways, the two characters reflect the prewar dichotomy Sven Møller Kristensen delineates in "Kunst og politik før og efter krigen" (Art and politics before and after the war) between the isolating, individualistic approach of liberalism and the organized, collective concerns of socialism. In his final work addressing the political and personal consequences of the war, Banner attempts to erase that dichotomy by ultimately uniting the two men into one cause: helping a group of refugees in a deserted building in Copenhagen.

The indictment of inertia and a dependency on empty words that characterized the earlier "Angst" protagonists resurfaces in *Ingen kender natten*. After Simon breaks into Tomas's villa, Tomas tells him, "There are so many other ways of taking people's lives. . . . The surest is to let nature take its course without doing anything at all" (Branner 1958: 188).[28] Tomas reinforces this warning when, after agreeing to help Simon, he admonishes himself later in the book (at a pivotal moment when he has been given a chance to escape capture and aid others): "Remember who you are, you have killed people before by sitting still and waiting" (Branner 1958: 268).[29] Møller Kristensen places this focus on action and involvement squarely in the prewar cultural radical camp: "It was not enough to interpret the world. It had to be changed. The bystander, the passive observer, the one who remained neutral, was an opponent" (Kristensen 1970: 94).[30] In Tomas's conversion one perceives a longing for the change in behavior that Denmark's cultural radicals believed was the only hope for the future.[31]

Late in the novel, Branner moves focus to a group of refugees hiding in a safe house in Copenhagen, and his prose becomes less stream-of-consciousness and more objective. Through his depictions of members of the resistance, Branner employs a range of attitudes from occupied Denmark in this scene: the humanist, the Marxist, the nationalist, the religious—each character espousing a point of view—and ties them in with the existential demand for authenticity. A nationalist, for example, mentions his fealty to "father land," which sets off bells at this time, Branner uniting this militaristic attitude with the Nazis. A minister offers the closest commentary to the position Branner proffers in "Humanismens krise": "But we forget the most important thing. Our responsibility. The individual person's responsibility for the common cause" (Branner 1958: 223).[32] Here, the minister sounds more like an existentialist, acknowledging the irreligiosity of the other characters and calling responsibility "life itself" (Branner 1958: 223). However, words once again prove deceptive: the minister confesses to the others that on the pulpit he read his church's encyclical against the persecution of the Jews to positive response—but that he then fled to this safe house after his life was threatened for speaking out. The pastor feels his own angst for abandoning his responsibility to his congregation in the face of death threats. "I fled from my responsibility. I betrayed the many who had taken me as an example. Yesterday I was part of a living fellowship, today I'm a dead man" (Branner 1958: 225).[33] In these scenes, with the two doppelgänger main characters offstage, the war becomes a more direct presence, an acute factor forcing the characters to face the central dilemma of life: responsibility to self contra responsibility to others.

As in "Humanismens krise," Branner has moved Christianity out of the realm of religion, in the conventional sense, and onto the personal and political stage (two poles that, as his career progressed, became more inseparable, particularly following the war). Considering the postwar division between the West and the Soviet Union, Branner pleads for a renewal of Christianity's original universalism, which he contends "will undoubtedly be the best way to advance a mutual understanding," while rejecting the West's current version of Christianity as "compromised by the church's unholy alliance with nationalism" (Branner 1950: 13).[34] Branner wants to replace religion with a socially active humanism. In *H. C. Branner—splittelse og kontinuitet* (H. C. Branner—division and continuity), Janne Jarlby sees *Ingen kender natten* as "an expression of Branner's will to believe in humanism, and to believe that existence has meaning—while in reality he is in an entirely different place" (Jarlby 2003: 51).[35] Jarlby feels that Branner's ultimate postwar novel indicates that he is caught between a longing for reality and a longing to run from it. However, this paradox or tension seems elemental not only in Branner's war-driven short stories and novels but in the broader existential concept of angst. Writing in an afterword to Kafka's *Der Prozess* (*The Trial*, 1958), Walther Killy observes that "angst may not simply be fear, however, but rather a longing for something more than what is arousing angst" (Killy 1958: 167).[36] Branner's use of World War II throughout his fiction illustrates this yearning; he does not construct a meaning to existence because he cannot find one in reality. Instead, he wants to replace the bifurcated one in the reality he finds—the failed one that has led the world to the brink of disaster with World War II and created a paralyzing personal angst—with one he views as more viable. He wants to resurrect the individual's initiative to care about the universal.

From "Trommerne" to *Ingen kender natten*, Branner's angst-ridden war stories present a movement from characters of narcissistic obsession to those of self-effacement and social concern. He summarized this movement and its relation to the war in the same 1959 New Year's talk in which he described war's unyielding presence in his youth:

> The time for angst has passed; escape from reality is no longer possible, and despair has become a meaningless thing. . . . It's pointless, as an artist, to say to yourself that you're not the only one who can give people back their lost faith in life, that with your poor understanding you cannot think the new thoughts and create the new images that will teach the world to live without war. For there are no others who are capable of doing so. (Branner 1959: 31)[37]

Doing so meant reminding readers that responsibility for the horrors of World War II could not simply be laid at Germany's doorstep, nor could the Danes wish away their personal or political complicity in myth and revisionism. Throughout his war-themed fiction, Branner struggled to propel readers out of inertia and into a shared sense of responsibility, so that they would become more than mere bystanders in their own lives and on the world stage.

Mark Mussari (PhD, University of Washington, Seattle, 1999) is Affiliate Assistant Professor of Scandinavian Studies at the University of Washington and an independent scholar, professional translator, and author of numerous scholarly articles on literature, art, and design, including articles on Christian Kampmann, Karen Blixen, and H. C. Branner published in *Scandinavian Studies*. His book *Danish Modern: Between Art and Design* (2016) is published by Bloomsbury Press.

Notes

1. In his essay "Kunst og politik før og efter krigen," Sven Møller Kristensen observes that in the postwar years "de nye modgående bevægelser" (the new opposing movements) took issue with the tenets of prewar cultural radicalism and "forenklede billedet af fortiden og formede myterne" (simplified the picture of the past and formed myths) (1970: 95). All translations are mine except where indicated.
2. "Besættelseshistorien var blevet et led i et forestillet fælleskab eller en del af den kollektive erindring" (Bryld and Warring, 1998: 181).
3. Jens Nyholm sees the underground or "illegal" press as essential to the inception of the resistance movement: "Spiritual and intellectual opposition through the press was the first step in the fight against the Nazis" (Nyholm 1947: 261). Nyholm also cites Branner's "Angst" thematically as an avatar of underground literary endeavor.
4. Translated by Villy Sørensen and Anne Born as *Anguish* (Copenhagen: Wind-Flower Press, 1953).
5. "Men krigen var kommet ind i mit liv og den har været der lige siden. Min Barndom blev borte i den. Hele min ungdom var efterkrigstid, mellem krigstid og førkrigstid. Saa blev ogsaa den borte i den sidste store krig og nu, i min manddom, er det den kolde krigs tid" (Branner 1959: 31).
6. ". . . Angsten brænder tørt bag ved Øjnene" (Branner 1944: 50).
7. "Du har at gøre med en Fjende, som er dybt fortrolig med alle negative Kræfter i Mennesket. Overtro, Fejghed, Uvidenhed, Løgnagtighed, Skadefryd, Ødelæggelseslyst, Sensationshunger, blind Egoisme—han ved, at de Ting findes i os alle, og hans Rige er grundlagt paa dem. Ogsaa du har været med til at støtte og hjælpe ham, skønt du ikke selv ved det, hans Sejre havde slet ikke været mulige uden dig. Du har hjulpet ham med din Tavshed og Passivitet, din Hang til at sprede Tvivl og Usikkerhed omkring dig, din Afstumpethed over for andres Lidelser. Endnu i dette Øjeblik virker du for hans Sag ved at forgifte Luften med din Frygt" (Branner 1944: 51).
8. ". . . en Ting man kan tage i Haanden og se og føle paa" (Branner 1947: 8).
9. ". . . en Bekræftelse paa alt hvad du ved om mig i Forvejen" (Branner 1947: 8)
10. "Saadan vil du slæbe paa et Brev som en død Ting du ikke kan slippe af med, skønt den ikke længere hører til dig" (Branner 1947: 9)
11. "Anxiety can be compared with dizziness. He whose eye happens to look down into the yawning abyss becomes dizzy. But what is the reason? It is just as much his own eye as the abyss, for suppose he had not looked down? It is in this way that anxiety is the dizziness of freedom that emerges when spirit wants to posit the synthesis, and freedom now looks down into its own possibility and then grabs hold of finiteness to support itself. In this dizziness freedom subsides" (Kierkegaard 2014: 75).
12. "In *Angst*, Da-sein finds itself *faced* with the nothingness of the possible impossibility of its existence. *Angst* is anxious *about* the potentiality-of-being of the being thus determined, and it discloses the most extreme possibility. Because the anticipation of Da-sein absolutely individualizes and lets it, in this individualizing of itself, become certain of the wholeness of its potentiality-of-being, the fundamental attunement *Angst* belongs to this self-understanding of Da-sein in terms of its ground. Being-toward-death is essentially *Angst*" (Heidegger 1996: 245)
13. This translation is mine. Sørensen and Born use the stilted "in the town's darkness of people" (Branner 1953: 42).
14. ". . . mine fortrolige Ting . . . skal faa Lyden af Trommerne til at forsvinde helt" (Branner 1947: 14).

15. "... kan man faa gode Kager igen ... kan I købe alle de uldne Sokker I har Brug for" (Branner 1947: 43).
16. Historian Niels Aage Skov reinforces the attitude Branner depicts in this scene: "More than three years into the Occupation, the public's concern was still focused on avoiding hardships, not on resisting the Germans" (Skov 2000: 94).
17. "Krigen fremstilles af danske forfattere kun i meget løs forbindelse med den konkrete politiske situation, den opfattes snarere som et cvilisationsfænomen, som gjorde sig gældende både for det enkelte individ og for hele samfundet" (Krysztofiak 1983: 139).
18. Branner saw images such as these when he toured Germany shortly after the war's end and lectured in German.
19. Elliott observes that the expressionist arts "are recognized not by any superficial similarity but by the specific confluence of ideas and subject matter which gave them meaning... a kind of art in which social, historical, political, philosophical, even scientific and medical ideas, crystallized into a series of widely held attitudes and beliefs" (Elliott 1993: 48f.).
20. The original Danish is, as I have translated it, "et mumlende Mørke" (a mumbling darkness, 45). Unfortunately, Sørensen and Born translated the Danish phrase as "pitch darkness" (45), which destroys Branner's inventive blend of sight and sound.
21. "... det var som de flammede op i et Nu og blev til Aske, som graa Genfærd forsvandt de i en høj hvid Bygning ... som et Tog af livløse Skygger" (Branner 1947: 46).
22. "Jeg sagde til mig selv at jeg vilde blive i Strømmen og føle mig som eet med den, men samtidig var jeg bange, for jeg mærkede at den var i Opbrud, den tog Fart frem imod noget stort og ukendt som ventede ude i Mørket—en jublende, grænseløs Frihed eller en Rædsel uden Navn, maaske et lodret Fald ned i Agrunden" (Branner 1947: 52).
23. "... jeg talte først om Troen paa Gud, og saa om Troen paa Mennesket og dets ukendte Bestemmelse, og til sidst kun om Troen paa selv det mangetydige Liv. Nu er jeg hinsides alle de Ting, nu prøver jeg at tro paa Gud. Men hvis du spørger om Navnet paa min nye Gud saa er der ikke noget Navn, og hvis du vil vide noget om min nye Tro saa er der ingenting at vide" (Branner 1947: 10–11).
24. "Humanist er den, som går ud fra troen på mennesket, idet han respektere det enkelte menneske som et mål i sig selv men samtidig erkender sin åndelige og materielle samhørighed med hele menneskeheden og vedstår sin del af ansvaret for denne helhed" (Branner 1950: 13).
25. Erik Skyum-Nielsen comments on the intellectual's experience of war in Branner's oeuvre: "Oplevelsen af anden verdenskrig med dens ufattelige ødelæggelse og elendighed har fremfor at vække til modstand lammet den enkelte, hvad der særligt grelt viser sig hos de intellektuelle som er blevet ribbet for illusioner, berøvet initiativ" (Instead of arousing opposition, the experience of World War II with its unimaginable destruction and misery has paralyzed the individual, particularly among intellectuals who have been stripped of their illusions, robbed of their initiative) (Skyum-Nielsen 1980: 75).
26. "... kan ingen tro på et transcendent princip længere befri den enkelte for ansvarets angst. Menneskets frelse er blevet menneskehedens frelse" (Branner 1950: 27).
27. The title comes from an old Danish hymn by B. S. Ingemann: "Ingen kender dagen før solen går ned" (No one knows the day before the sun goes down). Jørgen Egebak traces a direct line from "Trommerne" to *Ingen kender natten* in both characters' paralytic states and in the impotence of their words (Egebak 1981: 371–73).
28. "Der er så mange andre måder at tage livet af mennsker ... den sikreste er at lade tingene gå deres gang uden at gribe ind i noget som helst" (Branner 1955: 196).
29. "Husk hvem du er, du har før dræbt mennesker ved at sidde stille og vente" (Branner 1955: 278).

30. "Det var ikke nok at fortolke verden. Den skulle forandres. Tilskueren, den passive iagttager, den neutrale, var en modstander" (Kristensen 1970: 94).
31. With roots in Georg Brandes's critiques, socialism, Freud, and Marx, the cultural radicals were anti-Victorian rationalists and freethinkers. In the interwar years, they were especially influenced by Poul Henningsen's journal *Kritisk Revy* (1926–29) as well as his antifascist views.
32. "Men vi glemmer det vigtigste: Ansvaret. Det enkelte menneskes personlige ansvar for den fælles sag" (Branner 1955: 232).
33. "Jeg flygtede fra mit ansvar. Jeg svigtede de mange som havde set et eksempel i mig. I går var jeg en del af et levende fælleskab, i dag er jeg en død mand" (Branner 1955: 235).
34. ". . . den bedste vej til fremme af en gensidig forståelse . . . kompromitteret gennem kirkens ukristelige pagt med nationalismen . . ." (Branner 1950: 13).
35. ". . . et udtryk for Branners vilje at tro på humanismen, og til at tro på, at der er en mening med tilværelsen—mens han i virkeligheden befinder sig et helt andet sted" (Jarlby 2003: 51).
36. "Allerdings ist diese angst vielleicht nicht nur angst, sondern auch Sehnsucht nach etwas, was mehr ist als alles Angsterregende" (Killy 1958: 167). Branner translated Kafka's *The Trial* into Danish in 1945.
37. "Angstens tid er forbi, flugten fra virkeligheden er ikke længere mulig, og fortvivlelsen er blevet en meningløs ting. . . . Det nytter ikke man som kunstner siger til sig selv, at man ikke ene af alle kan give mennesker deres tabte livstro tilbage, at man ikke med sin ringe forstand kan tænke de nye tanker og forme de nye billeder som skal lære verden at leve uden krig. For der er ingen andre som formår det" (Branner 1959: 31).

References

Branner, H. C. "Angst." 1944. *Der brænder en Ild*, 49–53. Copenhagen: Folk og Frihed.
———. 1947. *Angst*. Copenhagen: Boghallen.
———. 1950. "Humanismens krise." *Menneske i tiden*, 7–30. Copenhagen: Hans Reitzels Forlag.
———. 1953. *Anguish*. Translated by Villy Sørensen and Anne Born. Copenhagen: Windflower Press.
———. 1955. *Ingen kender natten*. Copenhagen: Gyldendal.
———. 1958. *No Man Knows the Night*. Translated by A. I. Roughton. London: Secker & Warburg.
———. 1959. "En nytårsklokke." *Politiken* (4 January): 30–31.
———. 1966. "Trommerne." In *H. C. Branner*, edited by Sven Møller Kristensen and Karen Margrethe Branner, 50–75. Copenhagen: Gyldendal.
Bryld, Claus, and Anette Warring. 1998. *Besættelsestiden som kollektiv erindring*. Roskilde: Roskilde Universitetsforlag.
Egebak, Jørgen. 1981. "H. C. Branner." In *Danske digtere i det tyvende århundrede*, edited by Torben Brostrøm and Mette Winge, 3:371–73. Copenhagen: Gad.
Elliott, David. 1993. "Expressionism: A Health Warning." In *Expressionism Reassessed*, edited by Shulamath Behr, David Fanning, and Douglas Jarman, 40–49. New York: Manchester University Press.
Grieg, Nordahl. 1938. *Ung må verden ennu være*. Oslo: Gyldendal Norsk Forlag.

Heidegger, Martin. 1966. *Being and Time*. Translated by Joan Stambaugh. Albany: State University of New York Press.

Jarlby, Janne. 2003. *H. C. Branner—splittelse og kontinuitet*. Odense: Syddansk Universitetsforlag.

Kierkegaard, Søren. 1887. *Either/Or Part 1*. Translated by Howard V. Hong and Edna H. Hong. Princeton: Princeton University Press.

———. 2014. *The Concept of Anxiety: A Simple Psychologically Oriented Deliberation in View of the Dogmatic Problem of Hereditary Sin*. Translated by Alastair Hannay. New York: Liveright Publishing Co.

Killy, Walther. 1958. "Afterword." In Franz Kafka, *Der Prozess*. Frankfurt am Main and Hamburg: Fischer Bücherei.

Kristensen, Sven Møller. 1970. "Kunst og politik, før og efter krigen." *Litteratur: Sociologiske essays*. Copenhagen: Munksgaard.

Krysztofiak, Maria. 1983. "Æstetiseringen af besættelsestiden i dansk kortprosa: Et bidrag til prosaens poetic i Danmark." In *Kortprosa i Norden: Fra H.C. Andersens eventyr til den moderne novelle*, edited by Mogens Brøndsted, 139–50. Odense: Odense Universitetsforlag.

Nyholm, Jens. 1947. "Danish Underground Publications." *Scandinavian Studies* 19(7): 261–69.

Sartre, Jean-Paul. 1984. *Being and Nothingness: A Phenomenological Essay on Ontology*. Translated by Hazel E. Barnes. New York: Washington Square Press.

Skov, Niels Aage. 2000. "The Use of Historical Myth: Denmark's World War II Experience Made to Serve Practical Goals." *Scandinavian Studies* 72(1): 89–110.

Skyum-Nielsen, Erik. 1980. *Ideologi og æstetik i H.C. Branners sene forfatterskab*. Copenhagen: Gyldendal.

Chapter 10

CRISES OF MEMORY IN NORWAY'S OCCUPATION NOVEL

Sigurd Hoel's *Meeting at the Milestone*

Dean Krouk

The Nazi occupation of Norway from April 1940 to May 1945 has a special place in Norwegian historical memory. It is the period in the twentieth century that has been most frequently memorialized, represented in film and literature, written about by historians and scholars, and taken as the subject of memoirs. Representations and perspectives continue to multiply as we move further into the twenty-first century, including new films, novels, and television programs, new public acts of remembrance, and new historical studies and works of nonfiction. These are all part of the ongoing process that embodies, transmits, and reshapes the collective memory of a nation's shared past. In postwar Norwegian history writing and memory culture, as Synne Corell has argued, a dominant representation of World War II was centered on a small, young, democratic nation in resistance to the Nazis, with a dichotomy of "good Norwegians" set against the collaborating members of the fascist Nasjonal Samling (Corell 2011: 101–26). Although Sigurd Hoel's 1947 novel *Møte ved milepelen* (translated as *Meeting at the Milestone*, 2002) quickly achieved canonical status as the classic work of fiction about the occupation, it has never actually fit the dichotomous model that Corell argues has been a persistent feature of Norwegian historiography (which is discussed in further detail by Tom Kristiansen in chapter 3 of this volume). Rather, *Meeting at the Milestone* is a critical and problematizing literary representation—a modern psychological novel that enacts a crisis of memory by introducing multiple predicaments, dilemmas, and ambiguities to the representation and memory of the occupation period.

The term "crisis of memory" comes from the work of Susan Rubin Suleiman, who defines it as "a moment of choice, and sometimes a predicament or a conflict, about remembrance of the past, whether by individuals or by groups" (Suleiman 2006: 1). Suleiman helpfully adds that what is at issue in a crisis of memory is not only knowledge of the past but also an individual or group's self-representation in the present. This essay proposes that Hoel's *Meeting at the Milestone* engages with crises of memory at two related levels: the collective (national) level of its immediate historical context during the legal purge in post-occupation Norway, and the individual level of the fictional narrator.

Hoel's novel was completed and published at the moment of *landssvikoppgjøret*, a term that refers to the legal purge of collaborators or traitors after the war. An important feature of the novel's historical moment was this nationwide moral, political, and legal attempt to come to terms with the very recent past of the Nazi occupation, during which a vastly unpopular puppet government led the country. The name of Vidkun Quisling, the founder and leader of the small Norwegian fascist party (Nasjonal Samling), became a byword for traitors and sympathizers not only in Norway but also in the English-speaking world. The postwar situation of a reckoning with the recent past of the occupation, with its heroes of the resistance contrasting to its traitorous quislings, Nazi sympathizers, and opportunists, presented the nation with concrete predicaments of punishment as well as tough questions of identity and memory.

At the fictional and individual level, the novel tells a complicated psychological story of self-deception and unmasking. Hoel's anonymous narrator, nicknamed *den plettfrie* (the blameless one) is a middle-aged member of the resistance who, through a crisis of memory in the fictional time of writing (1943–47), confronts his repressed guilt about past betrayals of loved ones. In this way, the narrator's mask of blamelessness falls, and he takes a more penetrating look at how his life has been intertwined with the lives of Nazi collaborators. His ethical and political identity as a resistance member is destabilized when he is confronted with the consequences of the newly remembered past actions, namely that he has fathered a young man who is now a zealous Nazi sympathizer.

The novel's individual, fictional crisis of memory, experienced by *den plettfrie*, is connected to the historical moment of *landssvikoppgjøret*, with its acute debates about responsibility and just punishment. The narrator's complicity comes to stand in for a wider collective complicity. Hoel understood this complicity through the lens of Wilhelm Reich's psychosexual analyses of Nazism as an expression of the pathologies of patriarchal culture in an extreme form. Similarly, the narrator's self-deceiving mask of innocence or blamelessness becomes an image of a more general collective self-deception or self-righteousness. This contentious idea, that the allegedly innocent ones are self-deceivers who are in fact responsible for what they seek to punish, has volatile critical implications in the context of the divisive *landssvikoppgjøret*.

This chapter will focus on the distinctive features of Hoel's thought and fiction, emphasizing his psychoanalytic, specifically Reichian, understanding of Nazism and patriarchy, as well as his subtle use of a first-person narrative form to register the protagonist's shifting mental landscape of self-deception and resurfacing memories. Hoel's novel is to a great extent a document of midcentury culture, with its antiquated use of a psychosexual paradigm for understanding Nazism and its intricate connections to Norway's postwar historical process of working through responsibility, complicity, and guilt. At the same time, *Meeting at the Milestone* retains its fascinating psychological subtlety and its power to destabilize the *spotless* self-images of individuals or nations.

Landssvikoppgjøret: The Postwar Context of the Norwegian Legal Purge

It was to be expected that Sigurd Hoel, a major figure of interwar leftist cultural radicalism, would be involved in the resistance to the Nazi occupation of Norway. Indeed, before starting *Meeting at the Milestone*, Hoel wrote around fifty articles for the illegal resistance press in the early occupation years, from 1941 to 1943. He also helped to organize the resistance efforts of teachers and authors in Oslo. Eventually, he and his wife were forced to flee occupied Norway, arriving in Sweden by boat in October 1943 (Tvinnereim 1975: 209). Hoel began work on a novel about the question of Nazism as early as 1942, but most of *Meeting at the Milestone* was written in haste in 1947 (Lyngstad 1984: 97).

At that time, the postwar *landssvikoppgjøret*—the legal purge, or more literally, the reckoning with treason—had already been in progress for a few years. Norwegian society was in the midst of a debate about the severity of punishment for those who had collaborated with the Nazi occupation. An ordinance called *landssvikanordningen* was enacted "retroactively" on 15 December 1944, stating that all those who had joined Nasjonal Samling (Norway's National Socialist Party) after 8 April 1940 would be punished. During the purge, thirty Norwegian collaborators were sentenced to death, and thousands more faced imprisonment or hard labor (Andenæs and Sulland 2017). The death penalty was reintroduced in both Norway and Denmark at this time. Quisling was among the twenty-five Norwegian collaborators who were executed. At one level, the novel can be approached as a contribution to this debate, although not one that provides simple answers to the controversial questions about guilt, responsibility, and severity of punishment (Egeland 1960: 15).

Although critics at the time of *landssvikoppgjøret* and afterward have argued that it was excessive in its punishments, the Norwegian purge can actually be seen as one of the more lenient judicial processes against collaborators when compared to other countries occupied by the Nazis (Høidal 2016: 291). There were more collaborators imprisoned after the war in Denmark and the Netherlands than in Norway, taken as a percentage of the population. The number of imprisoned collaborators in Norway was fourteen thousand as of 1 July 1945, and it sank to eight thousand by the start of 1946. Comparable numbers in the Netherlands, with a population three times the size of Norway's, were ninety-six thousand in October 1945, and fifty-one thousand in August 1946 (Andenæs [1979] 1998: 81). The most severe sentences in Norway were the initial ones in 1945, because the process was modified after criticism that the concept of treason was being applied too widely.

A significant critic at the time was Johannes Andenæs, a professor of criminal law who published two books in the postwar years: *Omkring rettsoppgjøret* (Concerning the legal purge) in 1945 and *Nazisme og landssvik* (Nazism and treason) in 1947. Later, in 1979, Andenæs published the most important historical account of this period, *Det vanskelige oppgjøret* (The difficult reckoning). According to Andenæs, popular opinion among Norwegians after the war favored an angry condemnation and punishment of all NS members as individuals who should be held guilty of treason (Andenæs [1979] 1998: 83). The public desired a quick and thorough reckoning, and newspapers such as the leftist *Dagbladet* and the communist *Friheten* were especially fervent in their support for severe punishment. These organs of opinion were also critical of those who called for moderation or greater attention to shades of complicity or extenuating circumstances (Andenæs [1979] 1998: 84).

A prominent example of those calling for moderation was Minister of Justice Johan Cappelen, who claimed that "the demand for a quick handling and adjudication of the cases of treason was an expression of a Nazi mentality" (Andenæs [1979] 1998: 84).[1] Later, in his 1957 novel *Under en hårdere himmel* (Under a harsher sky), Jens Bjørneboe made a similar point when he wrote the following about the purge: "The uniformity in the press, in literature, and in the legal procedure was frightening. The true fascist period in Norwegian history came not during Quisling's time, but afterwards. You have to go to Hitler's Berlin or Stalin's Moscow to find a similar legal practice" (Andenæs [1979] 1998: 177).[2] Clearly, this is a polemical statement that should be taken with a grain of salt, but it indicates how charged the

Figure 10.1. Portrait of Sigurd Hoel in 1947, the year that *Meeting at the Milestone* was published. Although Hoel's novel quickly achieved canonical status as the classic work about occupied Norway, *Meeting at the Milestone* is a critical and problematizing literary representation of the period—a modern psychological novel that enacts a crisis of memory. Photographer: E. Rude, 1947. Courtesy of the National Library of Norway, Wikimedia Commons.

debate about the process of the legal purge was in Norwegian society, and also the extent to which this debate was capable of challenging Norway's liberal-democratic political identity.

Hoel's position was quite different from Cappelen's or Bjørneboe's. He did not accuse the leaders of the legal purge of being so severe as to have a "Nazi mentality" or of being the real fascists in Norwegian history. This is because Hoel understood the essence of Nazism quite differently from Cappelen or Bjørneboe. For Hoel, the salient quality of Nazism was neither its severe legal practice nor its insistence on a rigid conformity of opinion. Rather, the essential feature of Nazism in Hoel's understanding—especially after his contact with Wilhelm Reich and his ideas in the early 1930s—was its patriarchal regulation and repression of erotic life (Rottem 1991: 212–13). I will return to the issue of patriarchy and Hoel's Reichian analysis of Nazism below.

As a major leftist intellectual and cultural radical, Hoel was steadfastly opposed to Nazism, writing during the war that, "for many of us, it has become a mission in life, to eliminate Nazism . . . the most important mission in our lives" (Hoel 1945: 153).[3] Although Hoel was unmistakably situated on the side of the resistance, his novel of the occupation eschews dichotomous thinking about "good Norwegians" against Nazi collaborators. One of Hoel's repeated ideas was that the problem of Nazism in the occupied countries was different from that in Germany, in that it was patriotic and nationalistic *to oppose* Nazism in an occupied country like Norway. He was troubled by the thought that the good, patriotic Norwegians were not necessarily motivated by anti-Nazism and might actually have deeper similarities with the Nazi mentality than one might expect (Tvinnereim 1975: 265). In 1944, in the wartime magazine *Norges-Nytt*, which was issued from Stockholm by the Norwegian Legation during the occupation, Hoel wrote that "in each person—in each of us—there is a little place, often a cherished little place, where there is a little seed of—not of Nazism, far from it. But of something with a troubling resemblance to it" (Jensen 1981: 96).[4] In many ways, vigilance about this potential or "seed" (*kime*) influenced Hoel's political identity into the postwar era. The vigilant self-inspection that Hoel called for from even his most politically and morally blameless compatriots became a major theme in *Meeting at the Milestone*.

A Psychoanalytic Plot: Self-Deception and the Return of the Repressed

The fictional crisis of memory in *Meeting at the Milestone* concerns the narrator, a member of the resistance known as *den plettfrie* (the blameless one). In the course of the novel, the mask of *den plettfrie* is removed to reveal a man who is in fact worthy of blame, but not for any ideological crime or act of treason. He is not simply revealed to be a Nasjonal Samling member or a collaborator. He does, however, come to regard himself as complicit in causing *another* person to become a Nazi—the son that he fathered with the woman he loved and betrayed in his youth, twenty years before the occupation. Hoel's psychological novel subtly shows this narrator coming to terms with the guilt that he has repressed under the mask of blamelessness. In wartime he finds occasions to be punished (in a scene in which he is tortured by the boy's stepfather, a collaborator) and to confess (to the woman he loved all along, but betrayed), as he reaches a greater understanding of his individual culpability. The narrator also recognizes, at least in a fragmentary way, the collective responsibility of the patriarchal culture and society that produced him—Hoel's central Reichian theme.

Meeting at the Milestone is a curious work in terms of genre: it contains both a story of first love and an espionage thriller within an intricate retrospective narrative reminiscent of Joseph Conrad.[5] The novel's individual crisis of memory follows a psychoanalytic plot of the return of the repressed. As with earlier novels and essays by Hoel, this novel was greatly influenced by psychoanalysis, including Reich's critique of patriarchy and Nazism. Hoel's major essay on Nazism, "Om nazismens vesen," displays this influence, and was originally composed as part of a draft of *Møte ved milepelen*.[6] Hoel had earlier spent several years in training analysis with Reich, when the latter was living in Denmark, Sweden, and Norway, after being expelled from the International Psychoanalytic Association in 1934. Influenced by Reich's ideas in works such as *Massenpsychologie des Faschismus* (The mass psychology of fascism, 1933), Hoel argued that the roots of Nazism are to be found in the "human structure that is engendered by sexual repression," and he saw the main culprits of this repression as traditionalist fathers, the men of the older generation (Lyngstad 1984: 105).

To understand the narrator's crisis of memory, we need to consider the novel's complex structure, with its layering of documents written at different moments in Norway and Sweden during and after the occupation. *Meeting at the Milestone* is composed of the narrator's writings from three different years. Part 1 contains notes written in 1947 that tell of events from the summer of 1943. Part 2 contains notes written after the summer of 1943, many of which are recollections of events from the narrator's youth around 1920. Part 3 consists of notes from Sweden in 1944, which tell of events from September 1943. In addition, there is a brief introductory chapter, "Frontkjemperen" ("The Stormtrooper"), as well as a postscript, both of which are from 1947.[7]

"The Stormtrooper" presents tantalizing information that the reader will not understand until much later in the novel. The narrator introduces an unnamed man in his twenties who, during *landssvikoppgjøret*, was sentenced to eight years of imprisonment for collaboration. He also mentions that this young man's father drowned himself on 7 May 1945 (Victory in Europe Day). The young man will turn out to be Karsten Heidenreich and his "father" Carl Heidenreich, although we later learn that Karsten's biological father is actually the narrator. This opening chapter also refers to a third character, a woman to whom the narrator has not spoken since 1945. This will turn out to be Karsten's mother, Maria Heidenreich, also known as Kari, the young woman with whom the narrator broke off a passionate love affair in the early 1920s when she became pregnant.

Although *den plettfrie* insists in this tiny introductory chapter that these collaborators are merely strangers of no concern to him, this is an unreliable statement that masks his intimate connection to them. Criticism of *Meeting at the Milestone* has often focused on the twofold nature of the unreliable narrator's motivations. The narrator's rational, stated intention is to sort out the wartime papers that make up the bulk of the novel, but his irrational motivation is to examine his own guilt and complicity.[8] His underlying motivation for writing can be considered irrational in that he suffers a "reflexive breakdown"—for most of the novel, he himself cannot give a full account of what he is really doing by writing these notes (Lear 2005: 26). Instead, he offers feeble pretenses that readers are expected to see through, even before discovering the extent of his involvement with the other characters.

In part 1 (notes from 1947 that tell of events from 1943), we learn that the narrator bought a house in an affluent area of Oslo shortly before the war, which he used as a hiding place for endangered members of the resistance. One day, a nervous and worn-out resistance member called Indregård comes to stay with the narrator. Indregård eventually starts a conversation about a common friend from their youth, Hans Berg, who has now become a Nazi. Twenty years before the occupation, Indregård and Berg taught at the same school in Oslo, where they both fell in love with the same student. When Berg won this competition, Indregård's jealous disappointment led him to report the illicit relationship to the school authorities. Berg was fired and left Oslo in the early 1920s. Now, Indregård's inflated sense of guilt for betraying Berg convinces him that *he* is the one responsible for Berg *and* his family becoming Nazi sympathizers: "I know today that I'm directly to blame for another person, in fact a whole family, going to hell—because it means going to hell, in my opinion. I'm to blame for it" (Hoel 2002: 38).[9]

The tale about Indregård's betrayal of Hans Berg is important because it shows how a person can take the blame for someone else becoming a Nazi. In this way it provides a thematic starting point for the narrator's own crisis of memory and identity (Inadomi 1968: 29). The Indregård incident uncannily mirrors the narrator's own past and prompts his further recollections. After Indregård is taken to Sweden in August 1943, the narrator begins to write about Berg and other men he knew in his youth. Part 2 (notes from 1943) begins with a sketch of Berg's puritanical and dehumanizing upbringing, followed by brief vignettes of other former friends who also became Nazis, in a chapter called "Gallery of the Damned." The narrator examines each of the "damned," finding varied motivations and backgrounds, only to be confronted with his own past when he comes to Carl Heidenreich. It becomes impossible for him to ignore the past that Heidenreich resurrects; the inspection of other people's motivations gives way to self-inspection and memories of his childhood, his father, and his time as a student in Oslo, including his erotic experiences with several women, the most significant of whom was Kari.

While part 2 of *Meeting at the Milestone* is retrospective and nostalgic, concerned with events from the 1920s and with a love story that seems to have little to do with the war and occupation, part 3 resembles a spy thriller set in the context of the Norwegian resistance. The narrator is writing from Sweden in 1944, having been forced to flee Norway after being sent to a small town to discover who was leaking information to the Nazis about the resistance effort. While in this small Norwegian town, he discovers something that ties together the wartime plot and the 1920s love story: the leaker was none other than Karsten, his son with "Kari," whose actual name is Maria Heidenreich. Karsten has been raised with the narrator's former friend Dr. Carl Heidenreich as his father. The mask of *den plettfrie* falls as the narrator comes to perceive his betrayal of Kari/Maria as the true cause of Karsten's zealous commitment to National Socialism. Replicating Indregård's scrupulous and overanxious reasoning, the narrator regards himself as complicit in the production of a Nazi collaborator.

While in the small town to discover the leak, the narrator is captured and tortured by none other than Dr. Carl Heidenreich. The outward reason for the torture is that the Nazis want to know what the narrator has been doing in town for the resistance movement. But, inwardly, the torture scene is both an act of atonement (for the narrator) and an act of revenge (for Dr. Heidenreich). As Heidenreich and the other Nazis pull up their sleeves to interrogate him, a thought occurs to the narrator, which he describes as "sharp and painful but still holding some comfort. He has every reason for doing this. Now you're paying an installment on your debt" (Hoel 2002: 234).[10] He views Heidenreich as largely justified in this "private settling of accounts" ("privat oppgjør") and finds relief from his guilt-induced anxiety in the torture. Being tortured by Heidenreich is a liberating experience for the narrator because he feels that he is unloading a burden of debt to Heidenreich. Hoel allows it to remain unclear whether Heidenreich understands the repayment, although the narrator imagines that Heidenreich has at least a half-knowledge of the truth: "I realized one more thing as I lay there—he both knew and didn't know that the boy was my son" (Hoel 2002: 237).[11]

After being tortured, lying bloody on the floor, the narrator experiences what he calls *the vision*, which I will discuss further below. In a plot convenience, it is Kari/Maria who saves him from dying on the floor of the torture room. Before the narrator leaves for Sweden, the two of them have an intimate discussion, which ends with another important moment in the narrator's working-through of his guilt. Whereas the torture scene is the moment of punishment that alleviates his guilt-induced anxiety, the conversation with Kari/Maria is the moment of confession, when the narrator articulates an as-yet-not-fully-understood sense of guilt for the death of his wife and son. The narrator's wife drowned herself and their son after misunderstanding the seriousness of her husband's arrest by the Gestapo near the start of the occupation period. In the narrator's view, the Germans were not truly to blame for this suicide, as he tells Kari/Maria: "In reality, I'm afraid, I was to blame. I married her because I was lonely and she loved me. But I didn't love her as much as—well she deserved. I've never forgotten you, and—I believe I used you as a shield against a new love" (Hoel 2002: 254).[12] Only at the moment of confessing does the narrator fully realize how blameworthy he was in his marriage. He reveals that he made his wife suffer to the point of nervous illness because of his fixation on his youthful romance. This confession scene reveals another way in which *den plettfrie* is to blame: he betrayed his wife by being caught in his never-forgotten love of Kari, and he has been silently suffering from intense feelings of guilt about the death of his wife and son.

Hoel's use of first-person narration carefully tracks the power of the narrator's willingness to repress knowledge and deceive himself. After recognizing Karsten as his son, he has a moment of lucidity about his past and present guilt: "The other case was also crystal-clear. . . . The boy's resemblance to me as I was at that time [in my youth] was so striking that I had a feeling—unreal, but more powerful than reality—that I was the one who stood down there, that I was a traitor, spy, pimp—because he, that youthful portrait of myself down there on the stage, was precisely *that*" (Hoel 2002: 215).[13] The narrator's identification with his Nazi son is "unreal" in the sense that it is not factual—he is not in reality a Nazi, traitor, or pimp. But subjectively the resemblance has an irrational power that is greater than any literal outward truth, because it provides an outlet for his guilty feelings about betraying Kari and passing her off to another man. Why else would he feel like a "pimp"?

At a later moment, the narrator engages in a characteristic sort of self-questioning about what he really knew about the true paternity of Karsten and at what level he knew it. He recalls that, after breaking up with the pregnant Kari/Maria, he heard about Heidenreich's marriage from some medical student friends. They said the marriage had taken place in a hurry, and none of them knew the woman. "I didn't pay much heed. Heidenreich didn't interest me any longer. Heidenreich's marriage—it never occurred to me to connect it with anything having to do with me and my affairs. Really? It didn't?" (Hoel 2002: 225).[14] The questions at the end of this passage suggest that the narrator did at some level know something about Carl Heidenreich and Kari/Maria, but that he repressed this knowledge, and that those acts of repression are now becoming clear in retrospect during his crisis of memory.

The narrator's self-interrogation continues, as he recalls an occasion when he didn't even bother to check when he thought he saw Heidenreich and Kari/Maria together, since the thought would be too absurd: "After all, I didn't suspect that . . . I didn't suspect? Why did it become so important to me, as I sat writing my notes, to include that story about Kari? And why had I totally forgotten where on earth Heidenreich was living? Why did I look out of the window time after time today? Was there someone I hoped, and feared, to see?" (Hoel 2002: 225).[15] The narrator now questions his motivations for writing the youthful recollections that make up part 2 of the novel. He wonders whether the act of forgetting Heidenreich's residence when he came to the small town on the resistance operation was perhaps intentional. Finally, he admits to himself that, even on this very day, he had at some level been expecting to recognize his own son through the window marching in the small Nazi parade. Despite his apparent newfound clarity, the narrator concludes this passage with uncertainty, by claiming that the shock of seeing Karsten was so great that it affected his memory of what he knew in the past: "I no longer remembered how [the world] had looked before—didn't remember what I'd known or not known, what I'd suspected or not suspected." (Hoel 2002: 225).[16] The shock of recognizing Karsten represents the novel's climax of the narrator's individual crisis of memory. He is no longer worthy of the nickname *den plettfrie*, and thus his self-understanding and his identity are thrown into a state of uncertainty.

Betrayal and Guilt at an Individual and Collective Level

By viewing his betrayal of Kari/Maria as the root cause of Karsten's Nazism, the narrator understands himself as blameworthy in the sense introduced by Indregård in part 1. While hiding at the narrator's house, Indregård criticizes the "barbarism" of the legal purge (*landssvikoppgjøret*): "Who among us is so pure that he can stand up in public and say, I'm innocent? I'm not a Nazi, neither openly nor secretly, neither inwardly nor outwardly, neither in thought, word or deed. Nor am I to blame for anybody else having become one" (Hoel 2002: 37).[17] When Indregård reasons this way, the narrator initially responds with impatience and skepticism, seeing him as a confused and emasculated figure on the brink of a breakdown. By the end of the novel, however, Indregård's reasoning has become the narrator's own. The name

"Indregård" itself suggests that he is a figure of the narrator's masked inner self (Inadomi 1968: 33). Indeed, the questions about responsibility and complicity introduced by Indregård in part 1 were the very questions Hoel intended to develop in this novel, according to working manuscripts: could we all have become Nazis, and are we to blame for those who did become Nazis (Tvinnereim 1975: 213)?

A skeptical reader might wonder: couldn't it be that the narrator's guilty conscience gives him an inflated sense of control over the actions and decisions of others? By the end of part 3, *den plettfrie* has unmasked himself as guilty of two love betrayals (*kjærlighetssvik*)—the first of Kari in his youth, and the second of his wife during their marriage. He then holds himself morally accountable for actions by others taken decades later, which he interprets as direct consequences of his betrayal of Kari (Inadomi 1968: 33). He never questions the conclusion that he is responsible for causing the Heidenreich family to become Nazis, even though this might very well be a misinterpretation or cognitive distortion. The narrator is so scrupulously focused on his own complicity that he views others as lacking agency and responsibility for their actions, just as Indregård's understanding of Hans Berg and his family accords them little choice in their own political decisions.

At a more general level, beyond the narrator's understanding of his individual complicity, the novel ultimately blames patriarchy in accordance with Hoel's Reichian perspective. In a key passage in part 2, the narrator imagines mankind's primordial freedom in a time before the "thousands upon thousands of years of tradition, bondage, commands and prohibitions" (Hoel 2002: 159).[18] This is probably an imaginary primordial era, he admits, but he believes in it nonetheless as a regulative ideal free from the partitions created by patriarchal prohibition. The narrator is careful to add that this dream of a "proud, sovereign being" is not a racial fantasy—the primordial man can be "a negro or a Mongolian, a Jew or a Scandinavian" (Hoel 2002: 159).[19] Still, the fantasy of the free person is male, just like the "we" of all the narrator's youthful recollections, and his main appeal in this passage seems to be his *sexual* freedom. Shortly after this dream of liberated being, the narrator considers the "invisible tether around his foot" that made him meek and fearful of desire, so that during a night of promiscuity with a young woman named Ida, he "suddenly thought [he] could see [his] old father sitting in the chair over in the darkest corner of the room. He looked stern and threatening" (Hoel 2002: 159).[20] The distant, loveless, prohibitive father figure is pictured as a restrictive force limiting sexual exploration and freedom. Moreover, the narrator recalls that his younger self had internalized the father's "course puritanical sneer" (*puritansk pøbelflir*)—an oppressive inheritance from many generations of "moralists and paragons of virtue" (Hoel 2002: 160). Passages like this emphasize that, while the narrator's father is not the physically abusive pietist who scarred Hans Berg, he is a milder patriarchal figure of prohibition and insidious repression, and one with deep roots in Norwegian culture.

In the postscript written in 1947, the narrator ruminates further on guilt and the power of self-deception, and he also records fragments of his posttorture vision. These fragments are closely connected to the theme of the distorting influence of patriarchy.[21] He writes, "It was youth and the life of youth that I saw—in a world led and governed and driven into the abyss by old men. Those old men lift their trembling fingers and say, it's a sin, it's a sin! All that your body and soul desire is sin. Remember, you are bad and all you desire is bad" (Hoel 2002: 279).[22] These old men conceive of the purpose of life as a well-organized, prohibition-laden "higher freedom" that rejects the chaos of the body—and its desires and needs for sex and love—in favor of ideals of duty, obedience, and dignity. Hoel's novel holds this ethic of duty and renunciation responsible for the psychological damage that led to the narrator's betrayal of Kari. Therefore, the patriarchal ethic is ultimately responsible for the narrator's complicity in the production of a Nazi collaborator, just as in the Reichian framework it is patriarchal repression that lies behind the mass psychology of Nazism. For both Hoel and Reich, Nazism was an expression of a sickness that would not disappear with the defeat of Nazi Germany: a cancer or a plague that required introspection and cautious self-scrutiny to exterminate it.

By expanding the question of guilt from the limited context of the Nazi occupation of Norway, with its dichotomy of resistance and collaboration, to the broad, even ahistorical, issues of patriarchy and sexuality, Hoel might be accused of muddying the waters. Do the actions of *den plettfrie* really bear comparison with the misdeeds of the Norwegian Nazi sympathizers? Does the novel not sacrifice clarity of moral distinction by spotlighting the internal dynamics of guilt of its narrator, an obsessively scrupulous resistance member? As Indregård does in part 1, the novel as a whole introduces moral ambiguity to an issue that many find clear-cut: the difference between a "good Norwegian" and a Nazi collaborator. However, the purpose of this ambiguity is not moral equivalence or any type of vagueness about the evils of Nazism. Rather, the purpose is to promote vigilance about the self-deceptive masks of innocence or self-righteousness that allow people to become complicit in what they ostensibly oppose. This message was especially pointed during the intense and controversial historical moment of the Norwegian *landssvikoppgjøret* or legal purge.

Meeting at the Milestone is important in twentieth-century literary history both as a first-person novel of interiority, with subtle depictions of the narrator's acts of repression and insight, and as a sociopolitical novel that advances a midcentury psychoanalytic critique of Nazism and patriarchy. It shows how the narrator's feelings of guilt for betraying Kari and driving his wife to suicide lead him to seek irrational punishment and to view himself as complicit in the actions of collaborators during the Nazi occupation. In one of the fragments of the vision he records near the end of the novel, he writes, "I saw Nazism as our illegitimate child. Begotten blindly and cowardly, betrayed in his mother's womb and left to fend for himself. And I saw us, the blameless and self-righteous ones, stand there and look at this creature, our child of flesh and blood, and say, 'We do not know you!'" (Hoel 2002: 280).[23] In this allegorical vision, the narrator highlights the complicity of people like him—"the spotless and self-righteous ones"—who cannot recognize the bastard child of Nazism as their own. The rhetorical purpose of this passage is clear: by drawing attention to the responsibility of the blameless ones, the novel provokes a deeper self-questioning, perhaps even self-suspicion, in its readers. It sparks crises of memory and identity, prompting its readers to search their pasts and to remove their self-congratulatory masks of blamelessness.

Dean Krouk (PhD, University of California, Berkeley, 2011) is Associate Professor of Scandinavian Studies at the University of Wisconsin-Madison and has published *Fascism and Modernist Literature in Norway* (2017) and a variety of articles on modern and contemporary Norwegian literature.

Notes

1. "Kravet om summarisk behandling og pådømmelse av landssviksaker ga uttrykk for en nazistisk mentalitet."
2. "Ensrettingen i presse, litteratur og juridisk fremgangsmåte var av skremmende karakter. Ikke under Quisling, men etter krigen kom den fascistiske periode i norsk historie. Man må til Hitlers Berlin og Stalins . . . Moskva for å finne lignende rettspraksis."
3. "For mange av oss er det blitt noe av en livsopgave, dette å få nazismen tilintetgjort. . . . Den viktigste livsopgaven."
4. "Fordi det i noen hver—i noen hver av oss—fins et lite punkt, ofte et meget kjært lite punkt, hvor det sitter en liten kime til—ikke til nazisme, å langt ifra. Men til noe som ligner ganske betenkelig."
5. The Danish novelist Tom Kristensen noted this resemblance in a review (*Politiken*, 11 June 1948). In the years around 1930, Hoel translated three of Conrad's novels, which may account for his use of a similar method of composition.
6. For an extended discussion of this essay, see Krouk (2017).
7. I will be quoting from Sverre Lyngstad's English translation in the main text, with the original Norwegian in the endnotes.

8. This emphasis on dual layers of motivation is a standard feature of most critical readings of the novel, which tend to view the narrator as motivated by repressed guilt, or as a self-deceiver. For example, see Tvinnereim, who writes, "Det er ubevisst eller halvt bevisst skyldfølelse, trang til å skrifte og til å forklare seg, som driver ham til arbeidet. Men dette motivet er flettet uløselig sammen med nazismeproblematikken i romanen" (1975: 263).
9. "Jeg vet i dag at jeg er direkte skyld i at et annet menneske, ja en hel familie, er gått til helvete—for jeg mener jo at det er å gå til helvete. Jeg er skyld i det" (Hoel 1947: 34).
10. "Og det meldte seg en annen tanke, som var skarp og ond, men allikevel rommet en trøst: Dette har han grunn til. Nå betaler du av på en gjeld" (Hoel 1947: 225).
11. "Jeg forsto en ting til der jeg lå—han både visste og ikke visste at gutten var min sønn" (Hoel 1947: 229).
12. "I virkeligheten er jeg redd for at skylden var min. Jeg giftet meg med henne, fordi jeg var ensom og hun var glad i meg. Men jeg var ikke så glad i henne som—ja, som hun fortjente. Jeg har aldri glemt deg, og—jeg tror nok at jeg brukte deg som et vern mot en ny kjærlighet" (Hoel 1947: 246).
13. "Den andre saken var også blinkende klar. . . . Guttens likhet med meg fra den gang var så slående at jeg fikk en følelse—uvirkelig, men sterkere enn virkeligheten—at det var *jeg* som sto der nede, jeg som var forræder, spion, hallik—for *det* var han jo også, dette ungdomsportrettet av meg der nede på scenen" (Hoel 1947: 206).
14. "Jeg hørte ikke nøyere efter. Heidenreich interserte meg ikke mer. Heidenreich's giftermål—det falt meg aldri inn å se det i sammenheng med meg og mitt. Så? Ikke det?" (Hoel 1947: 217).
15. "Tanken forekom meg så absurd at jeg ikke engang gikk inn for å se efter. Jeg ante jo ikke at. . . . Ante jeg ikke? Hvorfor ble det så viktig for meg, da jeg satt og skrev notatene mine, å få med den historien om Kari? Og hvorfor hadde jeg totalt glemt hvor i verden Heidenreich holdt til? Hvorfor gikk jeg og kikket ut av vinduet gang på gang nå i dag? Var det en jeg håpet og fryktet å få se?" (Hoel 1947: 217).
16. "Jeg husket ikke lenger hvordan den så ut før—husket ikke hva jeg hadde visst og ikke visst, hva jeg hadde ant og ikke ant" (Hoel 1947: 217).
17. "Hvem av oss er så ren at han kan stå frem på torvet og si: Jeg er uskyldig. Jeg er ikke nazist, hverken åpent eller i det skjulte, hverken i sinn eller skinn, hverken i tanke, ord eller gjerning. Og jeg er heller ikke skyld i at noen annen er blitt det" (Hoel 1947: 33).
18. "Tusen på tusen års tradisjon, trelldom, påbud og forbud" (Hoel 1947: 152).
19. "Et suverent, stolt vesen . . . mannen kan være neger eller mongol, jøde eller skandinav" (Hoel 1947: 151–52).
20. "et usynlig tjor rundt foten. En ting husker jeg: En gang den natten med henne, gasellen, som jeg kalte henne, tenkte jeg meg med ett min gamle far sittende i stolen borte i den mørke kroken. Og da var han streng og truende" (Hoel 1947: 152).
21. Tvinnereim has compared this vision to passages in Wilhelm Reich. See Tvinnereim (1975: 275).
22. "Det var ungdommen og ungdommens liv jeg så—i en verden ledet og styrt og kjørt i avgrunnen av gamle menn. De gamle menn løfter skjelvende pekefinger og sier: Synd og atter synd! Alt det kroppen din og sjelen din vil, er synd! Husk, du er ond, og det du vil er ondt" (Hoel 1947: 270).
23. "Jeg så nazismen som vårt uekte barn. Avlet i blinde og i feighet, forrådt i mors liv og overlatt til seg selv, til lut og kaldt vann. Og jeg så oss, de plettfrie, og selvrettferdige, stå der og se på dette vesenet, vårt barn av kjøtt og blod, og si: Vi kjenner deg ikke!" (Hoel 1947: 271).

References

Andenæs, Johannes. [1979] 1998. *Det vanskelige oppgjøret*. 3rd ed. Oslo: Tano Aschehoug.
Andenæs, Johannes, and Sulland, Frode. 2017. "Landssvikoppgjøret." *Store norske leksikon*. Retrieved 25 September 2020 from https://snl.no/landssvikoppgjøret.
Corell, Synne. 2011. "The Solidity of a National Narrative: The German Occupation in Norwegian History Culture." *Nordic Narrative of the Second World War: National Historiographies Revisited*, edited by Henrik Stenius, Mirja Österberg, and Johan Östling, 101–26. Lund: Nordic Academic Press.
Egeland, Kjølv. 1960. *Skyld og skjebne: Studier i fire romaner av Sigurd Hoel*. Oslo: Gyldendal.
Hoel, Sigurd. 1945. *Tanker i mørketid*. Oslo: Gyldendal.
———. 1947. *Møte ved milepelen*. Oslo: Gyldendal.
———. 1961. *Essays i utvalg*. Edited by Nils Lie. Oslo: Gyldendal.
———. 2002. *Meeting at the Milestone*. Translated by Sverre Lyngstad. Copenhagen: Green Integer.
Høidal, Oddvar K. 2016. "Vidkun Quisling and the Deportation of Norway's Jews." *Scandinavian Studies* 88 (3): 270–94.
Inadomi, Masahiko. 1968. *Den plettfrie: En analyse av Sigurd Hoels "Møte ved milepelen."* Oslo: Universitetsforlaget.
Jensen, Brikt. 1981. *Sigurd Hoel om seg selv*. Oslo: Den norske bokklubben.
Krouk, Dean. 2017. *Fascism and Modernist Literature in Norway*. Seattle: University of Washington Press.
Lear, Jonathan. 2005. *Freud*. London: Routledge.
Lyngstad, Sverre. 1984. *Sigurd Hoel's Fiction: Cultural Criticism and Tragic Vision*. Westport, CT: Greenwood Press.
Reich, Wilhelm. [1933] 1970. *The Mass Psychology of Fascism*. Translated by Vincent R. Carfagno. 3rd ed. New York: Farrar, Straus, and Giroux.
Rottem, Øystein. 1991. *Sigurd Hoel: Et nærbilde*. Oslo: Gyldendal.
Suleiman, Susan Rubin. 2006. *Crises of Memory and the Second World War*. Cambridge, MA: Harvard University Press.
Tvinnereim, Audun. 1975. *Risens hjerte: En studie i Sigurd Hoels forfatterskap*. Oslo: Gyldendal.

Chapter 11

THE BATTLE OVER FINNISH CULTURAL MEMORY OF WAR

Väinö Linna's *The Unknown Soldier*

Julia Pajunen

In Finnish culture and war history, *Tuntematon sotilas* (*The Unknown Soldier*) has been a dominant narrative. Published in 1954, the novel is set during Finland's Continuation War (1941–44), in which Finland was allied with Germany in a military conflict with the Soviet Union during World War II. The writer, Väinö Linna (1920–92), was a veteran who had served as a non-commissioned officer in a machine-gun company during this war and wrote the novel based on his own experiences. *The Unknown Soldier* has generally been considered a radical microhistorical narrative of the war told from the perspective of an ordinary soldier who fought in it (Stormbom 1992: 119; Varpio 2007: 270). It is the story of a machine-gun platoon's hardships from the beginning of the war until the peace treaty between Finland and the USSR. Only a few of the soldiers depicted in the novel survive the war. Linna, who had a working-class background, explained that his aim was to remove all the glory from the war and portray Finland's soldiers as they really were (Stormbom 1992: 119). When the book was first published, it sparked wide and heated public discussion (Stormbom 1992: 126; Jäntti 1980: 79; Kurjensaari 1980: 60–61; Varpio 2007: 342). The novel was criticized for its representation of Finnish army officers and the *Lottas* (members of the women's auxiliary services) as well for the crude vulgarity of the soldiers' language. Nonetheless, it became an instant bestseller. Since the novel was published only a decade after the war had ended, it has been seen to have had a great therapeutic effect in Finnish society, providing a way to deal with the war's trauma (Eskola 1984; Stormbom 1992: 62).

This chapter investigates the extraordinary status enjoyed by *The Unknown Soldier* in Finnish culture and demonstrates how the cultural memory of Linna's story has changed since the work's initial publication in 1954 from that of an antiwar novel to patriotic national discourse. Over a period of sixty years, during which over eight hundred thousand copies were sold, three film adaptations were produced, and numerous theater productions were staged, Linna's work has evolved into the dominant narrative of the Finnish collective memory of the entire war. By examining the position of this novel through the concept of collective memory, I will demonstrate how the narrative of *The Unknown Soldier* has gradually been separated from the original novel and has come to constitute an imaginary construction in Finnish culture. This construction is cultivated separately from the context of war for the purpose of cultural capital and prestige. Further, this chapter will argue that *The Unknown Soldier* as the war's dominant narrative has been dependent on its ritualization as a celebration of the nation's independence.

The concept of collective memory is useful in understanding the position of the narrative of *The Unknown Soldier* in Finland. The term "collective memory" has its roots in Maurice Halbwachs's studies on *memoire collective*.[1] The concept has been criticized in particular because Halbwachs seems to transfer the concept of individual psychology to the level of the collective (Erll 2008: 1). In this chapter, I make use of the term "collective memory," rather than "myth" or "tradition," because it leaves room to connect this concept with institutional legitimacy and power, such as research and media. At the same time, the term is practical when the aim is to examine knowledge that is shared, maintained, or relayed by a community or group of people, such as *The Unknown Soldier* has been in Finland. Collective knowledge that creates collective memory comprises, for example, views of history, important generational events, and historical traumas (Siltala 2014: 2449). Critical theorist Linda Hutcheon compares stories retold in different ways using new material in new cultural environments to genes and the process of genetic evolution. Like genes, stories adapt to new environments through mutation (Hutcheon 2006: 31). Considered in this light, every adaptation of *The Unknown Soldier* reflects the values of the director in a certain political and cultural situation. The adaptations always connect with the battle of the power to define the cultural memory of war and qualities of heroism in the Finnish culture. Linna's novel, through adaptations, is thus nowadays a part of the hegemonic and conservative discourse of remembering the war (Tepora 2015).

As discussed by Juhana Aunesluoma in chapter 1 of this volume, the Continuation War began just fifteen months after the Winter War had ended. Lasting more than three years, it greatly affected the entire nation, from the frontline military hardships to the mass civilian evacuations, which included both adults (over four hundred thousand Karelian refugees) from eastern Finnish territories as well as tens of thousands of children who were evacuated to Sweden as *krigsbarn* (war children), when the threat of war and food shortages were at their most extreme. Further, because the number of military fatalities in the Finnish army was high (Meinander 2013: 153–55), the events of the war were traumatic for the entire Finnish population and needed to be processed during the postwar period; the narrative of *The Unknown Soldier* became a means for this collective process. The Continuation War was seen as an ordeal of initiation for Finland that became a description of the country, and the collective memories of war became the foundation of national self-understanding. People and communities need stories to be able to connect themselves with the history in a way that is comprehensible and affirmative. This requires simplifications and conscious acts of forgetting (Meinander 2012: 392–94). At the same time, the historical memory helps to create a shared past and a perception of unity. For this kind of memory work, a fictional narrative is very often appropriate.

The Unknown Soldiers

As mentioned, Linna's *Tuntematon sotilas* (originally translated into English as *The Unknown Soldier*, 1957; and later as *Unknown Soldiers*, 2015) is the story of a machine-gun platoon's hardships from the beginning of the war until the peace treaty between Finland and the USSR. The platoon consists of soldiers from different social-class backgrounds and regions of Finland. The characterizations of these men are based on regional stereotypes and dialects. The novel also builds on a particular sociopolitical perspective in relation to the class distinctions of wartime Finland as well as to the politics of the war itself by means of the characterizations of the soldiers. A handful of men represent the core group (the platoon) which is central to the novel; in addition, there are numerous secondary soldier-characters who suddenly appear and then disappear or die. Linna's realistic prose relies on descriptions of the bonds of brotherhood forged between men in one platoon, as the text constitutes a "collective novel," in that it has no single main character or protagonist. The title of the most recent translation—*Unknown Soldiers*—by American translator Liesl Yamaguchi, thus underscores the work's status as a collective novel. There is no single "unknown soldier"; rather, Linna has depicted the internal dynamic within a group of soldiers, and the plot is thus determined by the development of the group of soldiers.

Thus, there are no conventional war "heroes" in this novel; instead, the author Linna depicts the meaninglessness of the soldiers' (often horrific) deaths rather than a patriotic narrative of "sacrifices for the fatherland." Linna puts faces on all his soldiers, so that they become humans (indeed flawed), memorable, and more than faceless "unknown soldiers." For example, among the important characters belonging to this core group is Second Lieutenant Koskela, a country boy hailing from a small farm in Häme. He gets nicknamed "Quiet Koski" since he speaks so little. Koskela is uncomfortable giving orders in general, and formulating commands is particularly difficult, because somehow or other he is embarrassed by the contrived formality army commanders use to say such simple things. He is widely respected by his soldiers because of his humble character, and his motto: "The things we have to do, we do—otherwise, we might as well be Lulu's chickens on the loose" (Linna 2015: 289).[2] His closest soldiers-in-arms are Private Rahikainen, the unconcerned, perennial truant from North Karelia; Corporal Hietanen, a humor-loving bloke from the southwestern part of the country around Turku; Private Vanhala, a quiet chubby fellow; Corporal Lahtinen, a big guy from northern Häme with evident communist sympathies; and the shady Corporal Lehto from the outskirts of the working-class town of Tampere, who has been without his parents since he was a little boy. The superior for this platoon is Lieutenant Lammio, a career officer from Army Academy, possessed of self-assured arrogance, who figures as the most hated character in the novel, as Linna demonstrates: "The sound of Lammio's voice alone is enough to prick the men's hostility" (Linna 2015: 5).[3] The other central member of the officer ranks is Second Lieutenant Kariluoto, who is a more versatile character. Kariluoto dreams of becoming a young career officer, and he is promoted during the war to lieutenant, and finally to captain, just before he dies. Kariluoto is the only character who marries during the war. His love for Sirkka brings a female character into the novel, even though she is a dreamlike virgin maiden whose protection seems to justify the war. Then there is Corporal Rokka, who joins the core group midway through the novel but evolves into one of the most respected soldiers. Rokka is older than the others, with a wife and children too. This insubordinate family man from the "Karelian isthmus" takes every opportunity to take it easy, but "you go where you gotta go when'na situation calls for it, and otherwise you keep it low." As a soldier, he performs brilliantly, a cool-headed killer. His line, "Where do you need a real top-notch fella? Cause you're lookin' at him" (Linna 2015: 276),[4] has become one of the most referenced lines of Linna's famous novel.

Linna employs regional dialects to characterize the distinct personalities of each of his soldiers. The differences in their speech patterns reveal qualities, moods, and personalities, and they also "assert class, authority, defiance, belonging and comedic intent," according to the translator (Yamaguchi 2015: 470). In the 2015 English translation, Liesl Yamaguchi has solved the problem of dialogue spoken in the various Finnish dialects by inventing

Figure 11.1. Graphic designer Martti Mykkänen (1926–2018), who became the leading name in postwar Finnish applied graphic arts, made the cover image of *The Unknown Soldier*. The image that is now an icon was an emergency order to WSOY with only a few days' notice in 1954. Cover image by Martti Mykkänen, from database of the publisher WSOY, courtesy of Raili and Riitta Mykkänen.

for each of the soldiers, a speaking style of his own in order to express the regional dialect that is impossible to translate directly into English. Yamaguchi thus developed an array of compensatory maneuvers in her English translation—pronounced idiolects: particularly distinctive, individual voices crafted through speech patterns, rhythm, and word choice, but also partly through systematic misspellings (Yamaguchi 2015: 471). Corporal Rokka, for example, who does not respect his commanding officers, uses a signature slack salutation, "Lissen here, Lieutenant," instead of formal grammar. Yamaguchi also stresses syllables to signal differences between the characters. For example, the humoristic tone of Corporal Hietanen is conveyed this way: "Nah, you got me on that one, I'm stumped. Pre-tty damn strange if you ask me. Just thinking about it makes me feel like somebody dropped an anvil on my head" (Linna 2015: 15).[5] Private Riitaoja, the coward of the group, mumbles his lines with disarming childishness and a stutter: "You should not talk that way. The medics were almost c-c-c-crying" (Linna 2015: 101).[6] Although Linna does not describe the backgrounds of the various soldiers in the novel, they are each identified by their dialects, and these regional identifications have led to imaginative episodes about the characters' backgrounds and pasts in subsequent adaptations.[7]

Linna's war novel thus depicts the lives and deaths of the soldiers of this platoon from their initial mobilization, to the advance to the front lines, to inhuman trench warfare, and, finally, to the chaotic retreat from the Karelian isthmus. The novel concludes at the point of the armistice, a bittersweet defeat for Finland, which meant the loss of significant territories, although the Finnish army had prevented a Soviet occupation of the entire country. As Private Vanhala puts it, "The Union of Soviet Socialist Republics won, but racing to the line for a strong second place came feisty little Finland" (Linna 2015: 466).[8] Thus, as an antiwar novel, in the European tradition of *All Quiet on the Western Front* (also a collective novel), Linna's narrative is full of sardonic irony and bitter sarcasm regarding any patriotic war narrative.

Indeed, the publication of the novel marked a turning point in the Finnish cultural memory of the war. In Ville Kivimäki's opinion, "Many earlier taboos were openly discussed and front-line soldiers were given human faces instead of idealized images, which seemed to be much more realistic and acceptable to the soldiers themselves" (Kivimäki 2012: 484). Linna thus challenged the earlier nineteenth-century romantic depictions of Finland's soldiers, who were depicted heroically by Finland's national romantic (albeit Swedish-language) poet Johan Ludvig Runeberg in his poetic epos, *Fänrik Ståls Sägner* (1848; translated as *The Tales of Ensign Stål*).[9] Linna offers an alternative portrayal of the Finnish soldier that appealed to the veterans who had actually fought on the twentieth-century battlefield. The intention of Linna's very realistic portrayal of Finnish soldiers was to shatter the old myth that they were uniformly noble and obedient. At the same time, he created characters whose grouse became to portray another kind of heroism and a new myth of Finnish men. The characters of *The Unknown Soldier* gradually became archetypes of the Finnish male, as passages from Linna's work drifted into everyday use in Finland.

Before *The Unknown Soldier*, Linna had published two, relatively poorly received novels, *Päämäärä* (The goal, 1947) and *Musta rakkaus* (Black love, 1948). They do not enjoy the same popularity as *The Unknown Soldier*. After the success of *The Unknown Soldier*, the author continued his literary career with the trilogy *Täällä Pohjantähden alla* (translated as *Under the North Star*) published in 1959, 1960, and 1962, which relates the nation's history via the story of the Koskela family, covering a period of seven decades, from 1880 to the 1950s. The trilogy describes the family history of Second Lieutenant Koskela, one of the most loved and appreciated characters of *The Unknown Soldier*. It is the story of a family of farmers, particularly poignant when national independence was gained and during the civil war that followed only weeks later in 1918. Together with *The Unknown Soldier* and the trilogy, Linna became a leading national novelist and a public figure in Finland. Yrjö Varpio has observed that the position of Linna became institution-like already in the 1970s (Varpio 2007: 649). The institutionalization of Linna encompassed the writer, his work, and also a famous film adaptation by Edvin Laine.

The Unknown Soldier has today been translated into twenty-four languages. The majority of the translations are from the 1950s; for instance, the translations into Swedish, German, Danish, and Dutch were all published already in 1955. Nonetheless, Linna's novel never made a major breakthrough in international literary markets. Literary historian Juhani Niemi has speculated that in the 1950s there was little demand for a hard-boiled realistic war novel in the marketplace of the aesthetic European novel (Niemi 1980: 58). Perhaps *The Unknown Soldier* never gained international status as one of the great European war novels due to the regionalism of the specific setting and the characters. Further, the colorful dialects that offer a significant literary element in Linna's realistic prose are extremely difficult to render in any translation. This fact highlights the exclusive connection to Finnish culture and inhibits the appreciation of an otherwise universally relevant war novel.

Canonization: Stage and Screen Adaptations of *The Unknown Soldier*

Over the years, several Finnish adaptations further solidified the position that Linna's novel had gained in the postwar decades. Most important in the context of collective memory are the films by Edvin Laine (1955), Rauni Mollberg (1985), and Aku Louhimies (2017), as well as theatrical performances by the Pyynikki Summer Theatre (1961–69) and Kristian Smeds's adaptation by the Finnish National Theatre in 2007. In addition to these adaptations, thirteen other professional stage productions have been based on *The Unknown Soldier*, three of them for summer theater. The novel was also adapted as radio drama in 1966, 1979, and 2014. Finally, Linna's masterpiece was the first Finnish work of literature to be published in English in the Penguin Classics series in 2015.

Furthermore, Linna's novel has been interpreted as a work of historiographical value. Scholarly research has impacted interpretations of the work, beginning with Knut Pipping, who compares his findings on the sociological hierarchies of warfare with *The Unknown Soldier* and asserts that they are similar (Stormbom 1992: 152). For example, Pipping concludes that *The Unknown Soldier* is not only a "great literary masterwork but it became also a documentation of real life" (Pipping 1980: 291–302). For his part, the author Linna announced that the novel "lives with the power of truth" (Stormbom 1992: 140). *The Unknown Soldier* represents Finnish soldiers as honest and prone to humor, at times playful. Real life paragons were discovered in the novel and named. The battle to define the truth about Finland's war influenced the inclination to legitimize the narrative as reliable as history writing.

Because of its multiple adaptations, it is worth examining the dominant narrative of *The Unknown Soldier*, not strictly the novel itself, in the Finnish collective memory. The narrative engages to various degrees with the audience's collective and individual memory of previous adaptations (Carlson 2003: 165). In the case of *The Unknown Soldier*, these chains of memories are endless for a Finnish audience because of these prior adaptations. At the same time, the narrative of *The Unknown Soldier* has become an inconstant memory structure: since the memory about the story does not conform to one specific adaptation, it is a construction of memory traces. This inconstant memory structure of *The Unknown Soldier* also enables the projection of the differences of the meaning of the story.

In 1955, only one year after the novel was published, the first film version directed by Edvin Laine premiered in Finland. This initial film adaptation already made significant departures from the original text. For example, the most controversial scene in the novel, where Lieutenant Colonel Karjula executes Viirilä for not obeying his order when the troops are withdrawing, was omitted. In the scene, the overly aggressive Karjula sees Viirilä, an indecent, apelike soldier, as a repulsive personification of everything that turns the army into a flock of deserters and loses his head, shocking other soldiers with his action. Also, the scene with the *Lotta*, Raili Kotilainen (a member of the women's auxiliary services) is also omitted. In the novel, the sexual behavior of Kotilainen is portrayed in a judgmental tone, and she is ridiculed for trying to find a husband at the front. Women who had served in the Finnish army as volunteer nurses at the front felt that the depiction of the female character in Linna's novel had dishonored their efforts (Kinnunen 2006: 117). The film producers also worried that the image of Finnish women would suffer if they were presented as they had been in the novel (Kinnunen 2006: 118, 120). It was safer to avoid the sensitive topic altogether and omit Kotilainen.

The most significant change was the national pathos that marked Edvin Laine's 1955 film. In the novel, Linna often satirizes the characters when they express any ideological sentiments. The film, on the other hand, represents a melodramatic nationalization of Linna's novel that would become the officially acceptable version of the Continuation War, as John Sundholm demonstrates in chapter 19 of this volume, as well as in his other publications (Sundholm 2007: 124). Laine's film adaptation affected how the novel was remembered. Yrjö Varpio has demonstrates how the actors in the film gave distinct faces and voices to the novel's characters (Varpio 2007: 374, 378). It has also been argued that Laine's film "ate the novel" with its popularity, including the almost 2.8-million-strong movie theater audience (Seppälä 2000: 15). The scenes from the novel that were chosen for the screen version thus became dominant in the collective memory of *The Unknown Soldier*.

The first theater production based on the novel, also directed by Edvin Laine, was produced in 1961 at the Pyynikki Summer Theatre. The production proved especially popular. Altogether 372 performances were staged over nine consecutive summers (Paavolainen 1992: 164–67). The trips to this summer theater production became a kind of ritual and a way to remember the war and express gratitude to the veterans (Varpio 2007: 543–44). Still, considering the popularity of Linna's novel and Laine's film, there are surprisingly few theater productions of *The Unknown Soldier*. To date, only fourteen productions have been professionally staged in Finland. Most were in the 1960s and 1970s, when the war was otherwise not a particularly popular theatrical topic. At that time, *The Unknown Soldier* was used to exemplify the importance of acknowledging conflicts (Kettunen 2005: 14).

Exactly thirty years after the first film adaptation by Laine, a second screen adaptation directed by Rauni Mollberg premiered in 1985. Finnish society had experienced industrialization, international cultural influences, and urbanization. Mollberg felt that the generation born in the 1960s had little contact with the realities of wartime, and he wished to pass the narrative to the next generation (Jokinen and Linko 1987: 40). He thus emphasized realistic premises, concentrating on the horrors of the war. The film was recorded by handheld cameras and natural lightning was simulated. The actors were younger, closer to the age among the soldiers who served. The film concentrated on Riitaoja, the "coward" among the cadre of soldiers. The interest was no longer on the therapeutic function for the nation—the emphasis shifted to interpreting the humanity of the characters (Jokinen and Linko 1987: 5). As film director, Mollberg reinstated in the narrative some of the elements that Laine had cut out. The female character, *Lotta* Kotilainen, is presented as an escort for the officers. Also, the controversial scene in which Lieutenant Colonel Karjula executes private soldier Viirilä for no apparent reason during the last moments of war, when the troops are withdrawing from the battlefield in panic, is included in the film. The characters are more versatile and deeper, so that Mollberg avoided Laine's tendency toward caricatures of the soldiers.

Despite its favorable reviews, the film attracted an audience of only about 600,000; that is, very few viewers, when compared with Laine's film and its 2.8 million viewers. Laine's film had already gained the status of "original" adaptation. The second was considered an interesting experimentation that was constantly compared with the first. It did not alter the collective perception of *The Unknown Soldier*. Thus, Mollberg's film did not change the discourse around *The Unknown Soldier* and was quickly forgotten (Sundholm 2007: 131).

The discussion surrounding *The Unknown Soldier* again escalated in 2000 when the original unedited version of Linna's novel was published in Finland as *Sotaromaani* (A war novel). The passages and paragraphs that had been censored and cut from Linna's original 1954 manuscript were restored and visually highlighted in the new edition, which facilitated a comparison between the two different texts. The publication created a discussion about how and why the original text had been censored in the 1950s, during the Cold War period. When the novel was originally published, the war was still close and the political relations with the Soviet Union still had to be taken into consideration (Varpio 2007: 364). This may also be why the process of editing received unusual attention.

Upon closer inspection, the differences between the two versions are interesting; it is likely that some of the revisions are part of the usual editing of the novel. What was deleted was some of the vulgar language, crude humor, and cursing in the dialogue of the soldiers, as well as their talk about the loose morality of the women at the front. More importantly, Linna's harsh criticism of the Finnish High Command and officers was censored and much of it deleted entirely from the 1954 edition. The restored *Sotaromaani* also contains longer sections on the general philosophy of war. However, despite this editorial censorship, these were in fact the topics that heated the discussion when the novel was first published in 1954.

Significantly, when Kristian Smeds took his stage adaptation of *The Unknown Soldier* to the Finnish National Theatre in 2007, the playwright declared that his work was based on Linna's uncensored manuscript, *Sotaromaani*. Many of the lines deleted in 1954 rang out on the stage of the Finnish National Theatre, such as a joke at the expense of Vladimir Lenin and the monologue of the communist Lahtinen about the war as an example of the greediness of the leaders. Thus, Smeds's theater adaptation strongly challenged the widely accepted narrative of *The Unknown Soldier*. Smeds took the themes of the novel, incorporated the elements of contemporary theater into the work, and expanded the scope to address present-day issues. In addition, the Finnish National Theatre is an exceptionally important venue in Finland since its history derives from 1872, as the Finnish Theatre, and since 1902, as the Finnish National Theatre, fifteen years before Finland declared independence from Russia. Its position in the cultural sphere increased the importance of Smeds's work. Smeds's production was the first time any performance based on Linna's work was presented at the Finnish National Theatre. It was intended to honor Finland's ninetieth year of independence (1917 to 2007). After the premiere, the performance was declared as "the theatre event of the decade" (Yle TV1 Aamu-tv 30.11.2007). Tabloids played a significant part in creating sensation around the performance. Headlines announced the consensus that Smeds's interpretation was a radical theatrical revolution. They also evoked the question of whether the adaptation tainted and even violated both Linna's novel and the Finnish National Theatre as institutions (Pajunen 2017: 86). The debate was heated.

At the textual level, Smeds was loyal to Linna's narrative. But contrary to expectations, he employed an associative way of interpreting the well-known novel and rewrote unfamiliar elements into the war classic. The dominating aesthetic element was a camera crew on stage filming during the whole performance. A wide onstage screen was used to feed the online and recorded video material. The use of video challenged the position of the audience, as the actors moved throughout the auditorium during the performance. The performance created a performative tension between presenting and representing the well-known war story.

The parts that challenged the shared memory of *The Unknown Soldier* and cultural memory of war the most were not publicly discussed. For example, director Smeds included a scene of a gang rape by Finnish soldiers. The topic is not explicit in Linna's text; however, there are hints of sexual violence, as one of the soldiers is trafficking girls while the troops are occupying the city of Petrozavodsk. Smeds also embodied the mental effects of the war through the character Riitaoja, who suffers from war psychosis. In the play, he is executed for being a coward. In the novel, he dies in battle, together with the bravest soldier, Lehto. Smeds contests the conventional appropriation of Linna's characters by performing their unpleasant qualities, and, in this manner, restores the narrative to a version perhaps closer to Linna's original novel, in which the characters are presented as flawed human beings, not as heroes. Smeds's perspective could be seen as postnational (Kinnunen and Jokisipilä 2012: 474). The characters are also interpreted through the lens of contemporary personality types. Lieutenant Lammio, the most hated character of the novel, was depicted in the reviews as a caricature of a business manager. The youngest soldier, Hauhia, who dies on his first watch, is presented as a teenaged TV host, highlighting his youth. Smeds thus returned *The Unknown Soldier* to its critical context. However, in the context of collective memory, the problem with theater as an art form is that the performance disappears. *The Unknown Soldier* at the National Theatre sold out for the two-year period. It attracted a total audience of seventy-six thousand (Finnish theater database). Despite this evident success, theater cannot compete in distribution with the film industry.

When the novel was first published in 1954, it divided opinions strongly. The novel was debated in the press for months, more than any novel before or since (Varpio 2007: 309, 342). It also challenged the prevailing conservative nationalism (Kivimäki 2012: 487). Hence it is interesting that as time went on the narrative became tightly bound to a celebration of the nation's independence. Almost all stage presentations of the work, excluding summer theater productions, are near Finland's annual Independence Day, 6 December. The tradition of televising Laine's film on Independence Day began in 2000. Each year almost a million Finns, nearly 20 percent of the population, watch the Finnish Broadcasting Company's airing of the film. This television ritual greatly impacts the memory culture surrounding the story, becoming part of the official and institutional remembrance of Finland's engagement in World War II.

The novel's criticism of the military authorities and its challenge to the image of the Finnish heroes does not fit with *The Unknown Soldier* as a revised and patriotic narrative that is enacted as a ritual of remembrance. As discussed earlier, the original novel, *The Unknown Soldier* was highly critical toward war and the Finnish authorities. Nowadays, such criticism is forgotten, and only the "heroes" of the novel are celebrated. The fact that nearly all the soldiers in the platoon perish and that Finland loses its defensive war with the Soviet Union (although the nation remained independent) is forgotten. The novel is used as a testimony to national unity because it witnesses how men fought alongside one another, despite Finland's bloody civil war in 1918 that had divided the young nation only thirty years earlier (Kivimäki 2012: 486). However, in Linna's novel, the depiction of the soldiers' solidarity only applies to their own platoon, whereas their attitude toward others, especially the higher command, is generally hostile.

This tendency can be analyzed according to Richard Schechner's idea of cultural ritual. He emphasizes public life as a stage for collective performances and defines performance as restored behavior (Schechner 2006: 28). According my interpretation, the status of *The Unknown Soldier* and its adaptations in collective memory can be defined using Schechner's definition of restored behavior. The idea of the narrative has become independent in relation to Linna's novel. In other words, the idea is merely a number of values connected with its status as well as a certain kind of accumulation of experiences, opinions, and accents. By Schechner's definition, the origin of these meanings has become unknown, because it is distorted by repetition and the myth that is connected with the narrative (Schechner 2006: 34). This link to the national holiday also explains why the adaptations in the twenty-first century have been interpreted through national questions. Portraying the real nature of Finnish men is a strategy of reading that the new adaptations cannot escape. It is also always considered a cultural exploit, and those who direct adaptations of *The Unknown Solder* redeem their position in Finnish cultural history.

Conclusion

In contemporary discourse in Finland the references to *The Unknown Soldier* employed to describe Finnish people or Finland as a country have mostly lost their connection to Linna's original novel. The fact that the novel describes a time of crisis and extreme violence has largely been forgotten. Writer and cultural critic Tommi Uschanov, for example, states that the war becomes a value that should be a source of gratitude because it gave Finnish people an opportunity to show what they are capable of doing (Uschanov 2006: 330). This sentiment is completely opposite from Linna's depiction of war in his novel, in which war is an interruption to normal, human life. *The Unknown Soldier* and its characters have been used in ways that are foreign to the perspective in Linna's novel (Välimäki 2011: 51). They are taken out of their original relationships and moved into contemporary society in the form of different kinds of persons; for example, in a leadership guidebook the characters are cultivated as models of business leaders (Lundberg 2005). The idealistic image of the characters suits educational examples, where Second Lieutenant Koskela is the most admired (See Kettunen 2006: 119). It does not matter that in the novel Koskela is actually humble and fair to his soldiers, but at the same time he is a man who hides his emotions that burst out into violent behavior when he gets drunk and beats his fellow officers. Although Koskela has been used as a paradigm of management in change (Arnkil 2005: 40–41), in a closer reading, the character does not submit to the demands of the twenty-first century. The use of the idealized image of Koskela has been criticized in that in professional life today, he would be too soft: in modern late capitalism, the ones who survive the best have no emotional attachments to their subordinates (Siltala 2004: 315). The use of characters to represent the Finnish nation is questioned, and the position of Linna as universal authority has been questioned as well (see for example Arnkil and Sinivaara 2006).

Yet, despite these new interpretations and the scholarly criticism of the patriotic use of *The Unknown Soldier*, the latest cinematic adaptation by Aku Louhimies (2017) continues to reproduce an uncontested, patriotic representation of the novel. The film premiered in October 2017 as part of Finland's centennial. This most recent cinematic version of *The Unknown Soldier* is the most expensive movie production in Finnish history, and has already attracted an audience of a million viewers, making it the fourth most popular domestic production in Finland. The film's popularity shows that the meaning of *The Unknown Soldier* as a ritual of remembrance still holds, as John Sundholm illuminates in chapter 19 of this volume.

Although the most recent film adaptation is still based on the original text by Linna, it continues to narrow the narrative that circulates in Finnish cultural memory. Louhimies concentrates on just a few of the novel's main characters, those who have most often been viewed as the "heroes," that is to say Rokka, Koskela, Hietanen, and Kariluoto. Although the home front is not described in the novel at all, director Louhimies and scriptwriter Jari Olavi Rantala have added scenes in which the soldiers visit home, which creates a more psychologized image of the soldiers. Overall, there are minor changes compared with earlier renditions of the work that further strengthen the patriotic reading of the narrative.

The continual return of Linna's story is due to its enormous importance in Finnish collective memory and historiography, as demonstrated by numerous scholars. In Finland, World War II signifies both the emergence of a modern civic state as well as a unifying national sacrifice. In the Finnish context, the mythical elements of wartime offer ageless content that leaves no room for other subjects of remembrance (Tepora 2015). Louhimies draws on a reading of *The Unknown Soldier* as the great narrative that unifies the whole nation, despite the fact that Linna's text is harshly critical of national patriotism and does not offer nostalgic "monuments" of Finnishness (Arnkil 2005: 39). The same occurs in political speeches in which *The Unknown Soldier* has become a safe term for making cultural references and appealing to the national spirit. The institutional position that Linna has gained has over time disconnected him from his working-class background, and he is referenced conveniently by both left- and right-wing politicians (Niemelä 2006: 293). The work is suitable to any situation or context. *The Unknown Soldier* has become a symbol of national unity, even though Linna's success was based on the way he communicated the end of unity in his novel (Arnkil and Sinivaara 2006: 21).

In summary, this chapter has explored *The Unknown Soldier* as a national narrative that is repeated from one decade to the next as an actively maintained national ritual. The use of *The Unknown Soldier* continually connects with the battle of defining Finnishness and heroism in Finnish culture. It is important to challenge these existing models and narratives that dominate the shared collective cultural memory. Adaptations that deconstruct the contemporary use of the narrative and question the prior approaches are therefore crucial in this process of defining and redefining the meaning of *The Unknown Soldier* in Finland.

Julia Pajunen (PhD, University of Helsinki, 2017), an independent scholar, worked as a postdoctoral researcher at the University of Helsinki 2017–19 on theater relations between Finland and Estonia. Her PhD dissertation explores the adaptation of *The Unknown Soldier* by Kristian Smeds. She coauthored, with Professor Hanna Korsberg, "Performing Memory, Challenging History: Two Adaptations of *The Unknown Soldier*" (2017) in *Contemporary Theatre Review*.

Notes

1. Maurice Halbwachs began developing the term in *Cadres sociaux de la mémoire* (1925).
2. "Asialliset hommat suoritetaan, muuten ollaan kuin Ellun kanat" (Linna 2000: 334).
3. "Miehet vihasivat Lammion ääntäkin" (Linna 2000: 37).
4. "Kuule, vänskä. Mis sie tarviit oikein hyvää miest? Täs siul on sellanen" (Linna 2000: 320).
5. "Ei, mää olen mahdottoman hämmästynyt. Mää ihmettelen oikein kauhiast tämmöst ja olen niinkun klavul päähä lyöty" (Linna 2000: 47).
6. "Ei soa puhua. Lääkintämiehilläkin veet silmissä" (Linna 2000: 135).
7. See, for example, Ilkka Malmberg's *Tuntemattomat sotilaat*, 2007. In his book, Malmberg writes about the characters' backgrounds and pasts. He also compares the conditions of wartime with today's society (Malmberg 2007).
8. "Sosialististen Neuvostotasavaltojen Liitto voitti, mutta hyvänä kakkosena tuli maaliin pieni ja sisukas Suomi" (Linna 2000: 466).
9. *The Tales of Ensign Stål* is an episodic collection of Swedish poems that describes the events of the Finnish War (1808–9). The poems feature an image of the Finnish soldiers where the greatest value of all is the love for the fatherland and the greatest honor for a soldier is to die for his country. *The Tales of Ensign Stål* offers patriotic ideology that Linna challenged in his alternative portrayal of the Finnish soldier.

References

Arnkil, Antti. 2005. "Huomautuksia Väinö Linnasta ja muistista." *Nuori Voima* 3: 39–43.
Arnkil, Antti, and Olli Sinivaara. 2006. *Kirjoituksia Väinö Linnasta*. Helsinki: Teos.
Carlson, Marvin. 2003. *The Haunted Stage: Theatre as Memory Machine*. Ann Arbor: University of Michigan Press.

Erll, Astrid. 2008. "Cultural Memory Studies: An Introduction." In *Cultural Memory Studies— An International and Interdisciplinary Handbook*, edited by Astrid Erll and Ansgar Nünning, 1–15. Berlin: Walter de Gruyter.
Eskola, Katarina. 1984. "30-vuotias Tuntematon sotilas—kansallisesta terapeutista ihmisten toiminnan tulkiksi." *Sosiologia* 21(4): 325–32.
FILI—Finnish Literature Exchange. The Finnish Literature in Translation database. Retrieved 18 September 2018 from http://dbgw.finlit.fi/kaannokset/lista.php?order=author &asc=1&lang=ENG.
Finnish Theatre Database. Retrieved 18 September 2018 from http://ilona.tinfo.fi/esitys_lista .aspx?lang=fi.
Hutcheon, Linda. 2006. *A Theory of Adaptation*. New York: Routledge.
Jokinen, Kimmo, and Maaria Linko. 1987. *Uusi Tuntematon: Rauni Mollbergin ohjaaman Tuntematon sotilas -elokuvan ensi-illan aikainen vastaanotto*. Jyväskylä: Jyväskylän yliopisto.
Jäntti, Yrjö A. 1980. "Päämäärästä Tuntemattomaan sotilaaseen." In *Väinö Linna—Toisen tasavallan kirjailija*, 70–81. Porvoo: WSOY.
Kettunen, Pauli. 2005. "Tuntematon sotilas ja kansallinen suorituskyky." *Hiidenkivi* 1: 11–14.
———. 2006. "Tuntematon sotilas ja kansallinen suorituskyky." In *Kirjoituksia Väinö Linnasta*, edited by Antti Arnkil and Olli Sinivaara, 119–30. Helsinki: Teos.
Kinnunen, Tiina. 2006. *Kiitetyt ja parjatut: Lotat sotien jälkeen*. Helsinki: Otava.
Kinnunen, Tiina, and Markku Jokisipilä. 2012. "Shifting Images of 'Our Wars': Finnish Memory Culture of World War II." In *Finland in World War II: History, Memory Interpretations*, edited by Tiina Kinnunen and Ville Kivimäki, 435–82. Leiden: Brill.
Kivimäki, Ville. 2012. "Between Defeat and Victory: Finnish Memory Culture of the Second World War." *Scandinavian Journal of History* 37(4) (September): 482–504.
Kurjensaari, Matti. 1980. "Tuntematon ja kansakunta." In *Väinö Linna—Toisen tasavallan kirjailija*, 59–69. Porvoo: WSOY.
Linna, Väinö. 1954. *Tuntematon sotilas*. Helsinki: Werner Söderström.
———. 2000. *Sotaromaani*. Juva: WSOY.
———. 2015. *Unknown Soldiers*. Translated by Liesl Yamaguchi. New York: Penguin Books.
Lundberg, Tom. 2005. *Tuntematon sotilas ja johtamisen taito*. Lahti: Motto-julkaisut.
Malmberg, Ilkka. 2007. *Tuntemattomat sotilaat*. Jyväskylä: Gummerus, Helsingin Sanomat.
Meinander, Henrik. 2012. *Suomi 1944: Sota, yhteiskunta, tunnemaisema*. Helsinki: Siltala.
———. 2013. *A History of Finland*. New York: Oxford University Press.
Niemelä, Kyösti. 2006. "Linnan ironia ja ideologia." In *Kirjoituksia Väinö Linnasta*, edited by Antti Arnkil and Olli Sinivaara, 293–304. Helsinki: Teos.
Niemi, Juhani. 1980. "Tuntematon sotilas sodankuvauksen perinteessä." In *Väinö Linna— Toisen tasavallan kirjailija*, 47–58. Porvoo: WSOY.
Paavolainen, Pentti. 1992. *Teatteri ja suuri muutto. Ohjelmistot sosiaalisen murroksen osana 1959–1971*. Jyväskylä: Kustannus Oy Teatteri, Gummerus.
Pajunen, Julia. 2017. *Tulkintojen ristitulessa: Kristian Smedsin Tuntematon sotilas teatteri- ja mediaesityksenä*. Helsinki: Unigrafia.
Pipping, Knut. 1980. "Kaksi konekiväärikomppaniaa." In *Väinö Linna—Toisen tasavallan kirjailija*, 291–302. Porvoo: WSOY.
Schechner, Richard. 2006. *Performance Studies—An Introduction*. New York: Routledge.
Seppälä, Juha. 2000. "Tuntemattomat kuvat." In *Väinö Linna, Kootut teokset II. Tuntematon sotilas*, 5–19. Juva: WSOY.
Siltala, Juha. 2004. *Työelämän huonontumisen lyhyt historia*. Keuruu: Otava.
———. 2014. "Kollektiivinen muisti—kuka on se joka muistaa." *Lääketieteellinen Aikakauskirja Duodecim* 130(24): 2449–58.
Stormbom, N.-B. 1992. *Väinö Linna: Kirjailijan tie ja teokset*. Juva: WSOY.

Sundholm, John. 2007. "The Unknown Soldier: Film as a Founding Trauma and National Monument." In *Collective Traumas: Memories of War and Conflict in 20th-Century Europe*, edited by Conny Mithander, John Sundholm, and Maria Holmgren Troy, 111–41. Brussels: P.I.E. Peter Lang.

Tepora, Tuomas. 2015. "Mikä tekee sota-ajasta muistettavan." Ennen ja nyt, Historian tietosanomat. Retrieved 12 September 2018 from http://www.ennenjanyt.net/2015/08/mika-tekee-sota-ajasta-muistettavan-sota-ja-kollektiivinen-muistaminen/

Uschanov, Tommi. 2006. "Toisen tasavallan moralisti." In *Kirjoituksia Väinö Linnasta*, edited by Antti Arnkil and Olli Sinivaara, 307–56. Helsinki; Teos.

Varpio, Yrjö. 2007. *Väinö Linnan elämä*. Porvoo: WSOY.

Välimäki, Susanna. 2011. "Ihanaa leijonat ihanaa: päällekirjoittava adaptaatio Kristian Smedsin Tuntemattomassa sotilaassa." *Lähikuva* 3: 41–57.

Yamaguchi, Liesl. 2015. "Note on the Translation." In Väinö Linna, *Unknown Soldiers*, 467–73. New York: Penguin Books.

Chapter 12

INVESTIGATING SWEDEN'S POSTWAR NEUTRALITY
Ethics in Per Olov Enquist's *The Legionnaires*

Jan Krogh Nielsen

Baltutlämningen (the extradition of the Balts), the 1945–46 Swedish extradition to the Soviet Union of 146 Baltic soldiers, is a controversial chapter in Swedish postwar history, one surrounded by much political debate. The event was revived with the publication in 1968 of Per Olov Enquist's documentary novel *Legionärerna* (translated as *The Legionnaires*, 1973), which won the Nordic Council's Literature Prize in 1969. The 146 extradites were part of a group of 167 Baltic soldiers who had either volunteered or been conscripted into Nazi German forces in 1941, when the Baltic states were occupied. Not wanting to surrender to the invading Russians in 1944, they fled to Sweden. The extradition was controversial, particularly because of the uncertainty of the soldiers' fate in the hands of the Soviet Union: Would they get a fair trial? Would they be treated as traitors and executed? According to the Hague Conventions, as a neutral country, Sweden was not required to extradite any soldiers. In other words, Swedish politicians were not bound by international conventions, and therefore the choice they had to make was an independent political one. Adding to the complications and the considerations was the fact that the United States and Great Britain, not acknowledging the 1940 Soviet annexation of the Baltic states, refused to return Baltic prisoners of war to the Soviet Union, allowing them instead to emigrate to Great Britain, the United States, and other Western countries (Braconier 1994; Nollendorfs and Neiburgs 2015). Any decision by the Swedish government to extradite the Balts would be the result of a political choice rather than an obligation.

The narrator of *Legionärerna*, referred to as *undersökaren* (the investigator),[1] seeks to understand the political and ethical circumstances surrounding the decision to extradite the Baltic (primarily Latvian) soldiers, despite serious doubts about their judicial fate in the Soviet Union. Although the novel's narrator-investigator claims to fail in his attempt to get a clear understanding of the political, personal, and emotional factors underlying the decision, Enquist's novel succeeds in deconstructing this national political trauma, showing that it cannot be fully understood without considering as essential an appreciation of its individual and personal consequences on all levels, from the level of those making the decision to the level of those most severely affected by it.

Despite being a work of fiction, *Legionärerna* revived, more than twenty years after the extradition, the public debate about the decision. This was due not to the failed accomplishment of the narrator's clearly stated explanation of the political logic of the extradition (and by extension, political decisions) but to the fact that the novel, beyond simply analyzing and describing the events, invoked an interpersonal ethics irreducible to ideology or politics, which showed that a national historical narrative of guilt-free innocence can

Figure 12.1. Baltic legionnaires behind barbed wire in the internment camp Ränneslätt, Sweden. A total of 146 Baltic refugee soldiers were extradited to the Soviet Union in January 1946, despite doubts that they would receive a fair trial there. The Swedish government officially apologized for the extradition in 1994. Per Olov Enquist's 1968 documentary novel *The Legionnaires* explores the political and ethical dilemmas posed by the extradition. Unknown photographer. Courtesy of Scanpix, SIPA USA.

only be maintained temporarily at a simplistically ideological and naïve political level. *Legionärerna* dramatized and evoked the kind of trauma that is integral to the experience of individual and, by extension, collective, ethical responsibility.

Enquist's novel might thus be viewed as a literary representation of this political question, and maybe also, in a deeper, more general sense, part of the debate about Sweden's role during World War II, a debate that is still continuing, as discussed by John Gilmour in chapter 5 of this volume.[2] In the epilogue to the 1970 edition of the novel, Enquist argues that the extradition of the Balts led to the collapse of the dominant self-image of Swedish postwar humanitarianism, "an image of Sweden as the promised land of humanitarianism" (Enquist 1970a: 402).[3] This image of Sweden was not so much based on Sweden's official actions during the war itself, in which Sweden had, as Enquist puts it, "certain German-friendly actions on its conscience" (Enquist 1970a: 401–2),[4] but more on its postwar aid as well as the achievements of Raoul Wallenberg and Folke Bernadotte in saving Jews and negotiating the freedom of prisoners from German concentration camps.

Investigation of a Trauma

In the novel, the narrator sees the long Swedish "fixation" with the extradition of the Balts as possibly a part of a Swedish or Western European "trauma," "a part of a guilt, a manifestation of schizophrenic Europe's secret illness" (Enquist 1973: 505–6).[5] The significant impact and importance of *Legionärerna*, not just in Swedish literature but also in Swedish public debate, is no doubt tied to this broader historical and political context of Swedish and European postwar guilt. However, although the novel revived this Swedish trauma, it would take another twenty-six years before, in 1994, the Swedish government officially apologized and criticized the extradition, inviting the forty-four still-living Baltic extradites to Sweden. Of these, forty came and met with King Carl XVI Gustaf. Minister of Foreign Affairs Margaretha af Ugglas apologized for the suffering caused by the extradition: "I apologize for the human suffering that you and your fellow soldiers experienced as a result of the extradition decision. The Swedish government agrees wholeheartedly with the criticism of this decision" (Ehrensvärd 1994).[6]

The novel tells the story of the narrator-investigator's research into the facts behind the extradition of the Balts through documents and interviews with former Baltic soldiers, Swedish military guards, Swedish politicians, etc. It is divided into four main parts that to some extent reflect the chronology of the extradition. Part 1, "Sommaren" (Summer), describes the historical World War II background for the Balts' escape to Sweden, their arrival and internment in the summer of 1945, and the first stage of the decision to extradite them. Part 2, "Ränneslätt," describes episodes from the internment camp Ränneslätt, including a hunger strike among the Balts, as well as the political events and debate surrounding the extradition decision. The final phase of the events, the actual extradition of the Balts in January 1946 to Latvia (then annexed by the Soviet Union) is described in part 3, "Legionärernas uttåg" (Exodus of the Legionnaires). The fourth, and last, part, "Hemkomsten" (Homecoming) focuses on the investigator's visit to Latvia in 1967 and describes his interviews with former legionnaires and his attempts to find out what happened to the extradites.

Reading *Legionärerna* as an Ethical Work

Presumably as a consequence of the documentary approach, Enquist's novel was initially read by some critics solely with a focus on its historical accuracy and representation. According to Rolf Yrlid's study of the reception, out of the sixteen reviews that followed the publication of the book in 1968, six *only* reviewed the novel as a historical account (Yrlid 1975). Reflecting this common impression of the work, Arturs Landsmanis in 1970 authored a small book, *De misstolkade legionärerna* (The misinterpreted legionnaires), intent on, as the publisher, Lettiska Nationella Fonden (Latvian National Foundation) states it in the preface, "correcting the errors"[7] in Enquist's novel (Landsmanis 1970: 2). Viewed as a work of fiction, the novel has frequently been read as a description of the narrator's (and for some critics, that means the author, Per Olov Enquist's) attempt to reconcile the conflict between the personal and the political, in most cases concluding that this reconciliation proves impossible. Other readings have focused on the tension between fiction and facts, literature and nonfiction. Enquist himself has never claimed or pretended that his book was a historical work, although he clearly acknowledges the blurred lines between fiction and facts. Hence, in the preface he writes, "This is a novel about the extradition of the Balts, but if the word *novel* gives offence, *documentary report* or *book* can be used instead" (Enquist 1973: vii).[8]

It is not my aim here to analyze where the lines between the fictional and the historical are being crossed. Regardless of its exact historical accuracy, *Legionärerna* is a work with an emphasis on politics and ethics that has implications for the understanding of Swedish postwar guilt, specifically in relation to the extradition of the Balts. The novel's impact is due to its emphasis on the fact that the political decisions and consequences of the extradition of the Balts are not only a matter of ideology and politics, they are also tied to ethical, interpersonal, and human questions.

This approach is not the way the novel has typically been read, although many critics have focused on the contrast between the personal and emotional on the one hand and the political and the ideological on the other. Most notably, Erik H. Henningsen emphasizes this dichotomy in his 1975 study of the novel, *Per Olov Enquist*, a study frequently referenced by subsequent readers of the novel. Henningsen argues that the central project of the novel, namely to connect the individual and the world, fails. As do other scholars, such as Ross Shideler and Thomas Bredsdorff, Henningsen quotes the very last sentence of the novel—"I'll never understand anyway" (Enquist 1973: 508)[9]—and reads it as a concluding statement regarding the impossibility of understanding the political, a position that Shideler and Bredsdorff do not embrace to quite the same degree, although they too see this concluding sentence as expressing the limits of a clear understanding of the logic of political events.

Although the cited passage is the last sentence in the book, and therefore does carry some interpretative weight, it is not the final, nor sole, conclusion that the narrator draws. Indeed, the narrator states in the beginning of the last chapter that, "after all, something had to come at the end, though it seemed unreasonable to suggest that the building was finished, that the picture was complete" (Enquist 1973: 501).[10] The passage that Henningsen quotes appears in a description of the narrator's memory of his experiences and emotions a year earlier, on the deck of a ferry back from Latvia in 1967, before he has finished the work on the book. However, the immediately preceding paragraph, the second-to-last, in which the narrator reflects on the whole experience of writing the book, before he returns to the scene at the ferry, represents the actual chronological end of the narrative and tells a somewhat different story, namely the one that describes the narrator as being unable to ignore the faces and fates of the people he has encountered. In this concluding paragraph, the narrator focuses on the intersubjectively ethical, not on politics or ideology but on human beings, as *individuals*:

> He didn't know it himself, but what he was now experiencing was the last happy phase of the investigation. The summer would still be relaxed, the work dispassionate; for a month or two yet he would still be able to play about with the extradition and the extradited as if he were playing a game. Then all the faces and voices would overpower him, their destinies become too obtrusive, the general picture unclear, the trauma complicated and diffuse, his own life far too close to theirs. For they were alive, and they would go on living even if they were dead. And when, on a spring day of 1968, he wrote the last lines, it was with an almost desperate feeling of relief, as if at last he were to be given the chance to breathe, to live his own life, to leave the prison they had built for him. (Enquist 1973: 507–8)[11]

Margareta Zetterström has argued that this passage seems to be contradicted or negated by the following paragraph, the last in the novel, in which the narrator, as mentioned above, states that he will "never understand anyway," but the narrative chronology, along with the novel's general illumination of the (inter)personal ethics, suggests a different conclusion (Zetterström 1970). In this particular passage, the narrator—unable to uncover the political, ideological logic—describes an ethical responsibility that is beyond thematization and ideology, a responsibility ignited by faces and voices, bringing to mind Lithuanian-French philosopher Emmanuel Levinas's insistence on the face as the phenomenological site of the ethical experience. Levinas argues in *Totality and Infinity* that "the epiphany of the face is ethical" (Levinas 2005: 199). When the narrator states that he feels imprisoned, having lost his own life, he is describing an experience that is remarkably similar to the description of being subject to an ethical responsibility for the Other that Levinas describes in *Otherwise than Being, or, Beyond Essence*, in which he characterizes the experience of responsibility as a "trauma of persecution" that leads to a state of being a "witness that does not thematize what it bears witness of, and whose truth is not the truth of representation, is not evidence" (Levinas 1998: 146). The narrator-investigator—and/or Enquist, the author, if one likes—intends to be a traditional witness who thematizes and represents the story of the extradition of the Baltic soldiers. It is for the reader to judge, as Enquist writes in the epilogue to the 1970 PAN/Norstedts edition of *Legionärerna*: "In my book, I do not provide a final truth, I provide no clear final answers to questions such as these [regarding the underlying motives on both sides of the conflict]. I think it is more important that each reader search the heart and test the mind and provide the answers they can justify to themselves."[12] But despite the epilogue's explicitly stated aim for objectivity, the narrator-investigator's experiences transcend the roles of both investigator and traditional witness. What he describes is not the desired order or clarity of a witness seeing the events from the distance; it is, rather, the experience of being caught up in the trauma of persecution, experiencing that, as he says, "faces and voices ... overpower him, ... destinies become too obtrusive, the general picture unclear, the trauma complicated and diffuse, his own life far too close to theirs" (Enquist 1973: 507–8).[13] It is the experience of being overwhelmed by an ethical responsibility that transcends politics and ideology. It is, I will argue, the novel's emphasis on this personal dimension of the political that resulted in its significant impact on the postwar debate concerning the extradition of the Balts.

People and People's Faces: The Individual Stories behind the Trauma

While the novel is inspired by the Swedish collective political trauma of the extradition of the Balts, and a wish to understand it, it is in conveying the complex individual experiences behind that trauma that the novel encourages the reader to reflect critically on this political event. Emmanuel Levinas has described the reading of books (especially "national literatures"—he mentions canonical authors such as Dostoyevsky, Tolstoy, and Shakespeare, among others) as a "*modality* of our being" (Levinas 1985: 22) in which "initial shocks become questions and problems, giving one to think" (Levinas 1985: 21). Levinas's response is a remarkably precise description not only of Enquist's project and his narrator's situation but also of the role of Enquist's book. Furthermore, Enquist's inquisitive style of writing invites the reader to think, which is consistent with what Enquist wrote in a letter to Margareta Zetterström explaining his faith in a novel that makes the reader think for themselves. He does acknowledge, however, in the same letter, that he has a feeling that he might have led the reader into taking a (particular) stand—"Somewhere, a feeling that I, *nonetheless*, have steered him [the reader] into taking a stand"[14]—but from Zetterström's references to the personal letter, it is not clear whether Enquist indicates in which direction he might unintentionally have led the reader, and Zetterström concludes her article about *Legionärerna* by emphasizing that "to the question of whether it was correct to extradite the Balts, Enquist provides no answer."[15] But more important than whether the novel may influence the reader in one direction or the other is the fact that it casts a human and ethical light on this Swedish collective trauma, a light that both illuminates and simultaneously transcends the darkness of politics and ideology that surrounded the Balt extradition for more than twenty years.

In the beginning of the novel, the narrator describes his experiences in Jackson, Mississippi, where he witnesses the end of the 1966 civil rights movement March Against Fear, an experience that leads him to question his own overly emotional engagement and sows the seed for the "investigation" of the extradition of the Balts. The narrator wonders, "What does the mechanism behind a political action look like?" (Enquist 1973: 47).[16] An answer should not, however, simply replace feeling; the emotional engagement must remain, and one should "keep one's feeling but reduce one's ignorance" (Enquist 1973: 47).[17] A perfect balance of knowledge and feeling, participation and analysis, is the goal.

Although the novel ultimately depicts this as an impossible abstraction, the narrator's aspiration is a worthy one: to be able to be moved by the political, but at the same time remain critically aware of context and facts. However, it is evident from his personal encounters with the Balts, with former politicians, guards, etc., that the narrator increasingly experiences an ethical responsibility that is not intellectually based. This is concretely and symbolically represented in the narrator's description of a departure on a ship from Riga on 17 July 1967, a scene that appears toward the very end of the novel, suggesting its significance. The narrator is on the ship, one of only two every year to visit Riga, bringing tourists and relatives from Stockholm and the Western world for just a short visit, after which some will have to leave behind family members they probably have not seen since 1944, "mothers and fathers, brothers and sisters and cousins" (Enquist 1973: 502).[18] It is a gripping scene, showing the human pain caused by the politically motivated isolation of the Soviet population, the separation of families and friends. The narrator's awareness of the pain of witnessing the "brief, painfully intimate point of contact between two peoples who had once been one people" (Enquist 1973: 502)[19] is palpable.

While waiting to board, the narrator is approached by a woman, who tells him that she is German but is unable to get out of the Soviet Union after having followed her husband to a prison camp in Siberia, where he left her for a Russian woman, after which she brought up their children alone. Now that the children have left home, she wants to leave but cannot get permission from the Soviet authorities. In the narrator's description, the woman comes alive, along with her history, her aging, a glass of lemonade, as a "människa" (human being), a term that throughout the novel seems to evoke and emphasize a sense of the individual as more than just a piece of a political puzzle, more than a comma in an ideological narrative. The narrator's description is unusual exactly in regard to its use of the word "människa," indeed so unusual that the translator, presumably puzzled by this seeming redundancy, simply left it out in the English translation, which reads, "At one time she must have been very pretty. There she sat with her glass of fruit juice and her clear-cut profile and her brushed-back hair" (Enquist 1973: 501–2), leaving out the phrase "she herself was a human being [or person] . . ."[20] As the narrator boards the ferry, leaving the woman behind, he notes that she was "not even a parenthesis in his investigation, a comma at most" (Enquist 1973: 502),[21] as if to distance himself from the impression the meeting has made on him, a metaphor he repeats the moment after as a rhetorical question, presumably to convince himself that there is nothing more he can do: "Could he waste time on commas?" (Enquist 1973: 502).[22] Later, as he is watching the crowd of people on the quay from the ferry, he is still affected by the encounter, but, clearly without any logical connection, he concludes that since she is not visible in the crowd, "she was a comma he could rub out for good" (Enquist 1973: 502)[23]—which of course the description of the episode in the novel shows he could not.

The ensuing series of questions further reveals that this encounter cannot be made to fit neatly into the pattern the narrator is trying to detect: "Which moral-political conflict could she be fitted into? In which pattern was she the irrational factor? Of which colliding principles had she become a victim?" (Enquist 1973: 502).[24] It is as if the narrator consistently attempts to organize his experiences intellectually, to find the principles according to which this woman can be reduced to an "irrational factor"—thematized, invisible in the crowd. He does not succeed; the description of the woman is so personal and colored by feelings that she becomes much more than just a comma in the story—she becomes a symbolic representation of the narrator's failed attempt to organize and understand the political, while keeping his feelings at bay.

Even when the woman is not visible in the crowd, other familiar faces are. The narrator recognizes "E," one of the former prisoners, and concludes that the story he is writing, the mechanics he is trying to uncover, the metaphorical puzzle, keeps changing: the "tiny puzzle-piece" that he holds "seemed to come alive, to change, to be influenced" (Enquist 1973: 503).[25] The puzzle that the narrator is trying to piece together is, of course, life. The pieces are human beings.

As the ferry leaves the quay, the narrator sees another piece of the puzzle on the ship, a Latvian forestry officer he met on the way to Riga. He had left Latvia in 1944 and was now here to see his sister and brother one last time. The narrator describes the face almost photographically, seemingly unaffected, consumed by his role as observer: "He saw his face quiver, as if great uncertainty or weakness had moved it from within; saw the whole face quiver and twitch and then break into a ludicrously dry sobbing" (Enquist 1973: 503).[26] But when the narrator wants to document the officer's grief, photograph the face, he cannot: "But . . . he could not press the release, though he was aware that this was what he had been doing during the whole of the investigation: standing with his camera in front of him, awaiting the moment when the human being became visible" (Enquist 1973: 503–4).[27] The documentation of this human suffering is a betrayal of the ethical, of the "människa" (the human being). The experience is clearly outside of the narrator's conceptual understanding, as he twice states: "He could not press the release"; "He couldn't" (Enquist 1973: 503–4).[28]

Not only can the narrator not bear to photograph the forestry officer, seeing the crying people on the quay also overwhelms him: "He couldn't look at them anymore; he just couldn't" (Enquist 1973: 504).[29] He then goes to the other side of the ferry, away from land, from where he reflects on his experiences and his attempts to understand and describe the political controversy surrounding the extradition.

The narrator's retreat to the other side of the ship symbolizes his frustrated desire for clarity based on analytical understanding. He describes this side of the ship as "empty, the sun was shining, it was lovely and warm" (Enquist 1973: 504).[30] On the quayside of the ship, there were "houses, industries, barges, ships. People" (Enquist 1973: 504),[31] who were calling out and crying. On the one side, solitude and emptiness; on the other side, human beings and their lives and emotions. The scene symbolically represents the tension the narrator experiences between, on the one hand, the intellectual ambition of an analytical understanding that got him started on the investigation, and on the other hand, the ethical-emotional reality of his experiences and the meeting with the human beings behind the political structures. He concludes,

> There was one level of life on which man's actions were deliberate and the results of his actions could be foreseen, and this was the level he had wanted to get at all along: a state in which man was responsible for his actions and in which he had learned at last to govern the reality surrounding him, had learned at last the mechanism of living. But there was also another level, a more diffuse and enigmatic level which seemed dominated by a suffering man's face: a man with no background or story, defeated by reality. He had always hated the expression "suffering mankind," because he hated the sentimental side of himself; but sometimes he imagined he had seen the suffering man quite naked, vulnerable, and exposed, like a victim, and this had shaken him in a way he had never expected. (Enquist 1973: 504–5)[32]

The narrator describes two levels of life; one level governed by reasoning and politics, and another level dominated by "a suffering man's face." The image of the suffering man's (or, rather, in Swedish, "human being's") face, a naked human being without background or history, seems to echo Emmanuel Levinas's description of the ethical moment of encountering the Other in a dimension that "takes apart the recuperable time of history and memory in which representation continues" (Levinas 1998: 88), a fitting characterization of the effect of Enquist's novel.

Even Politicians Had Faces

The depiction of the political as ultimately being about individual human beings, naked, vulnerable, exposed, is not limited to the depictions of the Balts. It includes all involved parties of the Balt extradition, not only the prisoners and the guards but also the people most directly responsible for the extradition: the Swedish politicians. Thus, even the politicians are described with compassion, with an obvious focus on their humanity and, significantly from a Levinasian ethical viewpoint, their faces. I will briefly point out just one such example, although there are several in the book.

The Swedish prime minister before, during, and shortly after the war, Per Albin Hansson, is described as having been broken by the responsibility and the agony surrounding the extradition of the Balts. The narrator notes that nobody knows exactly what Hansson thought and felt but includes what appears to be an interview with his successor, Tage Erlander, who emphasizes how difficult the decision was for Hansson, and that he had much doubt. Erlander states that he personally believes that this broke Hansson, and adds,

"He was never the same man again, and in less than a year after extradition he was dead" (Enquist 1973: 329).[33] But in addition to this interview information, it is the human details and emotions that the novel describes that bring Hansson alive. Hence, it is told that in the last year of his life, Hansson "returned over and over again to the Balts, as though unable to leave the problem alone" (Enquist 1973: 330).[34] Not only does Hansson here appear to be ethically affected by his responsibility for others, he is also placed, by the narrator, in *time* in a way that makes it possible for the reader to imagine him as a human being: the phrase "over and over" suggests time passing in a way that most descriptions of politicians and their decisions do not. In the context of an (albeit partly fictional) investigation of a political trauma, the image of Hansson transcends his role as simply a politician. This appears toward the end of the novel, when the narrator describes the complexity of the question of the extradition of the Balts and its relation to a more general Swedish or Western European trauma/guilt. Reflecting on his experiences of "Människornas ansikten" (people's faces; in Swedish also, human beings' faces), he adds the unusual, significant, phrase, "even politicians had faces" (Enquist 1973: 506),[35] suggesting that politicians are also individuals, Others, in an ethical sense.

Legionärerna bears witness to the trauma of ethical responsibility that must be felt in order to transcend the political, both individually and collectively. The novel enacts, and thus brings to light, the collective psychological and ethical processing ignored in the immediate aftermath of the Balt extradition by emphasizing the interpersonal interactions and consequences of this Swedish political trauma. As the narrator states toward the end of the investigation, "But the pure, crystal pattern of which he had dreamed, the logical game he had been chasing, seemed to be hidden all the time by people and people's faces, and by life. By life" (Enquist 1973: 507).[36] It is in this sense that Enquist's novel becomes not just an account of a particular political Swedish and Baltic collective trauma but, in a broader perspective, an appeal for an ethics that transcends the political. *Legionärerna* is an important example of the power of literature to remind us that there will always be "people and people's faces."

Jan Krogh Nielsen (PhD, University of Washington, 2019; cand. mag., University of Copenhagen, 2002) served as Visiting Lecturer of Danish at the University of Washington, 2004–9. Krogh Nielsen has published on Danish poetry in *The Princeton Encyclopedia of Poetry and Poetics*; his PhD dissertation, *"People's Faces": Levinasian Ethics in Per Olov Enquist, Villy Sørensen, and Knut Hamsun*, investigates modern Scandinavian prose fiction in the light of the ethical philosophy of Emmanuel Levinas.

Notes

1. Quotations from Alan Blair's 1973 English translation, *The Legionnaires*. The original Swedish is given in the endnotes.
2. See also Östling (2011).
3. "en image av Sverige som humanitetens förlovade land" (Enquist 1970a: 402, my translation).
4. "vissa tyskvänliga skulder på sitt samvete" (Enquist 1970a: 401–2, my translation).
5. "fixeringen," "trauma," "en del av en skuld, en yttring av det schizofrena Europas hemliga sjukdom" (Enquist 1970b: 394).
6. "Jag beklagar det mänskliga lidande som ni och era dåvarande kamrater utsattes för som en följd av utlämningsbeslutet. Den svenska regeringen instämmer reservationslöst i kritiken av detta beslut" (Ehrensvärd 1994, my translation).
7. "rätta de felaktigheter" (Landsmanis 1970: 2, my translation).
8. "Detta är en roman om baltutlämningen, men om beteckningen 'roman' förefaller någon stötande, kan den ersättas med 'reportage' eller 'bok'" (Enquist 1970b: 5).
9. "Jag kommer ändå aldrig att förstå" (Enquist 1970b: 396).
10. "Något måste jag ändå stå där, fastän det tycktes orimligt att antyda att bygget var färdigt, att bilden var hel" (Enquist 1970b: 391).
11. "Han visste det inte själv, men det han nu upplevde var undersökningens sista lyckliga fas. Sommaren skulle ännu vara avspänd, arbetet lidelsefritt, han skulle ännu någon månad kunna laborera med utlämningen och de utlämnade som sysslade han med ett spel. Sedan skulle alla ansikten och röster övermanna honom, deras öden bli alltför påträngande, överblicken oklar, traumat komplicerat och diffust, hans eget liv alltför nära deras. För de levde ju, och skulle fortsätta att leva även om de var döda, och när han en vårdag 1968 skrev de sista raderna var det med en nästan desperat känsla av lättnad, som om han äntligen skulle ges chansen att andas, leva sitt liv, gå ut ur det fängelse de byggt åt honom" (Enquist 1970b: 395–6).
12. "I min bok lämnar jag inget slutligt facit, lämnar inga entydiga slutsvar på frågor som de här. Jag tror det är viktigare att varje läsare själv rannsakar hjärtan och njurar, och lämnar svar som han får stå för inför sig själv" (Enquist 1970a: 405, my translation). Enquist appears to refer to Psalm 26 (*Bibel 2000*).
13. "ansikten och röster övermanna honom, ... öden bli alltför påträngande, överblicken oklar, traumat komplicerat och diffust, hans eget liv alltför nära deras" (Enquist 1970b: 396).
14. "Någonstans en känsla av att jag *ändå* styrt honom [läsaren] in i ett ställningstagande" (Zetterström 1970: 531, my translation).
15. "På frågan om det var rätt at utlämna balterna ger Enquist inget svar" (Zetterström 1970: 532, my translation).
16. "Hur ser mekaniken bakom en politisk handling ut?" (Enquist 1970b: 41).
17. "reducera inte sin känsla, men sin okunnighet" (Enquist 1970b: 41).
18. "mödrar och fäder, sina syskon och kusiner" (Enquist 1970b: 392).
19. "korta, smärtsamt intima kontaktpunkten mellan de två folk som en gång varit ett folk" (Enquist 1970b: 392).
20. "själv var hon en människa som en gång måste ha varit mycket vacker. Där satt hon med sitt saftglas och sin rena profil och sitt tillbakastrukna hår" (Enquist 1970b: 391).
21. "inte ens en parentes i hans undersökning, möjligtvis ett kommatecken" (Enquist 1970b: 391).
22. "Kunde han uppehålla sig vid kommatecken?" (Enquist 1970b: 391).

23. "hon var ett kommatecken som han kunde stryka ut för gott" (Enquist 1970b: 392).
24. "I vilken moralisk-politisk konflikt kunde hon fogas in? I vilket mönster var hon den irrationella faktorn? För vilka kolliderande principer hade hon blivit ett offer?" (Enquist 1970b: 392).
25. "liten pusselbit"; "tycktes leva, förändras, påverkas" (Enquist 1970b: 392).
26. "Han såg . . . hur ansiktet på honom liksom darrade till, som om en stor osäkerhet eller svaghet rört det inifrån, hur hela ansikte darrade och rördes och till sist föll samman i en löjligt torr snyftning" (Enquist 1970b: 392–93).
27. "Men han kunde till sist inte trycka av, fast han var medveten om att det var detta han gjort under hela undersökningen: stått med kameran framför sig, inväntande det moment när människan blev synlig" (Enquist 1970b: 393).
28. "han kunde till sist inte trycka av," "han kunde inte" (Enquist 1970b: 393).
29. "det gick inte at se på dem längre, det gick inte" (Enquist 1970b: 393).
30. "tomt, solen sken, det var underbart varmt och skönt" (Enquist 1970b: 393).
31. "hus, industrier, pråmar, fartyg. Människor" (Enquist 1970b: 393).
32. "Det fanns ett livsplan där människans handlingar var medvetna och resultaten av handlingarna överblickbara, och det var detta plan han hela tiden velat komma åt: ett tillstånd där människan var ansvarig för sina handlingar och till sist lärt sig att styra den verklighet som omgav henne, till sist lärt sig levandets mekanik. Men där fanns också ett annat plan, ett diffusare och gåtfullare plan som tycktes dominerat av en lidande människas ansikte: en människa utan bakgrund och historia, besegrad av verkligheten. Han hade alltid hatat uttrycket 'den lidande människan,' eftersom han hatade det sentimentala inom sig själv, men ibland hade han tyckt sig se den lidande människan alldeles naken, utlämnad, som ett offer, och det hade skakat honom på ett sätt han aldrig hade väntat" (Enquist 1970b: 393).
33. "Han gick inte ut ur den som samma människa, och ett halvår efter utlämningen dog han" (Enquist 1970b: 260).
34. "återvände gång på gång till balterna, som om han aldrig kunde släppa problemet" (Enquist 1970b: 260).
35. "Människornas ansikten: också politiker hade ansikten" (Enquist 1970b: 395).
36. "Men det rena kristalliska mönster han drömt om, det logiska spel han jagat, det tycktes ständigt skymmas av människor och människors ansikten, och av liv. Av liv" (Enquist 1970b: 395).

References

Bibel 2000. Svenska Bibelsällskapet. Retrieved 30 September 2018 from www.bibeln.se.
Braconier, Fredrik. 1994. "Kontroversiellt drama som satte djupa spår." *Svenska Dagbladet*, 21 June, 11.
Bredsdorff, Thomas. 1991. *De sorte huller: Om tilblivelsen af et sprog i P. O. Enquists forfatterskab*. København: Gyldendal.
Ehrensvärd, Amelie. 1994. "Balterna återvände." *Svenska Dagbladet*, 21 June, 11.
Enquist, Per Olov. 1970a. "Epilog: Januari 1970." In *Legionärerna*, 397–407. Stockholm: Bokförlaget PAN/Norstedts.
———. 1970b. *Legionärerna*. Stockholm: PAN/Norstedts.

———. 1973. *The Legionnaires: A Documentary Novel*. Translated by A. Blair. New York: Delacorte Press/Seymour Lawrence.
Henningsen, Erik H. 1975. *Per Olov Enquist: En undersøgelse af en venstreintellektuel forfatters forsøg på at omfunktionere den litterære institution*. København: Samleren.
Landsmanis, Arturs. 1970. *De misstolkade legionärerna: Ett baltiskt debattinlägg*. Stockholm: Lettiska Nationella Fonden.
Levinas, Emmanuel. 1985. *Ethics and Infinity*. Translated by R. A. Cohen. Pittsburgh: Duquesne University Press.
———. 1998. *Otherwise than Being, or, Beyond Essence*. Translated by A. Lingis. Pittsburgh: Duquesne University Press.
———. 2005. *Totality and Infinity: An Essay on Exteriority*. Translated A. Lingis. Pittsburgh: Duquesne University Press.
Nollendorfs, Valters, and Uldis Neiburgs. 2015. *Latvians in the Armed Forces of Germany in World War II*. Ministry of Foreign Affairs of The Republic of Latvia. Retrieved 29 October 2018 from www.mfa.gov.lv/en/policy/information-on-the-history-of-latvia/briefing-papers-of-the-museum-of-the-occupation-of-latvia/latvians-in-the-armed-forces-of-germany-in-world-war-ii.
Shideler, Ross. 1984. *Per Olov Enquist: A Critical Study*. Contributions to the Study of World Literature. Westport, CT: Greenwood Press.
Yrlid, Rolf. 1975. "Efter läsarens sinnesart och erfarenhetsbakgrund. Om mottagandet av Per Olof [sic] Enquists *Legionärerna*." In *Diktaren och hans formvärld: Lundastudier i litteraturvetenskap tillägnade Staffan Björck och Carl Fehrman*, edited by R. Arvidsson, B. Olsson, and L. Vinge, 367–78. Malmö: Allhems Förlag.
Zetterström, Margareta. 1970. "'Det finns ingen helgonlik objektivitet': En studie i Per Olov Enquists Legionärerna." *Bonniers Litterära Magasin* 39(8): 524–32.
Östling, Johan. 2011. "The Rise and Fall of Small-State Realism: Sweden and the Second World War." In *Nordic Narratives of the Second World War: National Historiographies Revisited*, edited by H. Stenius, M. Österberg, and J. Östling, 127–47. Lund: Nordic Academic Press.

Chapter 13

THE ALLIED OCCUPATION OF ICELAND

Indriði G. Þorsteinsson's *North of War*

Daisy Neijmann

Memories of World War II in Iceland are distinctly different from those in other Nordic countries affected by this conflict. Iceland was occupied on 10 May 1940 by the British, who were replaced for the most part by American forces one year later. While most Icelanders were relieved that they were not occupied by the Nazis, the occupation was not exactly welcomed. It was generally perceived as an infringement on Iceland's policy of neutrality and its long history of isolation and peace. The country has never employed a military, and armed conflicts were regarded as something profoundly un-Icelandic, something that happened elsewhere.

The arrival of a foreign army therefore came as a shock to most inhabitants. Reactions varied, including alarm at the proximity of soldiers armed with guns, dismay at the fact that a foreign conflict had been brought to Iceland's doorstep, and profound concern about the large presence of foreign young men who outnumbered the locals, but also excitement. The army brought work and money, and introduced a consumer economy and international popular culture into a country where modernity had only barely begun to make inroads. The result was an unprecedented economic boom, which provided opportunities for many but also caused great social upheaval.

The occupation came at a sensitive time. Iceland was preparing to sever its final ties with Denmark and declare itself an independent republic, and although the occupation was a "friendly" one and the occupying forces declared they would not interfere in Icelandic politics, there was profound concern that a foreign power had again taken over the country, and by military force. At the same time, it drastically accelerated a gradual and controlled development toward a modern society. This development had started earlier in the century with the motorization of the fishing fleet, the build-up of Reykjavík to fulfill its role as the capital of an independent country, and the growth of fishing villages along the coast. The Depression of the 1930s increased the migration from the countryside, when many gave up on living in poverty and trying to wrest a living from the land. This development meant the decline of a thousand-year-old pastoral way of life, its culture and values. As painful and disorienting as this was, however, the changes had at least been relatively measured. When the army arrived, with its technology, its money, and its foreign culture, it overwhelmed the Icelanders and caused severe tensions of various kinds.

This watershed, and rupture, in Icelandic history has significantly complicated public memory of the war years. The rapid and profound changes caused a moral, cultural, and identity crisis, as time-honored ways and values were abandoned without new ones having had time to develop. Meanwhile, on an economic level, Icelanders profited from a conflict that brought unspeakable horrors on an unprecedented scale to most other countries. The result was a profound polarization of Icelandic society, with some clinging desperately to nationalism and the old ways, while others gave themselves over completely to the new available opportunities. The situation was further complicated by the fact that the Americans did not leave the country at the end of the war, as had been originally agreed, but retained a military base in Iceland until 2006, which was extremely controversial throughout the Cold War era. This left Iceland in a situation where it was neither occupied nor *not* occupied. As a result, memories of the occupation have been conflicted, to say the least, while World War II itself has barely been commemorated in public ways at all. Publicly, the war in Iceland is primarily remembered as a period of unprecedented economic prosperity, while it has tended to get only superficial attention in historiography, as Guðmundur Hálfdanarson discusses in chapter 4 of this volume. In postwar Icelandic literature, on the other hand, its obsequiousness borders on obsession.

Literature can be instrumental in the construction of public memory and forgetting by giving narrative shape to confusing, uncontainable experiences, creating discursive order out of chaos, and providing convenient explanations and justifications to protect a national sense of self against profoundly unsettling anxieties in the face of a perceived overwhelming threat. Icelandic literature during the war and Cold War period is virtually exclusively concerned with "the great upheaval," that is, the demise of the pastoral way of life and its replacement by modernity, with its capitalist, mechanized, urban, and international ways and values. The occupation became, almost from the first, a part of this narrative rather than being treated on its own, and was portrayed in this particular light: as the invasion force that dealt the old ways a quick and final blow with its introduction of foreign capital, foreign temptations, and foreign ways, thereby contaminating and polluting Icelandic society and culture. While, in reality, Icelanders were all too happy not to look back to centuries of poverty and drudgery but to use the money and the infrastructure brought by the army to build up a modern postwar society, fiction remained backward-looking, trying to capture what had happened and giving voice to memories and emotions of loss and guilt for which there was no room in public, daily life (Kristjánsdóttir 2006; Eysteinsson 2006).

By the time Indriði G. Þorsteinsson's novella *Norðan við stríð* (translated as *North of War*) was published in 1971, the portrayal of the occupation had become completely standardized, as well as exaggerated in the overheated political climate of the Cold War. This becomes clear in the opening lines with which literary critic Ólafur Jónsson received the work: "Well. Never let it be said that there wasn't yet another description of the occupation in the offing—more than 25 years after the war."[1] Nevertheless, it was considered by many to provide a different and more comprehensive view of the occupation, and it quickly became *the* novel most people thought of in relation to the occupation. Indriði G. Þorsteinsson (1926–2000) was at this point a well-established and popular author, having made his mark with the novel *79 af stöðinni* (Taxi 79, 1951), which remains to date his most acclaimed work and one of the key works of Icelandic fiction of the period. Here, Þorsteinsson introduced the hard-boiled, terse, fast-paced, and no-nonsense style that would come to characterize many of his works.

In the novels that followed, Þorsteinsson moved back in time, in an attempt to understand the present by exploring the recent past as well as to preserve its memory for future generations, being himself of the generation that, as he put it, "straddled the watershed."[2] He claimed that, with his fiction, he aimed to map out where Iceland was just a few decades ago, where it was now and how it got there, thereby building a bridge between the generations who had lived the times before the great upheaval and those who had not, a generation gap so profound that critics have since it likened to *ginnungagap*, the "bottomless abyss" of Old Norse mythology (Valsson 1995: 108). As such, he became regarded as the primary author of the greatest social changes in modern Icelandic history (Jónasson 1998: 109), which is well reflected in the most recent republication of his three main novellas in one volume under the title *Tímar í lífi þjóðar* (Times in the life of a nation, 2004). *North of War*, although written last, forms the central part of this unofficial trilogy. It is nevertheless remarkable that, although it is difficult to divorce it from the particular context in which it was both written and has been read since,

Figure 13.1. The original Icelandic book cover for *North of War* (1971) portrays the essence of the Icelandic war experience: a scramble for money and a battle over male potency. Cover design by Auglýsingastofa Kristínar Þorkelsdóttur.

North of War also distinguishes itself from earlier occupation novels in the fact that the actual occupation does not remain in the background but is the main focus. In this regard, it is therefore more recognizable as occupation literature also in a wider, international context, just as its relative distance in time from the events it describes allows the author a more comprehensive overview.

Contemporary critics writing on *North of War* claimed they detected a more objective view of the occupation: instead of the usual, highly political representation of the detrimental influence of the occupation, characterized by an almost hysterically accusatory tone, this novel was perceived as describing the effects of the foreign army presence in a much more measured way and without judgment.[3] The opening chapter of the novel, however, immediately reveals that, despite the more measured tone, the narrative attempts to direct the reader toward a particular point of view. The lyrical, tender description of a small, peaceful community living in harmony with nature, far removed from the outside world and its wars, forms a striking contrast with the rest of the novel. This, of course, underlines the shock of the violent rupture that the occupation constituted in Icelandic life, but it also establishes from the start an emphasis on loss rather than on what was gained, particularly considering the distance in time from which it was written when Iceland had long been reaping the benefits of the occupation and had thoroughly transformed itself into a modern, progressive state.

In chapter 2, the actual occupation is described, first in Reykjavík and then, a few days later, in the town that forms the setting for the novel, which, although it is nowhere named, is quite recognizably Akureyri, the main town in northern Iceland. This location is quite interesting in itself, as it is neither quite the city, Reykjavík, nor the countryside but a little bit of both, allowing the author to create a microcosm of Iceland as a whole. The tone in this chapter is immediately quite different from that in the previous one. The omniscient narrator is much more distant, relating events in a slightly ironic, almost offhand manner, which has the effect of making the occupation seem mildly ridiculous. This effect is strengthened by the contrast that is consistently drawn up between the invading army, on the one hand, and the sleepy, bewildered community on the other that makes the armed soldiers trying to perform an organized invasion seem utterly out of place. In the end, even the army realizes the pointlessness of its performance and sits down to make tea. The most painful moment in the entire chapter is in fact the arrest of the German Otto Schueler, who settled in Akureyri several years earlier to escape the Nazi regime, thinking that the war would not reach this far north. This scene, like so many others in the novella, has its direct basis in historical fact: after their landing, the British army immediately set out to arrest and deport the German ambassador and other Germans living in Iceland. In an Allied World War II context, this is not unexpected: the Germans were the enemy. In Iceland, however, there was no Nazi presence to speak of, no war, and no enemy, and local Germans were regarded simply as individuals who had made their home in Iceland. Many Icelanders were horrified at the treatment these German residents received at the hands of the army. It is telling that *North of War* should include this fact in its portrayal of the occupation in such a prominent way, immediately casting the British army in the role of villain rather than ally and protector. Portraying the army as a villainous, iron-booted invasion force is nothing new in itself in Icelandic occupation literature, but the way in which it is done here is different. While it encapsulates a particularly Icelandic experience of the war, at the same time it places this experience in a wider, international context of war, which is uncommon in Icelandic literature. It is this war that the army brings to Iceland, for the first time in its history, and with it a culture based in war: weapons, technology, and a militarized approach that sees people only in terms of allies and enemies. The contrast between the remote, peaceful community and the war brought by the army forms the main framework of the narrative, making the novel's title entirely ironic: from this chapter on, nowhere is north of war.

Another important feature that distinguishes this occupation novel from many earlier ones is the fact that the army gets a voice.[4] Although there is an omniscient narrator, this narrator takes on the voice and point of view of a selection of different characters. Among these are officers and soldiers in the army. During the landing in Akureyri, the platoon officer considers the army's situation and realizes that the conventional ways of war hardly apply here. He concludes,

> This bears no relation to doing or dying. Nobody's going to waste ammunition on this dot on the map. . . . Sending troops to a place like this has more to do with courtesy than with warfare because, weapons and gas masks notwithstanding, they're not expected to shoot anybody. They're supposed to go ashore smiling, as if the armed men below deck were merely a group of ambassadors wearing boots. (Thorsteinsson 1981: 13)[5]

This reflection nicely encapsulates the awkward ambiguity of what is generally called a "friendly" occupation, for the army, and of course also for the "coerced hosts," the people who are occupied. As anthropologist Inga Dóra Björnsdóttir (1995: 152) has pointed out, even a friendly occupation represents a threat against society: an invading military is after all a legal and institutional form of power and aggression. By allowing the platoon leader to come to this conclusion, the narrative seems to imply that even the highest echelons of the occupying army itself realize they are in a ridiculous situation, although they still have to do their jobs. Ridicule is of course a common strategy of the powerless to deflate the power of those wielding it. At the same time, in the context of this text, it emphasizes the underlying message that the army had no business bringing the war to Iceland. The argument that the army was sent to protect Iceland from Nazi occupation is undercut by repeated references throughout the novel to the army's lack of proper equipment and inadequacy: a painted telephone pole, for instance, is meant to convince the enemy that it is in fact an antiaircraft gun, and "the more sandbags and barbed wire, the more real the war becomes" (Thorsteinsson 1981: 23).[6]

The army presence is not just one of military might but of overwhelming numbers. Directly after the landing, the army takes over most public buildings, and the soldiers are "all over the place" (Thorsteinsson 1981: 39). An infrastructure needs to be built up, roads and an airport, and suddenly, everyone can get regular, well-paid work. In addition, the army brings entertainment and excitement into the impoverished, dull lives and drudgery of the locals, driving around on their motorcycles and keen to pass the time with movies and dances. As a result, and as is common in most occupation literature generally, the text soon reverberates with moral ambiguities and civil tensions revolving around questions of resistance versus collaboration, guilt and shame (Atack 2008: 82).

The characters in the novel are a collection of community representatives: the fisherman, the milkman, the cobbler, the journalist, the publican, the coffin maker, the prostitute, etc. In this way, the novella portrays the forced cohabitation of army and locals during the first year of the occupation and its effects on life in the community. Although the point of view continually shifts among them, the most prominent is Jon Falkon, a real-estate agent recently returned from Canada. The army hires him as its interpreter in order to facilitate communications. Jon Falkon is not pleased at first, as he, a successful businessman who has lived abroad, is already regarded with suspicion by the community. He is, however, enough of a businessman to see an opportunity. As such, Jon Falkon becomes a main focus for the relations, frictions, and moral ambiguity that soon develop.

In contrast to earlier Icelandic occupation novels, the text does not draw up a black-and-white picture based on those who choose to work with the army by accepting its jobs and money vis-à-vis those who avoid contact with them as much as possible. The shifting point of view allows us to feel a degree of sympathy for most characters. Nikulas, the fisherman, chooses to continue fishing even though his crew abandon him to work for the army, because fishing is his life. As such, he is the clearest representative in the novel of the organic society that is violently disrupted by the arrival of the army and about to disappear forever, and has the obvious sympathy of the author. Although his crew actively contribute to the demise of this way of life by choosing to work for the army, however, their choice is not represented in condemnatory terms: they have families to feed, and fishing is an unreliable source of income. In addition, the peat-extracting machine sitting in a town field is a constant reminder of the unemployment during the Depression, as it had been purchased in order to provide work. For cobbler Vopni Danielsson, the unrecognized son of a local district officer who took advantage of a poor working woman, meanwhile, the occupation provides an opportunity to leave poverty and social stigma behind and realize his dream of starting a shoe factory with the financial help of Jon Falkon.

The portrayal of the communist journalist is, on the other hand, entirely unsympathetic: his articles denouncing the army and those who work for it are described as both ridiculous and damaging, and even his looks reflect his deficient personality, with his eye "full of savage mercy" and his lips "shaped into a perpetual, cruel grin" (Thorsteinsson 1981: 28).[7] It seems like a deliberately missed opportunity on the part of the author not to present the journalist's communist views to counterbalance the views of others in the town. It is difficult not to interpret this negative portrayal of the journalist as political. His views reflect those published in the communist paper *Þjóðviljinn* during the occupation. It was strongly opposed to the army presence, which it regarded as an invasion by bellicose foreign capitalist and imperialist forces, a view shared by many prominent Icelandic writers with communist sympathies, notably Halldór Laxness. Indriði G. Þorsteinsson was not one of them, and he always felt that his works were not recognized by this literary elite on political grounds (Sæmundsson 1985: 59–60). Despite his regret at the demise of the Icelandic pastoral society, he regarded the occupation as "a plus for Icelandic society, it flung us into the world. Before that, Iceland did not exist in the world."[8]

As the army presence increasingly proves to be a source of money and opportunities that had never been available before to so many and to such a degree, many old-fashioned ways and virtues fall by the wayside as everyone wants their share. Locals start selling hot dogs, skyr with berries, fish and chips, eggs and turkey, and whatever else the soldiers will buy. Teenagers no longer bother with school, while men have started digging the airport by hand. A dairy shop opens, putting the local milkman out of work. Jon Falkon plays a double game, pretending to spy on the workers for the army while using the inside information he has access to as army interpreter to profit from it. At the same time, the soldiers gradually start to become restless in this "waiting room" north of nowhere with nothing to do while their friends are fighting where "the war is a serious matter" (Thorsteinsson 1981: 54) and their families at home are in danger of being bombed. As winter approaches, the military and civilian authorities try to defuse the building tensions by agreeing to sponsor a dance:

> Thus, both sides try to make their coexistence bearable. . . . It's no damn joke to be stuck with nearly four thousand men in a spot no larger than the palm

of your hand far out in the Ocean of Nowhere, while the nearest Nazi bloke is in Norway and every house is filled with wives and daughters. (Thorsteinsson 1981: 56)[9]

The dance, however, only puts oil on the fire, fueling protests, fights between local boys and soldiers, and a publicly published list of invitees to shame those who fraternize with the occupying soldiers.

So far, the ways in which the occupation is experienced and portrayed thus seem quite balanced on the whole. The novella even includes occasional reminders of the reality and the horrors of the war elsewhere, something that is not at all common in Icelandic occupation literature with its almost exclusive focus on the local situation, the army presence, and the changes that followed it. The novella's emphasis on the remoteness and unlikeliness of location to introduce a war is used effectively to demonstrate that World War II did not only erase definitively the boundaries between combatants and civilians but that its scope was such that it left no one untouched: the most isolated of places were drawn into it. From now on, Iceland "exists in the world" and has become part of world events.

The most notorious aspect of *North of War*, however, is its representation of women, where it loses all balance and distance. In this, it conforms to a public, historiographical, and literary discourse that had been well established since the earliest postwar years. In fact, economic prosperity is only one of the two ways in which the war years have been remembered in Iceland, the other being the relations between foreign soldiers and Icelandic women, commonly referred to in Icelandic as *ástandið*, "the situation." This particular aspect of the war in Iceland has, during recent decades, been the subject of extended critical revision, a process initiated by feminist scholars that may indeed even be traced to feminist critiques of *North of War* as well as other fiction by Indriði G. Þorsteinsson during the 1970s.[10]

From the very first day of the occupation, women were cast in the role of collaborator in public discourse, historiography, and, later and most prominently, in Icelandic occupation literature (Neijmann 2014). There are several reasons why and how this happened. First, as the Icelandic historian Sigríður Matthíasdóttir (2000: 30–31) has demonstrated, Icelandic nationalist discourse, which had come to permeate every level of Icelandic society at the time of the occupation, was firmly rooted in masculine values. "The Icelander" was conceptualized as a rational being averse to showing emotions, independent and self-reliant, with a developed intelligence and a strong sense of freedom and self. Women were represented as opposite to the nature of the Icelander: emotional, irrational and unreliable. They had an important symbolic role to play, however. In nationalist discourse, it is common for the nation to be portrayed as a family, where women become icons of exalted motherhood and cultural guardians. In Iceland, as Inga Dóra Björnsdóttir (1998b: 93–95) has pointed out, the country was celebrated as Mother Nature, the essence of the nation, and the source of everything Icelandic. Thus, women became identified with and were seen as the representations of the realms that were believed to be purely Icelandic: Icelandic culture and nature. This intimate connection between Icelandic manhood and Iceland as mother is of crucial importance when we come to look at representations of men and masculinity in Icelandic literature of the occupation, when the sons of Iceland were powerless to defend their mother from being invaded. As her purity and independence were threatened, so was the source of Icelandic manhood. Moreover, her invasion was also men's humiliation, a sign of their impotence and guilt.

Second, the occupation constituted a direct threat to Icelandic patriarchy. In the traditional pastoral society, women were little more than slave labor, lacking any form of independence or opportunity other than becoming wives, mothers, and unpaid farm workers (Jónasson 2004: 12; Helgadóttir 2001). With the occupation, a world of excitement and opportunity opened up for women. Suddenly, they could earn their own money and even start their own businesses, they had access to all kinds of entertainment, and they could take their pick from a large selection of men who were clean and smart, good-looking, polite, and appreciative of them. In short, the army presence brought Icelandic women choice, independence, and freedom to find an outlet for their dreams, talents, and ambitions. The fact that many women jumped at the chances on offer, however, caused deep resentment among Icelandic men. The resentment, humiliation, and guilt experienced as a result of the military invasion and the threat to their manhood, together with the perceived enthusiasm with which Icelandic women received the army and the opportunities it brought them, were channeled into a discourse in which Icelandic women were depicted as unreliable, morally dubious, at the mercy of their emotions and instincts, traitors to their country, and therefore a danger to themselves and society. This discourse became extremely influential and long-lived, and has since been analyzed as a way for Icelandic men to transfer their feelings of guilt and humiliation on to women, who made a much easier scapegoat than a foreign military (Kristjánsson 1984). It was she who, due to her irrational nature, proved incapable of resisting her desire to be taken by force, thus allowing the national body to be occupied and polluted. In other words, through its relations with soldiers, the female body had blurred the boundaries between foreign and native, thereby threatening the very definition of Icelandicness and Icelandic masculinity. Theories on the importance of gender in cultural representations of war support this analysis. In his discussion of masculinity in politics and war, for instance, John Horne (2004: 29) argues that the "positive attributes of national masculine ideals were matched by the negative figures of the internal and external enemy—who might be pictured either as female or as a derided or feared type of masculinity."

Virtually all women characters in *North of War* occupy roles that patriarchy considers "unnatural," and are described with different degrees of contempt. The Manfred sisters are mildly ridiculous and hysterical spinsters who are regarded as holding up a prudish bourgeois propriety in the town. Antonia, the wife of Gudmund the Sleigh, is portrayed as an overly ambitious woman anxious to make money off the soldiers in whatever way she can, treading on her husband's dignity and territory as breadwinner while she does so. In actual fact, her husband, the milkman, has been put out of work by the new dairy shop and is unable to adjust to the new circumstances, and Antonia uses her entrepreneurial spirit to make ends meet for the couple. While these female characters are made fun of, the serious contempt is reserved for the women who enter into sexual relations with soldiers. In each instance, from the very first moment of encountering a soldier, they fall prey to an uncontrollable lust. Imba of the Forge and her sister are the unmarried daughters of the late blacksmith who, before the occupation, served the sexual needs of local men. When the army lands, Imba sees an opportunity to find herself a husband and thereby "become a person" (Thorsteinsson 1981: 40). Her attempts are of such a desperate nature that they evoke our pity. The narrator, however, portrays her ambition in dismissive terms: Icelandic men are no longer good enough for her, and even the soldiers see her for what she is. At the end of the novella, she is described as lying in the grass after a drunk soldier keeps rolling off her, her dress in a roll beneath her chin and her thighs blue with cold. It is a profoundly sad, pathetic image, but all the narrator has to say is: "It looks as if she's waiting for a new man" (Thorsteinsson 1981: 112).[11] Imba, in other words, is and always will be a whore, only now she is an army whore.

Then there is Halla, the unsatisfied wife of Jon Falkon. When Jon invites the platoon leader home, he thinks Halla might like the company, as "she sometimes talked about her loneliness. . . . Women were like that. They could remain content with shit-asses, thieves, drunks, morons, and good-for-nothings. Otherwise, they got bored." When Jon introduces the platoon leader to his wife, the atmosphere is described as follows:

> They drink each other in with their eyes, and the air is charged. Jon looks astonished at his smiling wife. All her reticence is gone. "She's like a child who's had a visit from Santa Claus," he thinks to himself, and feels like a fifth wheel in their company. (Thorsteinsson 1981: 36–37)[12]

Here, Halla is likened to a child, and, later, the attraction between her and the platoon leader is directly associated with prostitution. It is true that Halla is at least provided with an excuse: Jon Falkon is impotent. The point of view in the text, however, remains solidly with Jon Falkon, who tries to cover up his pain and humiliation with business deals and alcohol. He also has the last word when, during the dance organized by the army, he tells his wife, loud enough for everybody to hear, "Shut up, you British whore; you sell yourself for sixpence!" (Thorsteinsson 1981:78).[13] The reader's sympathy is clearly meant to be with Jon. The next morning, Halla Falkon is gone, making Jon yet another local man betrayed by his wife.

The most disturbing description, however, is that of Vopni Danielsson's wife, who hangs out the window with her breasts dangling out of her gown, fascinated by the soldiers and their motorcycles, the spectacle of which grips her with an all-consuming lust. One day, one of them enters the house with his iron boots and rapes her in his full army gear. Although she weakly protests, she is described as secretly enjoying being overpowered and taken against her will, a victim of her own unreliable nature: she cannot seem to help herself. During the rape, Vopni comes into the room, then flees in utter shock and disgust. It does not seem to occur to him to do anything. Instead, he seeks solace with Jon Falkon and his business plans. Vopni's wife is out of the story after this: her only role in the narrative is as an unnamed "everywoman" who falls prey to her own lust and enjoys her rape by a soldier. These female character descriptions seem to have their basis in a particular view of women: they are all the same, all whores at heart, and their lust can only be kept in check under patriarchal authority, which has to ensure it receives an outlet through the "natural" channels: marriage and motherhood. If this fails, "women are apt to become like live mines. Someone steps a bit too close to them, and they just explode" (Thorsteinsson 1981: 60).[14] When the occupation happens and patriarchal control over women breaks down, all hell breaks loose. While the obsessive and widespread repetition of this theme may be particular to Icelandic occupation literature, the theme itself is not. In her article on "Women writers and the war," Gill Plain (2009: 166) discusses the representation of women in war literature and points to a basic cultural assumption of women's unreliability, women's sexuality as a potential national security threat, and a public fear of the breakdown of patriarchal authority as a result of increased opportunities for women and the following shift in gender relations brought about by the war, which raises the specter of the unruly, undomesticated female.

In *North of War*, as in earlier occupation novels, this depiction of women exposes an underlying narrative of a deeply wounded masculinity in crisis, which becomes even more obvious in the descriptions of the soldiers vis-à-vis Icelandic men. The male Icelandic characters in the novel, who stand by and watch a group of armed foreign males occupy their land and homes, almost all share a powerlessness and inadequacy. They have no idea how to respond and seem incapable of adapting to the new circumstances. The one thing they do understand is that there is money to be made, although even in this they are not very successful in the end, with the exception of Jon Falkon. They are stuck in a way of life they used to rule but that suddenly has become obsolete. They lose, while the women, who never had anything to lose, only gain. In contrast, the impression we are given of the soldiers is one of an overwhelming power, one that Icelandic men clearly are incapable of matching (Eysteinsson 2006: 414; Neijmann 2013). This sense of impotence and fear in the face of a superior masculinity is sexualized in the novella: the soldiers are endowed with an irresistible sexual attraction and virility, and insatiable, even unnatural appetites, as in the case of Harry Rosenblum, a sexually obsessed soldier suffering from mental problems, and the soldier who avails himself sexually of a local farmer's cow. Meanwhile, the main Icelandic male characters all lose or die. Vopni loses his factory in a fire, as well as his wife whom he has left; Jon Falkon also loses his wife as well as his fish and chips shop, although he has plenty of money left; Gudmund the Sleigh loses his business and his beloved horses; and Nikulas the fisherman dies at the end of the novella due to warplane fire. Indriði G. Þorsteinsson (*Morgunblaðið* 22 December 1971, 21) himself explained his endings as indicating the loss of a way of life, and the fact that there is no way back, but he added that, in *North of War*, most survive. This is true as far as it goes: the fact that it is Nikulas who dies is easily interpreted as a way of life and of seeing the world that dies, an interpretation that is underlined by the final image of Nikulas's fishing boat lying on its side, surrounded by dead fish in a blood-colored sea. The fact that it is Jon Falkon who is the main survivor and the way to the future, however, does not exactly constitute a ringing endorsement of this future, either for Iceland or for Icelandic men, as Kristján B. Jónasson points out in his introduction to the trilogy: "An impotent man who makes money only to cover up his own faults, lost in an alcoholic haze, and incapable of facing his own pain. Was this perhaps the inheritance left by 'the blessed war'. . .?"[15] Despite the fact that *North of War* was written thirty years later, a sense of profound loss reverberates through the entire narrative, culminating in an ending tainted by blood and death, and lacking any sign of confidence in a new future for Iceland, even though its Icelandic readers had been living and enjoying the fruits of that future for decades.

In *North of War*, the occupation is thus viewed from a greater distance in time than had been the case until then, and is placed in the larger, international context of World War II, while it remains at the same time a part of the Icelandic textual narrative of the great upheaval. Despite the author's often stated aim of wanting to document history as it was lived and thereby bridge this profound temporal discontinuity, what marks the text most is the obvious fact that the author is himself unable to cross the divide (Kristjánsdóttir 2006: 562; Ólason 1981: 139–40). Instead, *North of War* is, at its core, a crystallization of the standardized Icelandic narrative of the occupation as it had developed during the postwar years and its incorporation into public memory. This is seen particularly in the profound sense of inevitability that informs the narrative, which is perceived in terms of impotence and loss rather than gain, and portrayed in highly gendered and sexualized terms. The survivors are war profiteers who are not condemned, because they are the men of an inescapable future. The occupation appears in the novella first and foremost as a bringer of money and technology as well as a place in the world for Iceland, but at the expense of a way of life in harmony with nature, of cultural purity, potency, and power—at least for men. The resulting temporal discontinuity and disorientation cause a complete breakdown of values and certainties and threaten the loss of manhood and self. These "perilous times" (Thorsteinsson 1981: 89) seem to have fueled a nostalgia for the prewar past, born from the needs of a generation that still remembers it, which has gradually moved it out of reality and into a closed, textual world, preventing any critical examination (Ólason 1981: 140).

Despite its enactment of an established, backward-looking occupation narrative, however, *North of War* does mark a turning point, in that it sparked influential critiques, and not long afterward, younger writers began to introduce fresh approaches to the literary representation of the occupation and its consequences.[16] The figure of Jon Falkon, meanwhile, can be seen as a remarkably apt embodiment of Icelandic memory of the occupation: making money to compensate for, rather than face, failure, impotence, and shame. The way forward, the way to survive, is money, denial, and a displacement of guilt. Indriði G. Þorsteinsson's legacy in this regard also lives on in a different way. The most critical and influential revisions of the Icelandic occupation narrative in Icelandic literature have come from his son, the celebrated crime writer Arnaldur Indriðason, who has, it seems, inherited his father's interest in this period of Icelandic history, but who approaches it in a contemporary and radically innovative way by effectively using the generic conventions of the crime novel while contesting established ways of seeing and representing the occupation.[17] Thus, one could say that *North of War* is a transitional work that points forward, despite itself.

Daisy Neijmann (PhD, Vrije Universiteit, Amsterdam, 1994) teaches Icelandic literature and culture at the University of Iceland. Neijmann is the author of *The Icelandic Voice in Canadian Letters* (1996) and *Colloquial Icelandic* (2000/2013) and the volume editor of *A History of Icelandic Literature* (2006), and she has published widely on Icelandic-Canadian literature, modern Icelandic fiction, Icelandic literary historiography, war memory and trauma texts, and Icelandic as a heritage language.

Notes

1. "Jæja. Aldrei fór það svo að ekki fjölgaði enn um hernámslýsingu—meira en aldarfjórðungi eftir stríð" (Jónsson 1979: 20). All translations from the Icelandic *not* from *North of War* are my own.
2. "sátu klofvega á tímamótunum" (*Morgunblaðið*, 22 December 1971, 17).
3. See, for instance, Jónsson (1979: 30–31); Þorvaldsson (1972: 225); Stefánsson (1986: 109).
4. On the voice of the occupying army in Icelandic occupation literature, see Neijmann 2016.
5. "Þetta er ekkert skylt því að hlýða og deyja. Enginn fer að eyða púðri á þennan punkt á landabréfinu. . . . Á svona stað höfðar koma þeirra meira til kurteisi en hernaðar, því þrátt fyrir vopnin og gasgrímurnar og skotbeltin er þeim ekki ætlað að skjóta neinn. Þeim er ætlað að stíga á land með bros á vör, eins og þetta vopnum búna lið niðri í skipinu sé ekki annað en hópur ambassadora á klossum" (Þorsteinsson 2004: 157).
6. "Eftir því sem meira verður um sandpoka og gaddavír verður stríðið raunverulegra" (Þorsteinsson 2004: 169).
7. "fullt af heiftúðugri miskunnsemi"; "leikur stöðugt grimmdarbros um varir hans" (Þorsteinsson 2004: 175).
8. "Hernámið var sko hvorki meira né minna plúsinn í íslenzku þjóðfélagi. Það þeytti okkur inn í heiminn" (*Morgunblaðið*, 22 December 1971, 17).
9. "Annars staðar er stríðið alvara" (Þorsteinsson 2004: 203). "Þannig leggja allir sig fram til að gera sambúðina bærilega. . . . Það er ekkert helvítis grín að sitja með nærri fjögur þúsund manns á lófastórum bletti langt út í ballarhafi, og ekki nokkra nazistablók að hafa fyrr en í Noregi. Auk þess öll hús full af eiginkonum og dætrum" (Þorsteinsson 2004: 205).
10. The most influential, groundbreaking review in this regard was by Helga Kress (1975). Her critique became the basis for further critical examinations of this particular aspect of Þorsteinsson's work, notably by Steinþórsdóttir (1979) and Kristjánsson (1984). Further and more recent discussions of the so-called *ástandskona* (the name for a woman believed to have had relations with occupying soldiers) include Bára Baldursdóttir 2002; Herdís Helgadóttir 2001; and Inga Dóra Björnsdóttir 1989a. The *ástandskona* is, to date, the only aspect of World War II in Icelandic history that has been subjected to critical revision and debate.
11. "Það er eins og hún bíði eftir nýjum manni" (2004: 269).
12. "Hún, sem stundum var að tala um einsemd sína. Þetta var þó félagsskapur. . . . Þannig voru konur. Þær gátu þagað hjá drullusokkum, þjófum, breinnivínsberserkjum, heimskingjum og ræflum. Annars leiddist þeim" (2004: 183). "Þau svelgja hvort annað í sig með augunum og loftið titrar. Jón Falkon horfir undrandi á bros konu sinnar. Allt fálæti er úr svip hennar. Hún er eins og barn sem hefur fengið jólasveininn beint inn úr dýrunum, hugsar hann og finnst hann vera kominn milli þils og veggjar í þessu samfélagi. . . ." (2004: 184-85).
13. "Þegi þú Bretamellan þín, sem selur þig fyrir sex pence" (2004: 230).
14. "Annars urðu konur eins og jarðsprengjur. Stigi einhver af nálægt þeim splundruðust þær" (2004: 211). See also Kristjánsson (1984). Indriði G. Þorsteinsson admitted later that the occupation turned young men like himself off sex and made them negative toward women (Sæmundsson 1985: 47).
15. "Getulaus maður sem græðir peninga til þess eins að bæta upp ágalla sína, fastur í áfengismóðu, ófær um að ganga á hólm við sársauka sinn. Var þetta kannski arfleifð 'blessaðs stríðsins'?" (Jónasson 2004: 13)

16. Some notable examples are *Punktur punktur komma strik* (1976) by Pétur Gunnarsson; *Kvunndagsfólk* by Þorgeir Þorgeirsson (1974); Þórarinn Eldjárn's short story "Tilbury" (1981); and "I" in Álfrún Gunnlaugsdóttir's *Af manna völdum* (1981). It should be mentioned here that two female writers had already begun to challenge representations of the occupation shortly before *Norðan við stríð* was published: Jakobína Sigurðardóttir in *Snaran* (1968) and Svava Jakobsdóttir in *Leigjandinn* (1969).
17. Notably in *Silence of the Grave* and *The Shadow District*, but also in his many other novels dealing with this period.

References

Atack, Margaret. 2008. "Sins, Crimes and Guilty Passions in France's Stories of War and Occupation." *Journal of War and Culture Studies* 1 (1): 79–90.
Baldursdóttir, Bára. 2002. "Kynlegt stríð: íslenskar konur í orðræðu síðari heimstyrjalda." In *2. íslenska söguþingið 30. maí—1. júní 2002—Ráðstefnurit I*, edited by Erla Hulda Halldórsdóttir, 64–74. Reykjavík: Sagnfræðistofnun HáskólaÍslands/Sagnfræðifélag Íslands/ Sögufélag.
Björnsdóttir, Inga Dóra. 1995. "Uheldlige kvinner i et heldig land." In *Kvinner, krig og kjærlighet*, edited by Dag Ellingsen, Inga Dóra Björnsdóttir, and Anette Warring, 149–71. Oslo: Cappelen.
———. 1998a. "Public View and Private Voices." In *The Anthropology of Iceland*, edited by E. Paul Durrenberger and Gísli Pálsson, 98–118. Iowa: University of Iowa Press.
———. 1998b. "They Had a Different Mother: The Central Configuration of Icelandic Nationalist Discourse." In *Is There a Nordic Feminism? Nordic Feminist Thought on Culture and Society*, edited by Drude von der Fehr, Bente Rosenbeck, and Anna G. Jónasdóttir, 90–103. London: University College London Press.
Eysteinsson, Ástráður. 2006. "Icelandic Prose Literature, 1940–1980." In *A History of Icelandic Literature*, edited by Daisy Neijmann, 404–38. Lincoln: University of Nebraska Press.
Helgadóttir, Herdís. 2001. *Úr fjötrum: Íslenskar konur og erlendur her*. Reykjavík: Mál og menning.
Horne, John. 2004. "Masculinity in Politics and War in the Age of Nation-States and World Wars, 1850–1950." In *Masculinities in Politics and War*, edited by Stefan Dudink, Karen Hagemann, and John Tosh, 22–40. Manchester: Manchester University Press.
Jónasson, Kristján B. 1998. "Rödd úr hátalara, skilaboð í tóttarvegg: Skráning, geymsla og miðlun upplýsinga í skáldsögunum 79 af stöðinni og Land og synir eftir Indriða G. Þorsteinsson." *Andvari* 123(1): 104–28.
———. 2004. "Formáli." In *Tímar í lífi þjóðar*, by Indriði G. Þorsteinsson, 7–15. Reykjavík: Vaka-Helgafell.
Jónsson, Ólafur. 1979. "Norðan við heiminn: Indriði G. Þorsteinsson." In *Líka líf: Greinar um samtímabókmenntir*, edited by Ólafur Jónsson, 18–33. Reykjavík: Iðunn.
Kress, Helga. 1975. "Kvinne og samfunn i noen av dagens islandske prosaverker." In *Ideas and Ideologies in Scandinavian Literature since the First World War*, edited by Sveinn Skorri Höskuldsson, 215–40. Reykjavík: Bókmenntastofnun Háskóla Íslands.
Kristjánsdóttir, Dagný. 2006. "Árin eftir seinna stríð." In *Íslensk bókmenntasaga*, edited by Guðmundur Andri Thorsson, 3:419–661. Reykjavík: Mál og menning.

Kristjánsson, Kristinn. 1984. "Konan, draumurinn og dátinn." *Tímarit Máls og menningar* 45(2): 194–212.

Matthíasdóttir, Sigríður. 2000. "The Nation as Golden Age Man: Gender and Nation in Twentieth-Century Iceland." In *Internationalisation in the History of Northern Europe, Report of the Nordsaga '99 Conference*, edited by Richard Holt, Hilde Lange, Ulrike Spring, 23–36. Tromsø: University of Tromsø.

Neijmann, Daisy. 2013. "'A Fabulous Potency': Masculinity in Icelandic War Literature." In *Men after War*, edited by S. P. McVeigh and N. Cooper, 152–69. New York: Routledge.

———. 2014. "'... Sem allur þungi heimsstyrjaldar lægi í skauti hennar': Ástandskonur í íslenskum hernámssögum eftir karla." In *Fléttur III: Jafnrétti, menning, samfélag*, edited by Annadís Gréta Rúdólfsdóttir, Guðni Elísson, Ingólfur Ásgeir Jóhannesson, and Irma Erlendsdóttir, 196–213. Reykjavík: RIKK/Háskólaútgáfan.

———. 2016. "Soldiers and Other Monsters: The Allied Occupation in Icelandic Fiction." *Scandinavian-Canadian Studies* 23: 96–120.

Ólason, Vésteinn. 1981. "Frá uppreisn til afturhalds: Breytingar á heimsmynd í skáldsögum Indriða G. Þorsteinssonar." *Skírnir* 155: 126–41.

Plain, Gill. 2009. "Women Writers and the War." In *The Cambridge Companion to the Literature of World War II*, edited by Marina MacKay, 165–78. Cambridge: Cambridge University Press.

Stefánsson, Gunnar. 1986. "Sjónarhóll sögumanns: Athugasemdir um sögur Indriða G. Þorsteinssonar." *Andvari* 111(1): 104–13.

Steinþórsdóttir, Gerður. 1979. "Mér finnst ég vera hóra: Um kvenlýsingar í Sjötíu og níu af stöðinni eftir Indriða G. Þorsteinsson." In *Kvenlýsingum í sex Reykjavíkurskáldsögum eftir seinni heimsstyrjöld*, 123–37. Reykjavík: Hið íslenska bókmenntafélag.

Sæmundsson, Matthías Viðar. 1985. "Útlagi í tímanum: Indriði G. Þorsteinsson." In *Stríð og söngur*, 37–62. Reykjavík: Forlagið.

Thorsteinsson, Indridi G. 1981. *North of War*. Translated by May and Hallberg Hallmundson. Reykjavík: Iceland Review.

Valsson, Páll. 1995. "Orrustan geisar í heitu höfði okkar." *Tímarit Máls og menningar* 56(2): 106–11.

Þorsteinsson, Indriði G. 2004. *Norðan við stríð*. Reykjavík: Vaka-Helgafell. First published in 1971.

Þorvaldsson, Eysteinn. 1972. "Indriði G. Þorsteinsson: Norðan við stríð." *Skírnir* 146: 224–27.

Part IV

WAR CINEMA: REMEMBERING AND FORGETTING

What do some of the most popular and recent war films tell us about the evolving cultural memory of World War II in the Nordic region? Feature films—whether based on war novels, veterans' memoirs, or resistance movements—have the power to shape the collective imagination and cultural memory of the historical past, particularly when national legacies are based on civil war, revolution, resistance movements, or defensive wars against powerful neighbors. One such example is the wide significance of the cinematic masterpiece *All Quiet on the Western Front* (1930), based on Remarque's collective war novel, which enacts the perspective of imperial Germany in World War I, that has shaped and defined the twentieth-century combat film and established the aesthetic mode of the antiwar film.

This book has investigated aspects of cultural memory produced about World War II by historiography (in part I), as well as by literary media, i.e. war literature (in parts II and III). In part IV of this volume, six chapters investigate feature films (as well as one television series) that imagine, reinforce, reinvent, or challenge the codified war narratives of each of the five Nordic countries. I am interested here in the war film as a powerful agent in functional cultural memory. These chapters explore how filmed narratives activate, unsettle, or disrupt and reimagine past historical episodes of World War II. These analyses demonstrate how cinema and television may actively interact with and contest national memory culture about traumatic or problematic events of the war.

These six chapters are ordered chronologically, according to the years in which the productions originally aired or premiered, beginning with the early 1970s Swedish television series *Somewhere in Sweden* and concluding with the most recent adaption of *The Unknown Soldier*, which premiered in late autumn 2017, coinciding with the centennial celebrations of the founding of the Republic of Finland. The chapters begin in countries with peaceful conditions (Sweden and Iceland), move toward the German-occupied nations (Denmark and Norway), and conclude with Finland at war.

The Swedish television series *Somewhere in Sweden*, in seven episodes originally produced in 1973, has replayed numerous times on prime-time Swedish television, most recently in 2010. Thus, it constitutes a classic that shapes the Swedish cultural memory of the war years, depicting Sweden's armed military defense force, a group of officers and their men actively guarding the national borders. In chapter 14, Erik Hedling of Lund University analyzes the television series in the context of the controversial historical questions regarding Sweden's neutrality and demonstrates that the televised drama is largely constructed on the basis of the master narrative of "small-state realism" that allowed Sweden to stay out of the war.

In chapter 15 on Icelandic cinema, Pétur Valsson examines how the Allied occupation extends through the postwar decades by means of the continued American military presence that became a consistent, opaque backdrop in postwar films produced in Iceland. This chapter delineates a shift in the negative representation of American soldiers in *The Girl Gogo* (1962) and the depiction of the NATO controversy in *Atomic Station* (1984) toward a more sympathetic portrayal of American cultural influences in *Devil's Island* (1996).

Chapter 16 connects Sweden's war experience to the Finnish "war children" who were evacuated to live with Swedish foster families during the war. In an analysis of the Finnish film *Mother of Mine* (2005), Liina-Ly Roos of the University of Wisconsin-Madison explores the melodramatic depiction of the Finnish war child displaced in Sweden, where the promises of safety and compassion in the Swedish welfare state fail to alleviate the trauma of separation. Roos demonstrates how *Mother of Mine* attempts a healing reconciliation with the past while also reigniting the painful collective memory of this overlooked chapter of the war; the airing of the film in 2005 sparked public debate about the evacuation of seventy thousand children from wartime Finland, a topic unfamiliar to many Finns and Swedes living today.

In 2015, Danish directors produced two unconventional war films in order to mark the seventy-fifth year of the German invasion of April 1940. In chapter 17, I investigate the shifting war memory in Denmark by means of the war film genre, as evinced in *April 9th* (about the humiliating border fight on the day of invasion) and *Land of Mine* (about German POWs forced to de-mine Denmark's west coast after the war). Situated in the framework of cultural memory as defined by Aleida Assmann, I argue that both of these recent Danish films draw from passive memories that had been "archived" or stored, and that these particular historical episodes have not previously been activated as part of the institutionalized cultural memory by means of museum exhibits, public monuments, school textbooks, political speeches, or films. The pair of films dramatizes forgotten or actively marginalized episodes in Denmark's World War II occupation narrative. The two films do not belong in the patriotic or established genre of the occupation drama, which still remains popular, but seem to represent a ground shift in the Danish cultural memory of the war.

In chapter 18, Gunnar Iversen of Carleton University demonstrates that the occupation drama remains hugely popular in Norwegian cinema. Iversen proposes that two recent films, *The King's Choice* (2016) and *12th Man* (2017), represent a new type of war film in Norway that interprets the war for new generations of Norwegians, who have neither experienced the war firsthand nor learned about it by means of communicative memory. These new occupation films employ dramatic intensity and melodramatic emotional appeal while remaining within the established framework of the patriotic national struggle. Iversen argues that these films represent "acts of remembering" and "non-banal" nationalism, filmic media that keep the wartime struggle (under German occupation) active in the working cultural memory of Norwegian citizens in the present day.

In concluding chapter 19, John Sundholm of Stockholm University offers an analysis of the most recent film adaptation of the canonical *The Unknown Soldier*, directed by Aku Louhimies, as "returning to war on screen in Finland." In the context of memory scholarship on the discursive formations of *The Unknown Soldier* in the previous cinematic adaptations, this chapter explores the changes that have occurred in this latest version, due to new premises of film production and changes in the political climate in Finland. Sundholm determines that the new adaptation is a prime example of "prosthetic memory" and that Louhimies's film confirms that the entrenched discourses of victimization and defensive victory still prevail; in short, the hybrid narrative of "The Unknown Soldier," which blends novel and film, remains a powerful founding myth for postwar Finland.

Chapter 14

SOMEWHERE IN SWEDEN

Quality Fiction and Popularized History in the World War II Television Series

Erik Hedling

There have not been very many films for the cinema or television made in Sweden about the Swedish experience during World War II. Certainly not as compared to some other Nordic countries, such as Norway, Denmark, and Finland. Whereas Norway and Denmark suffered German occupation during 1940–45, and Finland fought the Soviet Union in 1939–40, and then fought again, alongside Nazi Germany as co-belligerent, against the USSR in 1941–44, Sweden remained neutral. Arguably, this can partly explain the relative lack of filmed war narratives in Sweden; the story of Sweden during this period is just not as adventurous and spectacular as in the neighboring Nordic countries.

There are, of course a few exceptions, as indicated in a recent study of Swedish World War II films of the last decade (Zander 2014: 23–41). The major one is the television series *Någonstans i Sverige* (Somewhere in Sweden), produced by Sveriges Television (Swedish Public Television) in 1973 and broadcast in seven episodes (the episodes are from forty-eight to sixty-two minutes long, with an average length of fifty-three minutes) over two weeks during Christmas and New Year's 1973–74, prime-time television in Sweden. This series depicts a group of officers and men in a Swedish infantry company and their experiences of guarding the Swedish borders with Norway and

Finland during 1939–45. The public perceived the series as highly realistic in its depiction of military life, and the press gave much coverage to the meticulously recreated details in the series, not least due to the consultation with military experts for the creation of costumes and props (Sörenson 1973).

Någonstans i Sverige has been replayed on Swedish television several times, in 1975, 1979, 1995, and 2010. It is currently available at the open site oppetarkiv.se. According to Swedish film and television historian Bengt Forslund, *Någonstans i Sverige* outclassed all other TV productions in 1973 regarding ratings, claiming that 62 percent of the Swedish population saw it (Forslund 2006: 261). The series was directed by Bengt Lagerkvist (the son of Nobel Laureate Pär Lagerkvist), generally regarded for his contribution to what has been perceived as quality fiction on Swedish public television (Forslund 2006: 256–62). According to the encyclopedia *Tusen svenska klassiker* (A thousand Swedish classics), there has been no better attempt to describe the Swedish military preparedness during World War II on film or television (Gradvall et al. 2009: 373).

Swedish writer Jan-Olof Olsson, mostly known under the nom de plume Jolo, wrote the script for the series. Jolo was a well-known journalist, writing for the Swedish major newspaper *Dagens Nyheter*. He also published many books, mainly consisting of popular history or documentary reportage. Because of the success of this TV series, he also published a book based on his script for *Någonstans i Sverige* (Olsson 1974), in which he summarizes the narrative of the series and adds some historical background to the major political developments affecting Sweden during the war. In the TV series itself, this information is provided by intercut newsreel footage as well as voiceover by director Lagerkvist. Jolo's role as the writer of the TV series received much public attention during production, particularly the fact that he had himself been called up for military service as a private soldier for almost five years during the war, a fact that adds a considerable degree of realism to the depiction of events (Adrup 1973). Interestingly, the narrative of the series does not conform entirely to a realistic mode, with some references to the conventions employed by the contemporary European art cinema. One example is the replaying of a scene with an officer bullying a private soldier with a different voiceover, thus comparing different points of view. In this chapter, however, the main focus will be on the depiction of the historical circumstances of Sweden during the war.

A Few Notes on Ulla Billquist

All the episodes in *Någonstans i Sverige* begin and end with a Swedish song, "Min Soldat" (My soldier) performed by singer Ulla Billquist, a Swedish equivalent of Vera Lynn in Britain. This song was and still is immediately

Figure 14.1. Popular singer Ulla Billquist—her song "Min Soldat" (My soldier) epitomizes Sweden's wartime atmosphere and military preparedness during World War II. Screenshot from the documentary film *When the Clouds Clear* (2016), directed by Lasse Zackrisson. Courtesy of Lasse Zackrisson.

recognized by the majority of adult Swedes. Written by Nils Perne, the song was recorded by Billquist in 1940 and became an instant hit, selling in the first run seventy-five thousand copies (a huge success in 1940), and eventually "millions," as is claimed in Billquist's biography, written posthumously by her daughter Åsa (Billquist-Roussel 2005: 112). Ulla Billquist was also a highly popular field artist, touring northern Sweden and performing for the soldiers.

"Min Soldat" has a bittersweet feel to it, nostalgically referring to the hardships of the conscripted soldiers: "His shoes are too big, his cap is too tight / his trousers too narrow his coat too long/ but that does not matter because he is my soldier / somewhere in Sweden."[1] The TV series, of course, took its name from the three last words in the chorus. The song expresses what some would regard as an antiheroic attitude, celebrating as an ideal the neutral Swedish soldier as the quintessential antihero, a stance that is emphasized in the depiction of the men in the series (some of the officers included). This antiheroic connotation becomes particularly strong when one takes into consideration the generally antimilitarist and antiauthoritarian sentiment among young Swedes in the early half of the 1970s (Wiklund 2006: 179) when the series was produced. Interestingly, a press article from the time of production explicitly mentions that most of the male actors in the series were conscientious objectors to mandatory military service (Forsström 1973: 50).[2]

Analysis and Historical Questions

The focus of this chapter is the view of the chronological events of World War II pertaining to neutral Sweden that is presented for the audience. With the high ratings the series achieved, it is reasonable to assume that the series was of paramount importance regarding the public memory of this particular historical period in Sweden: 1939–45. Recent historiography on Sweden during the war offers important background, particularly *Att bo granne med ondskan: Sveriges förhållande till nazismen, Nazityskland och Förintelsen* (Living as the neighbor of evil: Sweden's relations to Nazism, Nazi Germany and the Holocaust) (Åmark 2011), and *Sweden, the Swastika and Stalin: The Swedish Experience in the Second World War* (Gilmour 2010), as well as many newspaper articles dealing with the series from 1973 onward. As Swedish historian Ulf Zander states, serious critical voices regarding the series are tough to find: "It would . . . have been hard to get attention when praise was so overwhelming from both tv-critics and tv-audience" (Zander 2014: 26).[3] It should also be noted that journalistic and other writing about television in the 1970s was different from what it is today; there was virtually no scholarship dealing with television at the time. Television was certainly not highly regarded and was placed low in the cultural hierarchy, whereas literature, art, opera, and even films for the cinema flourished. Thus, writing on TV was focused on personalities, decidedly antiacademic (sometimes even aggressively so), and distanced, as if TV was so commonplace that it did not really deserve serious critical attention. But there were some interesting deviations from the general pattern.

The following analysis will consider the series in the context of some general themes and controversial historical questions, which scholars have regarded as important regarding Sweden during the war. Sweden was neutral, but it had to bow to Nazi Germany with a governmental policy of concessions until the tide of the war turned in the latter half of 1943. The central historical questions are thus: Sweden's relationship to Finland and Norway respectively during the war; the transport of an armed German infantry division through neutral Sweden from Norway to Finland; the handling of Norwegian refugees; Sweden's bystander role in the Holocaust; Swedish social class divisions; and finally, the course of the war itself. It is reasonable to claim that *Någonstans i Sverige* depicts the Swedish policy regarding Finland's and Norway's wartime ordeals according to a master narrative, popularized during the postwar decades, which mostly justifies the Swedish neutrality policy. Because of this perspective, the series was harshly attacked in *Aftonbladet*, a paper owned by the Swedish trade union movement, which in the 1970s was closely connected to the ruling Social Democratic party; it should be noted that the most important architect behind the Swedish policies during the war was the social democratic prime minister Per Albin Hansson. In the press coverage, the TV critic Macke Nilsson bitterly complained that the series was "political mush, suffused by patriotism"[4] and that it did not dare to address the very real political conflicts characterizing the home front (Nilsson 1974). The chronicler Allan Fagerström, formerly editor in chief of the paper, and who, already as a student at Lund University in the 1940s, was known as a stout anti-Nazi, spoke of the series as unrealistically depicting a "shameful period" (*skammens tid*) in Swedish history and that it expressed (cheap) nostalgia (Fagerström 1974).

The Story

The story of *Någonstans i Sverige* begins on the Swedish-Finnish border after the breakout of World War II in early September 1939. Soon, the Winter War ensues, when Finland is attacked by the Soviet Union in late November 1939, which intensifies the Swedish military preparedness, at the time called the "neutrality watch" (*neutralitetsvakten*). When the Winter War ends on 15 March 1940 (with signing of the Treaty of Moscow), the Swedish soldiers are demobilized, only to be called up again three weeks later when Germany occupies Denmark and Norway on 9 April 1940. This time, they are on guard along the Swedish-Norwegian border in the Swedish county of Värmland, a watch that is to remain until 1944, when they return to the Finnish border. This border patrol was mustered due to the great number of Finnish refugees fleeing to Sweden after the outbreak in September 1944 of the Lapland War in Northern Finland, which erupted when the Finns had made peace with their victorious adversary the Soviet Union and were thus forced to drive out their former military allies, the two hundred thousand German soldiers in Finnish Lapland. The series ends with the end of the war in Europe and celebrations in Stockholm on 7 May 1945.

During the course of the series we learn also about the private relations of some of the conscripted soldiers, and how they spend their leave of absence in Stockholm. In the Swedish capital, we encounter, for example, the family of the fiancée of the platoon commander, Second Lieutenant Ancker (played by Per Ragnar), a young man of upper-class origin. We also meet the intended (Anna Sällström) of Staff Sergeant Hansson (Hans Klinga), a well-educated middle-class youth who enjoys an illicit affair with a pharmacist (Monica Nordquist) close to his posting. Loffe Olsson (Janne Carlsson) and his Stockholm wife are both represented as belonging to the working class; Loffe is depicted as a sympathetic and funny small-time Stockholm trickster—during the entire series he is busy with his black racketeering and general wheeling and dealing. Loffe's wife is played by highly popular Swedish jazz singer Monica Zetterlund, and Loffe himself by accomplished jazz and rock drummer Janne Carlsson, who became the star of the series and whose stardom as an actor and entertainer still lingers, being forever identified as "Loffe." Janne "Loffe" Carlsson's eternal star status was particularly emphasized by the press during the fourth run of the series in 1995 (Björkman 1995; Andersson 1995). (It was even more so during the writing of this chapter, when he suddenly died from cancer, accompanied by multiple pages in the Swedish press, for instance Lind 2017.) There is also an interior scene from the kitchen of the "Momma's Boy" (Per Waldwik), a Stockholm youngster, whose anxious mother in a comic scene treats her son's friends to Swedish *snaps* (a shot of alcohol) with egg and bacon after a drunken night on the town.

Back in the field we are also introduced to Andersson (Olle Björling), a farmer who worries about his family back home; the cook "Big Norrland" (Jan Nygren), a burly northerner; and Big Norrland's adversary "Black Rudolf" (Stig Törnblom), a devoted communist from Tornedalen who belongs to a recognized bilingual minority—"*Tornedalingar*"—from the Swedish-Finnish border area. Corporal Hugg (Tommy Johnson) is a professional soldier who failed all military schools, thus preventing him from ever being promoted from his lowly rank. Above them all is their company commander, Captain Borgman, played by Ove Tjernberg as a slightly cynical but warmhearted father figure. Borgman is constantly complaining about the lousy levels of military education, the general unpreparedness of the Swedish troops in case of real war, the crazy idea held by many Swedes to intervene on Finland's side against the Soviets, and his military profession in general (Borgman and Hugg are the only professional soldiers—all the others are conscripts or reservists). The bottle of cognac, not so discreetly kept in his locker, lulls Borgman's emotions.

Sweden, Finland, and Norway

The soldiers that we follow in *Någonstans i Sverige* are called up for duty along the Swedish-Finnish border when the Winter War breaks out on 30 November 1939; some soldiers had been called already at an earlier stage of the war because of the increasing tensions in Europe. Even if there was strong sympathy for Finland in Sweden, Sweden did not officially or militarily support Finland's cause. The series adopts a somewhat double-edged approach to this Swedish policy of neutrality and nonintervention.

On the one hand, a short newsreel in the first episode refers to the Scandinavian Heads of State Meeting in Stockholm on 18 and 19 October 1939 (Gilmour 2010: 37), where the three Scandinavian kings, Gustaf V of Sweden, Christian X of Denmark, and Haakon VII of Norway, met with Finnish president Kyösti Kallio in order to express a strong Nordic unity. In his voiceover, director Lagerkvist, however, describes this as a public "show," since Swedish prime minister Per Albin Hansson at the same time made it clear to the Finnish foreign minister Eljas Erkko that the Finns could not expect military aid from Sweden if attacked by the Soviet Union, which Finland was some five weeks later. Thus, the voiceover indicates something of a betrayal.

On the other hand, the sympathetic Captain Borgman, also in the first episode, ironically complains about fellow officers who have forcefully advocated a Swedish military intervention on the Finnish side. Winter training for the Swedish army, he claims, was abolished in 1925, and the Swedes do not in reality even possess the ability to defend themselves. In a review of the original series, a Swedish critic describes Borgman as the stand-in for the author Jolo, "providing his view of Finland-activists (senseless), the preparedness (lousy) and defense policies up until 1939 (otherworldly)" (Hansen 1973).[5] This lack of Swedish military preparedness at the time is also emphasized by historians Gilmour (2011: 209–11) and Åmark (2011: 88). Still, Sweden did contribute more than eight thousand military volunteers to Finland and some military arsenal to the Finnish army (Åmark 2011: 87–88). Among later well-known Swedes who volunteered were Harry Martinson, the Nobel Laureate author, and Olof Lagercrantz, editor of Stockholm daily *Dagens Nyheter* (Olsson 1974: 60).

When the viewer sees the Swedish soldiers return to the Swedish-Finnish border, it is the seventh and final episode, set in September 1944. The Continuation War between Finland and the Soviet Union has just ended. Now the Lapland War between Finland and its former German allies is raging, and the Germans apply scorched-earth tactics, causing Finnish refugees to pour into Sweden. The Swedish soldiers help Finnish women to wash themselves in a sauna, causing the Finnish women to complain, to which Captain Borgman replies that he has ordered only married men for this somewhat sensitive duty. Sweden received some fifty thousand Finnish refugees (Gilmour 2010: 97) during the Lapland War. The series also depicts the instability on the Swedish border (Gilmour 2010: 97), as portrayed in the episode when Captain Borgman and a few men go over the river to advise the Germans that they are firing on Swedish territory by mistake. The relations between the Swedes and the Germans, both the officers and their men, are shown as pleasantly jovial, with the officers sipping cognac and the men the somewhat cruder *Weinbrand*.

Most of *Någonstans i Sverige*, however, takes place on Sweden's western border with Norway between episodes 2 and 6. Two historically controversial issues are highlighted: the first is the rail transport between 25 June and 12 July 1941 of the armed German, 163 Division *Engelbrecht*, thirteen thousand men strong, from Norway to Finland (in response to Operation Barbarossa, the German attack on the USSR). According to the transit agreement, the Swedish army was to feed the German soldiers. This concession to German demands, which was clearly in breach of Swedish neutrality, caused a serious political crisis in Sweden in which the government finally decided to concede to German demands. The second controversial issue on Sweden's western border was the handling of Norwegian refugees who were escaping German occupation in Norway.

A part of the third episode is accordingly devoted to the transit of the German soldiers, the *Engelbrecht* Division. In this episode, the Swedish soldiers are on alert on a railway station, pointing their rifles toward the German soldiers who get off the train in order to receive their food. The Swedish officer accompanying the Germans, obviously pro-Nazi, is upset by the behavior of the Swedish soldiers, who are acting as if they were on guard against a potential invader: "It is a scandal that the Swedish army acts in this way—Swedes ought to feel grateful for the German struggle," he exclaims.[6] Actor Lars Amble plays him in a mode of caricature, differing from the otherwise naturalistic approach among the actors. He obviously embodies values attributed to several generals in the Swedish High Command at the time, not least the supreme commander of Swedish forces, Olof Thörnell, who, with support from his colleagues, advocated to the coalition government of Per Albin Hansson that Sweden should actively join Finland in the Continuation War against the Soviet Union (Åmark 2011: 90)—that is, on the side of Nazi Germany. Captain Borgman, despite his steady intake of alcoholic refreshment, a moral example for the viewers, however, stands his ground against the officer and defends his soldiers' stance, even if the pro-Nazi officer apologizes to the German battalion commander.[7]

The depiction of Norwegian refugees on the western border is taken up in episode 4, which shows how the Swedish soldiers temporarily go AWOL at night in order to help refugees through the Swedish-Norwegian border, which is heavily guarded by German soldiers. Here, the Swedish soldiers save French and Soviet POWs from forced labor in Norway, and a Norwegian girl whose mother is Jewish. This episode reflects the saving of over one thousand Norwegian Jews in 1942, even if it should be emphasized that this latter action was organized by the Norwegian resistance movement, hardly by the Swedish military (Åmark 2011: 535). Åmark also mentions the initially highly restrictive attitude toward the activities of Norwegian resistance fighters in Sweden, attitudes that gradually changed as the Allies tightened their grip on Germany (Åmark 2011: 577–80). A recent Norwegian book on the matter, written by journalist Eirik Veum, claims Sweden's role may have been one of betrayal, as Norwegians were often stopped on the border and information about them delivered to the Germans (Veum 2017).

Class Divisions in Wartime Sweden

Furthermore, *Någonstans i Sverige* addresses some of the political issues of the era, particularly when it pertains to different social class interests. Most of the soldiers have lower-class backgrounds—Corporal Hugg, "Loffe," and the small-time farmer Andersson—and generally they express their fatigue and lack of engagement for the higher cause: the protection of Swedish neutrality. One of them is given particular attention, the communist "Black Rudolf" Ketola.

Already in the first episode he is attacked by the cook, Big Norrland, as a "bloody Bolshevik" (*jävla bolsjevik*) who thinks that the Soviet Union's war (in 1939) is a defense against Finnish fascists. Further political quarrels ensue, until episode 5, set in 1943, where Ketola is informed by Captain Borgman that he is to be transferred to a work company since he is judged to be "unreliable." Ketola refers to having fought against "them" already during the Spanish Civil War, in the international brigade on the government side against Franco's fascists. Captain Borgman sympathetically claims to have protested against the order and admits that he finds Ketola to be a good soldier. When Ketola mentions having been unfairly transferred once before, Borgman, however, says that at that particular time he understood why, and he reminds Ketola that he had "dubbla lojaliteter" (double loyalties) during the Winter War in 1939, even if the fight now concerns the threat from Nazi Germany. When Ketola returns in episode seven, it is late 1944 and the tide has definitely turned. He immediately gets into a quarrel with Big Norrland, telling about his experiences in the "Koncentrationsläger" (concentration camp) and adding that if the officers and generals who supported a Swedish entrance into the war on Finland's side, implicitly letting the Germans in, "we had probably all been detained in camps."[8] He also emphasizes that the (victorious) Soviet Union is a society based on socialism and that they will not oppress a single country. "We'll see about that," concludes Big Norrland, a prophetic utterance that carries much more obvious meaning today than it did in 1973 when the series was made.

The treatment of Ketola is quite realistic, considering that the Soviet Union in the Swedish view still was "Russia," Sweden's centuries-old enemy. There were several actions against self-confessed communists at the time, and, as Gilmour states, "the military used conscription to isolate suspected party members and sympathizers in unarmed work companies, for example to build roads in remote Norrbotten [in the extreme the north of Sweden] as a form of internment. There were between 600 and 700 held in ten companies nationally" (Gilmour 2010: 144). These actions, however, were suspended after the Soviets dealt the Germans a devastating defeat at the battle of Stalingrad in February 1943, which began to turn the tide of the war against the Axis powers.

The existence of the ordinary men in the company is dramatically juxtaposed in the series with some interiors from upper-class life in episodes 3, 4, and 5. These scenes are based around the subaltern of the company, Ancker, who is promoted to lieutenant by the end of the series. Ancker, in dress uniform at the elegant dinner party, is engaged to be married to the daughter of a prominent Stockholm businessman, played by distinguished Swedish character actor Gunnar Björnstrand (of Bergman fame). Ancker is asked whether his platoon contains any communist troublemakers, and he tells about "Black Rudolf," something that causes expressions of disgust among the men at the party. A camera movement, slowly zooming in on a portrait of Adolf Hitler on a table, ends the episode. As the scene continues in the next episode, the men in their dinner jackets discuss (with the exception of Ancker—he and his fiancée keep their distance) various political issues sympathetically, such as the sterilization of the mentally ill (an aspect of recognized Swedish policy at the time) and the suppression of "professional paupers."[9] The conversation turns into the general war situation, with comments like, "I thought that England would give in,"[10] and, "England is nothing but a nation of peddlers. They just aim to make money. The only thing they wish is to gain time so that other nations will win their war for them. England wishes to divide and conquer.

Germany wishes to unite and sort things out."[11] They then turn to an anti-Semitic discourse, claiming that there is a Jewish problem also in Sweden and adding, "It would be wise to . . . keep the Jews under some observance."[12] It seems suitable that a series like *Någonstans i Sverige* should address the Jewish persecution, and thus implicitly the Holocaust, as it was one of the most horrific consequences of the entire war. These implicit references to the ongoing Holocaust are in fact a radical aspect of *Någonstans i Sverige*, since the Swedish bystander role in the Holocaust was notably left out of established Swedish historiography until the 1990s (Gilmour 2010: 271).

Further, the strong pro-Nazi views expressed in the dialogue of the series conform to historian Johan Östling's claim that sympathies for Germany and Hitler were common among what he calls Swedish right-wing radicals and various conservatively academic, military, and ecclesiastical circles (Östling 2008: 26-27), to which one can add the members of the higher echelons of capitalist enterprises, as depicted in *Någonstans i Sverige*. The narrative perspective of the series distances itself from these right-wing circles, however, since the next gathering in the luxurious Stockholm apartment—it is now post-Stalingrad—shows the photo of Hitler exchanged for a portrait of Winston Churchill. The daughter of the house confronts her Nazi father for his turncoat behavior and for having earlier dismissed the writings of the outspoken anti-Nazi Segerstedt, to which the father responds, "Of course, Segerstedt can sit and shout down there in Gothenburg—it is somewhat different for us businessmen."[13] Segerstedt here refers to professor Torgny Segerstedt, editor in chief of *Göteborgs Handels- och Sjöfarts-Tidning* (Gothenburg's trade and maritime news) and a devoted anti-Nazi voice in Sweden since 1933. Segerstedt's fierce anti-German rallying was famously often censored by the Swedish authorities, as depicted in Jan Troell's biopic of Segerstedt, *Dom over död man* (The last sentence, 2012).

Social class issues and political sympathies often inform the relations between officers and enlisted men; in episode 2, this is demonstrated most emphatically when Andersson, standing at attention, is severely verbally and physically abused by a lieutenant colonel during parade for slouching. The voiceover informs us that Andersson, with the aid of the staff sergeant, reports the officer, who is disciplined by the auditor with fifteen days in military prison. Another class-related complication is the risk run by the men when performing their military duties, for example when Andersson later (episode 6) is accidentally killed by the recoil of an antiaircraft gun, and Corporal Hugg perishes when saving "Momma's boy's" life during training with live hand grenades (episode 7).

This focus on social class divisions, and the somewhat biased dichotomy between lower and higher classes (the former good, and the latter bad, even if Captain Borgman, who is solid middle class, is depicted as a highly moral man) is somewhat characteristic of the period in which *Någonstans i Sverige* was produced. Historian Martin Wiklund has described the strong influx of what he labels as the "New Left" of the 1960s, with their harsh criticism of Sweden as a class-based and unjust society and their advocacy of "a new libertarian and anti-authoritarian socialism" (Wiklund 2006: 182).[14] Although neither Jolo nor Lagerkvist belonged to the "New Left," narratives circulating in a popular medium such as television are undoubtedly influenced by the radical times.

The Course of the War: A Popular Historical Narrative

Intercut newsreels and commentary by director Lagerkvist serve to recount the major events of the war. Initially, implicit guilt for the war is put on Germany (Germany "annexed" [*anslutit*] Austria and "crushed" [*krossat*] Czechoslovakia and aided the fascists in Spain) as well as on the Soviet Union (the attack on Finland). The respective declarations of war on Germany by France and Great Britain are labeled as "Äntligen sätta stop" (finally putting an end) to German aspirations, all indicating the pro-Western perspective of the series. "*Jävla Hitler!*" (bloody Hitler!) is a common exclamation in the dialogue of soldiers and their women throughout the episodes. When the Allies eventually start to gain victories, it is described through newsreel images from Stalingrad. The voiceover states: "In October 1942, the Germans had constantly advanced in the Soviet Union. . . . Suddenly the English struck back. In the North African desert, the English attacked the legendary German General Rommel."[15] Then, the voiceover returns to Stalingrad, as if the massive Soviet victory was dependent on the relatively minor British one (in terms of German divisions knocked out of the war) at El Alamein in October–November 1942. The next piece of information about the war appears in episode 6, when Operation Overlord—the invasion of France in June 1944—is emphasized. Here, we see British or Commonwealth soldiers advancing toward the beach in their landing craft, even though the voiceover declares that the "English" and American soldiers managed to get ashore. This scene is followed by imagery of General de Gaulle and the French (who were in reality backed by American troops) entering Paris.

The final selection of newsreel appears toward the end of episode 7, where Winston Churchill, speaking from 10 Downing Street, announces the German unconditional surrender to the Allied expeditionary force at General Eisenhower's headquarters and simultaneously to the Soviet Union. This footage is followed by images of cheering masses outside Buckingham Palace in London and footage of George VI, Queen Elizabeth, and the princesses Elizabeth and Margaret receiving the jubilee of the people on the balcony.

There is arguably a pro-British bias to *Någonstans i Sverige* in terms of its Churchillian reading of the historical course of World War II. The United States, with its gigantic contribution to the war in the Pacific and the combined war effort, is hardly mentioned, and the Soviet Union's decisive role is discreetly downplayed. This historical bias is not in accordance with modern scholarship on the subject, in which historians tend to put much more emphasis on the Soviet Union as the most important belligerent in the fight against Nazi Germany (whereas the United States defeated Imperial Japan); the point of the Soviet Union vanquishing Nazi Germany is most emphatically upheld by British historian Norman Davies (Davies 2006) and numerous other American and British scholars. This point is not intended to diminish the great British war effort but rather to point out that the British bias in *Någonstans i Sverige* could have had something to do with both an anti-American bias—popular in Sweden in the 1970s because of the unpopularity of the Vietnam War—along with general sentiments about the communist dictatorship in the Soviet Union.

The master narrative of this television series is one identified by historians Gilmour (2010: 271) and Åmark (2011: 667), as well as many other Swedish historians, as "small-state realism," a narrative that supports the concessions to Nazi Germany (although it was morally questionable in relation to strict neutrality), because it allowed Sweden to stay out of the war, a great advantage for the Swedish people. That this was a wise policy was how World War II was understood in Swedish historiography up until the 1990s, when a more morally inclined paradigm gained ground; according to the more recent "moral narrative," Swedes let other people do the necessary fighting while Sweden profited from other people's misery. In certain aspects, *Någonstans i Sverige* conforms to the narrative of small state realism, particularly in the depiction of Captain Borgman. That this ideological construction earned criticism already in the 1970s is obvious from the critique of the series leveled by journalists Nilsson and Fagerström. But the series does in fact also distance itself from the narrative of small-state realism by referring to Swedish Nazi sympathies among the upper classes and the military, by hinting at Swedish anti-Semitism, and by depicting the meeting of the Nordic heads of state in 1939 as a performance.

As demonstrated, *Någonstans i Sverige* was a huge success with the Swedish television audience, as well as with the press, and it did not seem to decline in popularity over the years. Legendary Swedish TV critic Hemming Sten claimed the series was a true "classic" (Sten 1974), and the commander of the Swedish army at the time, Lieutenant General Carl Eric Almgren, stated in an interview that it was simply "brilliant" (Sörenson 1973). It seemed to offer the Swedish public, despite the social criticism it put forward, a nostalgic, feel-good experience by successfully mixing tragedy and comedy. And, as the ratings were so high, and the level of appreciation so overwhelming, it probably also functioned as a piece of World War II infotainment, forming Swedish views and feelings regarding this vital period in world history.

Erik Hedling is Professor of Film Studies at Lund University, Sweden. Among Hedling's many publications are *Lindsay Anderson: Maverick Filmmaker* (1998), *Interart Poetics: Essays on the Interrelations of the Arts and Media* (1997), *Cultural Functions of Intermedial Exploration* (2002), *Regional Aesthetics: Locating Swedish Media* (2010), and *The Battle of Dybbøl Revisited: The Danish Press Reception of the TV-series 1864* (2015). He is the editor of the anthology *Ingmar Bergman: An Enduring Legacy* (2021).

Notes

1. "Han skor är för stora och hans mössa för trång./ Hans byxor för smala och hans rock är för lång./ Men det gör det samma för han är min soldat/ Någonstans i Sverige."
2. Another aspect of the song is the claim that its author, Ulla Billquist, was homosexual, and that she committed suicide at the age of thirty-eight in 1946. Billquist's alleged homosexuality is not mentioned in her biography, but it is the main point in the recent documentary film *När molnen skingras* (When the clouds clear, 2016), written and directed over a period of fifteen years by Lasse Zachrisson. Whereas her daughter Åsa Billquist-Roussel blames her mother's suicide on her unhappy marriages, the documentary film claims these marriages to have been unhappy because of Billquist's homosexuality.
3. "Det hade . . . varit svårt att få gehör när lovorden dominerade hos både kritikerkår och tv-publik."
4. "Politiskt snömos i sann fosterländsk anda."
5. ". . . gav sin syn på Finlands-aktivisterna (vettlösa personer), på beredskapen (usel) och på försvarspolitiken (verklighetsfrämmande)."
6. "Det är skandal att svenska armén uppträder på det viset—svanskarna borde känna tacksamhet mot Tysklands kamp," *Någonstans i Sverige*.
7. There exists a famous photographic image of this historical situation, in which Swedish soldiers armed and ready look on as German soldiers descend from "uncomfortable goods-trucks" at a Swedish railway station (Gilmour 2010: 282). In reality, claim historians such as John Gilmour, this is an image of POWs en route for exchange in 1944. The photograph may be juxtaposed to another photograph, which shows German soldiers who "travelled comfortably in carriages without close Swedish armed supervision" (Gilmour 2010: 283). This latter image is a rare one from the transits of 1941. Interestingly, the "fake" one is also reproduced as an illustration of the story of the transit—in all 105 trains—of Division Engelbrecht through Sweden in historian Olsson's work (1974: 135–39).
8. "Hade vi . . . hamnat på läger allihop," *Någonstans i Sverige*.
9. "De professionella understödstagarna," *Någonstans i Sverige*.
10. "Jag hade trott . . . att England skulle ge upp," *Någonstans i Sverige*.

11. "England är inget annat än en krämarnation. De vill bara tjäna pengar. Det enda de är ute efter är att vinna tid för att de andra skall vinna deras krig åt dem. England vill söndra och härska. Tyskland vill ena och ordna," *Någonstans i Sverige*.
12. "Jag undrar om det inte vore klokt att . . . hålla dem under en liten observans," *Någonstans i Sverige*.
13. "Det är ju klart att den där Segerstedt kan sitta och skrika där nere i Göteborg—det är lite annorlunda för oss affärsmän," *Någonstans i Sverige*.
14. "En ny frihetlig och anti-auktoritär socialism."
15. "I oktober 1942 hade tyskarna hela tiden gått framåt i Sovjet. . . . Nu slog plötsligt England tillbaka. I den nordafrikanska öknen gick engelsmännen till anfall mot den legendariske tyske generalen Rommel," *Någonstans i Sverige*.

References

Adrup, K. A. (Karl Anders Andersson). 1973. "Fem förlorade år för tusentals vanliga grabbar." *Dagens Nyheter*, 3 June.
Andersson, Jan-Olof. 1995. "Repmöte—22 år senare." *Aftonbladet*, 29 April.
Billquist-Roussel, Åsa. 2005. *Köp rosor: Boken om Ulla Billquist*. Stehag: Förlags AB Gondolin.
Björkman, Anders. 1995. "Här blir han 'Loffe' med hela Sverige." *Expressen*, 28 March.
Davies, Norman. 2006. *Europe at War 1939–1945: No Simple Victory*. London: Pan Books.
Fagerström, Allan. 1974. "Skammens tid—är det något att minnas." *Aftonbladet*, 8 January.
Forsström, Ingmar. 1973. "Det hände någonstans i Sverige." *Veckojournalen* 295(2): 50.
Gilmour, John. 2010. *Sweden, the Swastika and Stalin: The Swedish Experience in the Second World War*. Edinburgh: Edinburgh University Press.
Gradvall, Jan, Björn Nordström, Ulf Nordström, and Annina Rabe. 2009. *Tusen svenska klassiker: Böcker, filmer, skivor, tv-program från 1956 till i dag*. Stockholm: Norstedts.
Forslund, Bengt. 2006. *Dramat i tv-soffan: Från Hamlet till Svensson, Svensson; Svensk tv-dramatik under 50 år*. Lund: Arena.
Hansen, Björn Fabricius. 1973. "Omruskning—39." *Svenska Dagbladet*, 27 December.
Lind, Kalle. 2017. "Cancern tog mångsidig konstnär." *Sydsvenska Dagbladet*, 1 September.
Nilsson, Macke. 1974. "Någonstans i Sverige' ljuger om beredskapen." *Aftonbladet*, 6 January.
Olsson, Jan-Olof. 1974. *Någonstans i Sverige*. Stockholm: Bonnier.
Sten, Hemming. 1974. "Fina skådespelare gjorde TV-klassiker av Beredskapsserien." *Expressen*, 8 January.
Sörenson, Elisabeth. 1973. "En nyttig serie som erinrar om hur förhållandena var då." *Svenska Dagbladet*, 31 December.
Veum, Eirik. 2017. *Det svenska sveket: 1940–45*. Translated by Jan Wibom. Stockholm: Lind & Co.
Wiklund, Martin. 2006. *I det modernas landskap: Historisk orientering och kritiska berättelser om det moderna Sverige mellan 1960 och 1990*. Stockholm and Stehag: Symposion.
Zander, Ulf. 2014. "På vakt eller på krigsstigen? Andra världskriget i svensk 2000-talstappning." In *Den nya svenska filmen: Kultur, kriminalitet & kakofoni*, edited by Erik Hedling and Ann-Kristin Wallengren, 23–41. Stockholm: Atlantis.
Åmark, Klas. 2011. *Att bo granne med ondskan: Sveriges förhållande till nazismen, Nazityskland och Förintelsen*. Stockholm: Albert Bonniers förlag.
Östling, Johan. 2008. *Nazismens sensmoral: Svenska erfarenheter i andra världskrigets efterdyning*. Stockholm: Atlantis.

Chapter 15

ICELANDIC CINEMA AND THE AMERICAN MILITARY PRESENCE

The Girl Gogo, Atomic Station, and *Devil's Island*

Pétur Valsson

In the early hours of 10 May 1940, British warships entered Reykjavík harbor, invading neutral Iceland, where they remained, along with the Americans, as an occupation force for the remainder of World War II. Being occupied by Allied forces during the war meant that the experience of Iceland was quite different from those of the other Nordic countries: Nazi-occupied Denmark and Norway; neutral but landlocked Sweden; and Finland, at war with the Soviet Union. Although there were some minor clashes between the locals and the armed forces, Icelanders were mostly unaffected by the traumatic war experiences of their fellow Nordic nations. Instead, the war years have been remembered for economic prosperity and the end of a long struggle for full independence from Denmark. As historian Guðmundur Hálfdanarson has argued, little attention has been paid to the war in historical and political debates, in large part because it seems to contradict the national narrative of Iceland's struggle for independence from foreign rule (Hálfdanarson 2011: 79–80). The continuing presence of a foreign army in Iceland after the war, albeit on a smaller scale, complicates public memory of the occupation, as there were still remnants of it in place for decades following World War II. As Daisy Neijmann discusses in chapter 13 of this volume, occupation and Cold War literature is mostly concerned with the transition from pastoral life to modernity and changing values, where the occupation is in the background, serving as final push in this progression rather than to be treated as a subject in its own right. Apart from economic prosperity, the war has been remembered in Iceland for what is usually termed *ástandið* (the situation) referring to relationships between Icelandic women and foreign soldiers. In postwar occupation literature, the concentration on these relations borders on obsession (Neijmann 2016: 98). For the most part, Icelandic cinema has ignored the subject of the Allied occupation, and no Icelandic feature films have been made that take place in Iceland during the war.[1] Instead, the continued presence of a foreign military power in Iceland following World War II has served as a backdrop in Icelandic films taking place in the postwar years that address its cultural, social, and political implications for Icelandic society.

In these films, the members of the army are scarcely seen and function as mostly as minor characters, often unnamed. This near absence of the defense force onscreen is characteristic of Icelandic films taking place in the postwar period, its presence sensed and sometimes discussed but rarely seen. However, the social or cultural influences of the army permeate these narratives and comparison of three films, each highlighting different aspects of the controversies concerning the stationing of the American army in Iceland reveals how over time social and political debates have yielded to a general acceptance of social and cultural impact of the American army in Iceland. In *The Girl Gogo/79 af stöðinni* (Balling 1962), the focus is on social issues, specifically the relationships between Icelandic women and American servicemen; *Atomic Station/Atómstöðin* (Jónsson 1984) focuses on the political debates leading to the defense treaty between Iceland and the United States; and lastly, *Devil's Island/Djöflaeyjan* (Friðriksson 1996) portrays cultural changes in the postwar years as American pop culture made an impression on the Icelandic youth. Although it is the main subject in *The Girl Gogo*, transnational romance features in all of these films, to varying degree. The negative portrayal of women fraternizing with soldiers in *The Girl Gogo* yields way for a more sympathetic depiction of transnational romances in later films. It is especially through the depiction of these relationships that the change in public opinion is evident and illustrates how general attitudes toward the social and cultural impact of the American army has shifted from the immediate postwar years to the end of the twentieth century.

Foreign Soldiers in Icelandic Cinema

There are two main reasons that may explain the lack of Icelandic films about the occupation during World War II. First, there has been little need to address traumatic experiences of the nation or controversial issues to resolve; the Allied occupiers did not enter with force, nor have those Icelanders working for them been branded as traitors. Secondly, Icelandic film production was minimal for the better part of the twentieth century, and only a handful of films were produced in Iceland until the Icelandic Film Fund was established in 1979, igniting the start of steady production of Icelandic feature films.[2] Thus, the first generation of professional Icelandic filmmakers was born during or soon after the war and had no personal experience from the occupation. Instead, there seems to have been more interest in depicting the impact of the American defense force on Icelandic society during the postwar years. While the occupation during the war was generally accepted as necessity, or at least the lesser of two evils, many saw the postwar presence of the US army in Iceland as being a direct threat to the sovereignty of the republic. Debates about Iceland's NATO membership and the cultural and social impact of the US defense forces were prevalent in the postwar years and seeped into literature and consequently Icelandic films.

In many ways, foreign service members are still portrayed along similar lines in Icelandic cinema as in occupation literature; they are usually referred to by military titles rather than names, they lack individuality, and when personal looks are described, the emphasis is on common features that signify otherness. The occupying army is "a faceless, nameless presence" and becomes "symbolic of an act of aggression against Iceland and a sign of imperialist power violating the rights of small, peaceful nations" (Neijmann 2016: 100). In Icelandic films, the American soldiers are either nameless or have simple names, and seem to lack personality or individuality beyond their uniform.[3] Moreover, the presence of the army is felt rather than seen, and instead of being the subject of the films, it provides the context in which narratives about Icelandic characters take place. A case in point is the coming-of-age drama *Dot Dot Comma Dash/Punktur punktur komma strik* (Jónsson 1981), in which a family's livelihood is based on the father's work on the army base. The only interaction with the army is when the family attends a magic show at the base. A young boy gorges on candy floss, a lump of sugar with no substance, while his grandfather is asked on stage to take part in the illusionist's trick. The old man is humiliated as the illusionist picks his pockets and pulls his pants down, to the amusement of the American service members in the audience. This short scene conveys the sentiment that the army's ongoing presence was humiliating for Icelanders, especially the older generation who had fought for the country's independence, while the younger generation was being force-fed American culture, addictive like sugar but lacking any substance.

American cultural influences during the postwar years were most prominently transmitted through media; the army base broadcasted American pop music, TV programs, and movies throughout the southwest region years before Icelanders established their own national television station in 1966. These broadcasts were heavily criticized by socialists and the local intelligentsia who claimed that they had negative impact on the country's youth and culture. For those growing up, these broadcasts opened up a whole new world and are, for example, portrayed fondly in *Movie Days/Bíódagar* (Friðriksson 1994), where the young protagonist uses every opportunity to catch a glimpse of TV broadcasts from the base. However, the drastic cultural clash is felt as he goes for a summer stay at a farm and exchanges stories with an elderly farmer. The young boy is not particularly impressed by the farmer's gruesome tales of folklore and ancient legends, the stories passed down by Icelandic generations over centuries. He insists that these stories are mundane compared to all the action he has seen on TV, responding with descriptions of action-packed sequences from war films. The film contrasts the Icelandic cultural heritage with the new foreign influences to illustrate how fast society and culture was changing in the postwar years.

Much of the focus in both historical accounts and occupation literature has been on "the situation" and there are references to it in almost all of the films depicting the American army.[4] Women who associated with members of the occupation force were heavily criticized in public discourse, ostracized, and branded as whores. The government took steps to prevent fraternization, and even incarcerated some young girls for having relationships with the soldiers (Ingimundarson 2004: 73). It was not only that the actions of these women were considered immoral, they were also regarded as unpatriotic, traitors to their country and not least to the Icelandic men. In much of the literature depicting the relationships between Icelandic women and American servicemen, the "blame" is put on the women rather than the foreign occupiers, a sentiment that mirrors the official reports at the time. Kristinn Kristjánsson has argued that the negative representation of women who consorted with the foreign soldiers in Icelandic occupation literature are based on prejudiced views about women as subservient beings with no or little regard for their country. He further points out that these women served as scapegoats for the nation's guilty conscience, as it was much easier to condemn local women than to criticize the foreign army (Kristjánsson 1984: 211). The clearest film example of this is *The Girl Gogo*, in which a woman is blamed for her Icelandic lover's death after he finds out about her affair with an American officer.

The negative views were dominant during the postwar years and weren't seriously challenged and criticized until the 1980s, which resulted in changed public opinion toward these relationships (Helgadóttir 2001: 12). These changed attitudes are evident in later films, such as *Movie Days* and *The Devil's Island*, where the men who use profanities toward women consorting with foreigners are ridiculed. In the former, a woman who has an American boyfriend attempts to assist an intoxicated neighbor on the street. Instead of accepting help he shuns her away and shouts "*kanamella*" (Yankee-whore) as he lies in the gutter. In *The Seagull's Laughter/Mávahlátur* (Guðmundsson

2001), Freyja, an Icelandic woman, returns to Iceland from America after her husband, an ex-army officer, dies. She's now a cosmopolitan, impeccably dressed in the latest fashion, and possesses grace and allure far beyond any other woman in town, projecting an almost otherworldly figure. She's talked about behind her back by other women in town: "Isn't she the chubby one, who was with the Yankees during the war?" says one of them.[5] She has not only gained style and gracefulness during her years in America, she has also become magically thin. Mysterious, well-endowed and with long flowing hair, Freyja seems to have acquired some of the qualities of her namesake from Nordic mythology; the goddess of love and fertility as well as sorcery and death. Although these traits originate from her Icelandic heritage, they seem only to have emerged during her stay abroad. By marrying the American officer, she escaped the traditional Icelandic society, enabling her to become a modern woman and unleash her full potential. The idea that a woman might be empowered by her association with a foreign soldier is certainly a sign of changing attitudes toward these relationships and is in sheer contrast to the portrayal of Gógó in *The Girl Gogo*, the first film depicting relationships between Icelanders and American soldiers.

The Girl Gogo

The 1962, *The Girl Gogo*, directed by the Danish filmmaker Erik Balling,[6] is the only Icelandic film made in the postwar years that depicts the American military presence. The film is an account of a romance between the taxi driver Ragnar and Gógó, a married woman whose husband is undergoing medical treatment abroad and passes away during the course of the film. Prior to meeting Ragnar, Gógó has been having an affair with an American officer, which she continues without Ragnar's knowledge. The film is based on the novel *79 af stöðinni* (Taxi 79, 1955) by Indriði G. Þorsteinsson, whose occupation novels are explored by Daisy Neijmann in chapter 13. Made only a few years after the novel was published, the film offers a similarly negative portrayal of the Icelandic women who had affairs with Americans. Moreover, it depicts American soldiers as drunks coveting Icelandic women, as evident in the opening scene of the film; an American soldier drinking in a Reykjavík bar unsuccessfully makes passes at Icelandic girls before dozing off on his table. As he's being driven back to the army base in a taxi, the car passes another drunken soldier sleeping in the arms of an Icelandic woman on a public bench. However, if the American soldiers are seen as intoxicated philanderers, the real blame lies with the Icelandic women, who by their actions are betraying both the Icelandic nation and its men. Gógó is depicted not only as being promiscuous and boozy but also callous and destructive. Gógó's "situation" is implied from the start, as she is introduced lightly dressed in a broken-down car on the road to Reykjavík from the Keflavik army base right after midnight.[7] It is Gógó who seduces Ragnar and betrays him by continuing her affair with Bill, the American officer. Neither Ragnar nor Bill are condemned for sleeping with a married woman. Gógó is, on the other hand, doubly condemned, both for adultery and for betraying Ragnar. Thus, there is a double standard in the characterizations of Gógó and Ragnar, which follows the misogynist stance of the source work.[8]

Gógó and Ragnar are in many ways opposites. Ragnar is an innocent country boy, representing old Iceland, while Gógó is the modern city woman, an embodiment of the changes to the old pastoral ways of life. Gógó's home is decorated in the style of midcentury modernism, in contrast to Ragnar's meager old-fashioned bedsit. Ragnar is as much perplexed by her as he is by the huge modernist painting on her living room wall, where a traditional rural motif encounters modernism.[9] Gógó welcomes foreign cultural influences pouring over the country, and she listens to pop music on the American radio broadcast, in Iceland nicknamed *kanaútvarpið* (Yankee-radio). Gógó also has a more modern attitude toward sex than customary at the time and is not afraid to make the first advance to Ragnar, right after telling him about her hospitalized husband. Ragnar is reluctant at first, uncomfortable sleeping with another man's wife, but is quickly persuaded. Ragnar's views toward relationships are traditional, while Gógó could be viewed as an early example of the sexual liberation; she doesn't feel as if she belongs to her husband and she wants to make her own decisions regarding her sex life. However, this is not depicted as a positive factor in the film but rather as a sign of Gógó's debased morality.

If Gógó's affair with Ragnar is morally wrong, it is her fault and not Ragnar's; he is happy and does not show any remorse, while she is reserved and covert when she's in public with him, indicating that she has a guilty conscience and has something to hide. Ragnar finds out about her other affair as he is selling alcohol illegally. Taxi cabs served as illegal liquor stores, and taxi drivers often stocked their trunks with bottles of booze (Jökulsson and Guðmarsson 1989: 97). Ragnar is asked by a fellow taxi driver to provide a bottle of Scotch for a regular customer, an American serviceman who spends every weekend with a woman in town. This is another example of the film's double standard; it is fine for Ragnar to profit from selling the Americans illegal alcohol at spiked prices, while Gógó's romantic relationship with an American is unacceptable. Ragnar faces no moral judgment for either sleeping with a married woman or profiting illegally, while Gógó is called a common whore for sleeping around with "Yankees" by Ragnar's best friend. This is in line with the public discourse in Iceland both during and after the war; it's acceptable to benefit financially from the occupation but any sort of fraternization is considered immoral.

Ragnar is infuriated by Gógó's betrayal, speeding home to the farm he grew up at in order to escape the debauchery of the city. Determined to get back home to where he grew up, Ragnar drives all night until he falls asleep at the wheel and drives off a cliff. Although Ragnar's death is an accident, it is evident that the moral blame in the film lies with Gógó. It's her promiscuity and unwillingness to sever ties with her American lover that causes Ragnar to leave the city and drive without resting; it is her betrayal that drives him to his death. In their last phone call, after Ragnar has found out about her affair, she says, "You're a good man and I am a bad woman."[10] Gógó acknowledges her guilt and is obviously remorseful, but she's a destructive force, and her betrayal drives him to his death. At the end, there is some redemption for Gógó's character; she enlists Ragnar's friend to help find him as she worries he might do something rash, but it's too late. The film is a moral tale where Gógó's immorality and liaison with the foreign service members is to blame for the death of an innocent Icelandic country boy.

The contradictions of the old way of life and modernity are manifested in the characters of Ragnar and Gógó, and the narrative demonstrates how the social and cultural influences of the foreign occupation are destroying, rather than changing, the traditional way of life. Although the members of the American defense force are shown in a negative context, intoxicated and philandering, it is Gógó who is really at fault for accepting foreign influences and being promiscuous. This critique of social and cultural changes is highly misogynist, in that the woman takes the blame, whereas neither the foreign army nor the Icelandic men profiting from it are held responsible. As Neijmann writes in chapter 13 of this volume, Þorsteinsson's depiction of women in *North of War* conformed to the public, historiographical, and literary discourse and "exposes an underlying narrative of a deeply wounded masculinity in crisis." The same can be argued for the film adapted from Þorsteinsson's earlier novel that demonstrates how women, who already were ostracized for their relationships, were made scapegoats for societal changes. These views were remnants from the occupation during the war, but were still firmly in place, even though the army presence was by that time no longer involuntary but rather politically motivated. This is the main concern of another film adaptation of Icelandic postwar literature, *Atómstöðin* (*The Atom Station*, 1948), a novel by Nobel Laureate Halldór Laxness.

Atomic Station

The 1984 film *Atomic Station* was among the surge of Icelandic films in the 1980s benefitting from governmental film subsidiaries.[11] The film was adopted from Laxness's novel, originally published in 1948. Written right after World War II, the novel was in direct dialogue with the political debates in Iceland at the time: the 1946 treaty that gave the United States control over Keflavík Airport, the 1949 NATO membership, and the 1951 defense agreement between Iceland and the United States. Laxness, a socialist, was critical of those negotiations, and *The Atom Station*, his most overtly political novel, was a strong contribution to the debate. Although the filmed adaptation was produced more than three decades after the conflict, it emphasizes the political aspect of the original literary text, and it can be regarded as a contribution to the ongoing debate about foreign interest on Icelandic soil.

The film takes place shortly after the war, and the American army is negotiating about continuing their stay in Iceland. Ugla, a young country girl, moves to Reykjavík to learn how to play the organ and lodges with the family of a powerful politician, Búi Árland, with whom she grows close over time. He is involved in negotiations with the US government, serving as a sort of intermediary. During her stay in Reykjavík, Ugla gets involved with a young communist, Gunnar, who is active in the protest against the treaty with the United States. After she becomes pregnant with Gunnar's baby, she has to choose between the two men and the ideologies they represent.[12]

Whereas the political critique of the foreign army in *The Girl Gogo* is based on its social impact, it is purely political in *Atomic Station*. It is not Iceland's women who are betraying the nation by sleeping around with foreign soldiers but rather its politicians, who make shady deals in smoke-filled rooms. In the film's first scene, US officers arrive at Árland's home in the shadow of night. In a backroom of his house, they brood over maps and pictures of possible locations for a military base. The whole scene is without dialogue, but the implied secrecy of the meeting indicates that Árland is plotting with US officials against Icelandic interests. Árland is firmly established as a supporter of foreign military presence in Iceland and advocates for the deal throughout the film. Publicly he insists that an army base is an opportunity for a newly independent nation to break the chains of poverty. When trying to convince his fellow party men and the prime minister in a private meeting, he maintains that there will be no atom bombs there, but he makes it clear that the Americans will build a base there whether Icelanders want it or not. There is certain duplicity in Árland's words: he publicly declares the deal as an important chance to strengthen the nation's autonomy, but in private he admits that Icelanders have no say in the matter. Thus, Árland is not only "selling the land" but also doing it in secrecy without disclosing that Icelanders have no choice. From the film's standpoint, there is of course a choice, and it is a paradox for a nation that has just gained independence to subject itself to yet another foreign power. The defense agreement was much less controversial in 1984 than it was thirty-six years earlier, but there were still debates about foreign interests on Icelandic soil. Criticism about dam-building on the Icelandic highlands to produce hydroelectricity for foreign aluminum manufacturing bears many similarities to Laxness's earlier criticism about "selling the land" and explains the continued relevance of the topic.[13] In regard to criticizing foreign interest in Iceland, *Atomic Station* has more in common with eco films like *Dreamland/Draumalandið* (Guðnason and Magnason 2009) and *Woman at War/Kona fer í stríð* (Erlingsson, 2018) than it does with films like *The Girl Gogo*, where foreign social or cultural influences are forefront.

Relationships between Icelandic women and soldiers only play a minor role in *Atomic Station* and are depicted in a very different way than they are in *The Girl Gogo*. Two minor characters are involved with foreign soldiers; Kleópatra, a prostitute and a friend of Ugla's teacher, and Guðný, Árland's adolescent daughter. Ugla runs into distraught Kleópatra after a dreadful encounter with an Icelandic customer. She tells Ugla that Icelanders don't pay, and she hopes that the Americans will soon return with an atom bomb, implying that some of her patrons are Americans soldiers who reward for her services, unlike her Icelandic customers. Guðný frequently goes to military balls, and one night, after returning home late, she confides in Ugla that she's pregnant following an affair with a married man.[14] Ugla dissuades her from committing suicide, but soon Guðný finds another way to avert public shaming. She calls Ugla, telling her that she's engaged and hoping to get married in America. Although her plan doesn't transpire, as her father arranges an illegal abortion, an American soldier offers her a way out. By marrying him, Guðný would be saved from the embarrassment of having an illegitimate child and bringing shame to the family. In both cases, the Americans are presented as being more decent in their interactions with Icelandic women than Icelandic men are. Given that both Kleópatra and Guðný have worse experiences dealing with Icelandic men than foreign servicemen says more about the character of their countrymen than it does about them. The film's criticism of foreign military presence in Iceland is clearly not based on sexual morals but rather on political ideals.

The most obvious references in the film to actual events are the riots in front of Alþingi, the Icelandic parliament building on Austurvöllur square, on 30 March 1949, when the parliament voted to join NATO. Although these events occurred an entire year after the publication of Laxness's novel, they seem to fit directly into the film narrative, demonstrating the political relevance of the novel at the time of publication.[15] The riots are not enacted on-screen, occurring off-screen instead when Ugla is returning to Reykjavík toward the end of the film. Ugla sees smoke and men with helmets and nightsticks run past her and asks Árland what is happening, to which he responds that hooligans have attacked the parliament. The next morning Ugla walks through the downtown area and passes by Austurvöllur, which is in ruins after the previous day's frenzy. The information about what happened is secondhand, from either Árland or the radio, whose report matches the events in 1949; rocks being thrown at Alþingi, clashes between protestors and the police, and the use of tear gas to disperse the crowd. The riots are among the most politically debated events in Icelandic postwar history, with either side accusing the other of violent behavior. By not depicting any of the violence on-screen and relaying the information of events secondhand, the filmmakers avoid taking sides in this debate. However, the inclusion of the event in the film also highlights another point: that controversial decisions about the country's future are repeatedly made without a referendum and that protesters are often depicted as hooligans by those in power. Without seeming to take sides, the film's reference to the 1949 protest is true to the political message of Laxness's novel; namely, that the decision to sign a defense treaty with the Americans was considered a betrayal by many Icelanders of their neutral and newly independent nation.

By emphasizing the political message of the original novel, the film *Atomic Station* preserves Laxness's main criticism of the defense treaty; namely, that it was in violation of Iceland's sovereignty. The objection to the interest of foreign powers in Iceland, as put forward in the film, should also be considered in a larger context. The criticism of the foreign military base on Icelandic soil in the postwar years has been replaced with environmental criticism of foreign industry in Iceland, using similar rhetoric. The film does not take a moral stance against the relationships between Icelandic women and the foreign servicemen. There is neither a moral condemnation of Guðný and Kleópatra, nor are the foreign soldiers depicted as predators setting out to steal Icelandic women. Instead, the main focus of the film stays on the political aspect of the army's presence in Iceland, a critique of policy rather than of people. While this reflects the viewpoint of the source novel, it is also a sign of a shift in attitude around the time the film was made toward women who had socialized with the foreign soldiers, one from condemnation, as in *The Girl Gogo*, to general acceptance. This change is evident in later films set during the postwar years, such as *Devil's Island*, where the social and political criticism of *The Girl Gogo* and *Atomic Station* yielded to a more humorous portrayal of how the foreign cultural influences impact everyday lives of the capital's poorest citizens.

Devil's Island

The 1996 film *Devil's Island* by Friðrik Þór Friðriksson is adopted from two novels by Einar Kárason, *Þar sem djöflaeyjan rís* (*Devil's Island*, 1983) and *Gulleyjan* (The golden island, 1985). The film takes place in the mid- to late 1950s and depicts people living in a neighborhood of abandoned army barracks in Reykjavík.[16] At the center of the story is one large family, where generations live together in the largest barrack in the community. Housing shortages were a continuous problem in Reykjavík, and toward the end of the occupation, the empty barracks were allocated to poor Icelandic families. Thus, although the film focuses on the misfortunes of one family; the barracks are ever present as relics from the war and a constant reminder of the occupation of Iceland, as emphasized in the film's preface:

> Icelandic Vikings found America in the ninth century. But as Oscar Wilde said, they had the good taste to lose it again. A thousand years later, in World War II, the Americans occupied Iceland. But they were so set on not losing it again that they kept a military base there, long after the war ended. They moved out of the capital, though, leaving behind barracks for the benefit of homeless Icelanders.[17]

The preface gives the context for the film and makes clear the circumstances of families living in the barracks. They were quickly built as temporary housing, and many were more or less falling apart after a few years. These cold and damp remnants from the occupation supplied Reykjavík's poorest families with a roof over their heads, however substandard it might have been.[18]

The setting of the film serves to remind the viewer of the temporary remnants of the occupation, but also of the more lasting cultural and social influences. This is evident in the film's first scene, a wedding reception in the barracks for an American and his Icelandic bride. The groom and his fellow Americans are snappily dressed in uniform, while the Icelandic family of the bride appear as poor peasants by comparison, a reminder that Icelanders were still transitioning to modernization. The interaction between Icelanders and Americans at the reception also illustrates different levels of courteousness; while the Americans invite the women to dance, the Icelandic men get drunk and complain to each other. Upon seeing his wife dancing with an American soldier, a husband drunkenly grumbles, "What are those Yanks hanging around here for? The war finished ages ago but they're still here molesting our women."[19] This echoes a common sentiment at the time that these foreigners were "stealing" Icelandic women, a sign of male anxiety stemming from the fear that Icelandic women would prefer these foreign soldiers to their countrymen. However, it is the disgruntled husband who becomes a laughingstock in the film; he acts like a fool, as he falls headlong in the mud in a meager attempt to fight the American. The humorous portrayal of a common concern during and after the war indicates how perspectives had changed by the end of the twentieth century. It is neither the women nor the foreign soldiers who are condemned or ridiculed but rather these old-fashioned views.

Like in Friðriksson's previous postwar film *Movie Days*, the clash between Icelandic and American culture is portrayed humorously in *Devil's Island*. The occupancy of thousands of soldiers during the war seeking entertainment on their days off created conditions for wider selection of entertainment. Businesses quickly started to cater to the sudden influx of young customers, who outnumbered the local youth. The selection of American films at local movie houses grew, and contemporary pop music and jazz dominated public dances. While the cultural elite and politicians condemned this invasion of new, mostly American culture, the Icelandic youth embraced it, and it quickly started to impact everyday life. Although far fewer troops were stationed in Iceland in the postwar years, the presence of an army continued to have cultural impact, especially with the rise of American youth culture in the 1950s. The Americans established radio and TV stations in 1951 and 1955, respectively. These broadcasts reached well beyond the military base and introduced new trends in music and fashion to the local public.

In *Devil's Island*, the impact of American culture is represented through the character of Baddi. Upon returning from a visit to his mother, who had immigrated with her American husband to the United States, Baddi has fully embraced the American way of life. Dressed in his leather jacket, looking like a cross between Marlon Brando and Elvis Presley, Baddi becomes the embodiment of American cultural influences and their clash with Icelandic culture. He drives around in a Plymouth Fury and throws around American slang and phrases. When kids in the neighborhood ask him to say something in English, he replies, "Wipe the windows, check the oil, dollar gas."[20] Although he is brimming with knowledge about the American way of life, his adaption of the American customs seems to be rather shallow. Baddi also seems to have adapted all possible bad habits during his stay in America, he drinks too much and treats everyone around him unkindly. He's ungrateful and is constantly complaining about how boring things are in Iceland compared to America. In the film, his younger brother Danni becomes his polar opposite. Less spoiled by American influences, he might seem old-fashioned compared to Baddi, but Danni seems to represent optimism for Icelandic youth. While Baddi spends his days drunk or loitering in front of the TV, Danni covertly trains to become a pilot and becomes the pride of the family, shortly before his untimely death. Much of the tension in the film stems from the changes that were quickly reshaping Icelandic society in the postwar years, where the values of old Iceland are being replaced by new, more modern ways of living. Although Danni is very much a side character for much of the film, which mostly revolves around Baddi and his shenanigans, he emerges as a hope for the future toward the end. By contrasting the characters of the two brothers, the film shows that regardless of the foreign influences "spoiling" the Icelandic youth, they could still aspire to greater things. Although Baddi's many vices are augmented by his stay in America, there is no condemnation of American cultural influences, but rather a warmhearted and often humorous portrayal of them in contrast to Icelandic customs. The differences between Icelandic and American culture are emphasized to make fun of Icelanders rather than to criticize foreign influences.

Devil's Island has the advantage of being able to look back at the cultural clash between tradition and modern times, which in the case of Iceland arrived rather quickly during the war. Instead of negatively depicting the social impact or the political implications of the American defense force's presence in Iceland, such as in *The Girl Gogo* and *Atomic Station*, the film shows how it affected people's daily life. The family has somewhere to live thanks to remnants of the occupation, one member of the family marries an American and emigrates, while the young generation has to find its footing in a newly independent country where the conflict between tradition and foreign culture impacts everyday life. In *Devil's Island* the humorous portrayal of a society in the midst of modernization illustrates how public opinion had changed by the end of century. Moral condemnation of transnational romances or criticism of

Figure 15.1. *Devil's Island*: An American serviceman and his Icelandic bride pose for a wedding photo with her family in front of the abandoned army barrack that serves as the family home. The wedding attire of the couple contrasts the appearance of the bride's family, illustrating the difference between the life the bride is leaving behind in Iceland and the one waiting for her in the United States. Production still from *Devil's Island* (1996), directed by Friðrik Þór Friðriksson. Courtesy of Friðrik Þór Friðriksson.

cultural or political influences has yielded to a general acceptance, where it is up to the individual to decide how he embraces them.

Conclusion

The Girl Gogo, *Atomic Station*, and *Devil's Island* all offer a different perspective on the presence of the American military in Iceland, focusing on either the social, political or the cultural effects of it. There has been a shift in general attitude toward the overall effects of the occupation over time, as is evident in these films. The negative portrayal of intimate relationships with American servicemen in *The Girl Gogo* and the political criticism of the defense force in *Atomic Station* give way to a more sympathetic portrayal of cultural influences in *Devil's Island*. To a varying degree, all of these films depict relationships between Icelandic women and American soldiers, which goes to show how important the subject has been to Icelanders. Like in Icelandic occupation literature, Icelandic films that take place during the postwar years are obsessed with these relationships. However, as most of the films were produced after the time when attitudes shifted from condemnation to general acceptance of transnational relationships, it is only *The Girl Gogo* that displays a hard opposition to fraternization between Icelandic women and members of the American army. Although these relationships remain in the background of *Atomic Station* and *Devil's Island*, the turnaround is evident in that there is no blame directed at the women. Instead, Icelandic men who treat women badly are unfavorably compared to the Americans in *Atomic Station*, and those who complain are ridiculed in *Devil's Island*. Other, later films, such as *Movie Days* and *The Seagull's Laughter*, also display similar sentiments toward "the situation." The shift in representation of transnational romance, from *The Girl Gogo* to *Devil's Island*, demonstrates how public opinion changed from the postwar years to the end of the twentieth century.

Although transnational relationships are present in most of the films that reference the impact of the occupation and the defense treaty on Icelandic society, it is only in *The Girl Gogo* where they are the main concern. The film is also the only one made during the immediate postwar years, while later films, made after governmental subsidies became available in 1979, demonstrate a more accepting perspective on the subject. A shift in focus from the social or political criticism of *The Girl Gogo* and *Atomic Station* to portraying social and cultural influences humorously in *Devil's Island* indicates the revised perspective of a younger generation. No longer was the presence of a foreign army viewed as a threatening danger to Icelandic cultural and national heritage; rather, it became an important factor in driving forward social change and pushing a somewhat homogeneous society toward modernity.

Pétur Valsson is a PhD Candidate in Scandinavian Studies and Cinema and Media Studies at the University of Washington, and holds an MA in film studies from Columbia University and a BA in history and film from the University of Iceland. His PhD dissertation investigates the work of Danish film auteur Lars von Trier.

Notes

1. The biopic of Icelandic composer Jón Leifs, *Tears of Stone/Tár úr steini* (Oddsson 1995), partly takes place during the war, but not in Iceland, and thus the occupation does not play a part in the narrative.
2. There was no public financial support available for filmmaking in Iceland until the Icelandic Film Fund was established in 1979. The first Icelandic feature film, *Between a Mountain and a Shore/Milli fjalls og fjöru* (Guðmundsson), was made in 1949, and over the next few years a number of domesitic productions were made with tight budgets and limited technical knowledge. From 1954 to 1967 the film company Edda film attempted to raise the bar for Icelandic cinema by coproducing films with Scandinavian partners and experienced Swedish and Danish directors, including *The Girl Gogo*. After the success of *Murder Story/Morðsaga* (Oddsson) in 1977 proved that it was viable to produce domestic feature films, the Icelandic parliament, Alþingi, passed laws to subsidize Icelandic film production.
3. In the rare instances that American characters have names, they are short nicknames such as Bill (*The Girl Gogo*), Charlie, Tom, and Harry (*Devil's Island*), that seem generically American compared to Icelandic names.
4. The only exception is *Dot Dot Comma Dash*, which has no mention of these relationships.
5. "Er hún ekki sú þybbna, sem var í kananum á stríðsárunum?" (translations from DVD subtitles).
6. The film was a coproduction between the Icelandic Edda film and the Danish Nordisk Film. The film was fully financed in Iceland, while the Danes supplied the director and technical staff.
7. The novel is more explicit in implying what kind of character Gógó is; she is described as dressing like a bimbo: "Hún var glyðrulega klædd, í ekki nema léttri regnkápu yfir flegnum kjól, berhöfðuð og í rauðum skóm háhæluðum." [She was dressed flirtatious, only wearing a light raincoat over the low-necked dress, bareheaded and in red high-heeled shoes] (Þorsteinsson 1978: 27, translation mine).
8. Þorsteinsson has been criticized for repetitive mysogyny in his portayal of women, both in the source novel (Steinþórsdóttir 1979: 135) as well as in his other works, as Neijmann discusses elsewhere in this volume.
9. The painting is *Skammdegisnótt* (Dark winter night, 1954) by Gunnlaugur Scheving, one of the best-regarded twentieth-century Icelandic painters.
10. "Þú ert góður maður og ég er vond kona" (translation mine).
11. The novel and the film have the same title in Icelandic, *Atómstöðin*, but while the novel was translated into English as *The Atom Station*, the film was screened internationally as *Atomic Station*.

12. In the film, Gunnar is a combination of two characters from the novel: the young communist who gets Ugla to sell lottery tickets and the self-conscious policeman who fathers Ugla's child. This creates an ideological love triangle between Ugla, Gunnar, and Árland that does not exist in the source novel.
13. The aluminum smelter was built in Iceland by a Swiss company in 1970, and since then two more smelters have been built, in 1998 and 2008.
14. The father's nationality isn't established in the film, but as Guðný claims that he went home with his wife after the ball, it is presumed that he is Icelandic.
15. It is inferred that the riots in the film are against the defense agreement, as the film takes place a couple of years before the formation of NATO.
16. The novels take place from approximately 1951 to 1967, but the sequence of events is condensed considerably in the film. Historian Eggert Þór Bernharðsson compared car models used and references to events and estimated that the time frame of the film is approximately 1956–63 (Bernharðsson 2005: 170).
17. "Íslenskir víkingar fundu Ameríku, en eins og Oscar Wilde sagði voru þeir nógu smekkvísir til að týna henni aftur. Í seinna stríðinu hernámu Ameríkanar Ísland, en þeir vildu ekki glata því aftur svo þeir héldu áfram að reka hér herstöð þótt stríðinu væri löngu lokið. Þeir yfirgáfu þó höfuðborgina og skildu þar eftir braggana sína, húsnæðislausu fólki til gæfu . . ." (translation from DVD subtitles).
18. The highest number living in barracks in Reykjavík was in 1952, an estimated 2,320 people or 4 percent of the population (Bernharðsson 1998: 301).
19. "Hvað eru þessir helvítis Kanar að þvælast hérna ennþá. Stríðið er löngu búið og þeir eru hérna ennþá að gramsa í okkar kvenfólki" (translation from DVD subtitles).
20. The phrase is derived from a Chuck Berry song but seems rather banal on its own, like something Baddi might have overheard at a gas station.

References

Balling, Erik. 1962. *The Girl Gogo/79 af stöðinni*. Iceland: Edda Film.
Bernharðsson, Eggert Þór. 1998. *Saga Reykjavíkur: Borgin; 1940–1990. Fyrri hluti*. Reykjavík: Iðunn.
———. 2005. "Djöflaeyjan . . . vekur allt liðið úr Thulekampinum upp til nýs lífs . . ." In *Kúreki norðursins: Kvikmyndaskáldið Friðrik Þór Friðriksson*, edited by Guðni Elísson, 160–83. Reykjavík: Háskólaútgáfan.
Erlingsson, Benedikt. 2018. *Woman at War/Kona fer í stríð*. Iceland: Gulldrengurinn.
Friðriksson, Friðrik Þór. 1994. *Movie Days/Bíódagar*. Iceland: Íslenska kvikmyndasamsteypan.
———. 1996. *Devil's Island/Djöflaeyjan*. Iceland: Íslenska kvikmyndasamsteypan.
Guðmundsson, Ágúst. 2001. *The Seagull's Laughter/Mávahlátur*. Iceland: Ísfilm.
Guðmundsson, Loftur. 1949. *Between a Mountain and a Shore/Milli fjalls og fjöru*. Iceland: Loftur.
Guðnason, Þorfinnur, and Andri Snær Magnason. 2009. *Dreamland/Draumalandið*. Iceland: Ground Control Productions.
Hálfdanarson, Guðmundur. 2011. "'The Beloved War': The Second World War and the Icelandic National Narrative." In *Nordic Narratives of the Second World War: National Historiographies Revisited*, edited by Henrik Stenius, Mirja Österberg, and Johan Östling, 79–100. Lund: Nordic Academic Press.

Helgadóttir, Herdís. 2001. *Úr fjötrum: Íslenskar konur og erlendur her*. Reykjavík: Mál og menning.
Ingimundarson, Valur. 2004. "Immunizing against the American Other: Racism, Nationalism, and Gender in U.S.-Icelandic Military Relations during the Cold War." *Journal of Cold War Studies* 6(4): 65–88.
Jökulsson, Hrafn, and Bjarni Guðmarsson. 1989. *Ástandið: Mannlíf á hernámsárunum*. n.p.: Tákn.
Jónsson, Þorsteinn. 1981. *Dot Dot Comma Dash/Punktur punktur komma*. Iceland: Kvikmyndafélagið Óðinn.
———. 1984. *Atomic Station/Atómstöðin*. Iceland: Kvikmyndafélagið Óðinn.
Kárason, Einar. 1986. *Þar sem djöflaeyjan rís*. 3rd ed. Reykjavík: Mál og menning.
———. 1987. *Gulleyjan*. 2nd ed. Reykjavík: Mál og menning.
Kristjánsson, Kristinn. 1984. "Konan, draumurinn og dátinn." *Tímarit Máls og menningar* 45(2): 194–212.
Laxness, Halldór Kiljan. 1961. *Atómstöðin*. 2nd ed. Reykjavík: Helgafell.
Neijmann, Daisy L. 2014. "'Sem allur þungi heimsstyrjaldar lægi í skauti hennar': Ástandskonur í fyrstu íslensku hernámssögunum." In *Fléttur III: Jafnrétti, menning, samfélag*, edited by Annadís G. Rúdólfsdóttir, Guðni Elísson, Ingólfur Ásgeir Jóhannesson, and Irma Erlingsdóttir, 196–213. Reykjavík: Háskólaútgáfan.
———. 2016. "Soldiers and Other Monsters: The Allied Occupation in Icelandic Fiction." *Scandinavian-Canadian Studies/Études scandinaves au Canada* 23: 96–120.
Oddsson, Hilmar. 1995. *Tears of Stone/Tár úr steini*. Iceland: Tónabíó.
Oddsson, Reynir. 1977. *Murder Story/Morðsaga*. Iceland: Borg-film.
Þorsteinsson, Indriði G. 1978. *Sjötíu og níu af stöðinni*. 4th ed. Reykjavík: Almenna bókafélagið.
Steinþórsdóttir, Gerður. 1979. *Kvenlýsingar í sex Reykjavíkurskáldsögum eftir seinni heimsstyrjöld*. Reykjavík: Hið íslenska bókmenntafélag.

Chapter 16

WAR MEMORY, COMPASSION, AND THE FINNISH CHILD

Klaus Härö's *Mother of Mine*

Liina-Ly Roos

While the various depictions of World War II continue to figure in Finnish cinema, Klaus Härö's melodrama *Äideistä parhain/Mother of Mine* (2005) remains one of the very few films to portray the experience of Finnish war children in Sweden. A Finnish-Swedish coproduction, based on the Finnish novel *Äideistä parhain* (The best of mothers, 1992) by Heikki Hietamies, *Mother of Mine* gained unusually wide acclaim both in Finland and Sweden. The topic of the evacuation of approximately seventy thousand children from Finland to Sweden, Denmark, and Norway during World War II, which had attracted some academic interest already in the 1980s and 1990s, was actively revisited in the 2000s in the Finnish and Swedish media.[1] During World War II, Finland fought two defensive wars against Soviet Union: first, the Winter War of 1939–40, and then the Continuation War from June 1941 to September 1944. Finally, from October 1944 to April 1945, Finland drove out German troops in the Lapland War. The idea of inviting Finnish children to live with Swedish families came from Maja Sandler, the wife of the Swedish foreign minister in 1939 (Kavén 2010), but according to Finnish historian Aura Korppi-Tommola, there had not been any requests from the Finnish side for Sweden to evacuate the children (Korppi-Tommola 2008). Along with other activists, there were several organizations created to offer humanitarian help to Finland, and even though there was some criticism of the project in Finnish public discourse, the number of children sent to Sweden was about the same as the number born in 1939. As Finnish historian Pertti Kavén argues, if the Winter War were to continue, the number of refugee children to be evacuated would have been so large that the migration would have been seen as a distribution of the nation's genes in order to store them in other Nordic countries in case the nation were destroyed (Kavén 2010: 12).

The war children project was, thus, invested with strong emotions in both Finland and Sweden. Whereas having to send one's children away was traumatic and difficult—and the public discourse in Finland was critical of the idea—such an attitude was seen in Sweden as ungratefulness, and therefore the Finns forbade most criticism of it in the media. The many problems of the war children initiative that were brought up later included the difficult and dangerous transport of the children; challenges with readjustment to Finnish homes in the postwar years; conflicts over custody; and the hypocrisy of Swedish neutrality politics that saw helping the innocent children as one of the few ways to assist Finland at war.[2] The Swedish activists for the project had emphasized the figure of the innocent child under the motto, "Finlands sak är vår" (Finland's cause is ours) in order to create feelings of compassion among the Swedish public; however, the traumatic experiences of many of the children reveal the difficult conditions of adjusting to Swedish society where the underlying attitude was often contrastingly a lack of care and compassion for the Finnish children or the Finnish wars in general.[3] A number of war child narratives (mostly in the form of autobiographies and collected memoirs) describe the experience of "war children" (a status with which many have continued to identify themselves even decades after the end of war) as that of "rootlessness, lacking sense of self, and an inner unexplainable insecurity" (Edvardsen 1977: 5).

In this chapter, I will explore how Härö's *Mother of Mine* meditates this emotional memory of the war and the growing ontology of homelessness in the realm of the domestic spaces, where the individual and state-level decisions during the war caused a prolonged sense of "in-betweenness" for the child who, paradoxically, had been promised a better home by the Swedish state. Scholarship on depictions of the child in literature emphasizes that the child is constructed by adults (Rose 1993; Honeyman 2005; Hirsch 2012). In analyzing the cinematic portrayal of the child within war, film scholar Karen Lury writes that, while not providing facts of war, the child's "experience as visceral, as of and on the body, demonstrates how the interweaving of history, memory and witness can be powerfully affective" (Lury 2010: 7). On one hand, the fictional construction of the child's perspective allows the narrative to affect its audience by victimizing the child and creating strong feelings of compassion and pity in the audience. On the other hand, the typical image of the child in the midst of traumatic events is that of someone who is more aware of the traumatic memories and problematics of decisions made by adults—offering a defamiliarizing effect, a perspective of the marginalized—who will always be portrayed as the Other to the adult audiences.[4] Both of these aspects of the figure of the child are present in *Mother of Mine*.

Hietamies's novel that *Mother of Mine* is loosely based on has been read as a trauma narrative, where the child's focalization is articulated through an adult narrator,[5] but Härö's film applies the melodramatic mode to emphasize the contrast between the promise and the lack of feelings of compassion for the child, at the same time trying to solve the moral conflict in the collective memory that the child's perspective depicts. By "melodramatic mode" I mean the revised concept of melodrama in contemporary film studies, which argues that it is not simply a genre but rather a mode that can figure within different genres. Linda Williams argues in her seminal essay "Melodrama Revised" (1998) that films in the melodramatic mode begin and end in the space of innocence and focus on victim-heroes, and instead of simply opposing suffering and victimization, their goal is to depict moral and emotional truths and to "reconcile the irreconcilable" (Williams 1998: 73). In her recent article, Williams adds that essential to melodrama is "the dramatic *recognition* of good and evil and, in that recognition, at least the hope that justice might be done" (2018: 215, italics in original). Thus, according to Williams, melodrama adapts "the most recent awareness of social problems and failures of justice" and is constantly renewing and modernizing itself (2018: 216). Different from the traumatic mode that in literary and cinematic works implies a haunting memory of the past in the present, disrupted narratives, and an unresolved suffering or victimization, the melodramatic mode in *Mother of Mine* focuses on the failures of justice, moral and emotional truths in Swedish and Finnish contemporary societies regarding the collective memory of World War II.

This chapter explores the juxtaposition of a promise and a failure of compassion as a "proper" moral emotion in *Mother of Mine*, which reflects the general discourse on World War II in Finnish and Swedish collective memories. Finnish historian Ville Kivimäki argues that there are currently two perspectives in Finnish memory culture of the war: one is "critical" and the other is "patriotic" (Kivimäki 2012: 496). Whereas the former draws attention to the possibly wrong decisions during the war (such as the evacuation of children to Sweden or continuing the war after the Winter War had ended), the "patriotic" perspective tends to oversimplify the wartime past "whereby the war generation and its sacrifices are consigned to only monolithically conservative and even militantly nationalist meanings" (Kivimäki 2012: 497). John Sundholm discusses these changing narratives in Finnish cultural memory in chapter 19 of this volume, which examines the third adaptation of Väinö Linna's seminal war novel. Further, Swedish historian Johan Östling argues that, even though during the 1990s the Swedish foreign policy of neutrality and nonalignment during war was contested and "portrayed as an exercise in hypocrisy," nevertheless "the moral of the small-state realism remained" (Östling 2008, 210). The collective feelings of guilt in Sweden regarding neutrality and collaboration with Nazi Germany are also addressed in a Swedish television series of the 1970s, which reinforces the narrative of "small-state realism" and the recent "moral narrative," as discussed in chapter 14 by Erik Hedling.

With its melodramatic mode, *Mother of Mine* portrays the moral conflicts between these two perspectives in Finnish and Swedish societies by constructing a child who experiences greater emotional trauma in Sweden than he did in Finland during war. This depiction provokes feelings of compassion and empathy in the audience for the child who did not receive such compassion, even though the relocation of the war children had promised it to him. The film uses the child figure not only to depict the uncomfortable emotional memories of war but also to inspire moral and emotional healing of the grown-ups, by seeking justice for the child. The child in these examples is portrayed as outside politics and history, and even though his ultimate experience throughout his childhood remains that of homelessness, his affective impact on the grown-ups aids the film in reestablishing national and familial continuity. The child in *Mother of Mine* resembles the "melodramatic child," an "exemplary and a utopian inspiration for the adult world. Helping, communicating, initiating social change, or preserving the memory of the human race, it becomes a force of improvement" (Decker 2007: 324). Christof Decker has defined this kind of a child figure in his analysis of American narrative cinematic works, which have also inspired Klaus Härö's work. The construction of the war child in *Mother of Mine* allows the film to provoke and mediate feelings of disappointment caused by the unfulfilled promises of compassion in the Finnish and Swedish collective memories of war; further, in its search for a solution it offers an abrupt reconciliation and a restoration of national belonging and justice.

The Promise of Compassion

Mother of Mine portrays a Finnish child Eero (Topi Majaniemi), who is sent to live in Sweden during the Winter War and the Continuation War in Finland. Eero is independent, adapting to the circumstances, and rather stable in the midst of adults, of whom several, particularly and most importantly for him both his Finnish biological mother and his Swedish foster mother, are portrayed as morally or mentally unstable. After his father's death in the war, Eero's biological mother Kirsti (Marjaana Maijala) suffers from depression and is not able to care for Eero, and once her son relocates to Sweden, she considers moving to Germany with a German soldier. In the beginning of Eero's stay in Sweden, his host mother Signe (Maria Lundqvist) does not want to accept him to the family, because she had expected a girl. As the audience soon finds out, Signe would have treated a girl as a replacement for her own daughter, whom she had lost, and thus she treats Eero with an emphasized lack of compassion. The entire film is presented as an extended flashback, interspersed with some black-and-white clips of grown-up Eero (Esko Salminen) trying to find reconciliation with both of his mothers following nearly sixty years of silence after his return to Finland at the end of war.

Throughout the film, Eero's perspective is singled out, both in relation to the adults and to other children around him. In the midst of his difficult circumstances, he acts like an adult, taking care of his own mother after the news of his father's death. However, when he is sent away from home, already on the ferry, in the midst of other children, the voiceover of grown-up Eero distances himself from the hopes and promises that other children might have had:

> They had promised the girls dolls and the boys bikes. When we got to Sweden, they first picked the youngest and then the prettiest girls—the ones with the prettiest smile. Everybody was afraid of going to an orphanage and wanted their own Swedish family to take care of them. Only I didn't want that. (*Mother of Mine* 2005)[6]

Similar recognition through Eero's perspective of the contrast between promises and reality continues on the train ride, where he sits across from a smiling *Lotta* (a volunteer in the Swedish women's voluntary defense organization, *Lottakåren*) sitting with two young girls. Soon after, he sees the *Lotta* trying to separate these sibling sisters, who are forcefully divided and sent to different families. The film is, thus, emphasizing the contrast between the promise and lack of compassion that only the child witnesses in his immediate surroundings, both in the narrative level and with mise-en-scène that supports this dissonance. In addition to this characteristic of melodrama, and to the musical score that emphasizes emotional effects (Elsaesser 2012: 441) (which several reviewers criticized for being too dramatic[7]), the result of the contrast is further achieved through the depiction of landscapes and interiors.

When Eero is dropped off at the bus stop to meet his Swedish parents Signe and Hjalmar (Michael Nyqvist), he is surrounded by an open landscape that (also in several later shots) appears to be swallowing him up. Härö and his cinematographer Jarkko T. Laine's preliminary goal with filming in this particular location in Skåne (the most southern province of Sweden) was to portray a landscape as different as possible from Eero's home in Finland. There are, however, more contrasts that are created by the camerawork within the Swedish surroundings. Whereas the open landscapes appear to the viewer much less claustrophobic than the tight, vertical scenes of Finnish birch tree forests or the dark, closed spaces infused with the proximity of war as the children are saying farewell, Eero is filmed with close-ups in the midst of the Skåne landscape, reflecting his emotional Swedish experience and making him look more claustrophobic, alienated, and trapped in the Swedish state. For example, in one scene he finds a bunker on the beach and looks from a small opening in its wall at the open sea. His body is visually trapped in darkness, while he is located in the nation-state that has promised him safety, peace, and compassion.

Inside the home of his Swedish foster parents, doors become important in the positioning of characters and camera. Doors in cinema are, according to Thomas Elsaesser and Malte Hagener, a bodily concept that indicates crossing and transgression, where the spectator enters metaphorically into "another world" while being aware of entry and transition. Also on the narrative level in *Mother of Mine*, the depiction of doors supports the "in-betweenness" of Eero and offers another contrast between a promised home and the homelessness of a Finnish war child in a Swedish nation. In several shots inside the house throughout the film, there is at least one door in the background that is closed. In one scene, before Eero goes to sleep, he peeks through the door of his room, listening for any news about his mother as his new family converses about him. However, the door between his room and the family is then shut, and parts of the house are hidden from his gaze.

Härö also incorporates the motif of the doors in the scenes of Eero's Finnish home, in order to further bring out the parallels between the Swedish and Finnish home, family, and state by extension. For example, one scene finds

Figure 16.1. Eero (Topi Majaniemi) peeking through a doorway at his Swedish foster parents in *Mother of Mine* (2005), directed by Klaus Härö. The use of doorways accentuates the "in-betweenness" of Eero, highlighting the homelessness of an evacuated Finnish war child in Sweden. Still from *Mother of Mine*. Screenshot: Liina-Ly Roos.

Eero looking at his Finnish parents (before his father dies in the war) who are talking in the other room. His position is similar to that in the Swedish home where he is looking from his bed through the door before it is closed. In the Finnish home, however, he hears and understands the conversation about his father going to war, and when he expresses his concern about his father getting hurt, his father comes to his room and comforts him. After they have received news of his father perishing in battle, and after his mother has developed depression and is no longer able to take care of Eero, we find the representatives of the organization responsible for the war children transport talking to Eero's mother. In this scene, Eero is placed in the same bed, but a curtain separates him from his Finnish mother when she comes to convince Eero to go to Sweden. By using these parallelisms, Härö establishes the connection and a threat of disconnection between the familial and national continuity from the perspective of the child. In addition, the room of the Swedish family's daughter who has passed away remains hidden from Eero's knowledge, until Siv (Penny Loftéen), the neighbor girl, shows it to Eero (and the audience finds out along with Eero that this room was meant for Eero). Here, the camera shows the door to the hidden room slowly opening, but then Signe discovers the children and chases them away, declaring, "This is not your home!"[8]

Search for Reconciliation

Up to this point in the film, the child has served a function of emphasizing and dramatizing the contrasts of the promise of compassion and a safe home with the reality of the Swedish mother's cruelty that is not comprehensible to the child. By extension, Eero's experience in Sweden is that of disappointment and nonbelonging. The film, nonetheless, wants to provide the audience with a reconciliation after it has offered the challenging image of war children in Sweden. After the dramatic sequence in which Signe explicitly manifests to Eero that "this is not [his] home," there is an abrupt change in Signe's behavior and the positioning of the child in the Swedish family. The cause of the change is the letter from Eero's mother in Finland, who writes that she is planning to move to Germany with a German soldier with whom she has fallen in love, and wonders whether Eero could stay with Signe and Hjalmar. Now the lack of compassion is replaced with an excess of it—Signe cries as she reads the letter and decides to tell Eero about the daughter that they have lost. The film thus suggests that this change of maternal behavior comes about only due to the failure of Eero's biological mother. *Mother of Mine* offers a variation on analyses of global motherhood in adoption narratives where, as Raka Shome argues, "the white mother can only occupy the positions of a 'global mother' by erasing the non-white maternal body from visions of global domesticity. The white mother's subject position is thus ironically dependent on the necessary failure of the non-white native mother" (Shome 2011: 399). Even though in this film narrative the two mothers are from neighboring countries and both white, Finland has often represented a borderland between Western and non-Western countries. This is caused both by its geographical location between the other Scandinavian countries and Russia—having been part of the Russian empire during the nineteenth century—and by Finns making up the majority of immigrants to Sweden throughout most of the twentieth century, where they experienced condescending attitudes toward their language and heritage.[9] Only after the "morally wrong"[10] decision of the biological Finnish mother does Signe become a compassionate, loving, and caring mother to Eero, as she opens up the door to the hidden room in order to explicitly accept him into his new home.

Along with that change in Signe's behavior, Eero's position as a "victim" is now acknowledged in the eyes of the Swedish parents. The image of Eero peeking through the door from the dark background into a lit room that is hidden from his gaze is replayed as an image of Signe and Hjalmar looking at Eero from the dark interior of the barn while Eero is standing in the bright daylight. Although it is the Finnish mother's letter that causes Signe to see Eero differently and to provide the compassion and love that she had not expressed before, Eero's role in listening to Signe's confession about the death of her daughter also helps the audience to reestablish trust in Signe, whose story makes her previous behavior justifiable. In this sequence, which is approximately three minutes long, Eero listens to Signe as if he were a therapist, mirroring the emotions that Signe is expressing and providing his compassion to her, while she tells the story for the first time aloud. The compassion that Eero displays here is common to the melodramatic child figure, according to the previously mentioned analysis by Decker, where the child becomes the fixer of adult problems, as the child's purpose in the narrative has *really* been to heal the adult world around the child and often also to heal the whole nation. Namely, Signe's confession that becomes accessible to the audience via the listening child reduces the problematics of the war children project to a personal and familial level, as it explains Eero's difficult experience in Sweden by means of one family's unfortunate history.

Not soon after Eero has been accepted by his Swedish family, his Finnish mother Kirsti decides not to move to Germany and suddenly invites Eero back home to Finland. However, Signe does not disclose to Eero all the information in his mother's letter, causing Eero's transition to Finland to be even more difficult and triggering a decision by him not to have a relationship with either one of his mothers any longer. The rest of his life, until the present day of the film, is portrayed as a prolonged disappointment and an ongoing failure of the promises that he was given during the years of war. Grown-up Eero does not mention the end result of the war—he contributes neither to the narrative of victory nor to that of defeat. Uncharacteristically to the traditional narratives of Finnish wars, it is not important for him at all. Social scientist Anna-Kaisa Kuusisto-Arponen argues that *Mother of Mine* depicts convincingly the transnational sense of place that many war children experienced, but which was not addressed in Finnish society after the war. Eero's experience does in fact depict the sense of becoming transnational, and therefore it does not contribute to the national narrative about the outcome of war. However, instead, the film emphasizes Eero's relationship with his Finnish and Swedish mothers as the main cause of feeling out of place and absent from the Finnish collective memory of war, and the melodramatic mode of film seeks to resolve this feeling for the audience.

The short black-and-white scenes from Eero's adulthood portray him in a constant state of melancholy and sentimentality in a search for healing, as the entire narrative of mature Eero focuses on him going to Signe's funeral in Sweden and trying to reconcile with his Finnish mother. He was too late to reconcile with Signe, and his conversations with his Finnish mother throughout the film as well as a scene in which he reads a letter from Signe that he had rejected as a child offer a "teasing delay"—another feature of melodrama that injects suspense—as to whether or not Eero will find reconciliation with his Finnish mother. Even though the war child is depicted as developing a transnational sense of space, as discussed earlier, the mothers in the film represent their respective nations.[11] Thus, restoring his relationship with his biological mother Kirsti provides Eero, by extension, with a restoration of a national belonging in Finland. The film seeks to return to a place of moral certainty where the "in-betweenness" or homelessness of the war child is cured and portrayed as an effect of the mistakes of individuals whose actions are made justifiable or at least understandable. Thus, the very last image of Eero, right after he has left the conversation with his mother, takes the audience back to the beginning of the film where he is still a child in Finland, alone in a snowy birch tree forest, before the bombing has started. This ending could be read as a simplified resolution that the fictional account in a melodramatic mode can offer—after reconciling with his Finnish mother, in his mind Eero is now able to return to his "state of innocence" before the traumatic experiences began. His childhood and growing up after returning to Finland, however, remain in silence and are not represented. The child figure in this film thus demonstrates a critical perspective on the emotional memory of war and helps the adults enact a moral and emotional healing, while returning the audience to a nostalgic perspective in which the otherwise uncomfortable transnational sense of space of the war children is replaced with national continuity and a hope for justice.

As a film in melodramatic mode, *Mother of Mine* does provoke strong emotions of compassion for the innocent victims and offers abrupt reconciliations that seek to restore the national belonging and moral order in the collective memories of war. The perspective of the child as the Other to the adults, a marginalized subject who sees and speaks the truth, offers a contrast to promises of compassion and welfare in the Swedish state and families. Within the larger debates in Finnish and Swedish cultural memories of war, the child's perspective represents the more critical one that questions some of the decisions made during World War II. While he functions as a medium for the grown-ups in the film and for the audience to find healing and reconciliation, the child's prolonged trauma and transnational sense of place during the rest of his life remain in silence and are resolved for the audience only by means of the nostalgic restoration of the familial and national (Finnish) continuity of grown-up Eero.

The aspect of healing, along with the depiction of strong emotions, is considered among the strengths of the film in reviews, public discourse, and historical research on war children. Around the time of the screening of the film in 2005 and 2006, several newspaper articles in both Finnish and Swedish media discussed the memory of war children as both having extraordinary emotional intensity and remaining a topic that is still unfamiliar to many people. Several reviewers focus on the film as bringing out the trauma of the children who had to leave their family, while the actor Maria Lundqvist recounts her tearful first reading of the script as she imagined what it might feel like if she had to send away her own children.[12] These discussions reflect on dealing with the previously forgotten events in the transnational collective memory of Finland and Sweden. As a transnational coproduction itself, the film also received wide acclaim in both countries. According to the Lumiere database, the admissions of *Mother of Mine* between 2005 and 2013 were 217,566 in Finland and 144,530 in Sweden. Maria Lundqvist was given the premier film award for her role as Eero's mother in both Sweden and Finland (the Guldbagge and the Jussi Award, respectively). At the same time, many of the reviews and interviews with the actors that focus on the emotional story of Eero developing a sense of placelessness and transnational identity gloss over the problematic decisions and dominant narratives of collective memory in the shared history of Finland and Sweden.

The public discourse on the topic of the war children increased after the release of Härö's film in 2005, and that is also when Hietamies's novel received more popularity and was reprinted several times. The screening of Ylva Hemstad's short documentary *Med adresslapp om halsen* (With the address label hanging by the neck, 2007) in 2008 also increased the discourse on war children. Hemstad's film follows a group of grown-up "war children" on a bus trip back to their childhood places in Finland. It focuses on the return narrative, and the film was advertised as an emotional bus trip back to childhood (*Svensk mediedatabas*). The reality reflected in several memoirs and interviews with Finnish war child refugees is, however, that for many the return to childhood is never really possible, and the feeling of rootlessness and not belonging to either Finland or Sweden has continued until the present day. The utopian ending of Härö's film represents clearly the desire of fulfilling the goal of restoring and saving the future of the nation by incorporating the image of the child. The film provides the grown-up audience with an opportunity to condemn the lack of compassion and to express compassion now in retrospect for the war children on a more universal level.

Liina-Ly Roos (PhD, University of Washington, 2018) is Assistant Professor of Scandinavian Studies at the University of Wisconsin-Madison. Roos has published on imagining the post-Soviet trauma in Nordic cinema in *Baltic Screen Media Review* (2014). Her monograph in progress, *The Not-Quite Child: Invisible Structures of Memory and Migration*, demonstrates that the literary and cinematic constructions of the postwar child challenge the collective memories of war, migration, and childhood in the Baltic Sea region.

Notes

I am grateful to the American-Scandinavian Foundation for the fellowship that allowed me to gather material in Sweden. I also extend thanks to Ann-Kristin Wallengren for her helpful comments on an early draft of this chapter.

1. According to Irene Virtala, approximately sixty-five thousand children were sent to Sweden, four thousand to Denmark, and four hundred to Norway (Virtala 2004: 31). According to Finnish historians Tiina Kinnunen and Markku Jokisipilä, this time period saw also a more critical perspective that pointed out the mythologized position of the war in Finnish collective memory (Kinnunen and Jokisipilä 2012).
2. See, for example, Finnish historian Aura Korppi-Tommola's article "War and Children in Finland during Second World War," which offers an overview of the history and politics around the transfer of Finnish children to Sweden (Korppi-Tommola 2008).
3. Swedish historian Ann Nehlin argues that the humanitarian goals of helping children were often overshadowed by the wish to create goodwill for Sweden (Nehlin 2011). The first collection of war children memoirs that expressed feelings of nonsafety, rootlessness, and depression was Annu Edvardsen's *De får inte hända igen* (1977).
4. Rebecca Knight argues that a child's perspective can work like Shklovsky's concept of defamiliarization, "which can also allow the reader to see events or ideas in a new light," allowing for a space of dealing with more difficult topics, because the assumed innocent misinterpretations of children "allow interrogation of an idea without it being a direct attack" (Knight 2009: 801).

5. Ilona Latvala argues in her MA thesis, Traumaattinen matka: Sotalapsuudesta aikuisuuteen," that the novel is a classical "trauma narrative" while the film is not.
6. "Tytöille oli luvattu nuket ja pojille polkupyörät. Kun päästiin perille Ruotsiin, meistä vietiin ensin pienimmät ja sitten näteimmät tytöt. Ne joilla oli kaunein hymy. Kaikki pelkäsi joutuvansa lastenkotiin ja halus oma ruotsalaisen perheen, joka olis pitänyt heistä huolta. Mä vaan en halunnut" (*Äideistä parhain* 2005).
7. See Olli Kangassalo's review (Iltalehti, 30.09.2005), quoted at http://www.elonet.fi/fi/elokuva/1251008, or Gunnar Bergdahl's review (Helsingborgs Dagblad, 04.11.2005) at https://www.hd.se/2005-11-04/vackert-men-en-film-med-flera-problem.
8. "Det är inte ditt hem!"
9. Swedish racial biology placed Finns as inferior to the Nordic race, as argued by Suvi Keskinen (2019).
10. In their chapter "Shifting Images of 'Our Wars,'" Tiina Kinnunen and Markku Jokisipilä argue that in postwar Finland the images of Finnish women who decided to leave Finland with German soldiers were infused with moral contempt: "They were instrumental in symbolizing the morally troublesome nature of the Finnish-German alliance during the Continuation War, as Finnish women and especially the mothers have been important icons for the whole nation in the cultural imagery" (Kinnunen and Jokisipilä 2012: 477).
11. The film makes that explicit with the scene where the two mothers appear physically in front of Eero's eyes, both addressing him in their native languages.
12. See, for example, Karin Thunberg's review "Höstens hetaste morsa" (*Svenska Dagbladet*, 27.11.2005), retrieved 27 March 2020 from https://www.svd.se/hostens-hetaste-morsa.

References

"Äideistä parhain." *Elonet—Kansallisfilmografia*. Retrieved 11 August 2017 from https://www.elonet.fi/fi/elokuva/1251008.

Bergdahl, Gunnar. 2005. "Vackert, men en film med flera problem." *Helsingborgs Dagblad*. 4 November. Retrieved 10 September 2017 from https://www.hd.se/2005-11-04/vackert-men-en-film-med-flera-problem.

Decker, Christof. 2007. "'Unusually Compassionate': Melodrama, Film, and the Figure of the Child." In *Melodrama! The Mode of Excess from Early America to Hollywood*, edited by Frank Kelleter and Barbara Kahn, 305–28. Heidelberg: Universitätsverlag Winter.

Edvardsen, Annu. 1977. *Det får inte hända igen*. Stockholm: Askild & Kärnekull Förlag AB.

Elsaesser, Thomas. 2012. "Tales of Sound and Fury: Observations on the Family Melodrama." In *Film Genre Reader IV*, edited by Barry Keith Grant, 433–62. Austin: University of Texas Press.

Elsaesser, Thomas, and Malte Hagener. 2010. *Film Theory: An Introduction through the Senses*. New York: Routledge.

Hirsch, Marianne. 2012. *The Generation of Postmemory: Writing and Visual Culture after the Holocaust*. New York: Columbia University Press.

Honeyman, Susan. 2005. *Elusive Childhood: Impossible Representations in Modern Fiction*. Columbus: Ohio State University Press.

Kavén, Pertti. 2010. "Humanitaarisuuden varjossa: Poliittiset tekijät lastensiirroissa Ruotsiin sotiemme aikana ja niiden jälkeen." PhD diss., University of Helsinki, Helsinki.

Keskinen, Suvi. 2019. "Intra-Nordic Differences, Colonial/Racial Histories, and National Narratives: Rewriting Finnish History." *Scandinavian Studies* 91(1–2): 163–81.
Kinnunen, Tiina, and Markku Jokisipilä. 2012. "Shifting Images of 'Our Wars': Finnish Memory Culture of World War II." In *Finland in World War II: History, Memory, Interpretations*, edited by Tiina Kinnunen and Ville Kivimäki, 435–82. Leiden: Brill.
Kivimäki, Ville. 2012. "Between Defeat and Victory: Finnish Memory Culture of the Second World War." *Scandinavian Journal of History* 37(4): 482–504.
Knight, Rebecca. 2009. "Representations of Soviet Childhood in Soviet Texts by Liudmila Ulitskaia and Nina Gabrielian." *Modern Language Review* 104(3): 790–808.
Korppi-Tommola, Aura. 2008. "War and Children in Finland during the Second World War." *Paedagogica Historica* 44(4): 445–55. Education Source, EBSCOhost.
Kuusisto-Arponen, Anna-Kaisa. 2011. "Transnational Sense of Place: Cinematic Scenes of Finnish War Child Memories." *Journal of Aesthetics and Culture* 3.
Latvala, Ilona. 2012. "Traumaattinen matka: Sotalapsuudesta aikuisuuteen; Eeron tarina Heikki Hietamiehen romaanissa *Äideistä parhain*." MA thesis, Jyväskylä University, Finland.
Lury, Karen. 2010. *The Child in Film: Tears, Fears and Fairy Tales*. New Brunswick, NJ: Rutgers University Press.
Lumiere Database on admissions of films released in Europe. Retrieved 27 March 2020 from http://lumiere.obs.coe.int/web/film_info/?id=24699.
"Med addresslapp om halsen." Pan Vision, 2009. Svensk mediedatabas. Retrieved 22 October 2018 from https://smdb.kb.se/catalog/search?q=med+adresslapp+om+halsen&x=0&y=0.
Mother of Mine. 2005. Directed by Klaus Härö. Finland and Sweden: Matila Röhr Productions, Omega Film & Television AB, Film i Skåne. DVD.
Nehlin, Ann. 2011. "Att rädda barn—humanitet och en politisk nödvändighet." *Locus* 2: 39–57.
Rose, Jacqueline. 1993. *The Case of Peter Pan, or, The Impossibility of Children's Fiction*. Philadelphia: University of Pennsylvania Press.
Shome, Raka. 2011. "'Global Motherhood': The Transnational Intimacies of White Femininity." *Critical Studies in Media Communication* 28(5): 388–406.
Thunberg, Karin. 2005. "Höstens hetaste morsa." *Svenska Dagbladet*. 27 November. Retrieved 10 September 2017 from https://www.svd.se/hostens-hetaste-morsa.
Virtala, Irene. 2004. *Tystnaden talar: Om finländska krigsbarn i skönlitteraturen*. Web Reports No. 5. Migrationsinstitutet.
Williams, Linda. 1998. "Melodrama Revised." In *Refiguring American Film Genres*, edited by Linda Williams and Nick Browne, 42–88. Berkeley: University of California Press.
———. 2018. "'Tales of Sound and Fury . . .' or, the Elephant of Melodrama." In *Melodrama Unbound: Across History, Media and National Cultures*, edited by Christine Gledhill and Linda Williams, 205–17. New York: Columbia University Press.
Östling, Johan. 2008. "Swedish Narratives of the Second World War: A European Perspective." *Contemporary European History* 17(2): 197–211.

Chapter 17

THE WAR FILM AS CULTURAL MEMORY IN DENMARK

April 9th and *Land of Mine*

Marianne Stecher-Hansen

On 22 July 2017, debutant Danish film director Roni Ezra stated on Danish television that he was, "optaget af nederlaget!" (preoccupied with defeat).[1] The comment referred to the 21 July premiere of Christopher Nolan's *Dunkirk* (2017), the Hollywood production depicting the evacuation of three hundred thousand Allied troops stranded at Dunkirk in late May 1940. The precarious evacuation was hardly an Allied victory but a "barely averted catastrophe," which Churchill himself had apparently referred to as "a colossal military disaster" (Lane 2017: 80). On television, Roni Ezra and the other debate panelists observed that such recent war films reveal a greater tendency to depict the plight of "den menige soldat" (the ordinary soldier) rather than focus on high-ranking military figures and political leaders. This televised Danish debate raised some broader questions: Do some films produced several decades after World War II offer more nuanced narratives of war? More specifically, how do recent Danish war films differ from the World War II "combat film," and how are they distinct from the "occupation dramas" produced during the postwar decades? Finally, what do particular films have to say about the shifting Danish cultural memory of World War II?

This chapter investigates two Danish war films produced in 2015, namely *9. April/April 9th* and *Under Sandet/Land of Mine*, that each dramatize in distinct ways the consequences of military defeat, fiasco, or mismanagement by the political leadership.[2] In both cases, the films represent previously neglected or silenced episodes in Denmark's Word War II experience. The filmed narrative perspective in both productions is that of "ordinary soldiers" (whether Danish or German); both films focus on a small platoon of soldiers (or prisoners of war) as a collective (a trope of the war film); both films situate this collective in relationship to the platoon's commander, a lower-ranking officer who is caught in a life-and-death struggle with the consequences of higher administrative decisions beyond his reach. These officers struggle with a lack of information in wartime crisis situations and flounder in the quicksand of not knowing (or not having access to) all the facts. Nonetheless, both film narratives allow the main protagonist, who is a "second-in-command" officer, to emerge in the film's conclusion with moral dignity. Both *April 9th* and *Land of Mine* make use of elements of an established genre—the *krigsfilm* (war film) or World War II "combat film"—and both ultimately challenge Denmark's cultural memory of the occupation period. Who is the ordinary soldier, and who is in command? What are the soldier's orders, and should he carry them out? What might be the cost to himself and to the soul of the nation?

This pair of somewhat unconventional war films produced in Denmark in 2015 commemorates the seventy-fifth year of the German invasion on 9 April 1940. This chapter investigates how these film productions evince a shift in the Danish narratives of World War II, which Sofie Lene Bak has discussed from the perspective of historiography in the second chapter of this volume. This chapter furthermore argues that these two particular films depart from the genre of the "occupation drama" (Villadsen 2000; Iversen 2012), popular in Danish and Norwegian cinema. Thus, the chapter suggests that a visible shift in an active "cultural memory" of the war is evident in recent Danish cinema. How do these two filmed narratives challenge the popular occupation dramas that tend to mythologize national resistance, as exemplified by Danish films such as *Flammen og Citronen/Flame and Citron* (Ole Christian Madsen, 2008) and *Hvidsten Gruppen/This Life* (Anne-Grethe Bjarup Riis, 2012)? Do *April 9th* and *Land of Mine* engage more complex and humanistic perspectives, and in doing so, perhaps indicate the impact of the ongoing revisionism in Danish war historiography, which challenges the master narrative of unified resistance? It becomes evident that, taken as a whole, films about World War II in Denmark—like the historiography of the occupation period itself—offer a complex and nuanced fabric of representation, and also that there are some surprises running through it.

The first film, *9. April/April 9th* (2015), directed by Roni Ezra and written by Tobias Lindholm, depicts the initial day of German Occupation in 1940 that brought about Denmark's quick capitulation in the early morning hours. The Danish government issued a cease-fire order already at 6:00 A.M., following some sporadic fighting at southern border of Jutland, after the German troops had begun to cross the border at 4:15 A.M.—however, the cease-fire order took a few hours to reach the scattered Danish troops in this region. This delayed communication is at the crux of this cinematic drama. *April 9th* depicts the meager Danish defenses that were ordered to hold back the massive German advance until reinforcements arrived (which they never did). The film's perspective is that of a small bicycle platoon (six men) ordered in the predawn hours of 9 April to face a formidable column of German motorized troops and panzer tanks rolling over Denmark's southern border. *April 9th* is framed by documentary footage that lends it authenticity: the film opens with the historical radio broadcast of 9 April in which King Christian X (1870–1947) pronounces Denmark's capitulation, and it concludes with recent filmed interviews with several elderly veterans of the 1940 border fight. The main body of the cinematic production is a motion picture drama, starring Pilou Asbæk as "Second Lieutenant Sand," a loyal soldier attempting to carry out his orders to defend the border (even after the cease-fire order), despite the futility of the Danish defense.

The second film is *Under Sandet/Unter dem Sand/Land of Mine* (2015), a Danish-German coproduction, written and directed by Martin Zandvliet (the title is literally "Under the Sand" in Danish and German; however, in the English-language release, the title becomes an ironic play on words that questions the meaning of patriotism). The film is set in the immediate aftermath of the liberation in May 1945, when two thousand German soldiers, held officially by the Allies as British "prisoners of war" (POWs), were forced to de-mine the beaches of Jutland's west coast. In other words, the de-mining operation was ordered by the British authorities but supervised by Danish soldiers—the extent to which the Danes were responsible for this immediate postwar dilemma and the extent to which Danish soldiers directly supervised the German prisoners became the touchstone in a press debate, which followed the film's premiere in Denmark.

Zandvliet's film is indebted to a 1998 study, *Under Tvang* (By force), by lawyer-historian Helge Hagemann, the son of a Danish veteran, which seeks to challenge the myths of a national past (1998: 17–18). Hagemann's study documents that the direct supervision of the German prisoners was delegated to the Danish army (specifically, members of the "pioneer corps" of the Danish Brigade, which had trained in Sweden during the last twenty months of the war). It is this *Danish* role in the supervision of the mine-clearing operation by German soldiers that constitutes a Danish violation of the international treaties of the Geneva Convention—in other words, a war crime.[3] Historians who study this period point to evidence that the British and Danish commanders chose to label the German soldiers as "voluntarily surrendered enemy personnel" in order to avoid a direct violation of the Geneva

Convention. This precarious postwar situation arose because the occupying German army had buried approximately two million mines along the entire west coast of occupied Denmark as part of the greater "Atlantic Fortress" in order to inhibit an invasion of Nazi-occupied Europe by the Grand Alliance, an invasion that was ultimately carried out at Normandy's Utah Beach, "D-day," on 6 June 1944.

Similar to *April 9th*, the narrative perspective of *Land of Mine* is that of a small group of young men (fourteen in total) under the supervision of a Danish officer, Sergeant Carl Leopold Rasmussen (Roland Møller). This film is by no means a documentary film that seeks to inform on a shameful chapter in Denmark's past: it is an emotionally charged motion picture drama, informed by difficult historical facts. Questions about the film's status as motion picture drama emerged in the press debate that erupted after the film's premiere in the Danish daily *Politiken* in early December 2015, when historians such as Bo Lidegaard and Palle Roslyng-Jensen debated the accuracy of the representation of the Danish supervisory role in the de-mining operation and the film's lack of historical context for Denmark's ambiguous political situation in the immediate postwar period.[4] The contentious press debate speaks to the fact that the de-mining operation has never been dealt with adequately neither in official Danish historiography nor in public discussions.

Land of Mine dramatizes the relentless trauma inflicted on the young German prisoners by the extremely dangerous work of locating and defusing the mines. Affectively bringing the audience into a sympathetic relationship to the German prisoners, *Land of Mine* induces fretful tension, tears, and even nausea in the film's viewer who must deal with the visceral tension created by the handling of the live mines. The film constitutes a kind of postwar "epilogue"—to the established master narrative of Denmark's occupation history—that is based on historical facts that had been lost from the "communicative memory" of Danish viewers of 2015.

Occupied Denmark and the Occupation Drama

Neatly, these two cinematic productions of 2015 enclose or "bracket" either end of the occupation period: 9 April 1940 and 5 May 1945; the five-year period in Denmark's history that has been subjected to the most intense historical scholarship. Following the sudden invasion and capitulation on 9 April, the Danish government initiated a Policy of Negotiation (*forhandlingspolitik*) with Nazi Germany, which lasted for the first three and a half years of the occupation. The political cooperation meant that the Danish parliament, police force, and judicial system continued to function, so that Denmark might appear as a "model protectorate" in Nazi-occupied Europe.

When the tide of World War II turned against Germany in early 1943, this government policy of negotiation grew unpopular among Danish civilians, and acts of resistance and sabotage escalated, even though acts of violence were condemned by the Danish government. On 29 August 1943, the Danish parliament resigned, refusing to concede to a German ultimatum that demanded martial law, curfew regulations, and the death penalty for saboteurs. No longer the model protectorate, Denmark faced the implementation of harsher conditions when the Wehrmacht assumed executive power and installed a Nazi plenipotentiary, Werner Best (1903–89), who is known to have referred to Denmark as "this ridiculous little country." In October 1943, nearly all of Denmark's seven thousand Jewish citizens escaped, aided by ordinary Danes and resistance members, to neutral Sweden. For the remaining twenty months of the war, labor strikes in major cities halted productivity, and underground resistance and industrial sabotage grew increasingly organized. Nonetheless, the vast majority of Danes remained passive during the German occupation. When Nazi Germany capitulated on 4 May 1945, Denmark was liberated by British forces without fighting (Hong 2012). Although it had not directly contributed to the Allied war effort, Denmark was "allowed into the select company of the victors" and extended an invitation to join the United Nations on 26 June 1945 (Skov 2000: 103). A voice among the third generation of Danish occupation historians, Uffe Østergård has bluntly stated, that relative to the rest of occupied Europe, "Denmark had a good war" (2011: 51).

In the Danish cinematic archive, there exists about twenty-five Danish feature films depicting Denmark during World War II, produced after the liberation in 1945 (Villadsen 2000: 28).[5] According to Villadsen, these Danish films fall into two main categories: firstly, "occupation dramas" with resistance plots that depict sabotage activities, betrayal by an informer, often intertwined with a love story. Already in December 1945, the first occupation drama appeared as *De røde Engel/The Red Meadows*, a tribute to Danish resistance fighters, directed by Bodil Ipsen. A second category consists of socially and politically critical films that feature ordinary daily life under the occupation, including depictions of collaboration, war profiteering, and government hypocrisy; an example of such is *Tre år efter* (Three years later, 1948, directed by Johan Jacobsen) based on the screenplay by playwright C. E. Soya. There exists a modest, third category of occupation dramas that dramatize the rescue of the Danish Jews to Sweden in 1943, including *Oktoberdage/The Only Way* (Bent Christensen, 1970), *En dag i Oktober/A Day in October* (Kenneth Madsen, 1991) and *Fuglene over Sundet/Across the Waters* (Nicolo Donato, 2016), none of which achieved critical acclaim or box-office success.

Denmark's cinematic archive of occupation dramas demonstrates that, contrary to any assumptions about postwar occupation dramas, a nuanced portrayal of German subjects is not entirely new in Danish cinema. The portrayal of ordinary German soldiers in Danish occupation films, produced in the postwar decades between 1945 and the 1960s, is "exceptionally realistic and well balanced," according to Ebbe Villadsen (2000: 34). In the postwar occupation drama, the depiction of German soldiers does not conform to the Nazi caricatures of Hollywood cinema that viewers later came to expect, the explanation being that the Danish audience who had lived in proximity of German soldiers for five years could easily identify the difference between the SS or Gestapo officer and the ordinary conscripted German soldier stationed in Denmark. Villadsen observes that the "audience remembered them only too well in reality, with the result that they were never portrayed as caricatures" (2000: 34).

April 9th and Danish Defeat

April 9th is director Roni Ezra's feature film debut, with the screenplay written by Tobias Lindholm, a Nordisk Film and TV2 Danmark coproduction. The production coincided with national commemorations of 9 April in 2015. The action of the film is set entirely in the evening of 8 April and the morning hours of 9 April. As a footnote to the historical facts, an informed viewer ought to note that the Danish government, under social democratic prime minister Thorvald Stauning (1873–1942), had done nothing to strengthen or alert Danish forces until 8 April (neither in Copenhagen nor at the southern border of Jutland), even though some intelligence regarding the impending German invasion had been received a few days earlier. Having only a tiny army, an aging naval fleet, and a nearly defunct air force, the Danish social democratic government had deliberately demilitarized and pursued a pacifist policy since the 1920s. When the massive air, land, and sea invasion by the German Wehrmacht forces took place in the predawn hours of 9 April, Denmark was merely a stepping stone. Norway, on the other hand, was a country of enormous strategic importance to the warring powers, with its long Atlantic coast, strong naval seaports, and access (via the port at Narvik and railway lines) to the iron ore mines of northern Sweden (Häikiö 1983). In contrast, Denmark was a "Lilliput" nation with neither geographic nor military defenses, nor did it hold strategic interest (excepting the airfields in northern Jutland). Already by 6:00 A.M. on the morning of 9 April, the Danish government (the king and cabinet) ordered a cease-fire and capitulated, "under protest."

Ezra's film opens with a dark screen and the radio broadcast of the capitulation proclamation read by King Christian X; the following screen states, "Early in the morning of the 9th of April 1940 the German troops crossed the Danish-German border. The unprepared and poorly equipped Danish army faces Europe's strongest military power. The hardest fighting takes place in South Jutland."[6] In order to make sense of the film, the viewer comes to understand that the early morning cease-fire order did not reach some of the meager Danish forces, which had been called up in the border territory, and therefore some pockets of fighting continued for several hours. This sad historical fact is the frame for *April 9th*, starring Pilou Asbæk as Second Lieutenant Sand, who is charged with commanding a platoon of bicycle infantry, half a dozen young soldiers. The use of the shaky, handheld camera suggests the shaky nerves of the commanding lieutenants, Sand and Bundgaard, as they receive their initial orders. Likewise, the dark tones (gray, brown, and green) of much of the film's lighting is somber, indicating an ominous outcome (Donnerborg 2017: 20).

The representation of this small collective emphasizes the regional distinctions between the soldiers, particularly privates Gram and Justesen whose Danish dialect identifies them as *sønderjyder* (southern Jutlanders), with roots in the border territory of the invasion. In the afternoon before the invasion, the bicycle infantry platoons are engaged in a mobilization exercise: practicing changing bicycle inner tubes under a stopwatch timing order. In another "mobilization" scene, the privates are provisioned with "40 patroner til hver" (forty bullets each), another indicator of the impossible odds that lie ahead. In the subsequent scene, the sleepy, young men in the predawn hours peddle rickety bicycles with heavy rifles and backpacks toward the border to face the oncoming column of German divisions.

In *April 9th* the cinematic enactment of the futility of the impending encounter between Danish bicycle infantry divisions and German steel tanks and motorized troops is effectively imagined. Against an open horizon of a dawn sky across the full screen, the viewer sees a small, silhouetted column of six silent bicyclists in the lower part of the screen. Whereas the mood is one of fear and anxiety for the young soldiers, the scene confronts today's viewer with the absurdism of this military venture. The soldiers seek cover behind some pine trees in order to fire on the oncoming Wehrmacht forces; the Danish military order is to slow down the German advance until reinforcements arrive. At this point in the film, the first combat scene takes place, with exchanges of fire, that are dominated by the "shot/reverse-shot" cutting characteristic of the postmodern war film (Bender 2013: 80–81). Private Kolding (Mathias Lundkvist) is fatally hit by fire from a panzer tank and falls backward. The blood splatters toward the close-up camera's lens, with the red fluid of the soldier's fatal stomach wound breaking with the dark tones of the opening scenes of the film (Donnerborg 2017: 25).

A key element in *April 9th* as "war film" is the empathy displayed by Lieutenant Sand for the six young men of his group. Following the initial border battle, Sand orders his platoon to retreat by bicycle to a farmhouse where the men are given shelter; nonetheless, Sand resists the option to defy his orders and spare his men from further fighting. Later, the platoon retreats farther north to the provincial city of Haderselv (where the final scenes of the film were actually shot). There fighting in the narrow streets ensues, as the German forces advance. In this second exchange of fire, Private Justesen, another Danish soldier from the platoon, is killed, despite Sand's repeated orders to retreat. The fatal shot is dramatized by Justesen's intense agony, as the camera rests on a close-up of his face. Soon after, Lieutenant Sand makes the decision to capitulate to the occupying Germans and surrenders with his men; this scene involves moral ambiguity, as he is breaking his order in favor of protecting his platoon from further causalities. It is only then that Sand learns of the earlier Danish cease-fire order from a German commanding officer, when the officer questions him, "Why did you continue to fight? It was an unnecessary loss of life, as your government has long capitulated." In the concluding scenes of the film, the audience observes a stunned and disillusioned Sand returning in a military van to the Danish barracks with the four surviving men.

What is the implication of the filmed narrative? The fight has proved a futile, if not absurd, military exercise. The audience might view the second lieutenant as betrayed by an indifferent Danish high command or incompetent political leadership. Sand has been forced to lead his platoon unnecessarily into battle, and it has cost the lives of two young men. Nonetheless, the final scenes allow Sand to emerge as a Danish patriot, by emphasizing the fact that he has adhered loyally to the military orders he received. The authenticity of Sand's plight is furthermore enforced by the testimonies of the elderly veterans (who were interviewed in 2014), which make up the film's epilogue.

There are several obvious structural elements in *April 9th* that align it with the war film, and specifically with the formulaic elements of the World War II "combat film" as defined by formalist study of the genre (Basinger 1986: 73–75). Foremost is the focus on the collective (the platoon) and the role of the commanding officer (Lieutenant Sand), who bears leadership responsibility. Furthermore, there are numerous combat film elements: the mobilization scene (recruits are trained); the communication of the military objective (defend the border); the faceless enemy (the oncoming German column); internal group dynamics (which emphasize the regional distinctions and differing abilities of the privates); death in battle (Kolding and Justesen are killed by gunfire); a climatic battle (the street fighting in Haderslev); resolution (Lieutenant Sand learns of the earlier cease-fire order); and the "enlightenment" or ennobling of the audience (by the documentary testimony of the patriotic elderly veterans). *April 9th* thus remediates many of the conventions of the war film genre; however, there is little heroism or glory in this Danish rendition of a war film. This is yet another chapter in a history of Danish defeat.

In 2015, Danish viewers saw the filmed enactment of Denmark's brief military resistance to the German invasion of 9 April 1940 play out in the battleground of the southern border, the historical site of the crushing Danish defeat in the Dano-Prussian war, or Second Schleswig War of 1864. For example, in the scene at the farmhouse where Sand temporarily shelters his retreating bicycle platoon, the farm wife remarks to him that this border territory in southern Jutland (*Sønderjylland*) had only "twenty years ago" been under German rule (in other words, until the plebiscite of 1920, which reunited the northern half of the Schleswig province with Denmark).

In 2014, the year prior to the production of *April 9th*, the popular eight-episode TV series *1864*, written and directed by Ole Bornedal, consumed the Danish public and became the subject of a heated national debate and contentious "culture wars" about national identity in the Danish press (Hedling 2015). The *1864* television production, which was also produced as a motion picture *1864—Brødre i krig* (1864—Brothers at war), commemorated the 150th year of Denmark's crushing military defeat in the second Dano-Prussian war (the bombardment of Dybbøl and the conquest of Als) and dramatized how the Danish kingdom had been "gambled" recklessly in a political power play brought about by Danish political and military leaders. This view may indeed be a valid interpretation of historical fact, popularized by Tom Buk-Swienty in his documentary novels *Slagtebænk Dybbøl* (The butcher's block; Dybbøl, 2008) and *Dommedags Als* (The day of judgment; Als, 2010).[7] Buk-Swienty maintains that "the Battle of Dybbøl became a significant milestone in Danish history. . . . Denmark became a Lilliputian monarchy of little political consequence. The Danes became mired in defeatist self-pity, a mood that lingers even now . . ." (2015: xxii–xxiii). According to his interpretation, political and military administrative incompetence and blind nationalistic zeal had coalesced to lead the nation into total military catastrophe, which cost the kingdom of Denmark two-fifths of its territory (the three duchies of Schleswig, Holstein, and Lauenburg) as well as the needless slaughter of thousands of largely untrained and ill-equipped Danish soldiers, most of whom were conscripted peasant farmers. In 1864, the Prussians had outnumbered the Danes four to one and bore the newly minted "needle rifles" that easily outgunned the clumsy front-loaders of the Danish soldiers. The televised battlefield scenes of Danish soldiers butchered by Prussian troops, a military fiasco and a national humiliation, was likely fresh in the minds of many Danish viewers the following year. How do the decisions of politicians and military leaders have massive consequences for the ordinary soldier—and for the civilian population of an entire nation? It seems that Roni Erza's film depicting the imposing German tanks rolling over the border in April 1940 relies on remediated historical images, which resonated with Danish audiences in 2015 by creating an uncanny *déjà vu* in the viewer experience: those well-equipped, blue-uniformed Prussian soldiers of *1864* returning in the invasion scene in *April 9th* as motorized gray German troops and panzer tanks.

Land of Mine and Postwar Retribution

The second recent Danish war film, *Under Sandet/Land of Mine*, does not depict the invasion or conditions under the five-year occupation in Denmark, but it dramatizes an episode in postwar retribution that took place in the weeks and months immediately following the liberation. The opening screen caption states, "May 1945." In fact, the deployment of German POWs in the mine-clearing operation took place between 10 May and 1 October 1945 (Hagemann 1998). Thus, the action of this film drama begins immediately *after* the celebrated liberation, at the historical point in time when most occupation documentaries and dramas happily end. *Land of Mine*, by Martin Zandvliet, one of five nominees for Best Foreign Language Film Oscar in 2016—and praised in the Danish press as "Årets bedste film" (best picture of the year)[8]—explores the moral ambiguity of the immediate postwar period. The film made the rounds of select US theaters in 2017. It stars Roland Møller as Sergeant Carl Leopold Rasmussen, the Danish army officer charged with supervising a group of teenaged German POWs ordered to defuse and clear the live mines, which lay buried in the beguilingly pristine white beaches of Jutland. The young men under his supervision are played by young German actors.

The moral logic of the postwar period, apparently held by the Allied victors as well as by a majority of Danish civilians at the time, required that the mines that had been buried by German soldiers needed to be located and defused by Germans. The work was often fatal; many of the Germans were killed or seriously maimed when the mines accidently detonated. The controversial question of the number of German fatalities among the two thousand German POWs has earned a mere footnote in official Danish war historiography. Official Danish estimates made in 1945 were low, naming 179 fatalities and 165 wounded (Hagemann 1998: 69). Alternatively, German estimates indicate as many as 250 fatalities, 200 seriously injured, and an additional 400 wounded, according to Hagemann (1998: 69). It is apparently a rounding up of the German estimate of 850 causalities (fatalities and injured), that forms the factual basis for Zandvliet's screenplay. The concluding screen captions (white text on full black screen) state, "After the war 2,000 German POWs were forced to clear 1.5 million mines from the Danish west coast"; next screen: "Nearly half perished or were seriously injured"; next screen: "Many of them were just very young boys."[9] This claim that "nearly half" of the two thousand German prisoners were killed or seriously maimed was naturally one of the points of controversy taken up by Danish historians in the press debate following the release of the film in Denmark. Rather than engaging archival research into historical statistics, I would argue that *Land of Mine* has a broad agenda as a work of cinema that actualizes the very real moral ambiguity of the postwar period and challenges Danish cultural memory of the war.

Martin Landvliet's screenplay focuses on a group of fourteen teenaged prisoners (only four of whom survive the ordeal). Young male actors are cast in the roles of the prisoners in order to typify the ordinary German conscripted soldiers serving in Denmark, who were often very young or quite old during the last months of World War II, when Germany's virile human fodder had been depleted. One ought to point out that Zandvliet's screenplay actively encourages the presumption of the innocence of the German soldiers by presenting these "boys" in a vacuum; the film does not offer any context to their backgrounds or loyalties during the war. Instead, *Land of Mine* employs the teenaged boys to represent the forgotten victims of the machinations of war by featuring soldiers who perhaps never engaged in combat on any battlefront, least of all in Denmark, which was known ironically as *flødeskumsfronten* (the whipped-cream front), during World War II. The innocence of these "boy prisoners" is implied to the viewer (in the historical context—which the film does not provide—they are "innocent" in the sense that young German soldiers stationed late in the war in Denmark may have never engaged in combat). More generally, as a theme of the war film genre, the young men come to represent the "senseless human waste of war," especially the "waste of youth" (Chambers 382: 1994).

The governing trope of *Land of Mine* is the inversion of the power structure; the Danes, freed from German tyranny, now themselves become cruel perpetrators of violence. The film opens with a completely dark screen (as in *April 9th*); the audience hears only the sound of heavy, enraged breathing—it is the pent-up anger of the main male subject, Sergeant Rasmussen. The viewer soon witnesses Rasmussen vent his anger, screaming violently in German (spoken with a Danish accent) at the retreating soldiers, "Get out!" and shouting, "This is *my* land, do you understand!!?"[10] The retreating soldiers are marching southward toward the German border; it is early May 1945, Germany has capitulated. Rasmussen becomes a study in embittered postwar revenge and retribution in this opening scene, which evokes a canonical Danish poem of the period, "De tyske soldater" (The German soldiers), published in 1945 by Tove Ditlevsen, depicting the "trætte tyske soldater" (tried German soldiers), as retreating soldiers, who "går mod nederlaget" (walk toward defeat), while the Danes harbor vengeful hatred toward the departing enemy (Ditlevsen 1996: 120–21).[11] The sight of a German soldier carrying a folded Danish flag under his arm as a souvenir sends Sergeant Rasmussen into a fit of rage; he grabs the flag away and violently beats the soldier. When Rasmussen symbolically wipes the German blood from his fists, the viewer must understand that the Danes also have blood on their hands.

In *Land of Mine* this second-in-command officer Sergeant Rasmussen is cast as a callous figure who initially behaves as a coldhearted military disciplinarian. The Danish officer subjects his boyish German charges regularly to verbal and physical abuse while taunting them with the harsh rhetoric of the military to behave "like soldiers." These scenes evoke the World War II "combat film" genre, which typically includes scenes involving the "training of new recruits," i.e. making young men into soldiers (Basinger 61–62: 1986). However, the scenes in *Land of Mine* are painful inversions of such tropes, as the young soldiers are instead prisoners, and the audience experiences the terror and shame in bewildered juvenile faces.

It is not a coincidence that the film's male protagonist, Sergeant Rasmussen, bears a strong resemblance to Field Marshal Montgomery, who led the liberating Allied troops into Denmark on 5 May 1945. Historical photographs of Montgomery reveal that Rasmussen, attired in uniform and red beret, is a remediated image of the British general. In fact, Sergeant Rasmussen is wearing the uniform of the British Parachute Regiment (the camera zooms in on his shoulder emblem), an obvious tie to postwar Denmark's Allied status and a reference to the wartime collaboration between British SOE (Special Operations Executive) and Danish resistance groups (Hong 2012). The British insignia of the Danish army officer is also a reminder to the audience that the German POWs were officially *British* prisoners of war, although they fell under the supervision of members of the Danish Brigade. The film's use of symbolism is quite explicit.

Although Rasmussen exercises strict discipline over his group of men, the ultimate role of a cruel "Nazi-like" Danish commander is played by Rasmussen's superior, his Danish commanding officer, Captain Ebbe Jensen (Mikkel Boe Følsgaard). Viewers witness a scene in which visiting Allied British officers, accompanied by Captain Jensen, assault the German boys in the early morning hours, including sexually violating one of the boys at gunpoint. The middle-aged British officers, who are out for "a night of fun," urinate on the young German prisoner and hold a gun to his forehead. The assault is eventually interrupted by Sergeant Rasmussen. In a spat between Rasmussen and his commander (Captain Jensen) over the treatment of "the boys," Captain Jensen retorts with the oft-repeated Danish defense of the forced labor of the young Germans to defuse the mines: "If you're old enough to go to war, then you're old enough to clean up after yourself."[12]

In a further inversion of World War II filmic tropes, this screenplay visually stages the soiled and hallow-cheeked boyish Germans as the victims of wartime atrocities. They appear as a variety of "concentration camp prisoners";

they are held captive at night in an inhospitable shack on raw cots; they are subjected to sadistic and cruel outbursts and beatings; they are commanded to perform dangerous forced labor; and they survive on starvation rations (at one point they eat animal fodder contaminated by rat feces). Further, the prisoners are offered a false promise: when the forty-five thousand mines in their area are cleared within three months, then they will be allowed to "go home."

The conceptual theme of the cycle of violence perpetuated by aggression and victimization has often been thematized both in war films and in postwar literature; it is the idea that violent aggression breeds vengeance and that the potential for hatred, depravity, and cruelty lies within any person.[13] Nonetheless, there is also the motif of redemption in *Land of Mine*, and that is the ultimate point of this neatly choreographed cinematic production, which suggests that the potential for decency also lies within everyone. Sergeant Rasmussen, the prison-keeper (who comes to suffer from a "reverse Stockholm syndrome" by forming strong emotional bonds with his prisoners) is gradually affected by the emotional and physical suffering of "his boys" and begins to feed and care for them. Rasmussen softens up visibly following the deaths of three of the boys (Wilhelm from severe maiming, the loss of both arms; Werner in an accidental detonation; later Werner's twin brother in an intentionally suicidal detonation). He begins to comfort and understand his prisoners, as if they were teenagers longing for their parents. Toward the film's conclusion, ten of the remaining boys are killed in a single explosion, leaving only four survivors of the group. However, the four survivors are not "sent home" as promised by their commander but instead ordered to Skallingen, a peninsula of sand dunes and salt marshes in which thousands of uncharted mines lie buried—many still remaining to this day. Here the mine-clearing was extremely dangerous and the number of fatalities even greater (Hagemann 1998: 53).

At the conclusion of *Land of Mine*, Sergeant Rasmussen directly defies the orders of his superior, Captain Ebbe Jensen, and, in an act of redemption (and outright military insubordination), retrieves the surviving four boys from the death trap at Skallingen in order to drive them south toward the German border. There Rasmussen releases the prisoners out of captivity and orders them to run the final five hundred meters toward the border with Germany. The implied moral redemption of Rasmussen in the film's conclusion is neat, but also problematic. It allows the commander to be true to his promise to let his boys "go home." However, the film's viewer who looks beyond the lens of the camera knows that there is no "home" any longer. The young men are running toward another dark hell, as they flee southward toward the ruins and utter desolation of Hamburg and other German cities firebombed and decimated by Allied air strikes.

The War Film as Cultural Memory in Denmark • 295

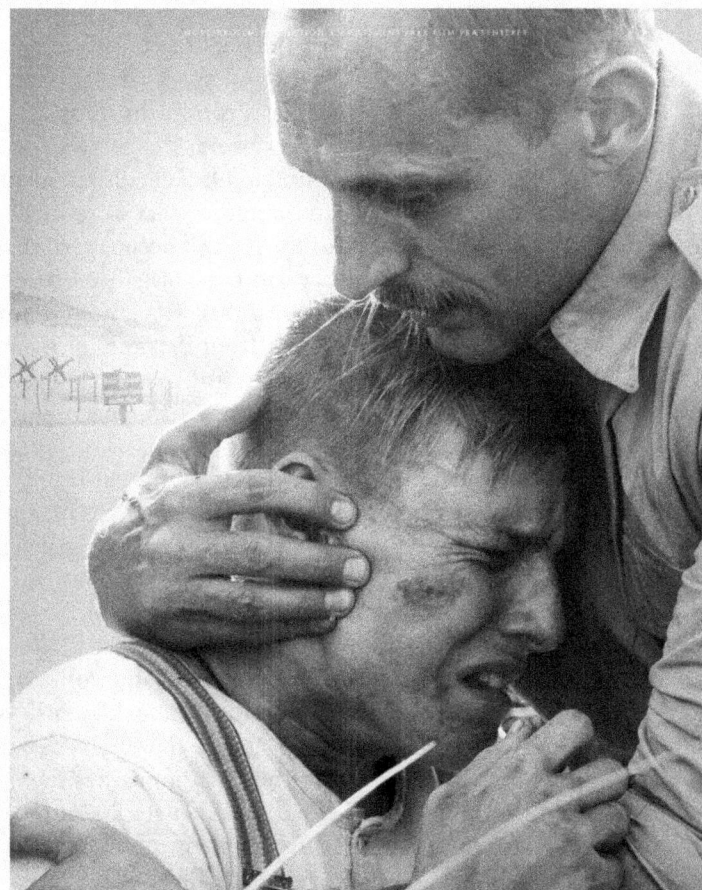

Figure 17.1. Poster for the Danish premiere of *Under Sandet* (titled *Land of Mine* in the English-language release) in early December 2015. The film enacts an inversion of the usual power hierarchy by depicting Danish soldiers harshly commandeering German prisoners—and it suggests that such brutal retribution may ultimately turn to compassion. In the featured image, the Danish sergeant Rasmussen (Roland Møller) cradles the young German prisoner Sebastian (Louis Hofmann). The promotional text states, "They survived the Second World War. Now they must survive the clean up." Courtesy of Nordisk Film.

Cultural Memory and the Archive

Both *April 9th* and *Land of Mine* dramatize the plight of the ordinary soldier caught in a bind created by political leaders and the higher military command. Neither one of the historical episodes depicted in these 2015 film productions (neither the neglected border troops nor the postwar treatment of German prisoners of war) have been central to Danish cultural memory of World War II. In relation to the dominant narrative (that of resistance) and counternarrative (that of collaboration) of the Danish occupation, these two recent films feature historical episodes that had previously been relegated to the footnotes or the "margins" of history (or to that which has been termed "storage memory"), and thus had been absent from the cultural memory of the war. One could say that these painful historical episodes did not until recently exist in the active memory that defines and supports the cultural identity of most Danes living today.

During the postwar decades, a resistance narrative was cultivated by historians, veterans, memoirists, and politicians; this narrative of anti-Nazi resistance allowed nearly all Danes to view themselves as active participants, thus the actuality of the active and organized resistance of the last year and a half of the war was conveniently extended backward in time in the collective memory to cover all five years and to include nearly every Dane (Skov 2000: 104; Bryld 2007: 90–94). In the 1990s, a second generation of occupation historians, who were not themselves veterans of the war, such Henrik Nissen, Henning Poulsen, and Hans Kirchhoff, engaged in the public debate that challenged the healing postwar cultural memory of unified resistance. This historical revisionism continues today with a third generation of historians. Still today the occupation period frequently enters into political discourse and public debates in Denmark, with references to Danish policies and conditions during World War II used to serve one political agenda or another without an accurate connection to historical facts (Bundgård Christensen 2013: 153).[14]

When situated in the theoretical framework of cultural memory studies, I would argue that both of these recent Danish films draw from passive memories that have been "archived" or stored. One could say they have belonged in "storage memory," which has not been cultivated as an active part of the institutionalized cultural memory by means of museum exhibits, public monuments, school textbooks, or political speeches (Aleida Assmann 2010: 99; 2011: 119–34). In other words, the story of the tiny army of Danish soldiers, inadvertently sent into battle against heavily armed German tanks and troops, was for the first time in spring 2015 the central subject of Danish institutional commemorations and museum exhibits, with the film's star,

Pilou Asbæk, attending the ceremonies on 9 April 2015 with aged veterans of the battle. With this film and the commemorating events of 9 April 2015, this archived historical chapter again became part of an active Danish cultural memory canonized by institutionalization. Perhaps the message being delivered to the Danish public by means of the enacted historical drama of *April 9th* is that the Danes had (after all) attempted to defend their border, but Danish political and military leadership had failed to provide adequate preparation, military support or equipment and troops. Like the catastrophic defeat of the Second Schleswig War depicted in *1864*, Danish soldiers had once again been recklessly or needlessly sent into battle.

In order to add documentary authenticity to *April 9th*, the epilogue features interviews with elderly veterans of the brief and hopeless border fight. The viewer hears the veterans speak haltingly about their efforts as soldiers on that fateful day. Their testimony constitutes what Jan Assmann refers to as "communicative memory" or the embodied memories of those who have actually experienced the events: "Communicative memory is non-institutional: it is not supported by any institutions of learning, transmission, or interpretation. . . . [It] has only a limited time depth which normally reaches no farther back than eighty years, the time span of three interacting generations" (Jan Assmann 2010: 111). The affect of the patriotic sentiments articulated by these honorable old veterans about the short battle seems inadvertently to add an apologia to the filmed narrative about the misguided Danish defensive battle, which the viewer has just experienced on screen.

With regard to the story of the Danish treatment of German POWs, depicted in *Land of Mine* as a form of cruel postwar retribution, there is evidence of deliberate marginalization or "active forgetting" in the collective memory. One could argue that this shameful chapter had previously belonged to taboo area of Danish cultural memory that was subject to negation or censorship. There will likely not be any institutionalized commemorations of Denmark's postwar de-mining operation along the Atlantic coast.[15] Nonetheless, both *April 9th* and *Land of Mine* are remarkable films in terms of illustrating the importance of stored cultural memory that is preserved in the historical archive, which "affords us the possibility of comparison and reflection for a retrospective historical consciousness" (Aleida Assmann 2010: 106). In other words, both these films to varying degrees offer narratives that contest the hegemonic cultural memory of World War II in Denmark. Furthermore, there certainly exists other controversial chapters in Denmark's storage memory of its war history—and there are other episodes that have yet to be activated in collective memory by means of cinematic productions or institutional commemorations.[16]

Conclusion

There are common traits, perspectives, concerns, and plots in these recent Danish war films, *April 9th* and *Land of Mine*—an anti-nostalgic sentiment and perhaps an antiwar film aesthetic. Both productions engage generic conventions belonging to the war film rather than the occupation drama, even at a time when the cinematic occupation drama remains a popular genre in Denmark as well as in Norway. Both of these Danish films are characterized by an overwhelming male subjectivity (Second Lieutenant Sand and Sergeant Rasmussen); the camera angle and the narrative perspective is focused on the inner, subjective struggle of these lower-ranking commanding officers, toiling under impossible leadership tasks. Both male protagonists are depicted as patriots, yet they are also portrayed as independent agents who, at crucial moments, are insubordinate to the higher command. Most obviously, both protagonists are in a sense "disenfranchised" (lower-ranking) military leaders, yet they hold the responsibility of life and death over a younger generation of men (whether a bicycle platoon of Danish soldiers or a group of young German prisoners of war). The camera often focuses the viewer's attention on anxious and bewildered faces of these younger males as they are traumatized collectively by conditions that force them to witness the random deaths and extreme suffering within their immediate group. Both lower-ranking commanders make efforts to "protect" and care for their charges—and one could say that, in the end, both films exonerate the male protagonist of the guilt for the deaths of their men.

This emphasis in *April 9th* and *Land of Mine* on the collective, on male subjectivity, and on the senseless waste of youth in war, as well as on moral redemption, extends to another recent Danish war film, *Krigen/A War* (2015) produced the same year. Written and directed by Tobias Lindholm, *A War* depicts Danish troops fighting the Taliban in Afghanistan rather than Germans in World War II. It is the most recent example of a small wave of Danish war films and literary works that has emerged since Denmark deployed troops to Afghanistan (Rothstein 2014). Again starring Pilou Asbæk, *A War* depicts the difficult circumstance of a Danish military company in Afghanistan under the command of a Danish officer. While saving the life of one of the men in his squad, the commander's decision results in eleven Afghani civilian deaths. He is accused of civilian murder, a war crime, but is eventually exonerated by the Danish court. The ruling is troubling, because the commander has lied under oath in order to avoid imprisonment; it is a morally ambiguous decision that is depicted in the film drama as an intentional choice made by the soldier in order to protect his Danish wife and children. In relation to the pattern of the other two war films, it is again the commander, loyal to the collective of young ordinary soldiers, who ultimately prioritizes his own men (and his own family, in this instance) against the judgments of the higher military command and judicial system.

The Danish World War II films *April 9th* and *Land of Mine* are focused on the plight of the ordinary soldier and his collective in wartime conditions, whether he is German or Danish. The real point being that he is young, he is innocent, and he will suffer as the victim of callous or incompetent higher command and political mechanizations beyond his control. This is the stuff of canonical war films such as *All Quiet on the Western Front*, Lewis Milestone's famous 1930 motion picture, a seminal work in cinematic history that simultaneously establishes the war film genre and attains the status of *antiwar film* (Chambers 1994). These recent Danish films, *April 9th* and *Land of Mine*, remind the viewer that the inhumane plight and absurd injustices of the ordinary soldier at war has often been the subject of war films and that, at its best, the war film is also an antiwar film.

Marianne Stecher-Hansen (PhD, University of California, Berkeley, 1990) is Professor of Danish and Scandinavian Studies at the University of Washington. She has authored *The Creative Dialectic in Karen Blixen's Essays: On Gender, Nazi Germany, and Colonial Desire* (2014), and the critical commentary for *Karen Blixen: Værker; Skygger paa Græsset—Essays* (2020), as well as edited *Danish Writers from the Reformation to Decadence 1550–1990* (2004) and *Twentieth-Century Danish Writers* (1999). She also published *History Revisited: Fact and Fiction in Thorkild Hansen's Documentary Works* (1997).

Notes

I wish to thank John Sundholm for his commentary on this chapter.
1. Roni Ezra, 2017, TV2 *Deadline*, 22 July 2017, "Jeg er optaget af nederlaget!"
2. An earlier version of this chapter was presented at the Society for the Advancement of Scandinavian Studies, University of Minnesota, Minneapolis, 12 May 2017.
3. Denmark signed the Geneva Convention in 1929, which forbids the use of prisoners of war for defusing land mines (Hagemann 1998: 16).
4. See Bo Lidegaard, "Hvad rager det filmen, at historien er forkert?" *Politiken*, 6 December 2015; Casper Bauerfeld Krogh, "Fremstilling af dansk ondskab er falsk," *Politiken*: Kronik, 4 December 2015; Eva Lange Jørgensen, "Historiker roser 'Under Sandet' selv om der skues 'liige lovligt meget på drama-knappen'—Interview med Palle Roslyng-Jensen," *Politiken*, 3 December 2015.
5. This figure is based on the twenty Danish war films chronicled by Ebbe Villadsen, plus the five additional war films produced in Denmark from 2000 to 2016, including *Flammen og Citronen* (2008), *Hvidsten Gruppen* (2012), *Under Sandet* (2015), *9. April* (2015), and *Fuglene over Sundet* (2016).

6. Zandvliet, *Under Sandet* (2015); opening screen captions in the Danish release: "Tidligt om morgenen den 9. April 1940 overskrider tyske tropper den dansk-tyske grænse. Den uforberedte og dårligt udrustede danske hær står overfor Europas stærkeste militærmagt. De hårdeste kampe finder sted i Sønderjylland."
7. See Tom Buk-Swienty's documentary novels, *Slagtebænk Dybbøl* (2008; translated as *1864*, 2015) and *Dommedags Als* (2010) that form the basis for Ole Bornedal's TV series and film.
8. See Stine Oksbjerg, "Begejstrede Anmeldere—Muligvis årets bedste film!" *DR Nyheder*, 3 December 2015.
9. Zandvliet, *Under Sandet* (2015); concluding screen captions in the Danish release: "Næsten halvdelen omkom eller blev hårdt sårede;" "Mange af dem var blot helt unge drenge."
10. Rasmussen shouts, "Heraus!"—"Das ist mein Land! Hast Die forstehen?!"
11. Tove Ditlevsen's poem "De tyske soldater," originally published in the Danish press in 1945, where it stirred controversy, was later included in Ditlevsen's collection, *Blinkende Lygter: Digte* (1947: Flickering Lights: Poems).
12. Zandvliet, *Under Sandet* (2015): "Hvis man er gammel nok til at gå i krig, så er man gammel nok til at rydde op efter sig selv."
13. In a postwar context, the allegory of a "latent Nazi," cultivated in the soil of hatred, who emerges at pivotal moments in history as a kind of "bastard child" of humanity, is employed in postwar Scandinavian literary masterpieces, for example in Pär Lagerkvist's *The Dwarf* (1945) and Sigurd Hoel's *Meeting at the Milestone*.
14. Former prime minister and NATO general secretary Anders Fogh Rasmussen has repeatedly criticized Denmark's wartime Policy of Negotiation, initially in August 2003 in a speech to the Danish Naval Academy in an effort to justify the current Danish foreign policy and military operations in Iraq and Afghanistan. In March 2010, Rasmussen called the Policy of Negotiation a "moral betrayal" and a "naïve understanding" of the Nazi German regime (Bundgård Christensen 2013: 153).
15. Notably, "Peace Sculpture," an art installation in 1995 by Danish artist Elle-Mie Ejdrup Hansen on the west coast of Jutland, which consisted of 532 miles of laser beams spanning from Skagen, Jutland's northernmost point, to the German island of Sylt, leaping from one fortification to the next in the (Danish-built, German-demanded) "Atlantic Fortress" of 6,000 bunkers, provoked indignant criticism from many Danes, precisely because the intended message was reconciliation between Denmark, Germany, and Europe at the fiftieth anniversary of the Liberation, when it was celebrated on 4 May 1995. According to Ejdrup Hansen, the laser sculpture was to be seen as "a celebration of life, of the world, of hope, of reconciliation" (Bryld 2007: 91).
16. There is no Danish cinematic production about the so-called *tyskertøser* (Danish women in intimate relationships with German soldiers), as researched by Anette Warring, nor a film depicting the internment of Danish communists (including many significant Danish writers for the period) in June 1941, the subject of Hans Scherfig's bitterly satirical novel, *Frydenholm* (1962).

References

Assmann, Aleida. 2010. "The Dynamics of Cultural Memory between Remembering and Forgetting." In *A Companion to Cultural Memory Studies*, edited by Astrid Erll and Ansgar Nünning, 97–107. Berlin: De Gruyter.

———. 2011. *Cultural Memory and Western Civilization: Functions, Media, Archives.* Cambridge: Cambridge University Press.
Assmann, Jan. 2010. "Communicative and Cultural Memory." In *A Companion to Cultural Memory Studies*, edited by Astrid Erll and Ansgar Nünning, 109–18. Berlin: De Gruyter.
Basinger, Jeanine. 1986. *The World War II Combat Film: Anatomy of a Genre.* New York: Columbia University Press.
Bender, Stuart. 2013. *Film Style and the World War II Combat Genre.* Newcastle upon Tyne: Cambridge Scholar Publishing.
Bryld, Claus. 2007. "'The Five Accursed Years': Danish Perception and Usage of the Period of the German Occupation, with a Wider View to Norway and Sweden." In *Scandinavian Journal of History* 32(1): 86–115.
Buk-Swienty, Tom. 2015. *1864: The Forgotten War That Shaped Modern Europe.* Translated by Annette Buk-Swienty. London: Profile Books.
Bundgård Christensen, Claus. 2013. "'The Five Evil Years': National Self-Image, Commemoration and Historiography in Denmark 1945–2010: Trends in Historiography and Commemoration." In *Hitler's Scandinavian Legacy*, edited by John Gilmour and Jill Stephensen, 147–57. London: Bloomsbury Academic.
Chambers, John Whiteclay, III. 1994. "*All Quiet on the Western Front* (1930): The Anitwar Film and the Image of the First World War." In *Historical Journal of Film, Radio and Television* 14(4): 377–411.
Ditlevsen, Tove. 1996. "De tyske soldater." In *Samlede digte*, 120–21. Copenhagen: Gyldendal.
Donnerborg, Mette. 2017. "Krigens affekt: En medievidenskabelig undersøgelse af det affektive potentiale." MA thesis, Aalborg University, Denmark.
Hagemann, Helge. 1998. *Under tvang: Minerydningen ved den jyske vestkyst 1945.* Copenhagen: Akademisk forlag.
Häikiö, Marttii. 1983. "The Race for Northern Europe, September 1939—June 1940." In *Scandinavia during the Second World War*, edited by Henrik S. Nissen, translated by Thomas Munch-Petersen, 53–97. Minneapolis: University of Minnesota Press.
Hedling, Erik. 2015. *The Battle of Døbbel Revisited.* Copenhagen: Kosmorama.
Hong, Nathaniel. 2012. *Occupied: Denmark's Adaptation and Resistance to German Occupation 1940–1945.* Copenhagen: Frihedsmuseets venners forlag.
Iversen, Gunnar. 2012. "From Trauma to Heroism: Cultural Memory and Remembrance in Norwegian Occupation Dramas, 1946–2009." In *Journal of Scandinavian Cinema* 2(3): 237–48.
Lane, Anthony. 2017. "The Current Cinema: 'On the Beach: Christopher Nolan's Dunkirk.'" *New Yorker*, 31 July, 80–81.
Rothstein, Klaus. 2014. *Soldatens år: Afghanistan-krigen i dansk litteratur og kultur.* Copenhagen: Tiderne Skifter.
Skov, Niels Aage. 2000. "The Use of Historical Myth: Denmark's World War II Experience Made to Serve Practical Goals." In *Scandinavian Studies* 72(1): 89–110.
Villadsen, Ebbe. 2000. "The German Occupation as a Subject in Danish Film." *Scandinavica: An International Journal of Scandinavian Studies* 39(1): 25–46.
Østergård, Uffe. 2011. "Swords, Shields or Collaborators? Danish Historians and the Debate over the German Occupation of Denmark." In *Nordic Narratives of the Second World War: National Historiographies Revisited*, edited by Mirja Österberg, Johan Östling, and Henrik Stenius, 31–53. Lund: Nordic Academic Press.

Chapter 18

ACTS OF REMEMBERING

Audiovisual Memory and the New Norwegian Occupation Drama

Gunnar Iversen

While the historic facts of the German occupation of Norway in the years between 1940 and 1945 remain unchanged, audiovisual representations of World War II have varied dramatically in Norway since 1946, strongly influenced by the changing conceptions and functions of the war in Norwegian society and changes in film production policies. War dramas have always been popular in Norway, but the recent Norwegian occupation dramas have been more popular than most films dealing with the events of World War II there.

Indeed, today the war seems more popular than ever in Norway. Every year a number of nonfiction books about the war years are published. Films are a good indication of the war's popularity too. The most-seen film in Norwegian cinemas in 2016 was the Norwegian *Kongens nei/The King's Choice* (directed by Erik Poppe), a film that explicitly presents itself as *the* story of the war and the national community. More than seven hundred thousand Norwegians saw the film in the cinemas, placing the film among the most popular films in the history of Norwegian film production.

During the first month of its release, *Den 12. mann/12th Man* (Harald Zwart, 2017), the most recent occupation drama, was seen by five hundred thousand Norwegians, one-tenth of Norway's population. This retelling of one of the most famous episodes of resistance and survival during the war is a very different story than an earlier film based on the same historical material.

Arne Skouen's *Ni liv/Nine Lives* (1957) was chosen as "the best Norwegian film ever made" during a national television event in Norway in 1991, but Zwart's film retells the story of resistance fighter Jan Baalsrud's dramatic escape from German soldiers with a new dramatic intensity and melodramatic emotional appeal.

Together with films like *Max Manus/Max Manus: Man of War* (Espen Sandberg and Joachim Rønning, 2008) and *Secondløitnanten/The Last Lieutenant* (Hans Petter Moland, 1993), *The King's Choice* and *12th Man* represent a new type of war film in Norway. These new Norwegian occupation dramas represent the war and interpret history for new generations of Norwegians who never experienced the war firsthand. These films do important cultural and political work in Norway, as they are obvious examples of "nonbanal" nationalism, and together with the many nonfiction books about the war published every year, they keep the values of the wartime struggle present in the public sphere. This chapter focuses on the most recent Norwegian occupation dramas and discusses the new occupation drama genre in the context of Norwegian film history and the changing representation of World War II in Norwegian feature films.

The Norwegian Occupation Dramas

Immediately after World War II ended, Norwegian filmmakers turned to topics and themes regarding the war. In 1946, six feature-length fiction films were made in Norway, and three of them were occupation dramas, as the new genre soon was called. Since 1946, around thirty occupation dramas have been produced in Norway. In addition, many other film and television series, as well as numerous documentaries, have been made that, in some way or another, deal with the war and the German occupation.

Even though many films have been produced in Norway representing the German occupation and war years, they use different strategies to approach their representations of the war. The occupation dramas have presented different narratives of historical events, demonstrating changing attitudes toward the war. Like most historical fiction, Norwegian occupation dramas have been selective in their choice of what stories to tell and how to tell them. Some highlight the authenticity of historical events and true stories, and others spin tales of pure fiction. Both types of war film can be seen as performative interpretations of the past (Sørensen 2015: 14), presenting these interpretations for contemporary purposes and experiencing changes in how they function in Norwegian society. The genre has gone through many changes since the very first films about the war made in 1946.

In the article "From Trauma to Heroism: Cultural Memory and Remembrance in Norwegian Occupation Dramas, 1946–2009," I proposed that the occupation drama could be divided into four distinct phases, with each period representing a distinct interpretation of the war years and having a special focus. This division into four periods emphasizes not only the development of the genre but also the changes in attitude toward the war and the representation of wartime experiences (Iversen 2012). In the first period (1946), the focus of the genre is on trauma; in the second (1948–62), ordinary collective heroism; in the third (1962–93), critique and revisionism; and in the fourth and last phase so far (1993–2017), on extraordinary individual heroism. I do not claim that these four phases or periods are all-inclusive, and a few significant exceptions do exist, especially within the transitional period of 1957–62, but the differences between the four periods are still striking. The war has been seen and represented in these four very different ways by Norwegian filmmakers from 1946 until today.

Although I do share film historian Tonje Haugland Sørensen's concern that such a focus on development can contain an implicit teleology—organizing the changes in the genre in a narrative with a clear beginning, middle, and end—the four phases still seem to be productive tools that can be used to interpret the occupation drama without downplaying some of the messiness of art and entertainment. Sørensen points out that all of the four phases contain elements of critical revision (Sørensen 2015: 18). However, the moments of critical revision are very different in terms of emphasis, importance, and frequency, especially in the second and fourth phases of the genre. All the films are representations, acts of remembering, and parts of an ongoing discourse about how to interpret and perform the Norwegian war experience, but the representations have very different concerns, interests, and functions. Even though it can be argued that all the periods contain critical revision as well as patriotic affirmation, very few films seem to subvert the general trend of the period during which they were made.

The first three occupation dramas, all produced and released in the year 1946, differ from the later war movies produced in Norway. They are more nuanced, troubled, and traumatic in their representation of the war years than the films made in the late 1940s and early 1950s as well as those made today. The term "trauma" in relation to these war stories refers not only to the fact that many Norwegians collaborated with the occupation forces, a deep wound that had to be dealt with in the immediate postwar years, but also to the fact that these films are so different in style and narration. The "story" of the war years seems not to have been established or formed, no hegemonic filmic narrative exists, and the three films focus on psychological strains, moral uncertainty, doubt, and inner fears. The films often question both masculinity and heroism, focusing not on heroic resistance fighters but on ordinary people forced to deal with traumatic experiences and placed in difficult moral and existential situations.

The second phase or period of the Norwegian occupation drama started with the famous *Kampen om tungtvannet/Operation Swallow* (Titus Vibe-Müller and Jean Dréville, 1948). This film is very different from the three previous films about the occupation. Emphasizing resistance, sabotage, and collective action and using a mixed docudrama form, *Operation Swallow* became the model for many later occupation dramas in the 1950s. A huge success, the film depicts two successful sabotage operations by Norwegians trained in England against the production of heavy water, *the* symbol of Norwegian resistance against German occupation, and the film contributed to making the saboteurs, some of whom played themselves in the film, into national heroes (Iversen 2005: 91; Iversen 2012: 241).

By focusing on resistance and sabotage, the film contributed to creating one of the "national grand narratives" of modern Norway and was important in healing the wounds of the war, but it also legitimated values in postwar society and formed the modern national culture in Norway (Iversen 2005: 91; Iversen 2012: 237–39). *Operation Swallow* and many war dramas made in the 1950s focus on resistance, combat, and male heroism. There are few moments of uncertainty and doubt in these resistance dramas, and the focus is on ordinary collective heroism. The films most often center on a group, depicting collective action. Men do what they have to do, women help them, and together they form a unified front against the Germans. Inner doubt, an idea important in the first phase of films in 1946, is replaced by external action. Collaboration with the Germans is certainly part of some of the stories, but this is always downplayed. Often the German soldiers are only one of many obstacles that saboteurs need to overcome, with the harsh Norwegian climate serving as an even more important enemy, especially in *Operation Swallow*.

The films that belong to the second period of Norwegian occupation drama, which highlight ordinary people's collective heroism, often take place in highly symbolic national landscapes, especially the barren winter mountains. However, in later films these symbolic landscapes also become the place of doubt and struggle. A categorical shift is signaled in the most celebrated occupation drama in the history of the genre, Arne Skouen's *Nine Lives* from 1957. The story of a Norwegian saboteur on the run through the barren mountains in the north of Norway during wintertime, *Nine Lives* marks a transition to a new period of revisionism. The story is about resistance and ordinary collective heroism, focusing as much on those who help the main character Jan Baalsrud as on his extraordinary abilities to survive hunger and cold, but external action is reduced to a minimum. The real enemy, as the director himself stated, is the natural Norwegian environment and not the German occupation army (Bjerke 1980).

The same highly symbolic and national landscape is the setting in another film by Arne Skouen, *Kalde spor/Cold Trails* (1962), which marked the beginning of a third phase of the occupation drama. This period is different from the previous ones, focusing on various forms of betrayal, doubt, and collaboration. The collective of everyday male heroes that just does its national and moral duty is replaced by tormented individuals who often betray their best friends as well as their country. *Cold Trails* extends its aim beyond betrayal, implying that not all of the people who had become heroes of the resistance actually lived up to their heroic image. As in the first phase, but with even stronger emphasis on betrayal and insecurity, the third explored inner subjectivities and transgressions. *Cold Trails* explicitly problematizes and questions resistance struggle, the collective and its attitudes toward the occupation forces, and sanctioned memory culture. Tonje Haugland Sørensen has shown how Skouen's film reverses almost all of the earlier positive elements of the genre. Even nature, the mountains and snow, regarded as integral to Norwegian identity in the normative film *Operation Swallow*, becomes negative and alienating (Sørensen 2011: 11–14, Sørensen 2015: 282). In the 1970s and 1980s, a number of films followed *Cold Trails* in revising and reversing the themes from the second phase of the genre. These films often focused on everyday life during the occupation and not on heroic resistance. Some also focused on the war in the far north of Norway, which had been largely ignored by the films and national memory culture based in the south.

In the third phase of the occupation drama, 1962–93, familiar themes and situations were reversed and reworked, focusing on collaboration and betrayal and debunking the myth of male heroism and national collective resistance. However, with Hans Petter Moland's *The Last Lieutenant* in 1993, the occupation drama changed once more and entered its fourth and last phase. The film centers on an old soldier who decides to join younger compatriots in defending the country when Norway is invaded in April 1940. Even though the film shows that the armed resistance against the German troops is ineffective and chaotic, especially because of bad political and military leadership, the focus of the film is on individual heroism. *The Last Lieutenant* can be seen as a transition film, signaling a new focus on extraordinary individual heroism, but at the same time it shows the ineptness of the Norwegian army and criticizes the lack of preparation for the war. Moland's film represented something new in the genre and became the first example of the new Norwegian occupation drama.

The New Occupation Drama

After the premiere of *The Last Lieutenant* in 1993, no occupation dramas were made in Norway until 2008's *Max Manus: Man of War*. The film was seen by more than 1.3 million people in cinemas (nearly every third Norwegian), inspiring other Norwegian directors and producers to turn to the occupation drama. After *Max Manus*, four occupation dramas were made, and the last two have been among the most popular Norwegian films of all time, pointing to the central position of the war in Norwegian culture and how the genre still contributes to shaping the public conception of the war and the nation.

The new occupation drama is characterized by its focus on extraordinary individual heroism as well as on more extravagant action. To a larger degree than before, these films have aligned themselves with the transnational war film genre, especially Hollywood war films. The exploration of inner subjectivities has been replaced by external spectacle. The occupation drama becomes a war drama with depictions of direct combat.

Max Manus: Man of War is a good example of the new Norwegian occupation drama. The film is an action-filled story about the saboteur Max Manus and his friends, who not only produce illegal newspapers but also blow up German ships in the Oslo harbor. Although Max Manus is troubled by nerves, because nearly all of his friends are killed by German soldiers, he has no doubt about his actions and his role as a saboteur. His inner demons are very different from the demons that cripple the main character in a film like *Cold Trails*. *Max Manus* focuses mainly on dramatic actions of sabotage: the myth of the autonomous heroic resistance fighter is no longer problematized but celebrated, and the more anonymous collective heroes of the genre's second phase are now replaced by extraordinary individual heroes. This tendency is even more pronounced in *The King's Choice* and *12th Man*.

There are probably many reasons why the more recent films are so much more action-oriented and portray individuals who are larger than life. One obvious reason has to do with the fact that there are fewer people still alive who experienced the occupation, making it easier to freely adapt war stories and make less nuanced films about individual heroism. Changes in the genre are also linked to larger cultural and political shifts, and especially to changes within the film production community as well as the support systems of the Norwegian government.

Since 1950, the Norwegian government has supported the production of feature films. Even though the support systems have varied and always maintained a balance between supporting art films and popular genre films, the financial assistance for popular genre films has increased, especially since the New Norwegian Film Policy in 2001. The explicit aim of the new policy was to provide the national film production sector with more freedom, and also to aid the production of popular genre films to a larger extent than before. This reflected changing attitudes among filmmakers, who no longer saw films as a sociopolitical tool but as a way of telling exciting stories. This changing attitude resulted in a turn to exciting genre-oriented stories, including a new type of occupation drama, depicting war in a new way through spectacular combat, as seen through the lens of the Hollywood war drama. This shift is especially clear in the two most recent occupation dramas, *The King's Choice* and *12th Man*.

The King's Choice: War as Family Melodrama

In a dramatic scene toward the end of *The King's Choice*, King Haakon VII (played by Jesper Christensen) flees from attacking German planes. Together with a large group of ordinary Norwegians caught in the rain of bombs from the German planes, the king and his family run to a forest to seek shelter among the pine trees. Hiding behind a tree, the king sees a young, terrified boy lying by himself in the snow. The king immediately crawls over to the boy and comforts him. We see the boy's mother running around in the background, calling out his name.

This scene goes to the heart of *The King's Choice*. The king himself is first and foremost presented as a family man, as we see him in the very first scene playing hide-and-seek with his grandchildren, among them the current monarch, King Harald V. Even though the film depicts the important historic moment when King Haakon refused the German ultimatum that would have forced Norway to accept the occupation and the puppet politician Vidkun Quisling as the new prime minister, a choice that amounted to an official declaration of war with Germany, the film is a family melodrama at its core.

The scene at the end of the film where the king comforts the boy in the snow is emblematic in many ways. It depicts the king not only as a selfless and caring father figure but also as a national father, caring for his Norwegian people. It is not accidental that the boy's name is Ola, thus making him not only a random scared little boy in the war but a symbol of Norway itself. The name "Ola," while a common nickname for a typical, average Norwegian man, is also a personification of the Norwegian people, most clearly in the name "Ola Nordmann," *the* Norwegian male. By comforting and taking care of the boy Ola until his mother has found him, the king demonstrates how he is the national father, taking care of his subjects. Nation and family meld together, becoming one and the same, in *The King's Choice*.

In many ways, *The King's Choice* is a good example of the new Norwegian occupation drama. Focusing on a heroic king selflessly fighting for his family and his people, the film has chosen one of the clearest examples of an extraordinary individual hero. But it also points to the resistance, since the king, with his government-in-exile in London, became an important figure opposing the Germans. Just writing his name (or his initials H7) on a wall was a crime during the occupation years. The presence of the current Norwegian king in the story, a very young boy in 1940, also strengthens the connection between royalty, family, and nation.

The King's Choice is also a political drama, about how the Norwegian government reacted to the German occupation, and a military drama, depicting the invasion itself through a series of combat scenes, most spectacularly when the Norwegian forces sink the warship *Blücher* in the Oslofjord. Furthermore, the film is about the relationship between a German diplomat, Curt Bräuer, and the king. In the depictions of the king and his family as well as politicians and diplomats, the family is the main metaphor and focus. This points to how the royalty are made human in the film, being depicted just like anyone else, and to the individualization of history that characterizes the new Norwegian occupation drama.

Traditionally Norwegian war films have depicted the Germans as faceless. With the exception of a few films, Germans are just there, de-individualized, an obstacle in the way of peace. In both *The King's Choice* and *12th Man*, the war and historic events are depicted as a duel between two men, one German and one Norwegian. In *The King's Choice*, the diplomat Bräuer is not a bad man; on the contrary, he tries to prevent combat and bloodshed, but he is flawed. This is most clearly seen in how he acts toward his family—in one scene he hits his wife in a moment of desperation and frustration. King Haakon VII is Bräuer's opposite, always calm and controlled, even though his choices are difficult, and many important decisions have to be made with far-reaching consequences.

As a typical melodrama, all conflicts in *The King's Choice* are reduced to personal strengths and weaknesses, and the king and the diplomat are symbols of the two countries at war. They are characterized and seen through the optics of family relations. The king is seen as the father of his country, helping a paralyzed Parliament. Clearly another symbol of Norway, the members of the Parliament, as well as the soldiers taking up arms against the German troops, have different accents and dialects, representing the whole country. They are stand-ins for the Norwegian people, and the film also repeatedly points to the fact that King Haakon VII in fact was a Danish prince elected king by the Norwegians in 1905, when Norway dissolved its Union with Sweden and became a sovereign nation.

By depicting the king first and foremost as a caring family man, a mild, playful grandfather and father, and representing the war as a duel between men, *The King's Choice* goes further toward the melodramatization of historical events than previous films in the genre. It is also striking that women are nearly absent and that the crown prince Olav accuses his mother, the dead queen, of being absent and a poor parent. In the occupation drama, women have mostly had roles as helpers and witnesses, and this focus on male melodrama is even clearer in *12th Man*.

12th Man: War as Masculine Duel

Immediately after the premiere of Harald Zwart's *12th Man* on 26 December 2017, op-eds were published in Norwegian newspapers that pointed out some of historical errors and controversial aspects of the film (Kvam Jr. 2018). As audiences embraced the film and filled the cinemas, historians and journalists discussed whether Zwart's film was a pure fantasy or if it had some connection to the real historical events. Together with *Max Manus: Man of War* and *The King's Choice*, the film was also seen as what historian Ivo de Figueiredo called "delayed nation-building" (de Figueiredo 2018).

Film historian Tonje Haugland Sørensen has pointed out that in many occupation dramas, Germans and especially German soldiers are not important. German soldiers are at the margins of the genre, and only one or two of the films depict German soldiers as evil (Sørensen 2015: 343). This perception has changed in the new Norwegian occupation dramas, and *The King's Choice* and *12th Man* are the most blatant portrayals of German stupidity and brutality.

The film *12th Man* is, like so many occupation dramas, based on real events, and the main character Jan Baalsrud certainly existed, but the film takes many liberties with historical events and truth and invents new characters in order to transform history into a Hollywood-like historical drama. The film tells the story of Baalsrud and his fellow English-trained saboteurs who traveled to the north of Norway to blow up an airfield and establish resistance groups in the area. The group itself is careless and is betrayed by a collaborator. In the fight with the Germans, only Baalsrud escapes. The other eleven men are either killed immediately or executed after being tortured. Baalsrud swims through ice-cold water, wades through deep snow, and, with the help of ordinary Norwegians, manages after three months to reach Sweden and freedom.

Arne Skouen made the story of Baalsrud's flight into a drama of ideas in his classic *Nine Lives*. In this film, the focus is not on the Germans but on harsh nature. The Germans are mere shadows, de-individualized and at the margins of the story. *12th Man* retells the same story, but in Harald Zwart's film the focus is on war and the Germans. In reality, when Baalsrud started his flight from the Germans in 1943, the German soldiers believed him to be dead and did not try to find him. In Zwart's film, Baalsrud is followed and attacked by German soldiers throughout the story, from the beginning to the very end. *Nine Lives* was a film about ideas, about the collective responsibility toward the individual. Contrarily, *12th Man* is an exciting, action-packed, emotional, and physical story of combat and war, a masculine duel.

Even though Baalsrud is the main character in *12th Man*, Zwart also focuses on the Germans hunting for the Norwegian saboteur. The second most important character in Zwart's film is the local Gestapo officer Kurt Stage. His character is based on a real person, but his actions are pure fiction. The film takes the melodramatic personification of *The King's Choice* even further, and Zwart retells the war drama not through the optics of family but of male melodrama. Baalsrud and Stage are personifications of the two nations, and the male body becomes the setting where the fight between nations is played out.

In a central scene in the film, the Gestapo officer Stage stages an experiment. He is sure that the twelfth man did escape, but his fellow officers say that he is dead. If he survived the explosion, he could not have swum across a fjord in the icy water, they reason. In order to prove that the twelfth man could have survived the icy swim, Stage stages a series of experiments. First, he uses some of the other resistance fighters. Prisoners are ordered to stand in the freezing cold water to see if it is possible to survive. When the abused and tortured prisoners break down, Stage strips and walks into the water himself to test whether survival in the water is possible. However, he has to give up because the water is too cold for him.

This emblematic scene sums up how *12th Man* is a male melodrama in which one German fights against one Norwegian. The war is represented as a duel between two men and reconceptualized as a test of masculine endurance. Stage is seen as the evil, weak man in this duel, and Baalsrud as the good man who wins the fight through his physical endurance. Simply by being Norwegian, and more closely connected to nature, landscape, and the geographical nation, Baalsrud wins over the German soldiers.

Acts of Remembering

No single hegemonic narrative about the occupation dominates in the history of the genre, and every generation of Norwegian filmmakers seems to have a different take on depicting the war. However, the recent Norwegian occupation dramas with few exceptions are different from all the previous films in their focus on extraordinary individual heroism. Films like *Max Manus: Man of War*, *The King's Choice*, and *12th Man* also depict war and occupation as military conflict, and include scenes of combat and patriotic violence to a greater extent than before.

Comparing one of the very first occupation dramas from the period of trauma, *To liv/ Two Lives* (Titus Vibe-Müller, 1946) with *Max Manus: Man of War*, film historian Tonje Haugland Sørensen points out that death is a heavy burden and an ethical dilemma in the first film while it has become a spectacle in the second (Sørensen 2015: 112). It is not only death that has become a spectacle in the new Norwegian occupation drama but also resistance, combat, and patriotism itself. Both *The King's Choice* and *12th Man* engage with a more patriotic pathos than most films in the genre.

Despite the many differences in their stories, *The King's Choice* and *12th Man* have many common elements, especially the melodramatization of historical events and representations of the war. Moral conflicts and events are simplified and reduced to oppositions of good and evil, and history is represented through personification and individualization. King Haakon VII and the saboteur Jan Baalsrud are examples of extraordinary individuals who personify the nation as well as specific national traits. The films are complex stories, but at the same time they are simple heroic narratives of national endurance, strength, and belonging.

The Norwegian occupation drama genre illustrates how historical events are depicted differently by different generations and in different historical periods. As historical fictions, they are acts of remembrance as well as performative interpretations of the past (Brinch et al. 2016: 59–60). The new occupation dramas are examples of a more patriotic memory than had been portrayed in previous periods and show a very different version of war events. Films like *The King's Choice* and *12th Man* make the connections between history and national identity more obvious than ever. They are not only examples of films made in a time when very few people remember the war through firsthand experience, and are therefore freer in their performance of history, but they are also examples of how Norway as a nation today seems to embrace the war to a larger extent than before, in a nationalistic ritual of creating and sustaining an imagined community called Norway.

Gunnar Iversen (PhD, University of Stockholm, 1992) served as Professor of Film Studies at the Norwegian University of Science and Technology from 1992 to 2016, and he is now Professor at Carleton University in Ottawa, Canada. Iversen has published numerous books and articles on Norwegian and Scandinavian cinema. In English, he cowrote *Nordic National Cinemas* (1998) and *Historical Dictionary of Scandinavian Cinema* (2012), and he coedited *Beyond the Visual: Sound and Image in Ethnographic and Documentary Film* (2010).

References

Bjerke, René. 1980. "Arne Skouen," *Kinoteket* 1, n.p.
Brinch, Sara, et al. 2016. *Forestillinger om fortid: Historisk fiksjon i film og fjernsyn*. Oslo: Scandinavian Academic Press.

de Figueiredo, Ivo. 2018. "Hvilke historier velger vi å fortelle om krigen." *Aftenposten*, February 2.

Iversen, Gunnar. 2005. "Kampen om tungtvannet / Operation Swallow." In *The Cinema of Scandinavia*, edited by Tytti Soila, 90–101. London: Wallflower.

———. 2011. *Norsk filmhistorie. Spillefilmen 1911–2011*. Oslo: Universitetsforlaget.

———. 2012. "From Trauma to Heroism: Cultural Memory and Remembrance in Norwegian Occupation Dramas, 1946–2009." *Journal of Scandinavian Cinema* 2(3): 237–48.

———. 2017. "Å hoppe etter Skouen." Rushprint.no, 28 December.

Kvam, Ragnar, Jr. 2018. "Tyskerne jaktet ikke på Jan Baalsrud." *Aftenposten*, 2 January.

Sørensen, Tonje Haugland. 2011. "Norsk krigsfilm og det erindringsteoretiske perspektiv: Tilfellet *Kalde spor*." *Norsk Medietidsskrift* 18(1): 4–20.

———. 2015. *The Second World War in Norwegian Film: The Topography of Remembrance*. Bergen: University of Bergen.

Chapter 19

FINLAND RETURNING TO WAR ON SCREEN

The Unknown Soldier of 2017

John Sundholm

The Finnish film *Tuntematon sotilas* (*The Unknown Soldier*, 1955), an adaptation of Väinö Linna's controversial novel of the same title from 1954, is something of a rarity: it serves as a national film. Many countries have a national literature or a national author, but few have a national film. That Finland has one is due to many reasons, but I think that two can be pointed out in particular. Firstly, Finland as a young and minor nation has been overtly focused on the task of building a nation and coherent identity; and secondly, the experiences of the civil war (1918) and the loss of World War II (1939–44) have been so overwhelming that the need to heal the scars and move on have been prioritized over a process of working through the events. Here Edvin Laine's 1955 film has been instrumental as survival story and cultural memory of the war. The popularity of the film adaptation of *The Unknown Soldier* and its recurrent repetition, as memorabilia and as periodical event broadcast on public service television regularly during Independence Day, indicate that the blending of the novel and the film, the hybrid narrative of "The Unknown Soldier," is a powerful founding myth for postwar Finland.[1]

The Finland-born Swedish political scientist Olof Ruin has claimed that whereas Sweden, the country that ruled Finland until 1809, has had a strong tradition of cultural radicalism with its liberal critique of authorities, in Finland most of the efforts and dynamism were devoted to creating a national consciousness, culture, and language (Ruin 2000: 49). This national, and often nationalist, strain has characterized much of Finnish culture, encompassing both the highbrow and the lowbrow, as well as academia. Ruin's explanation for this mindset and disposition is that the young nation of Finland is characterized by the fact that it is placed "in the shadow of great Russia" (2000: 49). However, the pressure has not only been external. When Finland gained independence from the Russian Empire in 1917, which was pushed into revolutionary turmoil, the young nation in turn faced a brief but grim civil war. Thus, the short and conflicting history of Finland has fostered a national and nationalist historiography in which the country is not only the frame for writing history but also the actual historical agent (Sundholm 2013b).

Finland's civil war was fought between left and right, or "the reds" and "the whites" as they were called. The reds, the socialists, had support from the Soviets, whereas the Germans supported the white side, the conservatives. The scars of the war and the events from 1918 never healed, nor were they worked through before Finland was thrown into yet another war, World War II, which started as the so-called Winter War in the fall of 1939. Yet again Russians and Germans would constitute allies and counterparts. The first stage of these war events ended in March 1940 and resumed as the so-called Continuation War in the summer of 1941, in which Finland was allied with Germany. It is this war, which lasted until 1944, that is depicted in *The Unknown Soldier* through the eyes of a machine-gun platoon.

Although the civil war had been short—it lasted for less than four months—the number of victims was high. It is estimated that up to thirty-six thousand died due to the war events, more than in the Winter War. The primary reason why the civil war became such a contested event is that a substantial part of the casualties were related to executions and the brutal detention camps that were established after the war by the Whites. About twenty thousand reds died after the actual war; also, women were executed and children imprisoned.

The Swedish-speaking general Carl Gustav Mannerheim was in command of the whites. He had served in the army of the Russian Empire—Russian was his second language and his Finnish was not particularly good—and would become appointed as commander in chief of Finland's army for World War II. Like Mannerheim, most Finnish officers of higher rank had a history of having fought for the whites during the civil war, and of these, practically every Finnish general in World War II had a background as an activist who had been trained in Germany during 1915–17. Hence, the sentiment was far from reconciliatory when the Winter War started in 1939. An indication of how charged the conflict was can be seen in the following statement by the press attaché at the Finnish Embassy in Berlin, Johannes Öhquist, who introduces Finnish history and culture for a German audience in a booklet from

1919: "For all its atrocities, this sinister catastrophe [civil war] was ultimately lucky for the Finnish people. Because it was not just a liberation. It was a great clean-up, a purification and cleansing of the body and soul, a bloodletting" (Öhquist 1919: 43–44, my translation).[2]

The politically charged prehistory of World War II, together with its transnational connections, is important to bear in mind as it forms an important backdrop to Linna's novel, but also because it explains both why the novel was so controversial at the time and why the following adaptation was so successful. Linna, a working-class writer with a left-wing agenda, stressed in his novel that the Finnish soldiers who entered World War II were sons of a society that was still characterized by political tension. Another of Linna's aims was to explicate that what the soldiers were facing was a brutal experience without any rationality. What the war events and actual battle showed was that there was no meaning whatsoever to the war. There was no higher cause, although the officers and the pastors claimed otherwise. A telling example of the historical situation and the terrible randomness of life at the battlefront is the fate of the Finnish film director Nyrki Tapiovaara, considered to be one of the most gifted Finnish filmmakers. As a left-wing activist who idealized the Soviet Union, Tapiovaara was under surveillance by the secret police during the 1930s. However, he began to change his mind about the Soviet Union after Stalin's purges became known, and especially after the bombings of Helsinki in September 1939. Thus, Tapiovaara volunteered for the war but was not accepted due to his political background. It was not until 20 February 1940, shortly before the Winter War would reach its end, that he was accepted for battle at the front. He would however never experience the peace of 13 March. Tapiovaara was killed two weeks after his deployment.

Linna's aim with the novel was to give meaning to those soldiers who had fought in the war, not by claiming that there was any higher cause, but by showing the irrationality and cruelty of war. Here are Linna's own words from a lecture that he gave during the winter of 1955, before the filming of the novel had started: "I wanted to repeal all value given to the war, but to give it to the soldiers" (Linna 2007a, my translation).[3] Linna thus gave meaning to the returning soldiers by claiming that there was no meaning to war. As a war veteran himself, Linna fully understood the schizophrenic situation that the soldiers found themselves in when they returned home, how they faced a sharp contrast between official national rhetoric and actual personal experience. Consequently, Linna does not let his heroes of the novel survive; instead, it is the buffoons and the everymen who last until the last page of the book. The joker of the machine-gun platoon, whose fate Linna's novel follows, utters one of the final and ultimate lines of the book when he says, "The Union of Soviet Socialist Republics won, but racing to the line for a strong second place came feisty little Finland," finishing his satirical statement with a laugh (Linna 2015: 466).[4]

The depiction of the political conflicts and tensions of the Finnish society as well as the contradictory experiences of the common soldiers were mostly erased and toned down by the 1955 film adaptation. Linna had in fact already faced a moderate censorship when the novel was published in 1954 (also the title was changed from the original *Sotaromaani* [A war novel]).[5] The publisher omitted not only the many four-letter words or expressions that were of sexual nature; the recurring political criticism and the disrespectful attitude toward religion were also toned down, especially parts that criticized the purpose of the war. The film adaptation, however, would take the revisionism even further.

Edvin Laine was given the task to direct the film. He was a trusty craftsman of the Finnish film industry, and *The Unknown Soldier* was the twenty-fifth feature that he directed. Juha Nevalainen, who had worked with Laine before, wrote the script, and Armas Vallasvuo and Osmo Harkimo edited together actual footage from battle with the aim and logic of the fictional narrative. In this way, the film came to both quote history (through the use of archival footage from the front) and construct memory out of the war events.

The making of the film was a delicate task. The original novel had been disparaged both by leading critics and the army. The critics had considered the aesthetics used by Linna as old-fashioned realist prose, whereas representatives of the army claimed that the officers and the women's organizations that supported the troops were depicted in a derogatory manner. Another widespread opinion among the critics was that the common soldier was caricatured too much. Furthermore, the minister of interior affairs was afraid that the making of the film would upset Soviet Union.

However, for the grand premiere, representatives of both the government and the army were present, and everyone was pleased with the result. An indication of the success of the film is that war films never became a popular genre in Finnish filmmaking; very few were made, although many became box office successes. It is rather *The Unknown Soldier* that became the genre, the monumental patriarch in the family of Finnish war films. The second adaptation for the screen from 1985, directed by Rauni Mollberg, and co-scripted by Linna himself, quickly fell to oblivion because it was considered far too pacifist and leftist, although it was widely seen at the time. Mollberg's adaptation is certainly at the top of the box office list of Finnish films, due to the interest in the new version of *The Unknown Soldier*, but it has never been able to compete with Laine's version.

The power of the original adaptation, with its fusion of both Linna's novel and historical representations of the war events, extends even to scholarly historiography of today. In *A History of Finland*, the historian Henrik Meinander not only reads Linna's writing through the reconciliatory eyes of the film but also substitutes the novel with the adaptation:

> In the autumn of 1954 Väinö Linna published his novel . . . in which Finland's progress through the Continuation War was depicted from the often-burlesque grass-roots perspective of the soldiers at the front. It immediately achieved tremendous popularity and was filmed the following year, ensuring its place as the national epic of a modern, independent Finland. Linna was obviously inspired by Finnish comedy films, which tended to make good-natured fun of classic conservative educational ideals. (Meinander 2011: 177)

In this symptomatic anachronistic description of Linna's novel, in which the original text disappears and is replaced by the film adaptation, not only are the boundaries between the novel and the film blurred, but the writing of Linna is also wiped out.[6] The film is thus treated as Linna's own narrative and characterized by its affinity with the adaptation, which in fact succeeded the original novel. The act of relating Linna's writing intertextually to other films downplays the war as the factual context and goes against the author's intentions to criticize the idealism of war propaganda and war narratives. An important context for Linna was to counter the national idealism and heritage of the national poet Johan Ludvig Runeberg and his heroic war epos *Fänrik Ståls Sägner* (1848), which depicted the Finnish war against Russia in 1808–9 and which constituted mandatory reading in Finnish schools.[7]

Meinander's foregrounding of contemporary intertextuality and genre conventions not only is characteristic of a cultural turn in historiography but also erases the conflict lines that typified Finland during the postwar era until the early 1990s. The political tensions of the war events were present in Finnish society throughout the Cold War and rose to the surface whenever a new war film was in the making. For example, in an article discussing the production of the film *Talvisota* (*Winter War*, 1989), it was stated that it was most welcome that Linna's novel had reproduced "the myth of the lost war and overt militarism" and had now received a proper counternarrative that would speak to a new generation (Kalima 1988, my translation).[8]

Meinander's account is symptomatic of Finnish postwar national consolidation in the spirit of a post-1989 Finland, in which Laine's film has become a master signifier and synonym for not only the novel but also for how the war events should be remembered and transmitted to later generations. Certainly *The Unknown Soldier* became a national epic—especially after the ritualistic broadcast every Independence Day on public TV since the 2000s. However, Linna's novel differs from the later uses of the narrative. This is evident not only from Linna's own essays and public lectures that he wrote and presented before the film had premiered but also from the reception of the adaptation at the time. Many of the Finnish critics were positive, but there were significant dissenting voices too. As expected, the left wing attitude was very unfavorable toward the adaptation, but high-profile film critics also had their doubts regarding Laine's and Nevalainen's nationalist adaptation.[9] One of the most respected Finnish film critics, Jerker A. Eriksson, characterized the film as "magnificent" in the literary review *Parnasso*, but he complained that Linna's critique against the officers had largely been omitted from the film adaptation (Eriksson 1956: 94). Eriksson stated that Laine's version had been criticized for being imbued with nationalist sentiment, something that was not "in coherence with the end of the novel by Linna," and added acidly that "a realistic depiction of war may be accepted if you frame it with enough of idealism, 'a defeat is made to victory'" (Eriksson 1956, my translation).[10] The latter was a comment that stressed how the ironic line at the end of the novel about Finland finishing second—and that fulfilled Linna's attack on all idealism associated with the war—was paradoxically changed into an emotional truth, framed and emphasized by Jean Sibelius's music.

It is symptomatic of the success of the film that the novel has fallen into its shadow, being read through its audiovisual narrative. The result is that film has become a national monument for postwar Finland at the expense of the novel. As one letter to the editor of *Helsingin Sanomat*, the largest Finnish newspaper, expressed during the time when the debate raged in 1981–82 over a remake of *The Unknown Soldier*, "It is as if the bombastic music of *Finlandia* was written just and only for *The Unknown Soldier*."[11] The audiovisual narrative of *The Unknown Soldier* had absorbed not only Linna's novel but also Sibelius's music and much of the war experiences.

Accordingly, the film from 1955 became the original narrative, and this out of necessity, of wish and urge to continue with nation-building. Finland was still fragile territory in the early 1950s, a teenage nation as it were, in urgent need of coherent narratives. In Linna's own words, "the war was still buzzing in your mind" in 1954, this coming at the same time that Finland found itself in a new historical situation characterized by Cold War geopolitics in which the Soviet Union not only exerted powerful political influence but also collected war debt and annexed land near Helsinki ("Sota saa puhua itseään vastaan" 1978: 66).[12] No wonder the actors who participated in the film have later reported how its production felt like revenge for the lost war.[13]

The Discursive Formation of *The Unknown Soldier*

I have dwelled on this prehistory of the first film adaptation because the historical background is so important and because the novel and the film have two different contexts, although they have later merged into one and the same narrative with identical imagery. In two previous studies, I have analyzed the legacy of Linna's novel and its first two adaptations and their reception, as well as how *The Unknown Soldier* has affected later war filmmaking, in particular after the end of the Cold War (Sundholm 2007; 2013a). In the first study, I explained the success of the film adaptation and the failure of the adaptation from 1985 by claiming that the first version constituted a founding trauma and a national monument. Whereas the novel, because of its criticism, was a revival of the painful war events, and therefore created debate and tension that had been present in Finnish society since the Civil War, the film was a reconciliatory albeit hegemonic response, a cultural trauma created to offer a survival story that would enable everyone to get on with their lives in 1950s Finland (Sundholm 2011). The more truthful adaptation from 1985, which Linna co-scripted, was a failure because Finland of 1985 was still in need of its cultural trauma.

In the second study, my aim was to analyze whether the adaptation from 1955 still held its grip, and if so, how it influenced other war films that were being made after the end of the Cold War. In that essay I discerned four discourses that characterized the discursive formation and the hegemony of *The Unknown Soldier*—the historical discourse, the discourse of the witness, the discourse of victimization, and the discourse of defensive victory—claiming that they kept their position and upheld the discursive formation although there had been a turn to postmodern memory culture. The historical discourse is the articulation of the view that every war film is foremost a historical document and only partly fiction; the discourse of the witness is one in which every war film is sanctioned by someone who had actually experienced the war events; the discourse of victimization is the articulation of the view that Finland was forced into the Continuation War (thus downplaying the alliance with Nazi Germany) and, because of the threat of extinction of the nation, Finland was a moral witness of the war events; and the discourse of defensive victory stresses Finland as victim and that the last battle during the summer of 1944 was a "defensive victory" against an overwhelming enemy.[14]

The ideological underpinnings of these discourses are the following: *The Unknown Soldier* of 1955 was built on a careful editing and inserting of archival material from the front into the fictive storyline. Thus, actual archival footage that, for example, ends in a close-up is cut to a scene that also starts with a close-up. In this way both history and memory is interwoven, not to deceive—the audience at the time was able to distinguish the two levels—but to stress the film as an actual depiction of what had happened. The other dimension of this strand, which emphasizes that the film is a historical document, is that it is being compared with the sanctioned history of the war events. Hence, the narrative has to follow history, not its own rationale as fiction. This opinion is evident in the comments that were given after the remake of 1985, where it was claimed that the version from 1955 was more historical, than Mollberg's and Linna's attempt to make a film that was more truthful to the spirit of the novel.[15] The ideological underpinning of the discourse of the witness is that an actual war witness sanctions every film after the premiere. The interviews with war veterans, who mostly act according to the sanctioned historiography and thus confirm the narrative, become testimonies that no one can question. Not because of epistemological reasons (that is, if the story is true or not) but because of ethics; everyone who has not been taking part in the war has to be considerate of these men who sacrificed their formative years of youth for the war and suffering. The ideology behind the discourse of the victim is that it offers a position from which one may escape the question of guilt (Sundholm 2013; Ylikangas 2004). That the last battles at the Eastern Front, when the Finnish troops at first withdraw in panic and then succeed in stopping the offensive (partly with help from German troops, partly because the race to Berlin had begun and therefore the Soviet offensive was weakened) receive so much attention in the narratives is so that the Continuation War may be depicted as a defensive struggle and a story about victimization. This had been the frame of the Winter War, which Linna commented upon on the first page of his novel in his distinctive ironic style: "Finland's Winter War had ended: the war that was, of all wars up to then, the best—seeing as both sides won. The Finns, however, won a bit less, in that they were obliged to cede some land to their opponents and retreat behind a new border" (Linna 2015: 1).[16] In fact, the Continuation War was fought in alliance with Nazi Germany during Operation Barbarossa, and thus was originally an attack on Soviet Union. This discourse of victimization is of course closely allied with the ideological underpinning of the discourse of the defensive victory. If Finland was a victim, if it had no choice, then the losses could be justified, and if it furthermore could be shown that Finland actually even partly won, achieving "a strong second place," all the better.

The Unknown Soldier of 2017

The reason why the discursive formation of the *The Unknown Soldier* of 1955 has been able to keep its hegemony, despite the collapse of the Soviet Union in 1991, the fact that Finland entered the EU in 1995, and the fact that communicative memory began to disappear, is due to a persistent nationalist and affirmative historiography. Thus, the question is—although the nationalist historiography in many ways prevails—how does the new adaptation relate to the abovementioned discursive formation and the position of the film as a national monument and founding trauma? In order to answer this question I will compare the film to the first adaptation and to the novel through a reading of the reviews in fifteen leading Finnish newspapers.[17] In my previous studies I have been able to follow the long-term discourse in the papers both before and after the premiere of the films and to relate these to a close analysis of them, but as this chapter is being written while the film is still being screened in the theaters—being an overwhelming box-office hit—I will only use the reviews from the premiere and relate them to the film that is not yet available for private viewing.[18]

The Unknown Soldier of 2017 is directed by Aku Louhimies and co-written by Louhimies and Jari Rantala. Louhimies and Rantala comprise a well-established team who have collaborated successfully since their much-appreciated feature film, *Paha Maa* (*Frozen Land*, 2005). Funding for *The Unknown Soldier* was given both by the Finnish Film Foundation and the Centenary Commission that was established in order to organize and program different events for Finland's celebration of its one hundredth birthday. However, the major part of the funding was collected from private investors. Six weeks after the premiere on 27 October, more than eight hundred thousand Finns had seen the film, which made it the most popular Finnish film since the Finnish Film Foundation established reliable and official statistics for ticket sales.[19] The film exists in two different versions. The original version for the domestic audience is 179 minutes long, whereas the international release is 133 minutes long. The difference in duration is significant for two reasons. It implies that the producers have acknowledged that this version of *The Unknown Soldier* also has a role as a commodity on the international market, but that the domestic market will view the film in the context of the original adaptation, thus constituting a visit to an already seen and heard story. This commercialization of *The Unknown Soldier* is not only a consequence of the substantial private funding behind the film but also a result of the fact that communicative memory has disappeared, and thus the discourse of the witness has weakened.[20] The shortened version that is made for an international market also has explications in the beginning of the film in order to give a historical explanation to why and for whom the Finnish forces fought. This also guarantees sales—war cinema culture has usually reproduced the juxtaposition of Nazi Germany vs. "the rest," whereas the fact is that Finland fought in alliance with the Third Reich—otherwise an international audience might find it difficult to be affected by the destiny of the soldiers that is being pictured on the screen.[21]

The reception of *The Unknown Soldier* among film critics is mixed when it comes to the evaluation of the film, although many agree on its core interpretation, which is that *The Unknown Soldier* of 2017 is a pacifist work that is made in order to honor everyone who took part in the war. In general it is the most established critics, who also write for the biggest newspapers, who tend to be more critical toward the new adaptation. Juho Typpö, who writes for *Helsingin Sanomat*, especially stands out, as he harshly criticized the new adaptation as pointless. He states that the new version is merely a remake of Linna's film because it does not offer a new interpretation or situate the narrative in an actual context of today.[22] Although Typpö appreciates the good acting and the craftsmanship behind the film, this alone cannot justify the making of the new adaptation, and he concludes by claiming that the *The Unknown Soldier* of 2017 is a risk-free and safe celebration of Finland's hundred-year anniversary that aims to please everyone. Many other critics are more appreciative and consider especially the professional update as welcomed because in this way the narrative may be handed over to a new generation. One of the more apt among Finnish film critics, Kari Salminen, summarizes well in his review what may be read from the reception as a whole, namely that the film is a story about heroes and heroic deeds, but an updated one in which (male) heroes also may be afraid; that it is large-scale entertainment in the style of a Hollywood production, albeit with a Finnish touch when it comes to characters and history; and finally that Louhimies's version is the most credible adaptation when it comes to acting and emotional affect, but that despite the professional production the film is merely an update, a translation of a national monument into contemporary cinema language.[23] The critics who were altogether positive in their response emphasized the position of the film as a practice of commemoration, that "we may never forget the ultimate prize for Finland's independence," as, for example, Juhani Nurmi wrote (Nurmi 2017).[24] It is also such reviews that most clearly adhere to parts of the discursive formation of *The Unknown Soldier*, namely the discourse of victimization and defensive victory.

Prosthetic Memory and National Consolidation

One may conclude that the version of *The Unknown Soldier* of 2017 confirms that the discourses of victimization and defensive victory still prevail. On the other hand, the critics neither invoked the historical discourse nor the discourse of the witness, the latter because there are hardly any war veterans left. The disappearance of communicative memory together with the overt intention of the filmmakers to make a professionally produced remake of a classic adaptation explains why the traditional historian's question of what actually happened is of less relevance. What is being offered is affective entertainment and prosthetic memory. Many a critic also described the film as a successful modern work that addresses a contemporary audience, and associations were made to both Terrence Malick's *The Thin Red Line* (1998) and production values and stylistic choices that are typical for Hollywood.[25] Louhimies and Rantala have also chosen to establish a few main characters out of the novel's larger collective, with the character Rokka as the hero and prime object of identification. Accordingly, in *The Unknown Soldier* of 2017 we are introduced for the first time to Rokka's wife and children at the home front. The film also establishes an emotional cliffhanger toward the end when we do not know if Rokka will survive, until the audience is finally relieved when Rokka returns to his nuclear family. In accordance with such an ideology of identification, many scenes that were depicted neutrally in the previous versions now become embodied in the point of view of the main characters. Another example is the well-known scene in which two Finnish soldiers who have ignored orders are being executed. In Laine's version the event is staged as a documentary scene that mostly uses long shots, as if the film is quoting history and addressing everyone, whereas Louhimies has chosen to show the scene as witnessed by Rokka.

The new adaptation is thus symptomatic of what has been coined "prosthetic memory" by Alison Landsberg, which she defines as "a sensuous engagement with the past" through mass-mediated representations that "become . . . the basis for mediated collective identification" (Landsberg 2004: 21). Landsberg claims that prosthetic memory often leads to the creation of counterhegemonic public spheres, a claim that I find doubtful, because you have to take into consideration the context and current discursive formation and hegemony. However, it is no doubt that in its aesthetics and commercial ambitions, *The Unknown Soldier* of 2017 is a prime example of prosthetic memory and builds in that sense on the tradition established by a previous successful Finnish war film, *Rukajärven tie* (*Ambush*, 1999). *Ambush* was arguably the first major Finnish war film that was not judged according to how it depicted history, instead being evaluated as a war film in its own right (Sundholm 2013a). It addressed through brilliant acting the individual rather than the nation and introduced female points of view, sensitive men, and love stories—ingredients that Louhimies and Rantala also use in order to update their version. However, *The Unknown Soldier* of 2017 does not challenge the discursive formation of "The Unknown Soldier" because it offers neither a new interpretation of the novel nor a timely update of Linna's interpretation, as the critic Typpö claimed. The new adaptation is instead faithful to the most common rationale of any war narrative, real or fiction, namely to act in the name of national consolidation. This is not what Linna had aimed at. He refused to accept the idealism of war rhetoric that upheld the idea of a coherent and unified people and nation. According to Linna, these were ideological discourses established in the name of the interest of the dominant social classes, whose victims were the common soldier and the common people. Among the examples of such discourses and war propaganda are writings by intellectuals like Johannes Öquist, who wrote a poem on how the Finns "for thousand years in the North / with sharp eyes day and night / against the uncounted hordes of the Asians / have faithfully guarded the borders of Europe" (Öhquist 1942: 5, my translation);[26] by the author Lorenz von Numers, who Othered Russian soldiers as "Tatar[s] with pitch black hair and coffee brown eyes" or "all kind of Asian trash";[27] and by significant cultural figures like Olof Enckell, who wrote during the beginning of the Continuation War that Finland's battle constituted a necessary "blood sacrifice" that would consolidate the young nation and give it a type of moral anchoring "that history always combines with glorious and powerful deeds" (von Numers 1942: 57; Enckell 1942: 145, my translation).[28] Such writing was Linna's target, positions and interpretations, which are compatible with Laine's and Louhimies's versions of the original narrative. Although *The Unknown Soldier* of 2017 depicts war as a tragic event, in which every soldier is a victim of an irrational cause, it never makes up with the image of Finland as one nation with a unified culture, in contrast to the Russian soldiers as the alien Others, all according to the quotes above by Öhquist and von Numers.[29] A case in point is the depiction of Captain Baranov, who is captured by the heroic soldier Rokka. Linna never describes what Baranov looks like, only depicting him with respect as "sullen and fearless" (Linna 1954: 333, my translation).[30] In the film by Louhimies, Baranov is shown as a dark and frightened man. In the adaptation by Mollberg, which uses a handheld camera and natural lightening, Baranov is barely shown, whereas he is big and stoic but an alien figure in Laine's version.

Väinö Linna's controversial novel was changed into a comforting story by Edvin Laine and Juha Nevalainen, a national monument and founding trauma that Rauni Mollberg with support from Linna tried but failed to unsettle thirty years later, and which is now being refurbished for future use by coming generations—all according to the tradition of nationalist and affirmative historiography.

John Sundholm is Professor of Cinema Studies at Stockholm University. He has published extensively on memory studies and minor cinemas. He is the coeditor of *Memory Work* (2005), *Collective Traumas* (2007), and *European Cultural Memory Post-89* (2013), and coauthor of *A History of Swedish Experimental Film Culture* (2010) and *Historical Dictionary of Scandinavian Cinema* (2012), as well as *Transnational Cinema at the Borders* (Routledge, 2018) and *The Cultural Practice of Minor Immigrant Filmmaking in Sweden 1950–1990* (Intellect, 2019).

Notes

1. I use the title *The Unknown Soldier*, although the recent English translation of the novel has the title *Unknown Soldiers*. Most quotations are from the English translation; in some cases, I have preferred to substitute with my own translation.
2. German original: "Trotz all ihrer Greuel war diese unheimliche Katastrophe für das finnische Volk letzten Endes ein Glück. Denn es war nicht bloss eine Befreiung. Es war ein riesiges Reinemachen, eine Läuterung und Säuberung am Körper und an Seele, ein Aderlass. . . ." Johannes Öhquist, the father of one of the prominent Finnish generals of World War II, Harald Öhquist, was born in Pavlovsk close to St. Petersburg into a polyglot environment with German as his mother tongue. He was appointed as lecturer in German at the University of Helsinki and also wrote extensively on Finnish art and art history. From 1915 he worked in Berlin for the two agencies that were set up in order to promote Finland for the Germans and which also helped Finnish activists of independence. When the first Finnish Embassy was inaugurated in Germany, Öhquist became its press attaché, and in 1925 he was promoted to professor for his service to the country. In the 1930s he resided mostly in Finland at famed architect Eliel Saarinen's combined studio and home, Hvitträsk, which Öhquist rented while Saarinen was in the United States. It was at this time that Öhquist became a devoted supporter of Nazi Germany.
3. "Sillä sodalta minä tahdoin riisua kaiken arvon, mutta sotilaille tahdoin sen antaa" (Linna 2007a: 86).
4. The Finnish original is a bit more brutal: "Sosialististen Neuvostotasavaltojen Liitto voitti, mutta hyvänä kakkosena tuli maaliin pieni sisukas Suomi." [The Union of Soviet Socialist Republics won, but feisty little Finland crossed the line as a good second] (Linna 1954: 444, my translation).
5. The original manuscript, *Sotaromaani* (A war novel), was published in 2000 with the omitted parts printed in italics.
6. As Jukka Sihvonen has pointed out in his book-length study on the film versions of *The Unknown Soldier*, a new book edition with images from the film was released just before the premiere of the film, which further contributed to the merging of the film and the novel at the expense of the latter (Sihvonen 2009). The images that were inserted into the middle of the book all had a page reference and sometimes also a direct quote from the corresponding part.
7. This was addressed by Linna himself in many essays, most explicitly in "Runeberg ja suomalainen kansalaismentaliteetti" (Linna 2007b). When the writer Olof Enckell toured in Sweden during the winter of 1941 to inform fellow authors about the situation of the Finnish writers, he was quoted expressing that "Johan Ludvig Runeberg was the Commander in Chief for all of us," (*Dagens Nyheter*, 21 February 1941). One of Linna's points in the essay on Runeberg is that his writing was pitched for a certain class and social strata and that it was this address and class-based idealism that upheld the notion of a unified people (Linna 2007b). Interestingly enough, the critics in Sweden pointed out that you could also read the novel as a nationalist contribution, seeing Linna as an updated Runeberg. For the reception in Sweden, see Järv 1971.
8. The two sentences in Finnish: "Suomalaisilla on lähihistoriasta ollut pitkälti se mielikuva, joka on syntynyt Väinö Linnan Tuntemattomasta sotilaasta. Myytti hävityksestä sodasta ja sotahulluudesta leimasi ajattelua pitkään."
9. The reception of the film is covered extensively in Sundholm 2007 and Sihvonen 2009.
10. "lopun isänmaallisuus ei ole sopusoinnussa Linnan kirjan päätöksen kanssa"; "realistinen sotakuvaus voidaan helposti hyväksyä, jos taisteluille annetaan sopivan idealistinen kehystys, 'tappio joka muuttui voitoksi.'"

11. "Tuntuu kuin Finlandian jyhkeä musiikki olisi sävelletty juuri ja vain Tuntematonta sotilasta varten." Letter to the editor, *Helsingin Sanomat*, 3 January 1982.
12. "sota vielä humisi tajunnassa."
13. For example, in an interview with Matti Ranin, *Helsingin Sanomat*, 5 September 2004.
14. It was the lieutenant general K. L. Oesch who launched the so-called driftwood theory—that Finland was a victim of historical forces—and that the last battle at the Eastern Front was a defensive victory. According to Meinander the latter view stretched "the concept of victory to an absurd degree" but "was essentially right" (1999: 262).
15. Rauno Velling in a column for the newspaper *Aamulehti*, 7 January 1986.
16. "Suomen talvisota oli sodittu, sota joka oli kaikista siihenastisista paras, sillä siinä voittivat molemmat osapuolet. Suomalaiset voittivat sikäli vähemmän, että heidän täytyi luovuttaa alueitaan vastustajilleen ja vetäytyä tämän johdosta syntyneen uuden rajan taakse" (Linna 1954, 5). The translation is somewhat missing the laconic and ironic style of the original that indicates a criticism of the postwar explanation of World War II, namely that Finland always seems to win the wars: "Finland's Winter War had been fought, a war that hitherto had been the best, because both sides won. The Finns won to a lesser extent as far as that they had to give up land to their opponents and therefore to withdraw behind a newly created border" (my translation).
17. Tiina Junttila at the National Audiovisual Institute of Finland has kindly provided me with copies of the reviews.
18. This is obviously a deficiency because repeated viewing is a premise for any close analysis of a film, and memory practices and historiographical habits are long-term dynamic processes that have to be studied over time (Sundholm 2007; 2011).
19. Statistics for the most popular Finnish films ever can be found at the website of the Finnish Film Foundation: http://ses.fi/tilastot-ja-tutkimukset/vuositilastot/kaikkien-aikojen-katsotuimmat/ (accessed 17 December 2017).
20. The difference between communicative and cultural memory is roughly that the former is living memory, present in everyday interaction, whereas the latter is materialized into objects and material remnants. Thus, a communicative memory is upheld as long as the generation is present that actually experienced the events. Cultural memory comes to the fore when there is no living memory left. A lot of merchandise was also launched in connection to the making of the film—coffee, mineral water, cleaning sets—thus making Louhimies's version the most commercially exploited one.
21. Due to this simplification of war history on the screen and the difficulties with putting Finland into such a scenario—the country being successful in its discourse of victimization—you may run into summaries such as the following one that advertised the screening of Laine's version in London in 2007: "Popular WWII feature based on Väinö Linna's novel about the trials of the young Finnish soldiers engaged in the desperate Winter campaign against the Nazis in the early 1940s" (Sibelius 2007: 96).
22. *Helsingin Sanomat*, 27 October 2017.
23. *Turun Sanomat*, 27 October 2017.
24. "Emme saa koskaan unohtaa Suomen vapauden äärimmäistä hintaa."
25. For example, Rane Aunimo in *Demokraatti*, 26 October 2017; Harri Hautala in *Aamulehti*, 27 October 2017; Jorma Valkola in *Keskisuomalainen*, 27 October 2017.
26. German original: "Wohl tausend Jahr hast du im Norden/mit scharfen Auge Tag und Nacht/vor Asien ungezählten Horden/Europas Grenzen Treu bewacht."
27. "tatar med becksvart lugg och kaffebruna ögon"; "allsköns centralasiatiskt patrask."
28. The full sentence in Swedish: "Men på den andra sidan föreföll det mig obestridligt, att Finlands folk—genom ett aktivt, målmedvetet och med blodsoffer hävda sin värdighet på samma gång som sin rätt—nu grundmurade sin unga självständighet och gav sin frihet

den moraliskt förankrade hävd, som historien alltid kombinerar med ärofulla, slagkraftiga handlingar."
29. When Soviet soldiers were imprisoned by Finnish forces, it was estimated that these represented eighty-seven different ethnic groups. Finns who belonged to the Jewish, Tatarian, or Roma communities fought in the Finnish army as well, as did the Swedish-speaking minority and volunteers, for example, from Sweden, Denmark, and Estonia. Of these, the Finnish Jews were obviously in the strangest situation. Taru Mäkelä has made a documentary about the situation of the Finnish Jews who fought for Finland (and with Nazi Germany) during World War II: *Daavid: Tarinoita kunniasta ja häpeästä* (Daavid: Stories about honor and shame, 1997); see Sundholm 2013b.
30. The English translation describes Baranov as "churlish, fearless" (Linna 2015: 349).

References

Ambush [*Rukajärven tie*]. 1999. Directed by Olli Saarela. Matila Röhr Productions.
Enckell, Olof. 1942. *Rapport från ödemarken*. Stockholm: Natur och kultur.
Eriksson, Jerker A. 1956. "Elokuvaa." *Parnasso* 2: 94–95.
Järv, Harry. 1971. "Linnakritiken i Sverige." In *Läsarmekanismer*, 367–83. Lund: Bo Cavefors.
Kalima, Tom. 1988. "Talvisota puhuttelee vasta nyt nuorisoa." *Uusi Suomi*, 6 December.
Landsberg, Alison. 2004. *Prosthetic Memory: The Transformation of American Remembrance in the Age of Mass Culture*. New York: Columbia University Press.
Linna, Väinö. 1954. *Tuntematon sotilas*. Helsinki: WSOY.
———. 2000. *Sotaromaani*. Helsinki: WSOY
———. 2007a [1955]. "Tuntemattoman sotilaan taustaa." In *Väinö Linna: Esseitä*, 82–87. Helsinki: WSOY.
———. 2007b [1964]. "Runeberg ja suomalainen kansalaismentaliteetti." In *Väinö Linna: Esseitä*, 238–51. Helsinki: WSOY.
———. 2015. *Unknown Soldiers*. Translated by Liesl Yamaguchi. London: Penguin Random House.
Meinander, Henrik. 2004. *Finlands historia 4*. Helsingfors: Schildts.
———. 2011. *A History of Finland*. London: Hurst & Co.
Numers, Lorenz von. 1942. "Eldlinjen förbyttes till etapp på en enda natt." In *I fält med Finlands armé 1941*, edited by Henrik Antell, 54–59. Stockholm: C. E. Fritzes.
Nurmi, Juhani. 2017. "Upeita näyttelijöitä modernissa sovituksessa." *Kaleva* 27, October 2017.
Ruin, Olof. 2000. *Sverige i min spegel*. Stockholm: Hjalmarson & Högberg.
"Sibelius on Film." 2007. *Time Out London* 1941: 96.
Sihvonen, Jukka. 2009. *Idiootti ja Samurai: "Tuntematon sotilas" elokuvana*. Turku: Eetos.
"Sota saa puhua itseään vastaan." 1978. [Interview with Väinö Linna]. *Suomen Kuvalehti* 2: 66–67.
Sundholm, John. 2007. "'The Unknown Soldier': Film as a Founding Trauma and National Monument." In *Collective Traumas: Memories of War and Conflict in 20th-Century Europe*, edited by Conny Mithander, John Sundholm, and Maria Holmgren Troy, 111–41. Brussels: P.I.E. Peter Lang.
———. 2011. "The Cultural Trauma Process, or the Ethics and Mobility of Memory." In *Migrating Memory: Multidisciplinary Approaches to Memory Studies*, edited by Julia Creet and Andreas Kitzmann, 120–34. Toronto: University of Toronto Press.

———. 2013a. "Finland at War on Screen since 1989: Affirmative Historiography and Prosthetic Memory." In *European Cultural Memory Post-89*, edited by Conny Mithander, John Sundholm, and Adrian Velicu, 209–39. Amsterdam: Rodopi.

———. 2013b. "Stories of National and Transnational Memory: Renegotiating the Finnish Conception of Moral Witness and National Victimhood." In *Finland's Holocaust: Silences of History*, edited by Simo Muir and Hana Worthen, 31–45. Basingstoke: Palgrave.

The Unknown Soldier. 1955. Directed by Edvin Laine. Suomen Filmiteollisuus.

The Unknown Soldier. 1985. Directed by Rauni Mollberg. Arctic-Filmi.

The Unknown Soldier. 2017. Directed by Aku Louhimies. Elokuvaosakeyhtiö Suomi.

Winter War [*Talvisota*]. 1989. Directed by Pekka Parikka. National Filmi OY.

Ylikangas, Heikki. 2004. "Muutokset tutkimuksen suuntautumisessa." *Historiallinen Aikakausikirja* 1: 29–32.

Öhquist, Johannes. 1919. *Finnland*. Leipzig: B.G. Tauner.

———. 1942. *Das Kämpfende Finnland*. Stuttgart: Alemannen Verlag, Albert Jauss.

Epilogue

There are still many unturned stones in the study of World War II history and cultural memory in the Nordic Region. Due to practical considerations, constraints of time, and the availability of scholarship, this volume is limited to the study of five national entities and linguistic groups in the Nordic region. Ideally, it might have covered more. Obviously missing are the former "colonial subjects" and Indigenous minorities of the Nordic region, including Greenland (an autonomous, self-governing territory of Denmark), and Sápmi (Lapland, reaching across northern Norway, Sweden, Finland, and Russia), both of which constitute important resource-rich territories in the Arctic region that held vital strategic interests for both Allied and Axis powers during and after World War II. The Inuit of Greenland and the Sámi peoples of Scandinavia's Arctic region were profoundly affected by the global conflict of 1939–45 and remain understudied in the context of World War II and the postwar decades. Future scholarship has yet to examine fully the effects of the war on these Indigenous communities, and their communicative and cultural war memory. Further, the volume also omits the Faroe Islands (today a self-governing territory of Denmark)—the Faroes were occupied by British forces in Operation Valentine within days of Germany's occupation of Denmark, and they withdrew shortly after the war's end. Last but not least, the volume might possibly have included chapters dealing with the three Baltic states in World War II, Estonia, Latvia, and Lithuania, which suffered three brutal occupations during this period (by the Soviet Union, by Nazi Germany, and again by the Soviet Union). Similar to Finland's geopolitical position in the war, the study of the Baltic States is vital to a broader understanding of the "eastern" pressure on the Nordic nations during the war. Including the histories and cultural memory of the Baltic countries in this collaborative study would have been an enormous, albeit highly relevant, undertaking; however, it reached beyond my area of scholarship and expertise.

Furthermore, I readily admit that the literary and cinematic texts selected from the five Nordic national entities for parts II, III, and IV of the volume also reflect the limitations of a single-volume project. Close readings of representational texts were favored over a more comprehensive approach, which might possibly have incorporated a wider range of literary and cinematic works. While I am aware of the shortcomings of this project, I am hopeful that this edited volume paves the way for continued scholarship in the field in the future.

As noted in my introduction to the volume, the autumn of 2019 marked eight decades since the outbreak of World War II on 3 September 1939, when the Allies (France and Great Britain) made the declaration of war in response to Hitler's invasion of Poland. Three months later, in late November 1939, the Soviet Union attempted a massive invasion into Finland, launching the mythic Russo-Finnish Winter War, an infamous disaster for Stalin's Red Army. At the time of this writing, the Nordic nations have already marked eighty years since the Wehrmacht (armed forces of Nazi Germany) swiftly invaded Denmark and Norway on 9 April—and since British military forces occupied Iceland on 10 May 1940.

At present, we stand at the end—or very near the end—of a *saeculum* (the potential lifetime of a person; approximately three generations), which was initiated by World War II. Soon eight decades will have passed since the totalitarian regimes of Nazi Germany and Soviet Russia carried out military aggressions, occupations, massive deportations, and genocide. I evoke the term *saeculum* as a measure of historical time, as its significance resonates with historians and sociologists as well as memory theorists. The passing of the generation of people that stored, silenced, transmitted, and ritualized communicative war memories signals a dramatic change in climate, not only in the field of cultural memory study but also in the cultural, social, and national politics of our planet. Notably, Fascism (or Nazism) as the "bastard child" or stunted "dwarf" of humanity—which Scandinavian writers Sigurd Hoel and Pär Lagerkvist illustrated metaphorically in their masterpiece novels of the 1940s—has reared its ugly face again on the European continent as well as here in the United States, under the guise of confederate flags and swastikas among counterprotesters at public demonstrations.

As a *postgeneration* scholar interested in history, literature, and cultural memory, I have strived to situate Denmark's occupation with respectful historical relativism—the wartime conditions in Denmark were hardly those of Poland or the Baltic states. Among the German forces in northern Europe, Denmark earned the ironic designation, "the whipped-cream front." Nonetheless, any study of violence, war, exile, trauma or displacement must not be reduced to a competition in human suffering. Late in the war, the leader (a woman) of my late father's resistance group in Copenhagen was arrested (she later escaped the prison under an RAF bombing), and young men in their underground group were also arrested. My father and his younger teenaged brother were hunted by German officers and fled to Sweden by boat—earlier, in October of 1943, they had assisted with the escape of Danish Jews by the same passage. In neutral Sweden, they both enlisted in the Danish Brigade (also known as Danforce), joining the five thousand trained Danish soldiers there—among them were many other resistance fighters. Several years after the war, my parents met in Copenhagen, married in 1953, and promptly immigrated, first to Canada and later to the United States. I now understand that my father's experiences during the five years of the occupation left deep psychic scars—even though we may count him among the most fortunate participants and witnesses during the war. In Sweden in 1944–45, my father apparently spoke with Baltic refugees who related the incomprehensible brutality of their experiences—and there he also witnessed the arrival of the thousands of skeletal survivors rescued from Germany's concentration camps by the Red Cross "white buses" in the early spring of 1945.

At the time of this writing, I find myself in Seattle. Here, like citizens around the globe, we are in the midst of two intersecting crises—a global pandemic (Covid-19) and mass public demonstrations over racial inequality and police brutality, sparked by the killing of George Floyd. This global tsunami of pandemic and protest could not have been foreseen three years ago when this book project was initiated. Nonetheless, over the past decade, the growing number of right-wing political parties, increasing populist politics, anti-immigrant sentiment, a rise in hate crimes and anti-Semitism, and blatant far-right extremism in both the United States and Europe—including, sadly, the Nordic countries—evince a radical and destabilizing shift in Western democracies that has not been witnessed to this extreme for three generations.

When political leaders, ordinary citizens, aged survivors, and elderly veterans recently commemorated the liberation of Germany's death camps and the seventy-fifth anniversary of VE day (Victory in Europe) on 8 May 2020, the global pandemic, which would soon reveal the deep ravines and divisions of our modern world and remind us of the persistent socioeconomic and racial inequities of our societies, had already swept the globe and inflicted populations in radically diverse national, regional, and local environments. Perhaps we could have anticipated the civic outrage and global protests that we are now experiencing and witnessing every day. It is my hope that the present study will engender further intellectual inquiry, historical insight, and personal reflections that are relevant to our current global crises, and that it will enhance understandings of the role of mass-mediated visual technologies in the shaping of public opinion and cultural memory.

—Marianne Stecher-Hansen
Seattle, 15 June 2020

Index

Aasen, Ivar, 141, 148n6
Act of Union (Iceland), 72
acts of remembrance, 52, 169, 312
Afghanistan, 298–99
aircraft invasion routes, 9
Allied/Axis powers: The Atlantic Charter of, 138; Germany's surrender to, 246; Indigenous minorities and, 330; Nazi Germany against, 5; *Return to the Future* for, 118, 137; Soviet Union joining, 143
Allies: fraternization, intimate relations with, 74–77, 224–28, 253, 255; Grand Alliance with, 50, 59, 62, 285; Western, 85, 88
Allies, in relation to Nordic countries, 8–10, 12–14, 137, 331; Grand Alliance and, 50, 59, 62, 285; Western Allies and, 85, 88
Allmänna Säkerhetstjänsten (STJ), 92
All Quiet on the Western Front (film, Milestone), 233, 299
All Quiet on the Western Front (novel, Remarque), 190, 233
Almgren, Carl Eric, 249
Åmark, Klas, 243, 245, 249
ambiguity, 82
ambivalence, 102, 117
Ambush (*Rukajärven tie*), 324
Andenæs, Johannes, 172
Andersen, Hans Christian, 129
Andrézel, Pierre (Dinesen; pseudonym of Karen Blixen), 131
The Angelic Avengers (Dinesen), 131
Angst (Branner), 151, 158; life and death narrative of, 159–62; potentiality-of-being in, 165n12; translations in, 166n20
"Angst" (Branner), 156
Anti-Comintern Pact, 36

anti-Semitism/anti-Semitic, 120–21, 247, 249; in Danish history, 39–40, 43; far-right extremism and, 332; in *Hitler Youth Quex*, 106; Western democracies and, 87, 332
anxiety, 165n11, 177
Arendt, Hannah, 116–17, 130
army border guards, 83
army mobilization, of Sweden, 84
Aryan race, 55, 102–4; Nordic people and, 137; in *Olympia* film, 107, 110
Asbæk, Pilou, 284, 288, 297, 298
Assmann, Aleida, 4, 8, 22, 235
Assmann, Jan, 2, 8, 297
Astarte (Boye), 103
The Atlantic Charter, 138
Atomic Station (film), 258–59, 264–65, 266nn11–15; defense treaty in, 253, 261; NATO controversy in, 234; women in, 260
The Atom Station (novel – Laxness), 258, 259, 261
atrocities, victims of, 293–94
August uprising (Denmark), 37
Aunesluoma, Juhana, 18, 186

Bak, Sofie Lene, 18, 155
Balling, Erik, 256
Baltic refugee soldiers, 203, 207–12
Baltic Sea, 4
Behrendt, Poul, 124
Being and Nothingness (Sartre), 156
Benjamin, Walter, 10
Berger, Stefan, 77
Berlin, Germany, 97–98, 128
Bernadotte, Folke, 89, 204
Best, Werner, 286

The best of mothers (*Äideistä parhain*, Hietamies), 269
Between a Mountain and a Shore (*Milli fjalls og fjöru*), 266n2
Bhabha, Homi K., 77
bicycle infantry divisions, 288–89
Billquist, Ulla, 238–40, 250n2
Billquist-Roussel, Åsa, 240, 250n2
Bíódagar (*Movie Days*), 255
Bjarnason, Ágúst H., 75
Björk, Leif, 108
Bjørneboe, Jens, 172, 174
Björnsdóttir, Inga Dóra, 221, 225, 230n10
Björnstrand, Gunnar, 246
Black love (*Musta rakkaus*, Linna), 191
Blixen, Karen. *See* Dinesen, Isak
blood-and-soil, 74, 141
bloody Hitler! (*Jävla Hitler!*), 248
Blücher (cruiser), 54, 309
Boëthius, Maria-Pia, 93
Bolshevik Revolution, 144
Bolshevism, 57, 87
Boye, Karin, 11, 97, 99; *Astarte* by, 103; cinema ambivalence of, 106–7; *Crisis* by, 103–4; erotic fanaticism from, 108–9; fascism view of, 103–4, 112; *Hitler Youth Quex* by, 106; Jewish culture admired by, 114n17; *Kallocain* by, 103, 106; National Socialism encounter of, 98, 103–4, 107, 109–10, 112; Nazi Germany opposition of, 112; on *Olympia*, 101–3, 107, 109–10; popular culture and, 105–6; Soviet Union trip of, 113n6; Third Reich experience of, 103; travel diary of, 105
Der brænder en Ild (A Fire is Burning), 156–57
Branner, Hans Christian, 151, 155–56, 162–64
Bredsdorff, Thomas, 206
Britain: *Någonstans i Sverige* bias to for, 249; Norway's alliance with, 60–61; ordered de-mining of Danish coast, 284; Reykjavík harbor with warships from, 252–53
British Navigation Acts, 59
British SOE (Special Operations Executive): resistance in Norway, 58; supported resistance in Denmark, 293
British soldiers, in Iceland, 71–74
Bryld, Claus, 152, 155

Büchner, Georg, 129
Buk-Swienty, Tom, 290
By force (*Under Tvang*), 284

Cappelen, Johan, 172
Carlsson, Janne, 242
Carl XVI Gustaf (king of Sweden), 204
censorship, 86, 119, 130
children: defamiliarization and, 279n4; Finland evacuating, 269–70, 279, 279n1; rights of, 138–40; Sweden and evacuation of, 187; war, 82, 143, 187, 278–79; as Winter War refugees, 270
Christensen, Jesper, 308
Christian X (king of Denmark), 243, 284, 287
Churchill, Winston, 60, 138, 247–49, 282
Churchillian view, 7–8, 249
cinema, 106–7, 253–56
civilian/military resistance, 42–43, 58
civil war, 3, 18, 22, 41, 315
Cold Trails (*Kalde spor*), 305–6
Cold War, 28–31, 93–94, 217–18; in "Angst," 156; Finland during, 25, 318–20; Iceland during, 67; 9th of April cry during, 43–44; *The Unknown Soldier* (Linna) during, 194
collaboration (political), 11, 18, 39, 53, 57–58
collaborators ("quislings"), 172, 174, 181–82
collective memory, 169, 234, 277–78, 296–97; of Denmark, 38; events shaping, 11; from "Freedom and Culture" exhibit, 19, 66; Halbwachs's concept of, 8, 186; of Iceland, 68; moral conflict in, 271; of occupation, 41–43, 45–46, 155; oral communications in, 3; Rothberg and, 10; from *The Unknown Soldier*, 186–87, 191–93, 196–98; through *The Unknown Soldier*, 191–92; of war experience, 151
collective novel, 75, 187, 190
commemoration, act of, 18, 22–23, 30, 38, 152, 297
communicative memory, 2, 8, 327n20
Communist Party, 38; disease of, 144; Norwegians in, 149n11; Soviet's fall of, 44
compassion, 272–75
compensation law, 38

Index • 335

concentration camps: Danish police sent to, 37; Jews transported to, 86–87; *Koncentrationsläger* as, 246
Conrad, Joseph, 175, 182n5
constitutional monarchies, 3
Continuation War, 24; of Finland, 152, 185–87, 272–73; during Operation Barbarossa, 321
Copenhagen, 41–42, 44
Corell, Synne, 169
coup d'état, 133n15
Crises of Memory and the Second World War (Suleiman), 11
Crisis (Boye), 103–4
The crisis of humanism (Humanismens krise), 161, 163
crisis of memory, 152, 170, 174–79
cruiser (*Blücher*), 54, 309
cultural hierarchy, 75–76
cultural influence, 254–55
cultural life, of Third Reich, 129–30
cultural memory, 8, 151, 153, 292; communicative difference with, 327n20; Danish, 296–97; of Finnish culture, 186, 190; historiography and, 13; of Holocaust, 10–12; Laine, E., and, 314; in "Letters from a Land at War," 118; of northern Europe, 4–12; from *The Unknown Soldier*, 195; from *The Unknown Soldier* (Linna), 152; war films as, 282–83; of World War II, 2–3, 233–35
cultural radicalism, 171, 314

Dahl, Ellen, 120, 130, 131
Dahl, Hans Fredrik, 53
Danforce (Danish Brigade), 284, 332
Dano-Prussian war, 155, 290
"Dante's Hell, above earth" (Dinesen), 129
The death of Danton (*Dantons Tod*), 129
death penalty, 171–72
Decker, Christof, 272
defamiliarization, 279n4
defense treaty, 261
de-mining operation, 284–85, 297
Democracy, 147
Denmark, 3; Act of Union with, 72; Afghanistan with troops from, 298–99; Anti-Comintern Pact signed by, 36; anti-Semitism in history of, 39–40, 43; brigades from, 284, 332; Christian X king of, 243, 284, 287; collective memory of, 38; concentration camps and police from, 37; cultural memory of, 296–97; Geneva Convention signed by, 299n3; German occupation of, 6, 9, 35–37, 45–46, 283–87; Germany's protection of, 35–37; hidden resistance of, 38–39; Iceland ties severed with, 67; Jews rescued from, 43, 88, 286, 332; *Land of Mine* film from, 282–84; "Letters from a Land at War" in journal from, 118; liberation of, 37–38; moral narrative in, 44–46; neutrality of, 120; *9th of April* film and, 282–83, 287–91, 298–99; Policy of Collaboration, 39–40; Policy of Cooperation, 18, 40, 43–44; Policy of Negotiation, 18, 40, 285–86, 300n14; *Politiken* newspaper in, 119–22, 285; Sweden with forces from, 92, 332; as Third Reich protectorate, 18, 36–37; Waffen-SS of, 40; war films produced in, 283–84; Wehrmacht fighting, 13; Wehrmacht's executive power of, 36–37; women of, 42; World War II experience of, 282–83
Devil's Island (film), 164, 234, 255, 261–65, 267nn16–20
Dinesen, Isak (Karen Blixen), 97, 99; *The Angelic Avengers* by, 131; in Berlin, 128; Blixen, Karen, as, 116, 128–30, 132n2, 134n30; cloak of neutrality of, 117; "Dante's Hell, above earth" by, 129; German National Socialists and, 127–28; National Socialism depiction by, 126–27; Nazi Germany observations of, 122–23, 125, 130–31; "Old Hero in Bremen" by, 123–24; *Out of Africa* by, 98, 119; political interest of, 118–19; *Seven Gothic Tales* by, 98; *Shadows on the Grass* by, 125; "Strength and Joy" by, 127; *Winter's Tales* by, 124; World War II aesthetic vision of, 131–32. *See also* "Letters from a Land at War"
Ditlevsen, Tove, 156, 292
"Do We Need a New History of the Second World War?" (Keegan), 7
Doxtater, Amanda, 98
Dreamland (*Draumalandið*), 260
driftwood theory, 28–29, 327n14
Dunkirk (Nolan), 7, 282
The Dwarf (Lagerkvist, P.), 1, 300n13

Edda film, 266n2, 266n6
Edvardsen, Annu, 279n3
Eichmann, Adolf, 130
1864 (television), 290, 297
Einsatzkommando (mobile killing squads), 30
Eisenhower, Dwight D., 248
Eisenstein, Sergei, 102
Ejdrup Hansen, Elle-Mie, 300n15
Ekelöf, Gunnar, 121
Elliott, David, 160, 166n19
Elsaesser, Thomas, 274
Enckell, Olof, 325, 326n7
Enquist, Per Olov, 152–53, 202–4
Eriksson, Jerker A., 319
Erkko, Eljas, 243
Erlander, Tage, 211
Erll, Astrid, 152
erotic fanaticism, 108–9
EU. *See* European Union
eugenics, 75
Europe, northern, 4–12
European Union (EU), 13, 321
expressionist arts, 166n19
Ezra, Roni, 282–83, 287

Fagerström, Allan, 241
family melodrama, 308–9
fanatic religion, 117–18
Fänrik Ståls Sägner (Runeberg), 190, 199n9, 318
De får inte hända igen, 279n3
far-right extremism, 332
fascism: Boye's view on, 103–4, 112; after Holocaust, 103–4; National Socialism and, 99; psychology of, 106; of Third Reich, 104
Faurschou-Hviid, Bent, 45
Figueiredo, Ivo de, 310
film industry: Iceland's production in, 254–56; Nazi Germany production in, 106–7, 129; under Third Reich, 129; Third Reich propaganda in, 106. *See also specific film*
Finland, 3; children evacuated from, 269–70, 279, 279n1; civil war in, 315; Cold War independence of, 25, 318–20; Continuation War of, 152, 185–87, 272–73; driftwood theory of, 28–29; EU entered by, 321; foreign policy of, 25–26;

German allegiance with, 5; historiography of cultural, 23, 27, 198; Hitler's visit to, 27; Holocaust's influence on, 29–30; Independence Day of, 22; independence earned by, 32; Jews from, 328n29; Laine, E., as viewed by, 318; *Mother of Mine* film from, 234; Operation Barbarossa joined by, 24–25; postwar revisionist view of, 25–28; reparations of, 32n3; Russo-Finnish War of, 6; soldiers campaign from, 327n21; sovereignty of, 17–18; Soviet aggression against, 24, 241–43; Soviet soldiers imprisoned by, 328n29; Sweden and importance of, 82–83; Third Reich's alliance with, 322; three wars of, 24; victimization discourse of, 327n21; war chosen by, 29–31; Wehrmacht and, 83; Winter War in, 327n16, 327n21; in World War II, 22–23, 198–99
Finland and World War II, 1939–1944 (Wuorinen), 28
Finnish National Theatre, 192, 194–95
Finnish War (1808–9), 199n9
A Fire is Burning (*Der brænder en Ild, Branner*), 156–57
Flame and Citron (*Flammen og Citronen*), 45, 283
Fogh Rasmussen, Anders, 44, 300n14
Folkestrejken (General Strike), 41–42
Følsgaard, Mikkel Boe, 293, 295
Fontander, Björn, 148n2
food and fuel rationing, 84
foreign policy, of Finland, 25–26
foreign service members, 254
foreign soldiers (American soldiers), 253–56
Forslund, Bengt, 238
Fourth Commandment speech, 138–40
fraternization, intimate relations with Allied soldiers, 74–77, 224–28, 253, 255
fraternization, intimate relations with German soldiers, 42, 53, 280n10, 300n16
Freedom and Culture exhibition, 65–67
Friðriksson, Friðrik Þór, 261–62
"From Trauma to Heroism" (Iversen), 303
Frozen Land (*Paha Maa*), 322
Frydenholm (Scherfig), 300n16
functionalism, 40

General Strike, 41–42
The Generation of Postmemory (Hirsch), 11

Geneva Convention, 284–85, 299n3
Gerhardt, Karl, 91
German Expressionism, 160
German National Socialists, 127–28
German soldiers, 42; at railway station, 250n7; women leaving with, 280n10
"The German soldiers" ("De tyske soldater," Ditlevsen), 292
German-Soviet Treaty of Nonaggression, 4
German tarts (*Tyskertøse*), 42
Germany, 3; Allied powers and surrender of, 246; army border guards of, 83; Berlin in, 97–98, 128; Denmark protected by, 35–37; Denmark's occupation by, 6, 9, 35–37, 45–46; Finland's allegiance with, 5; Hansson and conflict in, 91; historiography of occupation by, 39–41; master race of, 137, 142; mental illness of, 147, 181; moral defeat of, 128–29; Norway occupied by, 6, 54–58, 62; Soviet Union attacked by, 56–57, 84–85; Sweden concerned about war with, 83–84; Sweden's transit agreement with, 142–43; Sweden with troops from, 86–87; World War II tide turns against, 286
Gilmour, John, 19, 204, 243, 249
The Girl Gogo (film), 253–58, 264–65; dress in, 266n7; Edda film and, 266n2; U.S. soldiers in, 234
Gíslason, Gylfi Þ., 76
The goal (*Päämäärä*, Linna), 191
The golden island (*Gulleyjan*), 261
Gordon, Terri, 110
Göring, Hermann, 107
Grafström, Sven, 90
Grand Alliance, 50, 59, 62, 285
"Great Undertakings in Berlin" (Dinesen), 125
Greece, 102, 110–12
Grieg, Nordahl, 161
Grimnes, Ole Kristian, 53
"Grógaldr" (poem), 69
guilty conscience, 180
Gulleyjan (The golden island), 261
Günter, Martin, 122
Gustav V (king of Sweden), 83, 88, 243

Haakon VII (king of Norway), 49, 69, 243, 309, 312

Hæstrup, Jørgen, 39
Hagemann, Helge, 284, 291
Hagener, Malte, 274
Halbwachs, Maurice, 8, 186
Hálfdanarson, Guðmundur, 19, 217, 252
Hallgrímsson, Jónas, 69
Hamm, Christine, 98
Hanel, Margot, 108
Hansson, Per Albin, 241, 243–44; ambiguity used by, 82; German conflict and, 91; as Sweden's prime minister, 19, 211–12; Swedish army and, 84–86
Happy Times in Norway (Undset, S.), 148n2
Harald V (king of Norway), 308
Harkimo, Osmo, 317
Härö, Klaus, 12, 269, 272, 274
Hasager, Niels, 120
Hedin, Sven, 121–22
Hedling, Erik, 234
Heidenreich, Carl, 176–79
Heidenreich, Karsten, 176–77
Heidenreich, Maria ("Kari"), 176–77
Helgadóttir, Herdís, 230n10
Helgason, Hallgrímur, 76
Hemstad, Ylva, 278
Henningsen, Erik H., 206
Henningsen, Poul, 167n31
Hietamies, Heikki, 269
Himmler, Heinrich, 55, 89, 130
Hirsch, Marianne, 2, 11–12
"The Historical Text as Literary Artifact" (White), 7
historiography, 285, 315, 317–18; from Bak, 283; cultural memory and, 13; in Finnish culture, 23, 27, 198; of German occupation, 39–41; Iceland's war and, 217; literary imagination in, 7; in *Meeting at the Milestone*, 152; of *North of War*, 224; of Norwegian war, 49–54, 169–70; Soviet Karelia occupation in, 30; on Sweden, 240–41, 247, 249; in *The Unknown Soldier* (Linna), 192; from war veterans, 321; of World War II, 17–19
A History of Finland (Meinander), 317
Hitler, Adolf, 246; Finland visited by, 27; Germanic master race from, 137, 142; invading Russia, 4, 82, 138; mass appeal of, 104, 120; at Olympic games, 101–2; Sweden remarks by, 83

Hitler Youth Quex (Boye), 106
Hoel, Nic, 107
Hoel, Sigurd, 1, 11, 152, 169–71, 173, 300n13, 331
Hofmann, Louis, 295
Holmila, Antero, 30
Holocaust, 39–40, 241, 247; cultural memory of, 10–12; fascism after, 103–4; Finland influenced by, 29–30; "Letters from a Land at War" and, 121; survivor's guilt and, 93; World War II episode of, 87–90
the Home Front, 58, 61–62
homoeroticism, 110
homosexuality, 108, 250n2
Horne, John, 225
human being (*människa*), 209–12
The Human Condition (Arendt), 116
"Humanismens krise" (The crisis of humanism), 161, 163
humanitarianism, 204
Huntington, Constant, 119, 130
Hutcheon, Linda, 152, 186
Hvidsten Gruppen (*This Life*), 45, 283

Iceland, 3, 13; Act of Union with, 72; British soldiers in, 71–74; during Cold War, 67; collective memory of, 68; cultural hierarchy and, 75–76; Danish ties severed with, 67; film production in, 254–56; foreign soldiers in cinema in, 253–56; freedom regained by, 70; historiography of war in, 217; moral decay in, 74–75; national freedom in, 78; national rule in, 71–73; *North of War* and occupation of, 216–29; self-determination of, 70, 72, 78n1; the situation in, 253; survival struggle of, 74; U.S. defense of, 67; war experience of, 219; women in, 74–77; World War II and, 18–19, 66–67, 78, 216–17
Icelandic Film Fund, 266n2
in-betweenness, 270, 274, 277
Indigenous minorities, 330
Indriðason, Arnaldur, 229
Ingen kender natten (*No Man Knows the Night*), 162–64
internment camps, 32n4, 203, 300n16, 328n29
Ipsen, Bodil, 286

Isak Dinesen (Thurman), 119
Isak Dinesen's Art (Langbaum), 119
Islam, 126
Iversen, Gunnar, 54, 235

Jacobsen, Johan, 286
Japan, 99, 102, 137–38, 143, 145–46
Jarlby, Janne, 163
Jävla Hitler! (bloody Hitler!), 248
jazz music, 75–76, 263
Jews: Boye admiring culture of, 114n17; concentration camps transport of, 86–87; Danish, 43, 88; from Finland, 328n29; Norway's deportation of, 53, 88; Norwegian, 88; persecution of, 247; problem of, 43; Scandinavian, 88; Swedes protecting, 13, 89–90; Wallenberg rescuing, 88–89
Johansson, Alf W., 93
Jokisipilä, Markku, 279n1, 280n10
Jónasson, Kristján B., 228
Jónsson, Jón, 78
Jónsson, Jónas, 75
Jónsson, Ólafur, 218
Judt, Tony, 87, 90, 93

Kall, Leo, 106
Kallio, Kyösti, 243
Kallocain (Boye), 103, 106, 110
Kampen om tungtvannet (*Operation Swallow*), 305–6
Kárason, Einar, 261
Karelia, 24–26, 30, 32n4
Karelian isthmus, 24, 188
Karelian refugees, 25, 187
Kavén, Pertti, 270
Keegan, John, 6–8
Kekkonen, Urho, 25, 28
Kierkegaard, Søren, 129, 158–59, 161
Killy, Walther, 164
The King's Choice (film), 235, 302–3, 308–9, 311–12
Kinnunen, Tiina, 279n1, 280n10
Kirchhoff, Hans, 39, 296
Kivimäki, Ville, 190
Kjeldstadli, Sverre, 52
Knight, Rebecca, 279n4
Knopf, Alfred A., 136, 140
Koivisto, Mauno, 30–31
Kona fer í stríð (*Woman at War*), 260

Index • 339

Koncentrationsläger (concentration camp), 246
Kongens nei (*The King's Choice*), 302
Korhonen, Arvi, 29
Korppi-Tommola, Aura, 269
Kracauer, Sigfried, 110
Kress, Helga, 230n10
Krigen (*A War*, film), 298
krigsbarn (war children), 82, 143, 187, 269–70, 278–79, 279nn1–3
Kristensen, Sven Møller, 162
Kristensen, Tom, 182n5
Kristiansen, Tom, 18, 169
Kristin Lavransdatter (Undset, S.), 136
Kristjánsson, Kristinn, 230n10, 255
Kritisk Revy (journal), 167n31
Krogh Nielsen, Jan, 153
Krosby, Hans Peter, 29
Krouk, Dean, 152
Krudttønden (Powder Keg Cultural Center), 45–46
Krysztofiak, Maria, 160
Kuusisto-Arponen, Anna-Kaisa, 277

Laban, Rudolph, 110
Lagercrantz, Olof, 243
Lagerkvist, Bengt, 238, 248
Lagerkvist, Pär, 1, 111, 121, 238, 300n13, 331
Laine, Edvin, 191–94; cultural memory and, 314; Finland's account of, 318; *The Unknown Soldier* (2017) and, 317, 324–25; *The Unknown Soldier* directed by, 18, 21, 317
Laine, Jarkko T, 273
Land of Mine (film), 234; as Danish film, 282–84; moral redemption in, 294–95; postwar retribution in, 291–94, 297; war's forgotten victims in, 292; Zandvliet directing, 284–85
Landsberg, Alison, 10–11, 324
Landsmanis, Arturs, 205
landssvikoppgjøret, 171–75, 179, 181
Langbaum, Robert, 119
Lapland War, 17, 24, 242, 244
The Last Lieutenant (film), 303, 306
Laxness, Halldór, 223, 258–59, 261
Leander, Zarah, 106, 129
Lebensborn program, 53
Lefebvre, Catherine, 117

The Legionnaires (*Legionärerna*, Enquist), 152, 202; Baltic refugee soldiers in, 203, 212; trauma investigation in, 204–5
Lenin, Vladimir, 194
"Letters from a Land at War" (Dinesen), 116; Arendt not familiar with, 117; Berlin chronicles in, 97–98; cultural memory in, 118; in Danish literary journal, 118; film propaganda in, 106; National Socialism in, 130; postwar memories in, 130–32; racism in, 126; Third Reich and, 118–23
Levinas, Emmanuel, 207–11
liberation, of Denmark, 37–38, 130
Lidegaard, Bo, 285
life, levels of (Levinas), 211
Lindholm, Tobias, 283, 298
Linna, Väinö, 21, 271, 316–18, 325; *Black love* by, 191; Finnish soldiers campaign by, 327n21; *The goal* by, 191; *Under the North Star* by, 191; war depiction of, 197. *See also The Unknown Soldier* (novel, Linna)
literature, 7, 151–53
Loftéen, Penny, 275
Louhimies, Aku, 192, 198, 235, 322–23, 325
Lubrich, Olivier, 102, 118
Lundin, C. Leonard, 29
Lundkvist, Mathias, 288
Lundqvist, Maria, 273, 278
Luovutetut (Sana), 30
Lury, Karen, 270
Lynn, Vera, 238
Lyttkens, Alice, 142

machine-gun platoon's hardships, 187–91
Maijala, Marjaana, 272
Majaniemi, Topi, 272, 274
Mäkelä, Taru, 328n29
Malick, Terrence, 323
Malmberg, Ilkka, 199n7
Mannerheim, Marshal (Carl) Gustav, 26–27, 315
människa (human being), 209–12
March Against Fear, 208
Martinson, Harry, 243
masculine duel, 309–11
Matthíasdóttir, Sigríður, 224
Mávahlátur (*The Seagull's Laughter*), 255–56
Max Manus (films), 303, 306–7, 311

May the world stay young (*Ung må verden ennu være*, Grieg), 161
Meeting at the Milestone (*Møte ved milepelen*, Hoel, S.), 169–71, 173, 300n13; betrayal and guilt in, 179–82; crisis of memory in, 174–79; historiography in, 152
Meinander, Henrik, 317–18, 327n14
"Melodrama Revised" (Williams), 271
memoire collective, 186
memory study, 2, 7–10, 118, 331
Men in Dark Times (Arendt), 132n1
mental illness (Nazism as), 147, 181
merchant fleet, 51–52, 59, 61
The Merchant of Venice (theater production), 92
Mesterton, Erik, 105
Migel, Parmenia, 117, 132n1
Milestone, Lewis, 299
military preparations, 55–56, 58
Milli fjalls og fjöru (*Between a Mountain and a Shore*), 266n2
Milorg leadership, 58
"Min Soldat" (My soldier), 238–39
The misinterpreted legionnaires (*De misstolkade legionärerna*, Landsmanis), 205
Moberg, Vilhelm, 92
mobile killing squads (*Einsatzkommando*), 30
Moland, Hans Petter, 303, 306
Mollberg, Rauni, 191–94, 317, 321, 325
Møller, Roland, 285, 291, 295
moral conflict, 271–72
moral decay, 74–75
moral defeat, 128–29
morally superior, 148
moral narrative, 249, 272; in Danish politics, 44–46; postwar, 92–94; of World War II, 1, 6–7
moral redemption, 294–95
Morðsaga (*Murder Story*), 266n2
Moscow Peace. *See* Treaty of Moscow
Mother of Mine (film), 269–71; compassion in, 272–75; as Finnish film, 234; Härö directing, 274; reconciliation in, 275–79
Mother of Mine (Härö), 12
Movie Days (*Bíódagar*), 255, 262
Multidirectional Memory (Rothberg), 10
Munk, Kaj, 121
Murder Story (*Morðsaga*), 266n2
Museum of Danish Resistance, 39

Mussari, Mark, 152
Musta rakkaus (Black love), 191
Mykkänen, Martti, 189
My soldier ("Min Soldat"), 238–39

Någonstans i Sverige (Somewhere in Sweden), 237–38, 241, 243–49
Nansen, Fridtjof, 56
När molnen skingras (When the clouds clear), 239, 250n2
Nasjonal Samling (National Union), 56, 169–71, 175
national consolidation, 323–25
national essentialism, 148n7
national rule (Þjóðveldi), 68–69, 71–73
National Socialism, 148, 152, 171; Boye's encounter with, 98, 103–4, 107, 109–10, 112; Dinesen and German, 127–28; Dinesen's depiction of, 126–27; fascism and, 99; in "Letters from a Land at War," 130; Nazi regime and, 117–18; von Lettow-Vorbeck and, 124
National Socialist Party, 7–8
National Union (Nasjonal Samling), 56, 169–71, 175
Nation and Narration (Bhabha), 77
NATO. *See* North Atlantic Treaty Organization
Nazism / Nazi Germany: Allied power against, 5; Boye's opposition to, 112; Dinesen's observations of, 122–23, 125, 130–31; as fanatic religion, 117–18; film production in, 106–7, 129; gangsters in, 131; hypnotic lure of, 107–8; National Socialism and, 117–18; Norway occupied by, 12, 160–71; Öhquist, J., supporter of, 326n2; soldier's description from, 142; Sweden's cultural exchanges with, 91; zealots of, 125–27
Nazi-Soviet Pact, 4, 6, 143
"Negro music." *See* Jazz music
Nehlin, Ann, 279n3
Neijmann, Daisy, 153, 252, 256, 258
Nerman, Ture, 91
Neuengamme camp, 89–90
neutrality: of Denmark, 120; Dinesen's cloak of, 117; Finland's no option for, 31; Norway forced out of, 50; policy, 44, 93, 241; Sweden defending, 19, 94; Third Reich and, 118–23

Nevalainen, Juha, 317, 325
New Norwegian Film Policy, 307
Nielsen, Asta, 121
Niemi, Juhani, 191
Nilsson, Macke, 241
Nine Lives (Ni liv), 303, 305, 310
9th of April, 234; bicycle infantry divisions in, 288–89; Cold War cry of, 43–44; as Danish film, 282–83, 287–91, 298–99; Norway's conscripts and, 50; promises of, 46; structural elements of, 289–90
Nissen, Henrik, 296
Nolan, Christopher, 282
No Man Knows the Night (Ingen kender natten, Branner), 162–64
nonaggression pact, 35, 155
nonalignment, 13, 63, 272
Norðan við stríð. See *North of War*
Nordisk film, 266n6
"Nordmannen" (Aasen), 141, 148n6
North Atlantic Treaty Organization (NATO), 13, 43–44, 234, 254, 259–60
North of War (Norðan við stríð, Þorsteinsson), 153; historiography of, 224; Iceland's occupation in, 216–29; women represented in, 224–28
North Sea, 9
Nortraship, 60
Norway: anti-Bolshevik crusade in, 57; British alliance with, 60–61; conscripts of, 50; forces of, 61; German Campaign in, 6, 9; German occupation of, 6, 54–58, 62, 303–8, 311–12; Grand Alliance with, 50, 59, 62; Haakon VII king of, 49, 69, 243, 309, 312; Harald V king of, 308; historiography of war with, 49–54, 169–70; Home Front of, 58, 61–62; Jews deported from, 53, 88; merchant fleet of, 51–52, 59, 61; Nazi Germany occupying, 12, 160–71; neutrality forced out of, 50; New Norwegian Film Policy in, 307; *9th of April* and conscripts from, 50; Nortraship of, 60; Quisling regime in, 51; refugees from, 245; strategic importance of, 287; Sweden with refugees from, 61; Third Reich resistance of, 51; Waffen-SS of, 57–58; war experiences of, 18; Wehrmacht and, 13, 49–50, 54; World War II experience of, 302–3
Norway-in-exile, 51–54, 59–62

Norwegian Constitution Day, 49
Norwegians: in Communist Party, 149n11; Jews as, 88; as morally superior, 148; *Return to the Future* with self-controlled, 141–42; in Sweden, 61
Nurmi, Juhani, 323
Nygaardsvold, Johan, 61, 85
Nyholm, Jens, 165n3
Nyqvist, Michael, 273

occupation: collective memory of, 41–43, 45–46, 155; of Denmark, 6, 9, 35–37, 45–46, 283–87; German historiography of, 39–41; *North of War* and Iceland, 216–29; of Norway, 6, 54–58, 62, 303–8, 311–12; phases of, 303–4; Soviet Karelia, 30; threats against society from, 221–22; women influenced by, 230n14, 255–56
Oesch, K. L., 327n14
Öhquist, Harald, 326n2
Öhquist, Johannes, 315, 326n2
Olav Audunssøn (Undset, S.), 136
"Old Hero in Bremen" (Dinesen), 123–24
Olgeirsson, Einar, 66
Olsson, Jan-Olof, 238
Olympia (film), 11, 98; Aryan fanatics in, 107, 110; Boye on, 101–3, 107, 109–10; erotic excitement of, 108; gazing at bodies in, 111; by Riefenstahl, 109, 111; women in, 110
Olympic games, 101–2, 109
Operation Barbarossa: Continuation War during, 321; Finland joining in, 24–25; Hitler invading Russia in, 4, 82, 138; in *Någonstans i Sverige*, 244; national government after, 57
Operation Overlord, 248
Operation Swallow (Kampen om tungtvannet), 305–6
Operation West, 56
Öquist, Johannes, 325
Order of the German Eagle, 85
ordinary soldiers, in war films, 282–84
Oslund, Karen, 67
Østergård, Uffe, 286
Östling, Johan, 93, 247, 271–72
Out of Africa (Dinesen), 98, 119

Päämäärä (The goal), 191
Paasikivi, Juho Kusti, 25–26

Paha Maa (*Frozen Land*), 322
Pajunen, Julia, 152
Palace in Helsinki, 21
Paris Peace Treaty (1947), 24
patriarchal authority, 227
patriarchy, 180–81
Peace Sculpture, 300n15
Per Albin. *See* Hansson, Per Albin
Perne, Nils, 240
Per Olov Enquist (Henningsen, E.), 206
Petri, Erik, 119, 134n30
Pipping, Knut, 192
Plain, Gill, 227
Policy of Collaboration (Denmark), 39–40
policy of concessions (Sweden), 13, 19, 152, 241
Policy of Cooperation (Denmark), 18, 40, 43–44
Policy of Negotiation (Denmark), 18, 40, 285–86, 300n14
Politiken (Danish newspaper), 119–22, 285
Poppe, Erik, 302
Poppe, Nils, 92
popular culture, 105–6
Þorsteinsson, Indriði G., 153, 218, 223, 228–29, 230n14
postgeneration, 2
postmemory, 2, 11–12
postwar revisionism, 25–28
potentiality-of-being, 165n12
Poulsen, Henning, 296
Powder Keg Cultural Center (*Krudttønden*), 45–46
POWs. *See* prisoners of war
Prague, 110
prime-time television, in Sweden, 237–38
prisoners of war (POWs), 32n4, 284, 328n29
propaganda soldier (Undset), 139–40
prosthetic memory, 10–11, 235, 323–25
Prosthetic Memory (Landsberg), 10
psychology, of fascism, 106
psychosexual analyses (Reichian), 170–71
Pyynikki Summer Theatre, 192–93

Quisling, Vidkun, 54–58, 308; execution of, 172; of Nasjonal Samling, 170; National Socialist Party of, 7–8; Norway with regime of, 51; puppet government of, 49; Ruge's opinion on, 62

quislings, 170

racism, 126–27, 148n7
railways, 244, 250n7
Rantala, Jari Olavi, 198, 322
Rasmussen, Anders Fogh, 300n14
Ravensbrück camp, 89
Red Cross, 88–90, 332
Red guards (the Reds), 22
Rediess, Wilhelm, 55
The Red Meadows (*De røde Enge*), 286
refugees: Baltic soldier, 203, 207–12; children, 270; from Norway, 245; in Sweden, 61
Reich, Wilhelm, 170–71, 174–75, 181
Reich Commissariat, 55
reparations, 32n3
Resedagbok i Grekland (Travel diary in Greece), 97
resistance: civilian/military, 58; collaboration and, 53; Denmark's hidden, 38–39; movement, 58, 165n3; of Norway, 51, 59–62
retribution, 291–94, 297
Return to the Future (Undset, S.), 130; for Allied powers, 118, 137; memoir of escape in, 136–40, 147–48; Norwegians self-controlled in, 141–42; Russia as backward in, 144–45; Undset's goals in, 97–99, 118, 140; Western democracies future in, 146–48
Reykjavík exhibition, 65–68, 70, 77
Reykjavík harbor, 252–53
Ribbentrop, 88, 121
Ride this Night (*Ridd i Natt!*), 92
Riefenstahl, Leni, 98, 101–2, 104, 109, 111
De røde Enge (*The Red Meadows*), 286
Rønning, Joachim, 303
Roos, Liina-Ly, 234
Roosevelt, Franklin D., 49, 73, 138
Roslyng-Jensen, Palle, 285
Rothberg, Michael, 10
Rougemont, Denis de, 108
Ruge, Otto, 54, 62
Rukajärven tie (*Ambush*), 324
Runeberg, Johan Ludvig, 190, 199n9, 318, 326n7
Russia, 315; Hitler invading, 4, 82, 138; *Return to the Future* and backward, 144–45

Russo-Finnish War ("Winter War"), 6
Ryti, Risto, 26, 30

SA. *See* Sturmabteilungen
Saarinen, Eliel, 326n2
"The Sailor-Boy's Tale" (Dinesen), 124
Salminen, Esko, 273
Salminen, Kari, 323
Sana, Elina, 30
Sandberg, Espen, 303
Sandler, Maja, 269
Sartre, Jean-Paul, 11, 156
Scandinavian Jews, 88
Scavenius, Erik, 36, 44
Scharp, Vilhelm, 107
Schechner, Richard, 196
Scherfig, Hans, 300n16
Schmith, Jørgen Haagen, 45
Scholtz-Klink, Frau, 125
The Seagull's Laughter (Mávahlátur), 255–56, 265
Second Schleswig War (Dano-Prussian war), 155, 290
The Second World War (Keegan), 6
Secret Alliance (Hæstrup), 39
Segerstedt, Torgny, 91, 247
self-determination, 70, 72, 78n1
Seven Gothic Tales (Dinesen), 98
79 af stöðinni (Taxi 79), 218, 253, 256
sexual freedom, 180
sexual violence, 195
Shadows on the Grass (Dinesen), 125
Shideler, Ross, 206
Shome, Raka, 275
Sieg heil, 107
Sigurðsson, Jón, 78n1
Sihvonen, Jukka, 326n6
Silvennoinen, Oula, 30
"the situation" (Icelandic women and Allied soldiers), 74–77, 224–28, 253–55
the Situation Report, 74–75
Skodvin, Magne, 52
Skouen, Arne, 303, 305, 310
Skov, Niels Aage, 166n16
Slapgard, Sigrun, 140
"small-state realism," 19, 92–94, 234, 249, 272
Smeds, Kristian, 192, 194–96
Social Democratic Party, 76
society, threats against Icelandic, 221–22

Somewhere in Sweden (*Någonstans i Sverige*), 234, 237–38, 241, 243–48
Sørensen, Tonje Haugland, 304, 306, 310–11
Sotaromaani (A war novel), 194, 317
Soviet Karelia, 30, 32n4
Soviet Union: Allied powers joined by, 143; Boye's trip to, 113n6; Communist Party fall in, 44; Finland defending aggression of, 24, 241–43; Finland imprisoning soldiers of, 328n29; German-Soviet Treaty of Nonaggression of, 4; Germany attacking, 56–57, 84–85; separate war against, 28; Undset, S., visit to, 143–46
Soya, C. E., 286
stage presentations, 196
Stalin, Joseph, 86
Stalinism, 143
Stauning, Thorvald, 287
Stecher-Hansen, Marianne, 106
Steinþórsdóttir, Gerður, 230n10
Sten, Hemming, 249
STJ. *See* Allmänna Säkerhetstjänsten
storage memory ('reference memory'), 97, 296
"The Stormtrooper," 175–76
storytelling, 116–17
Stowe, Leland, 140
"Strength and Joy" (Dinesen), 127
"The Struggle" room (Freedom and Culture exhibition), 66
Sturmabteilungen (SA), 55
Suleiman, Susan Rubin, 11, 152, 170
Sundholm, John, 198, 235, 271
survivor's guilt, 93
Svedjedal, Johan, 112, 114n13
Sweden: army border guards of, 83; army mobilization of, 84; Bolshevism crusade of, 87; children evacuated to, 187, 269–70; class divisions in, 245–48; Danish forces in, 92; external threats to, 90–92; Finland's importance to, 82–83; food and fuel rationing in, 84; German troops transported through, 86–87; German war concerning, 83–84; Germany's transit agreement with, 142–43; Gustav V king of, 83, 88, 243; Hansson prime minister of, 19, 211–12; historiography on, 240–41, 247, 249; Hitler's remarks on, 83; Jews protected by, 89–90; Nazi Germany

cultural exchanges with, 91; neutrality defended by, 19, 94; Norwegian forces in, 61; Norwegian refugees in, 61; poems from, 199n9; policy of concessions, 13; postwar humanitarianism in, 204; primetime television in, 237–38; rail transport in, 244; refugees in, 61; Wehrmacht countered by, 91; during Winter War, 272–73; World War II impacting, 81–82, 93–94, 237–38

Täällä Pohjantähden alla (*Under the North Star*), 191
The Tales of Ensign Stål (*Fänrik Ståls Sägner*, Runeberg), 190, 199n9, 318
Talvisota (*Winter War* – film), 318
Tapiovaara, Nyrki, 316
Taxi 79 (*79 af stöðinni*), 218, 253, 256
television, 240–41
Terboven, Josef, 49, 55
theater production, 193–95
theatrical performances, of *The Unknown Soldier*, 191–92, 195
"They Bind Our Mouths and Hands" (song), 41
The Thin Red Line (Malick), 323
Third Reich/German Reich, 86, 97–99, 102, 107–10; Boye's experience with, 103; cultural life of, 129–30; Denmark as protectorate for, 18, 36–37; fascism of, 104; film industry propaganda by, 106; Finland's alliance with, 322; German film industry under, 129; great personalities of, 122; "Letters from a Land at War" and, 118–23; neutrality and, 118–23; Norway's resistance to, 51; Norwegian Waffen-SS and, 57–58; social revolution of, 125–26
This Life (*Hvidsten Gruppen*), 45, 283
Thörnell, Olof, 84–85, 244
Thors, Ólafur, 70
Three years later (*Tre år efter*), 286
Thurman, Judith, 119
Tilbake til fremtiden (Undset, S.), 136–37
Times in the life of a nation (*Tímar í lífi þjóðar*), 218
Titania (Migel), 117, 132n1
Tjernberg, Ove, 242
Totalitarian regime, 144, 147
Totality and Infinity (Levinas), 207

trauma investigation, 204–5
Travel diary in Greece (*Resedagbok i Grekland*, Boye), 97
Travels in the Reich (Lubrich), 102, 118
Tre år efter (Three years later), 286
Treaty of Moscow (1940), 29, 82, 241
Treaty of Versailles (1919), 3, 128
trench warfare, 190
Troell, Jan, 247
Trommer, Aage, 39
"Trommerne" (Branner), 156, 159, 162, 164
Tuntemattomat soti (Malmberg), 199n7
The 12th Man (film), 54, 235, 302–3, 309–12
Two Lives (*To liv*), 311
Typpö, Juho, 323–24
Tyskertøse (German tarts), 42, 300n16
"De tyske soldater" (The German soldiers, poem), 292

Ugglas, Margaretha af, 204
Under a harsher sky (*Under en hårdere himmel*, Bjørneboe), 172
Under the North Star (*Täällä Pohjantähden alla*, Linna), 191
Under Tvang (By force), 284
Undset, Hans, 141–45, 148n7
Undset, Ragnhild, 148n2
Undset, Sigrid, 130; children's rights speech of, 138–40; *Happy Times in Norway* by, 148n2; Japan criticized by, 145–46; *Kristin Lavransdatter* by, 136; memoir of escape by, 136–40, 147–48; *Olav Audunssøn* by, 136; as propaganda soldier, 139–40; *Return to the Future* by, 97–99, 118, 140; Soviet Union visit by, 143–46; *Tilbake til fremtiden* by, 136–37; in U.S., 139
Ung må verden ennu være (May the world stay young), 161
United Kingdom (U.K., Britain), 9, 58, 249
United States (U.S.): aircraft invasion routes from, 9; *The Girl Gogo* with soldiers from, 234; Iceland's defense by, 67; not acknowledging Soviet annexation of Baltic states, 202; troops from, in Iceland, 253–65; Undset, S., in, 139
The Unknown Soldier (*Tuntematon sotilas*, film), 235, 314; collective memory through, 191–92; discursive formation

of, 319–21; Finnish Independence Day broadcast of, 318–19; ideological discourses in, 320–21; Laine, E., directing, 18, 21, 317; Mollberg directing second adaptation, 193–94, 317; premier of, 192–94; remake debate of, 319; Smeds stage adaptation of, 192, 194–96; stage and screen adaptations, 191–97

The Unknown Soldier (film, 2017): Louhimies directing, 322–23; national consolidation in, 323–25; premier of, 198, 234–35; prosthetic memory in, 324

The Unknown Soldier (*Tuntematon sotilas*, novel, Linna), 21, 318; during Cold War, 194; collective memory and, 186–87, 196–98; cultural memory from, 152, 195; fictional account of war in, 29; historiography value of, 192; machine-gun platoon's hardships in, 187–91; Mykkänen' cover image of, 189; Sihvonen's film study of, 326n6; *Sotaromaani* published and, 194; stage and screen adaptations of, 191–97; theatrical performances of, 191–92, 195–96; unknown soldiers in, 187–91; war's microhistorical narrative in, 185–86

Upton, Anthony, 29
Uschanov, Tommi, 197

Vallasvuo, Armas, 317
Valsson, Pétur, 234
Varpio, Yrjö, 191
Vertov, Dziga, 102
Vibe-Müller, Titus, 305, 311
victimization discourse, 327n21
Vihavainen, Timo, 24
Villadsen, Ebbe, 286–87, 299n5
Virtala, Irene, 279n1
von Blücher, Wipert, 28
von Falkenhorst, Nikolaus, 56
von Lettow-Vorbeck, Paul, 123–24, 133nn15–16
von Numers, Lorenz, 325

Waffen-SS, 153; of Denmark, 40; of Norway, 57–58
Wallenberg, Raoul, 88–89, 204
war: collective memory of, 151; forgotten victims of, 292; historiography and veterans of, 321; historiography of Iceland in, 217; Iceland's experience of, 219; "Letters from a Land at War" and memories of, 130–32; Linna's depiction of, 197; Norway's experiences of, 18; *The Unknown Soldier* fictional account of, 29; victims of atrocities in, 293–94

A War (film), 298
war children (*krigsbarn*), 82, 143, 187, 278–79
war films: as cultural memory, 282–83; Denmark producing, 283–84; ordinary soldiers in, 282–84; Villadsen chronicling, 299n5
War of Liberation (Finland's civil war, 1918), 22, 315–16
Warring, Anette, 42, 152, 155, 300n16
wartime angst, 158
wedding photo, in *Devil's Island*, 164
Weel, Liva, 41
Wehrmacht, 86, 99, 286–87; Denmark fighting, 13; Denmark's executive power assumed by, 36–37; Finland and, 83; intimate fraternization with, 42; military preparations of, 55–56; Nordic nations and, 331; Norway and, 13, 49–50, 54; resistance movement against, 58; Sweden countering, 91
Western democracies, 85, 145; anti-Semitism and, 87, 332; *Return to the Future* and future of, 146–48
Western Europe, 87
When the clouds clear (*När molnen skingras*), 239, 250n2
White, Hayden, 7
white buses (Red Cross "White Buses"), 89–90, 332
the Whites (in Finland's civil war), 22, 315
Wigman, Mary, 110
Wiklund, Martin, 248
Wilde, Oscar, 262
Williams, Linda, 271
Winter's Tales (Dinesen), 124
Winter War, 24, 143, 241–43; children refugees in, 270; in Finland, 327n16, 327n21; Sweden during, 272–73; World War II started as, 315
Woman at War (*Kona fer í stríð*), 260
women, 84; in *Atomic Station*, 260; from Denmark, 42; German soldiers leaving with, 280n10; in Iceland, 74–77; *North*

of War representation of, 224–28; occupation influencing, 230n14, 255–56; in *Olympia* film, 110; patriarchal authority and, 227; as slave labor, 225–26

World War I, 3

World War II: aircraft invasion routes of, 9; Churchillian history of, 7–8; cultural memory of, 2–3, 233–35; Denmark experience of, 282–83; destruction and misery of, 166n25; Dinesen's aesthetic vision of, 131–32; in Finland, 22–23, 198–99; Finnish republic in, 22–23; Germany losing, 286; historiography of, 17–19; Holocaust episode in, 87–90; horrors of, 164; Iceland's experience of, 18–19, 66–67, 78, 216–17; literary representations of, 151–53; military resistance in, 58; moral narrative of, 1, 6–7; Nordic countries fates after, 12–14; Nordic narratives about, 8–10; Norway's experience of, 302–3; Sweden impacted by, 81–82, 93–94, 237–38; Winter War start of, 315

Wuorinen, John H., 28

Wyller, Thomas, 52

Yamaguchi, Liesl, 187–90

Yrlid, Rolf, 205

Zachrisson, Lasse, 239, 250n2

Zander, Ulf, 240

Zandvliet, Martin, 284, 291–92

Zetterlund, Monica, 242

Zetterström, Margareta, 206–8

Zwart, Harald, 303, 310–11

www.ingramcontent.com/pod-product-compliance
Lightning Source LLC
Chambersburg PA
CBHW070121110526
44587CB00017BA/2801